Red Army Order of Battle

Red Army Order of Battle

in the
Great Patriotic War

Including data from 1919 to the present

Albert Z. Conner   Robert G. Poirier

PRESIDIO

355.30947
C752r

Copyright © 1985 by Robert G. Poirier

Published by Presidio Press, 31 Pamaron Way, Novato, CA 94947

All Rights Reserved

Library of Congress Cataloging in Publication Data

Conner, Albert Z., 1943–
   Red Army order of battle in the Great Patriotic War.

   Bibliography: p.
   1. Soviet Union. Raboche-Krest′īanskaia Krasnaīa Armiīa—History. 2. World War, 1939–1945—Soviet Union.
I. Poirier, Robert G. II. Title.
UA772.C66 1985   355.3′0947   85-3676
ISBN 0-89141-237-9

Printed in the United States of America

Contents

Chapter One	Armies	9
Chapter Two	Honorifics for Corps and Divisions	75
Chapter Three	Corps	87
Chapter Four	Rifle Division Activations and Military District Summary	173
Chapter Five	Artillery Divisions	185
Chapter Six	Guards Divisions	197
Chapter Seven	Rifle Divisions	261

Introduction

In the Soviet Union and its Armed Forces, the study of military history *(voyennaya istoriya)* is an enterprise of enormous if not heroic proportions. It is first and foremost a practical activity that is a vital component of the Soviet military science *(voyennaya nauka)* process which influences the preparation of forces in peacetime and their employment in war. Research into military history provides the objective, scientific data for the analysis of the number, types, and deployments of forces to engage specific enemies on the battlefield.

Military historical study is secondarily an instructional activity. Through the systematic and uniform analysis of that subject, the USSR provides its past, present and future military leadership with a common public forum for the discussion of strategy, operational art, and tactics, the components which comprise Soviet military art. It is also closely connected with the military educational establishment in a way that is unknown in the West. It has come to play a major role in the self-education and self-improvement that is so valued in developing the Soviet officer corps. Through intensive and regular individual study, future military leaders are familiarized with both the processes and substance that are the foundation for higher military education and for practical work in higher command staffs.

Thirdly, military history plays an important socializing role. Through the analysis and study of war, predominantly the history of the Great Patriotic Fatherland War of the Soviet Union (World War II), military virtues, successful role models, and patriotic themes are disseminated and promulgated to citizens and officers alike. Thus, military history has served to form an important bond among the several generations of officers within the Armed Forces.

Finally, such research, and particularly its exposition through multimedia sources, provides a tremendous communications vehicle in a centralized and secretive society. Using a large number of professional military journals, the collective leadership can disseminate the content and context of current practices without explicit elaboration. In this way, the entire officer corps, and not solely those handpicked for higher responsibilities, can be informed in a coherent and pragmatic manner.

For anyone in the West interested in entering the collective Soviet military brain and viewing the world through *its* eyes, the study of military history is a fundamental prerequisite. Once initiated, we are exposed to a world that has its own order of hierarchical military thought, precise terminology and, everywhere, systemic complexity and numerical enormity. In this Soviet military world, and for that matter all military establishments, we find the embodiment of shared military virtues inherent in the history of formations and units and termed "combat traditions" *(boyevye traditsii)*.

We believe that this book fills a long-standing need for readers and students of Soviet military history and the Second World War. It provides a numerical reference describing the combat and historical trace of armies, corps, and divisions of the Red Army. When pertinent data was available for pre/postwar periods, it was included. This book provides its readers with data that will allow analysis of the awards and honors, battle record, composition, origin, and subordination of each unit. The entries are arranged in chronological order and have been augmented with information on key commanders as deemed appropriate.

It is also our belief that this compilation should appeal to a cross-section of readers. The data compiled on the "decisive front" should appeal to any student of World War II, particularly those who are intrigued by the war in the East. For wargaming enthusiasts, information on the actual combat effectiveness of units, the Soviet force generation process, and the quality of Red Army formations should be invaluable. Similar information on German forces has already been made available in copies and reprints of the War Department's Military Intelligence Division *Order of Battle for the German Army* for 1944. Lastly, for academic, corporate, and government researchers and students of the modern Soviet Army, it provides a handy, ready-made data base of source materials available nowhere else in an ordered form.

As stated above, no single reference is available to provide flesh to the skeletal framework of Soviet combat units and formations that abound throughout Soviet and Western military literature. This order of battle is the first effort to screen the vast amount of available open-source materials and to delineate the combat histories of the fully mobilized Red/Soviet Army. It has drawn on a myriad of sources for its information; the following are the most important:

1) The records of the German Foreign Armies East Branch (FHO) of the Army High Command (OKH). Formerly Secret, these files are now in the public domain at the National Archives and Records Service (NARS).

2) US War Department G2 and Military Intelligence Division Records at the NARS. These files contain declassified data which ranged from Top Secret to Restricted.

3) United Kingdom Ministry of Defense Records in the public domain in the Public Record Office (PRO). These files contain declassified data ranging from Top Secret Ultra to Secret.

4) *The Soviet Military Encyclopedia* (SME), Moscow: Military Press of the Ministry of Defense of the USSR, 1976–79. This unclassified reference contains extensive research analyzing Soviet military concepts, forces, and organization.

5) The Soviet *Military Historical Journal* (MHJ), Moscow: Military Press of the Ministry of Defense. This monthly publication is the primary medium of publishing military historical research in the Soviet Union.

6) The Soviet *Journal of Military Thought,* Moscow, is the monthly magazine of the General Staff Academy. Issues from 1974 to the present were used; many were formerly Confidential and are now in the public domain.

7) A variety of general Soviet and Western historical works on the war, the Eastern Front, and the Red Army.

The authors made a conscious, but regrettable, decision to dispense with the use of footnotes. Given the nature of this order of battle, a separate footnote would have been required for each line entry. The result of such an approach would have led to a reference section at least the same length as, and probably longer than, the original text. We trust this will not greatly inconvenience our readers. Some entries have source abbreviations in a general sense (e.g., FHO, SME, or MHJ).

This publication, owing to the availability of information on Red Army units, will inevitably require some updating. We envisage that it will be updated every three to five years in order to incorporate new information. Errors and oversights in a work of this type are unavoidable considering the large number of sources involved and the difficulties in verifying information and resolving conflicting data. The authors solicit assistance from any and all readers in expanding and improving this order of battle. Contributions to future editions will be gratefully acknowledged.

We would like to acknowledge the invaluable advice and assistance of Col. Frederick Turner, USA (Ret.). He showed infinite patience, encouragement, and a genuine willingness to share his expertise in Russian materials. We would also like to thank Messers. Robert Wolfe and Timothy Mulligan of the United States National Archives and Records Service for their assistance in locating German intelligence records on the Soviet forces.

Robert G. Poirier and Albert Z. Conner

Washington, D.C., November 1984

Prologue

This order of battle is arranged in army, corps, and division sections. In each part we introduce briefly the types of formations and then list the records of the specific units in numerical order. Where formations were named rather than numbered, they precede their numbered counterparts.

Individual entries for the formations follow the same format throughout. This includes the name of the formation; its origins or earliest known activity; achronological accounting of its history and combat service; and where known, its postwar activity. Also listed are unit honors: awards, decorations, honorary titles (honorifics), and other distinctions; key commanders; and subordinate units or formations. In the chronological listing, any known specific subordinations or associations are cited.

All Soviet military formations and units were provided with three essential components: a banner (color) and an accompanying certificate; a number or name designation; and, after 1943, a random code number of five digits. The latter numerical code was the military unit *(voinskaya chast)* or *VCh* number which was used as a ready unit reference for common usage such as mail and dealings with other units or civilian officials. *VCh* numbers frequently used the designation *PP* as a component of the number. This *PP (polevaya pochta)* or "field post" was often detected by the Germans who used it as an aid in tracking Soviet units.

The banner of a Soviet military unit was the literal embodiment of the combat traditions and honor of the unit or formation. Since the 1920s, Soviet writings have stressed several principles relating to the banner. The banner and its accompanying certificate remained perpetually with the unit regardless of modifications to the name or numerical designator; these were regarded as simple clerical changes. Both in garrison and in the field, the banner was kept and continually guarded within the headquarters area. If the colors were lost or captured, as was the case with the 24th Rifle Division, the unit could be disbanded and those deemed responsible for the loss severely punished. Though other banners could reside in the unit as "martial" or "sacred relics," only one banner could be designated as the "combat standard." The former could come from other units or formations that had been reorganized or absorbed into the active unit. During the course of the war, these evocative, symbolic colors were used to incite Soviet troops in defensive or offensive combat. In preparation for attacks, the banners were sometimes moved to and among the assault troops and carried into combat. In the defense, banners were often placed in the first defensive line to ensure defensive tenacity. Veterans who served with the unit in combat were motivated to fight literally "to the death" for the military honor of the unit or formation. At the end of hostilities, there were many emotional ceremonies of deactivation and farewell to the colors, which were recorded for posterity.

The banners of deactivated formations and units were retired to the Central Museums of the Armed Forces. As some units were deactivated some were absorbed into others during the demobilization process of 1945-47. The banners were then retained by the gaining unit. When a formation/unit was awarded the title of "guards," and a guards banner, the original color was retained by the guards unit. If a new unit was formed using the number of the unit that had become "guards," it was referred to as the "xth unit/formation of the second (third, etc.) formation/activation *(vtorogo formirovaniya)*. If a unit was destroyed or deactivated for any reason, a replacement could be activated in the same way. Some divisions, for example, had up to four reactivations due to destruction or one or more reorganizations into a guards unit.

The Soviets developed a large number of awards to acknowledge special achievements by individuals and units. In precedence, those assigned to formations/units were:

> Order of Lenin
> Order of Red Banner
> Order of Suvorov
> Order of Kutuzov
> Order of Bogdan Khmelnitskiy
> Order of Alexander Nevskiy
> Order of Red Star
> Order of Labor Red Banner

In addition, units were also awarded special titles or "honorifics" which became part of the permanent unit name. Titles related to place of origin, characteristic ethnic composition, or localities where the unit distinguished itself in combat, or to special or unique aspects of the formation, e.g., "Communist," "Komsomol," "Proletariat." Units could also be named in honor of distinguished heroes, leaders, or state organizations. These full titles often appeared in official correspondence, and numerous examples were captured by the Germans. One example of such a capture was a document of the "1 Ssevsk-Glukhov, Order of Lenin,

Red Banner, Order of Suvorov, Order of Bogdan Khmelnitskiy Artillery Breakthrough Division of the Reserve of the Supreme High Command." Those units either permanently or temporarily assigned to the Reserve of the Supreme High Command (RVGK) used that appelation in their official title.

Units or formations attached to the RVGK carried a special significance. They represented the VGK's ability to influence operations on the most important axes/sectors. The RVGK were qualitative and quantitative reinforcements committed to operations pursuing strategic objectives. By the end of the war, German intelligence estimated that nearly 50 percent of the Red Army were reserve formations of reinforcing divisions, corps, armies, and fronts. According to Soviet writings, twenty-three armies were assigned to the RVGK at least once, twenty-two were assigned twice, three were assigned at least three times, and two were assigned five times. Tank armies, tank and mechanized corps, and independent corps were RVGK assets. The RVGK could also be used for rebuilding units destroyed in combat, activating new ones, and as a conduit for the redeployment and regrouping of formations and units.*

*For further details on the RVGK, see the following articles by the authors: "Soviet Strategic Reserves: The Forgotten Dimension," *Military Review,* Vol. LXIII, No. 11, November 1983; and "Soviet Wartime Tank Formations," *Armor,* Vol. XCII, No. 3, May–June 1983.

CHAPTER ONE

Armies

Armies were the basic operational formations of the Red Army in the Great Patriotic War (GPW). These formations could be combined (or all) arms, cavalry, engineer, reserve, shock *(udarnaya)* or tank. A Soviet army consisted of a large, permanent headquarters which would be allotted combat, combat support, and combat service support units as required. The composition of an army was determined based on the axis of the operation, the mission, the terrain, and the composition of the enemy forces projected to be found on the attack axis. Great variation, therefore, was found in the composition of the forces from one army to another. Despite the fact that certain elements were common to each army, there was no "type" army. Found in all armies were the following: one signal regiment, one replacement regiment, two engineer construction battalions, one flame thrower battalion, one chemical warfare battalion, one road maintenance battalion, two reconnaissance battalions, two to four motor transport battalions, one security battalion, one penal battalion, an ordnance battalion, and various depots, workshops, and medical and veterinary facilities. The combat element of the army consisted of three rifle corps, normally with three rifle divisions. After July 1943, army artillery complements were standardized in that each army had at least a mixed artillery brigade, a tank destroyer regiment, at least one antiaircraft artillery (AAA) regiment, and a mortar regiment. Engineers were special troops that were assigned from the front or from the Reserves of the Supreme High Command (RVGK) as needed.

It was not unusual for combined arms armies to contain 12 or more rifle divisions. When an army, such as a shock army, was tasked with conducting a breakthrough *(proryv)* operation, it could have as many as 18 divisions. The most numerous formation was the combined arms army. More than 100 of these were organized at various times during the GPW. The Germans identified 70 existing in January 1945 while British ULTRA signals intelligence carried 75. Shock armies and tank armies existed in far fewer numbers. There were five shock and six tank armies functioning during the war. These armies were *always* assets of the Supreme High Command. They would be assigned to a front for a specific operation or operations, task organized as required. Upon completion of the mission, control would revert to the Supreme High Command. Shock armies, in prewar military writings, were meant to have 18 rifle divisions, 6–8 tank brigades, 12–14 RVGK artillery regiments, and 2–3 air divisions. They would be committed on the most important offensive and defensive sectors *(napravleniya)*. Tank armies were allotted to the front making the main effort on the decisive axis. These tank armies were tasked with conducting exploitation to operational depth. They normally had two tank and one mechanized corps, three artillery brigades, a tank destroyer brigade, an engineer brigade, two self-propelled artillery regiments, a rocket launcher regiment, and an antiaircraft regiment. Cavalry and engineer armies were not major factors in the GPW and are not examined here in great detail.

Certain armies were designated Guards by virtue of having distinguished themselves in combat or having been formed from elite troops. Eleven combined arms and the six tank armies were so designated between 1942 and 1945. By the middle of 1943, guards armies were tasked with missions on the key axes and functioned much as shock armies had been intended to function. In fact, ULTRA records show that allied and German intelligence treated shock, tank, and guards armies as elite "assault" armies and indicators of major efforts. Guards units had special tables of organization and equipment and select personnel. They were always more powerful than corresponding non-guards combined arms armies.

Reserve armies existed until 1943. There were ten reserve armies and these were converted into combined arms armies in the Stalingrad campaign. Prior to this conversion, they were employed in training regiments, brigades, divisions, and corps and forwarding them to the armies and fronts.

The listing of units as subordinate to the Army Headquarters is not necessarily all-inclusive but is confined to units that can be confirmed as subordinate for the date and location indicated.

Combined Arms, Cavalry, Engineer, Reserve, Shock,
and Tank Armies

Updated 1 Nov. 1984

Independent Coastal Army
—Odessa, July 1941.
—Sevastopol, May 1942.
—Formed from North Caucasus Front, 20 Nov. 1943.
—Kerch amphibious landing, Nov. 1943.

—Later the Independent Maritime Army, then Maritime Army, 18 Apr. 1944.
—Sevastopol, May 1944.
—Yalta, 16 May 1944.
—Army Headquarters used w/Headquarters 22 Army to form Headquarters Tauric Military District in the Crimea, July, 1945.
Key Commanders: A.I. Yeremenko, May 1944.
Units: May 1942: 2, 25, 95, 172, 345, 386 and 388 Rifle Division and 40 Cavalry Division and 7, 8, 79 Naval Rifle Brigades.
Jan. 1944: 11 Guards Rifle Corps w/2, 32, 55 Guards Rifle Divisions; 16 Rifle Corps w/227, 339, 383 Rifle Divisions; 89 Rifle Division, 128 Guards Mountain Rifle Division, 414 Rifle Division.
Apr. 1944: 11 Guards Rifle Corps w/2, 32 Guards Rifle Divisions, 414 Rifle Division; 16 Rifle Corps w/339, 383 Rifle Divisions; 20 Rifle Corps w/55 Guards Rifle Division, 89, 227 Rifle Divisions.

1 Army
—Created from volunteer units on eastern front, June 1918.
—Transformed into 1 Rifle Division, Jan. 1921.

1 Cavalry Army
—Activated, Nov. 1919.
—Commanded by Budyenny in Civil War, 1920.
—Deactivated, Oct. 1923.
—Far East, 1941–45.
—Transbaikal or Mongolia, 1946–47 (European Command Study, 1948– EUCOM Study).
—Lineage of selected regimental elements taken into the Strategic Rocket Force, 1960.

1 Combat Engineer Army
—Formed in the RVGK with ten engineer brigades of eight battalions each, Nov. 1941.
—Moscow axis, Dec. 1941.

1 Guards Army
—First formation created from 2 Reserve Army, Aug. 1942.
—RVGK on Southwest (Stalingrad) strategic axis/sector, Aug. 1942.
—Personnel transferred to 24 Army; Headquarters became Headquarters Southwest Front, Oct. 1942.
—Second formation raised, Nov. 1942.

—Stalingrad offensive as main attack army of Southwest Front, Nov. 1942.
—Redesignated 63 Army then 3 Guards Army, Dec. 1942.
—Third formation from troops of the operational group of the Southwest Front and elements of 4 Reserve Army, Dec. 1942.
—On the middle Don River, Dec. 1942.
—Thrust to Dnepropetrovsk, Jan. 1943.
—Penetrated German line east of Zaporozhye; in position to overrun Manstein's Headquarters, 18 Feb. 1943.
—RVGK, Feb. 1943.
—Badly battered in German attack east of Dnepropetrovsk, Mar. 1943.
—RVGK, Nov. 1943.
—From RVGK to Kiev axis, Dec. 1943.
—Radomysyl, Dec. 1943.
—One of main attack armies on Zhitomir-Berdichev axis, Jan. 1944.
—RVGK, June 1944.
—Lvov-Sandomir Op., July 1944.
—Carpathian Op. in Uzhgorod-Mukachevo area, Sept. 1944.
—Czechoslovakia, Apr–May 1945.
Key Commanders: Katukov, Feb. 1943; K.S. Moskalenko, 1942–43; A.A. Grechko, Sep. 1944 to May 1945.
Units: Sep. 1942: 38, 39, 41 Guards, 24, 64, 84, 116, 315 Rifle Divisions; 4, 7, 16 Tank Corps.
Nov. 1942: 1, 153, 197, 203, 208 and 226 Rifle Divisions.
Dec. 1942: 24, 25 Tank Corps.
May 1943: 4, 6 Guards Rifle Corps and 172 Rifle Division.
Jan. 1944: 11 Rifle Corps w/271, 276, 316 Rifle Divisions; 94 Rifle Corps w/30, 99, 350 Rifle Divisions; 107 Rifle Corps w/ 127, 304, 328 Rifle Divisions, 3 Breakthrough Artillery Division.
Mar. 1944: 11, 17, 30, 47, 94, 107 Rifle Corps.
July 1944: 24, 161, 226, 351 Rifle; 66 Guards Rifle Divisions.
Sept. 1944: 18 Independent Guards, 30, 107 Rifle Corps; 3 Mountain Corps; 66, 129 Guards Rifle Divisions; 30, 141, 151, 161, 167, 226, 237, 276, 317 Rifle Divisions.

1 Special Red Banner Army
—Formed at Voroshilov (Ussuriysk), Far East Military District on basis of the Special Red Banner Far East Army as 1 Coastal Army, 1938.
—Renamed 1 Independent Red Banner Army at Voroshilov; subordinate to NKO, 4 Sep. 1938.
—Khalkhin Gol, 1939.
—Converted to a Front, Jan. 1940.
—Reformed in Front Command Khabarovsk, Apr. 1943.

—Manchurian Op., Aug. 1945.
—Khabarovsk, Far East Military District, 1946; in Sep. 1947 Order of Battle (OB).
—Independent Army.
Key Commanders: Gen. G.M. Shtern, 1939; M.M. Popov, Jan. 1940.
Units: Apr. 1943: 22, 59, 66, 105, 108, 187, 199 (?) Rifle Divisions, 106 (Poltavka), Grodekovo Fortified Areas, 1, 42 Tank Brigades.
Aug. 1945: 22, 39, 59, 231, 300, 365 Rifle Divisions.

1 Reserve Army
—Formed from 24 Army (via Moscow Defense Zone), in Tula area, 1 May 1942.
—Reserve armies were RVGK formations. Stalingrad, June 1942.
—Redesignated 64 Army, July 1942.
—Administrative staff of this army used in forming 2 Guards Army, Oct. 1942.

1 Shock Army
—Formed in RVGK at Zagorsk, Moscow Military District from 19 Army, Nov. 1941.
—Committed from RVGK on Moscow Front, end of Nov. 1941.
—Klin, Moscow Counteroffensive, Dec. 1941.
—Airlifted to Staraya Russa, Jan. 1942.
—Lama River, Jan. 1942.
—RVGK, Jan. 1942.
—Demyansk, Feb. 1942.
—Demyansk Pocket, Dec. 1942.
—Northwestern Front, July 1943.
—Staraya Russa area, Jan. 1944.
—Ostrov area, June 1944.
—Pechory, Aug. 1944.
—Tukums, Oct. 1944.
Key Commanders: Gen-Lt F.I. Kuznetsov, Nov. 1941.
Units: Nov. 1941: 29, 44, 47, 50, 55, 56 Independent, 62, 64, 71, 82 Naval Rifle Brigades.
Feb. 1942: 1 Guards Rifle Corps.
July 1943: 23 Guards Rifle, 391 Rifle Divisions.
July 1944: 23 Guards Rifle, 33 Rifle Division.

1 Guards Tank Army (Formerly 1 Tank Army)
—Formed from 28 Army on Southwest Front with "combined composition," 22 July 1942.
—Headquarters formed from Headquarters 38 Army, 23 July 1942.

—Stalingrad area, Aug. 1942.
—Stalingrad counteroffensive, Nov. 1942.
—Temporarily ceased to exist, Dec. 1942.
—RVGK, Jan. 1943.
—Reconstituted in Northwest Front, Feb. 1943.
—In "Khozin's Special Group" w/68 Army, Demyansk, Feb. 1943.
—RVGK, Mar. 1943.
—Reformed as tank army of unified composition, Apr. 1943.
—Kursk salient; had 631 tanks, Apr–May 1943.
—Kursk, July 1943.
—Belgorod Kharkov Op., Aug. 1943.
—Dnieper at Lutezh Bridgehead, Sep. 1943.
—RVGK, Nov. 1943.
—From RVGK to Kiev axis, Dec. 1943.
—Badly beaten near Zhitomir, Dec. 1943.
—Had major elements destroyed in pocket near Cherkassy, Jan. 1944.
—Dniester River at Chernovtsy, Proskurov-Chernovtsy Op., Mar. 1944.
—Chortkhov, Mar. 1944.
—Trapped German 1 Panzer Army, Mar–Apr 1944.
—Designated Guards, 25 Apr. 1944.
—RVGK, June 1944.
—Lvov Sandomir Op. at Rava Russkaya, July 1944.
—Vistula Oder Op. (Magnuszew Bridgehead), Jan. 1945.
—Kolberg and Gdynia, Mar. 1945.
—East Pomerania, Apr. 1945.
—Berlin Op.; had 854 Tanks and Self-propelled (SP) guns, Apr. 1945.
—Germany, Jan. 1947 as 1 Guards Mechanized Army; (Feb. 1947 OB).
Key Commanders: K.S. Moskalenko, July 1942; M.Y. Katukov Jan. 1943– May 1945.
Units: July 1942: 13, 28 Tank Corps; 131 Rifle Division; 158 Tank Brigade.
May–Aug 1943: 6 (later 11 Guards Tk), 31 Tank Corps, 3 Mechanized Corps.
Aug. 1943: 2, 5 Guards Tank Corps; other units: 2 Mechanized (later 8 Guards Mechanized Corps), 93 Independent Tank Brigade.
Jan. 1944: 11 Guards Tank, 8 Guards Mechanized Corps.
Sep. 1946: 4 Artillery Division, 8 Guards Mechanized Division, 11 Guards Tank Division, 9 Tank Division.

2 Army
—Activated June 1918.
—Deactivated; Headquarters to Southern Front, July 1919.

2 Cavalry Army
—Activated on Southwest Front, July 1920.
—Reformed into 2 Cavalry Corps, 6 Dec. 1920.

2 Combat Engineer Army
—Moscow area, Dec. 1942.
—Southwest Front, Nov. 1943.

2 Guards Army
—Formed in the RVGK at Tambov on basis of the administration of 1 Reserve Army (SME), Aug–Oct 1942.
—May have been formed using elements of 1 and 4 Tank Armies (FHO), Aug. 1942.
—RVGK, Nov. 1942.
—RVGK to Stalingrad Axis, Dec. 1942.
—Opposed Manstein at Kotelnikovo and Mushkoma River, Dec. 1942.
—Stalingrad, Jan. 1943.
—To Caucasus near Taganrog, Jan–Feb 1943.
—Liberated Novocherkassk, 7 Feb. 1943.
—Melitopol Op. as main attack army with 5 Shock Army, Sep–Nov 1943.
—Broke through Wotan Line, Oct. 1943.
—Southern Ukraine w/4 Ukrainian Front, Jan. 1944.
—Crimea, Perekop, Apr. 1944.
—Sevastopol, May 1944.
—RVGK, May 1944.
—Regrouped via RVGK for Belorussian Op., June 1944.
—Polotsk, July 1944.
—Shauliai, July 1944.
—Kaunus axis, Aug. 1944.
—Lithuania, Sep–Oct 1944.
—Goldap, Poland, Jan. 1945.
—East Prussia, Jan. 1945.
—Vistula Oder Op., Jan. 1945.
—Dresden, 2 May 1945.
—Czechoslovakia, 8 May 1945.
Key Commanders: R.Ya. Malinovskiy Jan. 1943; G.F. Zakharov, Oct 1943–May 1944.
Units: Oct. 1942: 6, 7 Tank Corps, 4 Cavalry, 4 Mechanized Corps, 87 Rifle Division.
Dec. 1942: 2 Guards Mechanized Corps, 13 Guards Rifle Corps.
Jan. 1943: 2, 5 Guards Mechanized Corps, 3 Guards Tank Corps, 1 Guards Rifle Corps.
Jan. 1944: 1 Guards Rifle Corps w/33, 86 Guards Rifle Divisions;

13 Guards Rifle Corps w/3, 49, 87 Guards Rifle, 295 Rifle Divisions.
Apr. 1944: 13 Guards Rifle Corps w/3, 24, 87 Guards Rifle Divisions; 54 Rifle Corps w/126, 315 Rifle Divisions; 55 Rifle Corps w/87, 347, 387 Rifle Divisions; 2 Guards Breakthrough Artillery Division.

2 Independent Red Banner Army
—Formed in Far East Military District at Kuibyshev as 2 Army, 1938.
—After deactivation of 2 Independent Red Banner Front, reformed as 2 Independent Red Banner Army under the NKO, 1938.
—Khalkhin Gol, 1939.
—Elements used to form 15 Army, June 1940.
—Border defense, 1940–45.
—In "Front Command Khabarovsk," Apr. 1943.
—Manchurian Campaign, Aug. 1945.
—Army included in the Amur-Transbaikal Military District, Aug. 1945 (SME).
Key Commanders: I.S. Koniev, 1938–40.
Units: Apr. 1943: 3, 12, 107 Rifle Divisions; Blagoveshchensk Fortified Area, 43 Tank Brigade.
Apr. 1945: 3, 12, 396 Rifle Divisions.

2 Reserve Army
—Formed in Vologda area, spring 1942.
—Reserve Armies were part of the RVGK.
—Used to form 1 Guards Army, Aug. 1942.
—Apparently reformed as it was used as the basis for reforming 63 Army, May 1943.

2 Shock Army
—RVGK when formed from 26 Army, Nov. 1941 (SME).
—Volkhov Counteroffensive, Jan. 1942.
—Volkhov Pocket, Jan. 1942.
—Novgorod Chudovo rail line, Feb. 1942.
—Krasnaya Gorka, Feb. 1942.
—Trapped in Volkhov Pocket, Mar. 1942.
—Destroyed in Volkhov Pocket, June 1942.
—Lost seven divisions near Lake Ladoga, 1942.
—Leningrad Front, 1942–43.
—Leningrad Counteroffensive, Jan. 1943.
—Leningrad Front, Aug. 1943.
—Oranienbaum Pocket, Jan. 1944.

—Narva front, took Ropsha, Feb. 1944.
—Narva, July 1944.
—Dvinsk axis, Aug. 1944.
—Major role in Estonia, took Tartu, Sep. 1944.
—RVGK, Sep–Oct 1944.
—With 2 Belorussian Front, Nov. 1944.
—East Prussian Op., Jan. 1945.
—Marienberg, Jan. 1945.
—Pomeranian Op., Feb. 1945.
—Graudents, East Pomeranian Op., Mar. 1945.
—Danzig, Mar. 1945.
—Berlin Op., Apr. 1945.
—Elements in Leningrad Military District after war; 1946–48 OBs.
Key Commanders: A.A. Vlasov, Feb–June 1942; I.I. Fedyuninskiy Mar. 1945.
Units: 12 Jan. 1943: 11, 18, 71, 128, 147, 191, 239, 256, 314, 327, 372, 376 Rifle Divisions, 73 Naval Rifle Brigade.
Jan. 1944: 11, 43, 90, 131, 196 Rifle Divisions.
Sep. 1944: 30 Guards and 8, 108, 118 Rifle Corps; 98 Rifle Division.
Feb. 1945: 37, 142 Rifle Divisions.
Mar. 1945: 98, 108, 116 Rifle Corps, 46, 86, 90, 142, 281, 321, 326, 372, 381 Rifle Divisions.

2 Guards Tank Army (Formerly 2 Tank Army)
—Formed as a Tank Army of combined composition, summer 1942.
—Stalingrad axis, July–Sep 1942.
—Reformed in RVGK, Jan. 1943.
—Tank army of unified composition, Apr. 1943.
—Kursk; lost over 300 tanks; only 36 combat ready, July 1943.
—Zhitomir Berdichev Op., Dec. 1943.
—Korsun Shevchenkovskiy Op., w/2 Ukrainian Front to mid-June, Jan. 1944.
—Uman Botosani Op., Mar. 1944.
—Proskurov Chernovtsy Op., Mar. 1944.
—Dniester, south of Balta, (Ultra KV 332, 6 April 1944); had tank corps in the Jassy area, 29 Mar. 1944.
—Iasi River, Apr. 1944.
—Targul Frumos, Rumania, 2–5 May 1944.
—Regrouped from Rumania to Belorussia, June 1944.
—Lublin Brest Op.; took Lublin, July 1944.
—Lvov Sandomir Op., July 1944.
—Praga (Warsaw), July 1944.

—Warsaw area, Aug-Sep 1944.
—Redesignated Guards, 20 Nov. 1944.
—RVGK (MHJ), Jan. 1945.
—Vistula Oder Op. (Magnuszew Bridgehead), Jan. 1945.
—Kustrin Bridgehead, Feb. 1945.
—North of Stettin, Mar. 1945.
—Berlin Op., Apr. 1945.
—Northern Germany as 2 Guards Mechanized Army, (Feb. 1947 OB).
Key Commanders: Gen-Lt P.D. Romanenko Jan–Feb 1943; Gen-Lt A.G. Rodin Feb–Sep 1943; Gen-Lt S.I. Bogdanov, Sep. 1943–July 1944; A.I. Radziyevskiy, Aug. 1944–Jan. 1945; Gen-Col S.I. Bogdanov, Jan–May 1945.
Units: Jan. 1943: 11, 16 Tank Corps.
May 1943: 3, 16 Tank Corps.
May 1944: 3, 7, 16 Tank and 1 Cavalry Corps.
July 1944: 3 Tank, 8 Guards Tank and 16 Tank Corps; 24 RVGK Antiaircraft Artillery Division.
Jan. 1945: 9, 12 Guards Tank, 1 Mechanized Corps.

3 Army
—Activated from forces of Far East Front; suppressed anti-communist peasant revolt, June 1918.
—Renamed 1 Revolutionary Workers Army, Jan. 1920.
—Reactivated on Western Front on basis of Forces of Southern Group of 15 Army, 1920.
—Commanded by Tukhachevskiy in Civil War; at Warsaw, 1920.
—Deactivated, Dec. 1920.
—Reactivated in Belorussian Special Military District on basis of Vitebsk Army Group of Forces, Aug. 1939.
—Poland, Sep. 1939.
—North of Grodno as a covering army, Western Special Military District, June 1941.
—Destroyed near Bialystok, June 1941.
—RVGK, July 1941.
—With the Reserve Front, Sep. 1941.
—Bryansk Pocket, Oct. 1941.
—Kursk; main battle group of Bryansk Front, July 1943.
—Orel, Aug. 1943.
—North of Bryansk, Sep. 1943.
—Gomel Op., Nov. 1943.
—Belorussian Op., Rogachev, June 1944.
—East Prussian Op. as main assault group of 2 Belorussian Front, Jan. 1945.

—Berlin Op., Apr. 1945.
—Probably in Belorussia, 1946, EUCOM Study.
Key Commanders: Gen. V.I. Kuznetsov, 1939.
Units: June 1941: 4 Rifle Corps w/27, 56, 85 Rifle Divisions; 2, 50, 86 Rifle Divisions; 11 Mechanized Corps w/29, 33 Tank, 204 Motorized Divisions.
May 1943: 110, 269, 356, 415 Rifle Divisions, 41 Rifle Corps.
Nov. 1943: 17, 120, 121 Guards; 186, 269, 283, 363 Rifle Divisions.
June 1944: 35, 40, 41, 80 Rifle Corps.

3 Guards Army
—Formed from second formation of 1 Guards Army (SME), 5 Dec. 1942.
—Detection of this army in Don Bend by Manstein's intelligence led Germans to forecast a Russian attack, Dec. 1942.
—Mius Front, Jan. 1943.
—Voroshilovgrad, Jan. 1943.
—Southwest Front, Aug. 1943.
—Zaporozhye Bridgehead, 10–14 Oct. 1943.
—Melitopol Op., 18 Oct. 1943.
—Lutezh Bridgehead on Dnieper; 30% RVGK troops, Nov. 1943.
—South Russia w/4 Ukrainian Front, Jan. 1944.
—Lvov Sandomir Op. (Rava Russkaya), July 1944.
—Baranov Bridgehead, Warsaw area, Aug. 1944.
—Olesno, Poland, Jan. 1945.
—Leignitz, Poland, Mar. 1945.
—Berlin; a main attack army, Apr. 1945.
—Czechoslovakia, May 1945.
—North Caucasus Military District (EUCOM Study), Dec. 1945.
Key Commanders: Gen. Lelyushenko, Oct. 1943.
Units: Oct. 1943: 59, 61 Guards, 243, 266, 279 Rifle Divisions.
Jan. 1944: 32 Rifle Corps w/259, 266, 279 Rifle Divisions; 34 Guards Rifle Corps w/59, 61 Guards, 243 Rifle Divisions; 37 Rifle Corps w/248, 416, 417 Rifle Divisions; 7 Breakthrough Artillery Division.
July 1944: 21, 22, 76, 120 Rifle Corps.
Aug. 1944: 197 Rifle Division.

3 Reserve Army
—Formed spring 1942.
—Basis of 60 Army, July 1942.
—Reformed, basis of 21 Army, July 1943.
—Reserve Armies were RVGK.

3 Shock Army
—Formed in the RVGK by reforming 60 Army; had 104 Heroes of the Soviet Union (HSU), (SME), Dec. 1941.
—Nevel Offensive, Jan. 1942.
—Velikiye Luki, Feb. 1942.
—Demyansk Pocket, Vitebsk Sector, Feb. 1942.
—Velikiye Luki, Dec. 1942–Jan. 1943.
—Kalinin Front, Aug. 1943.
—Smolensk Op., Sep. 1943.
—Nevel Op.; took town, Oct. 1943.
—Fastov Zhitomir area, Oct. 1943.
—Northwest of Nevel, Dec. 1943.
—Belorussian Op., June 1944.
—Rezenka w/2 Baltic Front, Aug. 1944.
—Kaunata, Aug. 1944.
—South of Lake Luban, Aug. 1944.
—Riga axis, Sep–Oct 1944.
—RVGK (SME), Dec. 1944.
—Pomeranian Op., north of Stettin, Mar. 1945.
—Berlin, Apr. 1945.
—Furstenburg, Germany as 3 Mechanized Army, 1946–47 (Feb. 1947 OB).
Units: Dec. 1941: 23, 33, 257 Rifle Divisions.
Nov. 1942: 21, 46 Guards Rifle, 28, 257, 357 Rifle Divisions.
Apr. 1945: 79 Rifle Corps.
Oct. 1946: 18 Artillery Division; 12 Guards Rifle Corps w/22 Motorized Rifle Division, 23 Guards Rifle, 33 Rifle Division; 79 Rifle Corps w/150, 171, 207 Rifle Divisions; 175, 185, 260 Rifle Divisions.

3 Guards Tank Army (Formerly 3 Tank Army)
—Formed on basis of a combined arms army as most powerful single formation in Red Army; had three tank corps, three rifle divisions and an independent tank brigade, 14 May 1942.
—RVGK near Tula, Dec. 1942.
—Ostrogosh Rossosh Op., Jan. 1943.
—Took Krasnoarmeyskoye, 13 Feb. 1943.
—Mius River, 18 Feb. 1943.
—Destroyed near Kharkov (Krasnograd Pocket), as "Popov Armored Group;" 4 and 12 Tank Corps destroyed, Mar. 1943.
—Tank Army of "unified composition," May 1943.
—Reformed near Plavsk w/unified composition, July 1943.
—Orel Op.; had 731 tanks, 700 guns/mortars, 40,000 men, July 1943.

—Dnieper Op.; first to reach river w/40 Army, Oct. 1943.
—Kiev Op., Nov. 1943.
—Fastov, Nov. 1943.
—Zhitomir Berdichev Op., Dec. 1943.
—With 1 Ukrainian Front, Jan. 1944.
—Broke through 4 Panzer Army at Shepetovka, Mar. 1944.
—Lvov Sandomir Op., July 1944.
—Vistula Oder Op., Jan. 1945.
—Berlin Op., Apr. 1945.
—Took Zossen, Apr. 1945.
—Czechoslovakia, May 1945.
—Redesignated Guards, 14 May 1945.
—Luckenwalde, Germany, 1946 as 3 Guards Mechanized Army, (Feb. 1947 OB).
Key Commanders: Gen P. Romanenko, 1942; Gen-Maj P.S. Rybalko, May 1943–May 1945.
Units: May 1942: 4, 12 Tank Corps.
  Jan. 1943: 12, 15 Tank Corps, 111, 180, 184 Rifle, 48 Guards Rifle Division.
  May 1943: 12, 15 Tank, 2 Mechanized Corps.
  Oct. 1943: 6, 7 Guards Tank, 9 Mechanized Corps, 91 Independent Tank Brigade.
  Jan. 1944: 6, 7 Guards Tank, 9 Mechanized Corps, 91 Independent Tank Brigade.
  Aug. 1946: 6, 7 Guards Tank, 9 Mechanized Divisions.

4 Army
—Activated from separate detachments of the Red Army, Apr. 1918.
—Reformed as 2 Revolutionary Workers Army, Apr. 1920.
—Reactivated, Western Front on the basis of the Southern Group of Forces, 15 Army, May 1920.
—Deactivated, Mar. 1921.
—Reactivated in Belorussian Military District on basis of the Bobruysk Army Group, Mar. 1939.
—Poland, Sep. 1939.
—Brest Litovsk as a covering army, Western Special Military District, 22 June 1941.
—Smolensk, July 1941.
—Commander court-martialed, July 1941.
—Bobruysk pocket, July 1941.
—Subordinated to 21 Army, July 1941.
—Deactivated; Field Headquarters became Headquarters Central Front, July 1941.

—RVGK when reactivated (SME), Sep. 1941.
—Leningrad, directly subordinate to Stavka VGK, Nov. 1941.
—Volkhov area, Nov. 1941.
—Tikhvin, Nov–Dec 1941.
—Voronezh Front, Sep. 1943.
—Deactivated, Nov. 1943.
—New 4 Army was created by renaming the 34th Army (Caucasus), Jan. 1944.
—Iran, 1945.
—Transcaucasus, Jan. 1947, EUCOM study.
Key Commanders: V.I. Chuikov, Mar. 1939.
Units: June 1941: 14 Mechanized Corps w/22, 30 Tank Divisions, 205 Motor Rifle Division; 28 Rifle Corps w/6, 42 Rifle Divisions; 49, 62, 75 Rifle Divisions.
Sep. 1941: 285, 292, 311 Rifle, 27 Cavalry Divisions.
Nov. 1941: 4 Guards Rifle, 44, 65, 92, 191, 285, 310, 311 Rifle Divisions, 60 Tank Division.
Dec. 1941: Northern Operations Group had 44, 191 Rifle Divisions, 46 Tank Brigade; Central Operations Group had 60 Tank Division, 27 Cavalry Division; Southern Operations Group had 4 Guards, 92 Rifle Divisions; 65 Rifle Division in army reserve.

4 Combat Engineer Army
—Stalingrad axis, July 1942.

4 Guards Army
—Formed from 24 Army, 16 Apr. 1943.
—Kursk, July 1943.
—RVGK, Aug. 1943.
—RVGK to Akhtyrka, 17 Aug. 1943.
—Belgorod Kharkov Op., Aug. 1943.
—Korsun Shevchenkovskiy Op.; stopped breakout w/27 Army, Jan. 1944.
—Kirovograd w/2 Ukrainian Front, Jan. 1944.
—Uman Botosani Op. w/5 Guards Tank Army, Mar. 1944.
—Dniester River, Mar. 1944.
—Iasi Kishinev Op., Aug. 1944.
—Hungary, Nov. 1944.
—Lake Balaton; took main attack w/26 Army, Mar. 1945.
—Varpalota, Apr. 1945.
—RVGK Army, (MHJ), Nov. 1982.
—Belorussian Military District (EUCOM Study), July 1946.
Key Commanders: Aug. 1944: I.V. Galinin.
Units: July 1943: 21, 31 Guards Rifle, 20 Guards Airborne Corps; 8 NKVD Division.

Jan. 1944: 20 Guards Rifle Corps w/5 Guards Airborne, 66 Guards Rifle, 375 Rifle Divisions; 21 Guards Rifle Corps w/69 Guards, 138 Rifle Division.
Mar. 1944: 5, 6, 7 Guards Airborne, 41 Guards Rifle Divisions.
Aug. 1944: 5, 7 Guards Airborne Divisions.
Nov. 1944: 4, 34, 40, 41, 62, 69, 80 Guards Rifle; 3, 5, 6, 7 Guards Airborne, 84, 252 Rifle Divisions.

4 Reserve Army
—Formed in Kalinin area, spring 1942.
—Kalinin, June 1942.
—Formed 38 Army, third formation, Aug. 1942.
—All reserve armies were RVGK.
Key Commanders: Gen. N. Chibisov, Aug. 1942.

4 Shock Army
—Formed in the Northwest front from the 27 Army (SME), Dec. 1941.
—Southwest front offensive, drove towards Vitebsk, Jan. 1942.
—Toropets, Jan. 1942.
—Demyansk Pocket, Smolensk Sector, Feb. 1942.
—Velizh Op., Dec. 1942.
—Kalinin Front, Aug. 1943.
—Smolensk Op., Sep. 1943.
—Nevel Op., Oct. 1943.
—Dretun, Nov. 1943.
—Belorussian Op., June 1944.
—Took Daugavpils, 25 July 1944.
—Kaunas area, Aug. 1944.
—Dvinsk, Aug. 1944.
—Riga, Oct. 1944.
—Field Headquarters used to form Headquarters Steppe Military District, July 1945.
Key Commanders: Y. Yeremenko, January 1942; F. I. Golikov, Apr. 1942; Maklyshev, June 1944.
Units: Dec. 1941: 249, 332, 334, 358, 360 Rifle Divisions.
Feb. 1942: 249, 332, 334, 358, 360, 382 Rifle Divisions.
Aug. 1944: 14, 44, 100 Rifle, 5 Tank Corps.

4 Guards Tank Army (Formerly 4 Tank Army)
—Formed from 38 Army, July 1942.
—Kletskaya, July 1942.
—Stalingrad axis; remnants redesignated 65 Army, Summer 1942.
—Temporarily ceased to exist, Dec. 1942.
—Reformed at Naro Fominsk, Moscow Military District, July 1943.

—Orel, in breakthrough zone of 11 Guards Army, July 1943.
—Bolkhov, 24 July 1943.
—Zhitomir Berdichev Op., Dec. 1943.
—From RVGK to 1 Ukrainian Front, Feb. 1944.
—Seret and Dniester Rivers, Mar. 1944.
—Proskurov Chernovtsy Op., Mar. 1944.
—Resisted breakout of 1 Panzer Army, Apr. 1944.
—Lvov Sandomir Op., Koltov Corridor, July 1944.
—Vistula Oder Op., Jan. 1945.
—Krosno Odrozanskie, Poland, Jan. 1945.
—Guards, 17 Mar. 1945.
—Berlin Op., Apr. 1945.
—Prague, May 1945.
—Germany as 4 Guards Mechanized Army, Sep. 1946, (Feb. 1947 OB).
Key Commanders: Gen-Lt V.M. Badanov, July 1943– Mar. 1944; Gen-Lt D.D. Lelyushenko, Mar. 1944–May 1945.
Units: July 1942: 22, 23 Tank Corps, 18, 205 Rifle Divisions, 133 Tank Brigade.
May 1943: 11 and 30 Tank Corps (Ural Volunteers), 6 Guards Mechanized Corps.
May 1945: 10 Guards Tank Corps
Sep. 1946: 10 Guards Tank, 25 Tank Divisions.

5 Army
—Formed Kazan, 1918.
—Defeated "White Army of Siberia near Chelyabinsk;" Tukachevskiy Commander, 1919.
—Deactivated, 1924.
—Eastern Poland, Sep. 1939.
—Reactivated as a covering army, Kiev Special Military District, June 1941.
—Kovel, 22 June 1941.
—Counterattacked at Korosten and Novograd Volynskiy, July 1941.
—Chernigov pocket; commander captured, Aug. 1941.
—Borodino; referred to as "newly created," Oct. 1941 (MHJ, Jan. 1982).
—Reformed from 1 Guards Rifle Corps at Mozhaisk, Oct. 1941.
—Mozhaisk Defense Line at Volokolamts, Nov. 1941.
—Moscow, Dec. 1941.
—Mozhaisk, Jan. 1942.
—Secondary attack, Rzhev-Sychevka Op., July 1942.
—Smolensk; took city, Sep. 1943.
—Vitebsk Orsha Op. as a breakthrough army, June 1944.
—Southeast of Kaunus, July 1944.

—Vilnius, July 1944.
—Vistula Oder Op., Jan. 1945.
—East Prussia Op., in assault group of 3 Belorussian Front, Jan. 1945.
—Koenigsberg, Apr. 1945.
—Dresden, May 1945.
—Manchurian campaign, Aug. 1945.
—Kuibyshev, Far East Military District, 1946 (Sep. 1947 OB).
—Grigorenko Operations Officer of this army in early 1960's.
Key Commanders: D.D. Lelyushenko Oct. 1941; L.A. Govorov, Nov. 1941; N.I. Krylov, 1944–45
Units: June 1941: 15 Rifle, 22 Mechanized Corps 45, 62, 87, 124, 135 Rifle, 19, 41 Tank, 215 Motorized Divisions.
Nov. 1941: 32, 30, 82 Motorized Divisions and 2 Guards Cavalry Corps.
Dec. 1941: 32, 50, 82, 144 Rifle Divisions.
Jan. 1942: 19, 32, 50, 108, 144, 329, 336 Rifle Divisions, 82 Motorized Division.
July 1944: 45, 66, 72 Rifle Corps w/63, 93, 97, 144, 215, 277, 371 Rifle Divisions.

5 Combat Engineer Army
—Stalingrad, July 1942.

5 Guards Army
—Activated at Saratov, Volga Military District as 66 Army (former 8 Reserve), Aug. 1942.
—Designated Guards, 16 Apr. 1943.
—Orel, penetrated Army Group Center, July 1943.
—Kursk, at Prokhorovka, July 1943.
—Belgorod Kharkov Op., Aug. 1943.
—Vorskla River, Sep. 1943.
—Kremenchug, Sep. 1943.
—Poltava, Sep. 1943.
—RVGK (MHJ), Dec. 1943.
—Kiev Zhitomir Defensive Op., Dec. 1943.
—Kirovograd Op. w/2 Ukrainian Front, Dec. 1943–Jan. 1944.
—Attacked German 6 Army, Mar. 1944.
—Lvov Sandomir Op., July 1944.
—Mielec, Poland, Aug. 1944.
—Vikavishkis, 17 Aug. 1944.
—Czestochowa, Jan. 1945.
—Vistula Oder Op., Jan. 1945.
—Torgau, Elbe River (met Americans), 25 Apr. 1945.

—Prague, May 1945.
—Austria, Feb. 1946.
—Uzhgorod Mukachevo area, Carpathian Military District, 1947 (Feb. 1948 OB).
Key Commanders: Gen-Lt A.S. Zhadov, 1943–44.
Units: Oct. 1943-Apr. 1945: 32, 33, 34 Guards Rifle Corps; 13, 14, 15, 32, 33, 34, 58, 78, 95, 97 Guards Rifle, 9 Guards Airborne Divisions; 118 Rifle Division.
Jan. 1944: 32 Guards Rifle Corps w/6 Guards Airborne, 95, 97, 110 Guards, 214 Rifle Divisions; 33 Guards Rifle Corps w/9 Guards Airborne, 13 Guards, 111 Rifle Divisions; 35 Guards Rifle Corps w/93, 94 Guards, 78, 84 Rifle Divisions.

5 Reserve Army
—Formed by VGK Order, probably in Novo-Annenski, Don Bend, 28 May 1942.
—All reserve armies were RVGK.
—Redesignated 63 Army, 10 July 1942.
—Stalingrad axis, July 1942.
Key Commanders: V.I. Kuznetsov: June 1942.
Units: May 1942: 1, 127, 153, 181, 184 and 196 Rifle Divisions.
June 1942: 14 Guards, 1, 127, 153, 181, 184, 196 Rifle Divisions.

5 Shock Army
—Formed in the RVGK by reforming 10 Reserve Army; had 224 HSU (SME), 9 Dec. 1942.
—FHO thought it was formed from 27 Army, Jan. 1942.
—Stalingrad area; drove to Mius River, Dec. 1942.
—Caucasus, Jan–Feb 1943
—Mius River; had 25% RVGK troops, Aug. 1943.
—Melitopol Op.; main attack army, Sep–Nov 1943.
—South Russia w/4 Ukrainian Front, Jan. 1944.
—Iasi Kishinev Op.; deceived Germans into thinking they were the main attack army, Aug. 1944.
—Vistula Oder Op., Jan. 1945.
—Magnusew Bridgehead, main attack force, Jan. 1945.
—Main breakthrough army, Kustrin Bridgehead, Feb. 1945.
—Berlin, Apr. 1945.
—Zhukov appears to favor this army in his memoirs.
—Gen. Berzarin, their commander, became commandant of Berlin, May 1945.
—Schwerin, Germany, as 5th Mech Army, Jul. 1946 (OB).
—Transferred to Kaliningrad and deactivated, 1947 (EUCOM Study).

Key Commanders: M.M. Popov, Dec. 1942; R. Ya Malinovskiy, Dec. 1942; N.E. Berzarin 1944–45.
Units: Dec. 1942: 3 Guards Cavalry, 4 Mechanized, 7 Tank Corps, 4 Guards Rifle, 87, 258, 300, 315 Rifle Divisions.
Aug. 1943: 31 Guards Rifle Corps w/4, 34, 40 Guards Rifle Divisions.
Jan. 1944: 3 Guards Rifle Corps w/50, 54, 96 Guards Rifle Divisions; 63 Rifle Corps w/118, 267 Rifle Divisions.
Jan. 1945: 9, 26, 32 Rifle, 4 Breakthrough Artillery Corps.
Apr. 1945: 11 Tank Corps, 32 Rifle Corps, 60, 87, 94 Guards Rifle, 230, 248, 266, 295, 301, 416 Rifle Divisions.
Jan. 1947: 9 Rifle Corps w/30, 89, 94 Guards Rifle Divisions, 301 Rifle Division; 6, 41, 42, 248 Rifle Divisions.

5 Guards Tank Army (Formerly 5 Tank)
—Formed as tank army of combined composition on basis of an unknown combined arms army headquarters, 29 May 1942.
—Stalingrad axis; strongest of early tank armies, Aug. 1942.
—RVGK (MHJ), Nov. 1942.
—Main attack army, Stalingrad Counteroffensive, 19 Nov. 1942.
—Caucasus, Jan–Feb 1943.
—First tank army of unified composition, Jan. 1943.
—Designated Guards, 10 Feb. 1943.
—Kursk, at Prokhorovka; had 850 tanks, July 1943.
—Belgorod Kharkov Op., badly beaten, August 1943.
—RVGK (SME), Sep. 1943.
—Kremenchug, Oct. 1943.
—Kirovograd/Krivoi Rog axis, Nov. 1943.
—RVGK (MHJ), Dec. 1943.
—Kiev Zhitomir Defensive Op., Dec. 1943.
—Znamenka, Dec. 1943.
—Korsun Shevchenkovskiy Op. w/2 Ukrainian Front, Jan. 1944.
—Kirovograd w/2 Ukrainian Front, Jan. 1944.
—Uman Botosani Op. w/2 Ukrainian Front, Mar. 1944.
—Attacked 9 Army near Uman with 4 Guards Army, 4 March 1944.
—Targul Frumos; badly beaten, May 1944.
—Rumania, June 1944.
—Regrouped to Belorussia via RVGK, 3 Belorussian Front, June 1944.
—Belorussian Op.; captured Minsk, July 1944.
—RVGK (SME), July 1944.
—Lvov Sandomir Op., July 1944.
—Vilnius, Aug. 1944.
—Shauliai, Aug. 1944.

—Memel Op., Sep. 1944.
—RVGK, Oct. 1944.
—With 2 Belorussian Front, Nov. 1944.
—Vistula Oder Op. (Deutsche Eylau); 2 Belorussian Front mobile group, Jan. 1945.
—Memel, Feb. 1945.
—East Prussian Special Military District in 1946, (OB).
Key Commanders: P.L. Romanenko 1942; P.S. Rybalko, Fall 1942–Jan. 1943; P.A. Rotmistrov Feb. 1943–Aug. 1944; Gen-Lt V.T. Volskiy, Aug. 1944–Mar. 1945; Gen-Maj M.D. Sinenko, Mar–May 1945.
Units: July 1942: 2, 7 and 11 Tank Corps.
Nov. 1942: 1, 26 Tank, 8 Cavalry Corps, 14, 47, 50 Guards, 159, 346 Rifle Divisions.
May 1943: 17, 18, 19 Tank Corps, 5 Guards Mechanized Corps.
July 1943: 2 Guards, 2, 18, 29 Tank Corps, 5 Guards Mechanized Corps; 2 Guard Tank and 2 Tank Corps attached for Prokhorovka.
Jan. 1944: 18, 20, 28, 29 Tank Corps, 5 Guards and 8 Mechanized Corps.
June 1944: 3 Tank Corps.
Jan. 1945: 8 Guards Tank and 8 Mechanized Corps.

6 Army
—Formed under direct control of the Revolutionary Council and the Supreme Commander, Sep. 1918.
—Called 6 Independent Army. 1919.
—Murmansk area, 1920.
—Troops to 7 Army, Apr. 1920.
—Headquarters became Military Directorate of the White Sea Military District, 1920.
—Reactivated, Aug. 1920 to May 1921.
—Headquarters personnel used to form Headquarters Kharkov Military District, May 1921.
—Reactivated, Kiev Special Military District, Aug. 1939.
—Poland, Sep. 1939.
—Lvov as covering army, Kiev Military District, June 1941.
—Attacked near Kiev; commander captured, July 1941.
—Trapped in Uman Pocket; destroyed near Pervomaisk, Aug. 1941.
—Deactivated, 10 Aug. 1941
—Recreated on basis of 48 Rifle Corps, on Kharkov Sector, end-Aug. 1941.
—Izyum, Jan. 1942.
—Main attack army in Kharkov offensive, May 1942.

—Destroyed, June 1942.
—Field Headquarters deactivated, June 1942.
—Reactivated in RVGK on basis of 6 Reserve Army, June 1942.
—Kantemirov, Dec. 1942.
—Belgorod Kharkov area, Feb. 1943.
—Annihilated near Zaporozhye, 18 Feb. 1943.
—Kursk, July 1943.
—Dnieper River, Sep. 1943.
—South Russia w/3 Ukrainian Front, Jan. 1944.
—Forces sent to 37 and 46th Armies, June 1944.
—RVGK, July 1944.
—Transferred to 1 Ukrainian Front; troops from 3 Guards and 13 Army, Dec. 1944.
—Vistula Oder Op., Jan. 1945.
—Liegnitz, Mar. 1945.
—Breslau, May 1945.
—Field Headquarters used to form Headquarters Voronezh Military District, July 1945.
Key Commanders: F.I. Golikov, Sep. 1939; K.S. Moskalenko, Dec. 1941; F. Kharitanov, 1942.
Units: June 1941: 41, 97, 159 Rifle, 32, 84 Tank, 81 Motorized, 3 Cavalry Division.
June 1942: 106, 169, 226, 230, 255, 273, 277 Rifle, 26, 28 Cavalry Divisions.
Dec. 1942: 11 Tank Corps, 172, 267, 350 Rifle Divisions.
Jan. 1944: 66 Rifle Corps w/203, 244, 333 Rifle Divisions.

6 Combat Engineer Army
—Stalingrad, July 1942.
Units: July 1942: 3, 17, 18, 19 Combat Engineer Brigades.

6 Guards Army
—Formed from 21 Army, 16 Apr. 1943.
—Kursk (Oboyan), July 1943.
—Made major attack near Orel, July 1943.
—Belgorod Kharkov Op., Aug. 1943.
—Captured Belgorod, Aug. 1943.
—Voronezh Front, Sep. 1943.
—Pskov, Feb. 1944.
—Belorussian Op., June 1944.
—Lithuania (Memel, Riga), Oct. 1944.
—Baltic Military District in 1946; (Feb. 1947 OB).
—Riga, Lithuania, Nov. 1946, (EUCOM study).

Units: May-July 1943: 22, 23 Guards Rifle, 89 Rifle Corps, 2 Guards
Tank Corps, 51, 52, 67, 71, 89, 90 Guards Rifle Divisions, 375
Rifle Division.
June 1944: 2, 23 Guards Rifle Corps.

6 Reserve Army
—Formed at Novo-Khopersk, southeast of Voronezh, spring 1942.
—Reserve armies were in the RVGK.
—Used to form 6 Army, June 1942.
Key Commanders: F. Kharitanov, June 1942.

6 Guards Tank Army (Formerly 6 Tank)
—Formed as a tank army of unified composition in the RVGK on basis of 5 Mechanized and 5 Guards Tank Corps, Jan. 1944.
—Korsun Shevchenkovskiy Op., Jan. 1944.
—Uman Botosani Op. w/2 Ukrainian Front, Mar. 1944.
—Jassy area (Ultra), 29 Mar. 1944.
—Targul Frumos, May 1944.
—Rumania, June 1944.
—Iasi Kishinev Op.; had 398 tanks, 153 SP guns, Aug. 1944.
—Captured Bucharest and Ploesti, Aug. 1944.
—Designated Guards, 12 Sep. 1944.
—Hungary; in big tank battles near Debrecen, Oct. 1944.
—Budapest Op.; had 325 tanks and SP guns, Nov. 1944.
—Budapest, Feb. 1945.
—Lake Balaton Op.; had 406 tanks and SP guns, Mar. 1945.
—Vienna; had 286 tanks an SP guns, Apr. 1945.
—Czechoslovakia, near Prague; had 151 tanks and SP guns, May 1945.
—Manchurian campaign, Aug. 1945.
Key Commanders: Gen-Lt A.G. Kravchenko, Jan. 1944–May 1945.
Units: August 1944: 5 Guards Tank, 5 Guards Mechanized, 23 Rifle Corps.
August 1945: 5, 9 Guards Tank, 7 Guards Mechanized Corps.

7 Independent Army
—Activated for defense of Petrograd, Nov. 1918.
—Renamed Petrograd Revolutionary Worker Army, Feb. 1920.
—Became part of Petrograd Military District, Feb. 1920.
—Resubordinated to General Staff, Mar. 1921.
—Put down Kronstadt Rebellion, Mar. 1921.
—Deactivated, 10 May 1921.
—Reactivated in Leningrad Military District, Oct. 1939.
—Karelian Isthmus, Finland, Nov. 1939.
—Made main assault on Mannerheim Line; took Vyborg, Mar. 1940.

—Deactivated, Mar–Apr 1940.
—Reactivated in Leningrad, second half of 1940.
—Leningrad Military District, Jan. 1941.
—Leningrad Military District as a covering army north of Lake Ladoga, June 1941.
—Petrozavodsk Axis, July 1941.
—Svir River, Aug. 1941.
—Reformed as an Independent Army directly subordinate to VGK, Sep. 1941.
—Leningrad, Nov. 1941.
—Karelian Front, 1941–44.
—Between Lake Onega and Ladoga, Spring, 1944.
—Svir River Op., main attack army, June 1944.
—Took Petrozavodsk, June 1944.
—Finland, Sep. 1944.
—RVGK, Nov. 1944.
—Field Headquarters used to form field headquarters of 9 Guards Army, Jan. 1945.
Key Commanders: June 1944: A.N. Krutikov.
Units: Feb. 1940: 17, 28 Rifle Corps.
      June 1941: 54, 71, 168, 237 Rifle Divisions.
      Dec. 1941: 55, 69, 70, 73 Naval Rifle Brigades.
      June 1944: 37 Guards, 4, 94, 99 Rifle Corps, 3, 69, 70 Naval Rifle Brigades.

7 Combat Engineer Army
—Formed Apr. 1942.
—Southwest Front, Apr. 1942.
—Stalingrad, July 1942.
Units: Apr. 1942: 20, 21, 23 Engineer Brigades.
      May 1942: 12, 14, 15, 20, 21 Engineer Brigades.

7 Guards Army
—Formed from 64 Army, 16 April 1943.
—Kursk, July 1943.
—Fourth Battle of Kharkov, Aug. 1943.
—Dnieper, Sep. 1943.
—Kirovograd w/2 Ukrainian Front, Jan. 1944.
—Attacked German 6 Army, Mar. 1944.
—Targul Frumos w/2 Ukrainian Front, May 1944.
—Iasi Kishinev Op., Aug. 1944.
—Debrecen Op., Szolnok Bridgehead (Ultra), Oct. 1944.
—Budapest, Dec. 1944.

—Komarno, Czechoslovakia, Apr. 1945.
—Tabor, Czechoslovakia, May 1945.
—Yerevan, Transcaucasus Military District, June 1946 (Feb. 1947 OB and EUCOM Study).
Units: July 1943: 15, 24, 25, 35, 36, 72, 73, 78, 83 Guards Rifle, 24 Tank Corps, 213 Rifle Division.
Jan. 1944: 24 Guards Rifle Corps w/8 Guards Airborne, 36, 41 Guards Rifle Divisions; 25 Guards Rifle Corps w/72, 81 Guards, 409 Rifle Divisions; 303 Rifle Division.

7 Reserve Army
—Formed, probably in Stalingrad area, June 1942.
—Reserve armies were RVGK.
—Became 62 Army at Stalingrad, 10 July 1942.
Key Commanders: V. Kolpakchi, June 1942.
Units: June 1942: 33 Guards, 147, 181, 184, 192, 196 Rifle Divisions.

8 Army
—Activated, Sep. 1918.
—Deactivated; Headquarters to Caucasus Labor Army, May 1920.
—Activated on basis of Novogorod Op. Group, Oct. 1939.
—Finland, north of Lake Ladoga, Nov. 1939.
—To Baltic Special Military District, Aug. 1940.
—Baltic Special Military District as a covering army, 22 June 1941.
—Defended Latvia, June 1941.
—Estonia, Aug. 1941.
—Leningrad; had 100% losses in battalion/company commanders, Aug. 1941.
—Schlusselburg area of Leningrad, Dec. 1942.
—Leningrad Offensive Jan. 1944.
—Narva River, Apr. 1944.
—Narva, July 1944.
—Tartu, Sep. 1944.
—Estonia, Jan–May 1945.
—Deactivated in Estonia (SME), Oct. 1945.
—Krasnogvardeysk, Leningrad MD, Oct. 1946 (Feb. 1947 OB).
Units: Dec. 1939: 11, 18, 168 Rifle Divisions.
Jan. 1940: 18, 56, 75, 139, 155, 168 Rifle Divisions.
June 1941: 10, 11, 16 Rifle Corps, 48, 90, 125 Rifle Divisions, 23, 28 Tank, 202 Motorized Divisions.
Sep. 1941: 10, 11, 125, 168 Rifle Divisions.
Oct. 1946: 109 Rifle Corps w/109, 131 Rifle Divisions.

8 Combat Engineer Army
—Formed from miners of Donets Basin, Jan. 1942.
—Novocherkassk, Jan. 1942.
—Rostov, Apr. 1942.
—Stalingrad, July 1942.
Units: Apr. 1942: 10, 24, 25, 30 Engineer Brigades.

8 Guards Army
—Formerly 62 Army, designated Guards, 16 April 1943.
—Kursk, July 1943.
—Dnieper River, Sep. 1943.
—Zaporozhye Bridgehead, Oct. 1943.
—Krivoi Rog offensive, Oct. 1943.
—Nikopol and Krivoi Rog w/3 Ukrainian Front, Jan. 1944.
—Attacked German 6th Army, Mar. 1944.
—Odessa, Apr. 1944.
—Lublin Brest Op.; at Kovel, July 1944.
—Magnuszew Bridgehead, Aug. 1944–Jan. 1945.
—RVGK (MHJ), Jan. 1945.
—Vistula Oder Op.; breakthrough army, Jan. 1945.
—Poznan, Feb. 1945.
—Kustrin Bridgehead, Seelow Heights, Mar. 1945.
—Berlin Op.; main attack army, Apr. 1945.
—Weimar, Germany as 8 Guards Mechanized Army, Dec. 1946 (Feb. 1947 OB).
Key Commanders: V. Chuikov 1942–45.
Units: Oct. 1943: 27, 39, 50, 74, 78, 79, 82, 88 Guards Rifle Divisions.
  Jan. 1944: 4 Guards Rifle Corps w/35, 47, 57 Guards Rifle Divisions; 28 Guards Rifle Corps w/39, 79, 88 Guards Rifle Divisions; 29 Guards Rifle Corps w/27, 74, 82 Guards Rifle Divisions. (Same units to end of war).
  Dec. 1946: 11 Tank Division, 4 Guards Rifle Corps w/20 Guards Mechanized Division, 39 Guards Rifle Division; 27 Guards Rifle Corps w/21 Guards Mechanized Division, 82, 102 Guards Rifle Divisions; 28 Guards Rifle Corps w/19 Guards Mechanzied Division, 57, 88 Guards Rifle Divisions.

8 Reserve Army
—Formed in Saratov area, spring 1942.
—Used to form 66 Army, Aug. 1942.
—Reserve armies were RVGK.
Key Commanders: R.Ya. Malinovskiy, June 1942.

9 Army
—Activated, Sep. 1918.
—Kuban, Sep. 1920.
—Deactivated, June 1921.
—Finland's Polar Region, Jan. 1940.
—Formed from Odessa Military District upon invasion as 9 Independent Army, June 1941 (SME).
—Southern Front, July 1941.
—Rostov; good reputation in defensive battles, Nov. 1941.
—First Kharkov offensive, Jan. 1942.
—Second Kharkov offensive, May 1942.
—Only headquarters and "special units left," diverted to rear to be brought up to strength (prob. in RVGK), July 1942.
—Grozny, Sep. 1942.
—Caucasus, Jan. 1943.
—Krasnodar Op., Feb. 1943.
—Novorossiysk Op., Sep. 1943.
—Units to other armies; headquarters deactivated, Nov. 1943.
Key Commanders: F. M. Kharitanov, Nov. 1941.
Units: Jan. 1940: 14 Rifle Corps, 163 Rifle, 44 Motorized Divisions.
June 1941: 2, 18 Mechanized Corps, 3 Airborne Corps; 25, 30, 51, 74, 95, 116, 147, 150, 176, 206 Rifle Divisions; 2, 5, 9 Cavalry Divisions.
Oct. 1941: 30, 136, 150, 339 Rifle, 56, 66 Cavalry Divisions.
Aug. 1942: 11 Guards Rifle Corps, 151, 176, 417 Rifle Divisions.
Nov. 1942: 10, 11 Guards Rifle Corps, 3 Rifle Corps, 275, 276, 319, 351, 389 Rifle Divisions.

9 Combat Engineer Army
—Stalingrad area, July 1942.

9 Guards Army
—Activated as Independent Airborne Army, Oct. 1944.
—RVGK, Dec. 1944.
—Formed as 9 Guards Army on basis of the administration of 7 Army and Airborne Forces Headquarters (VDV), Dec. 1944–Jan. 1945.
—Southeast of Budapest, Feb. 1945.
—North of Lake Balaton, divisions had 11,000 men, Mar. 1945.
—Vienna, Apr. 1945.
—Prague, May 1945.
—Hungary, early 1946 (Feb. 1947 OB).
—Hungary and Rumania, as 9 Parachute or Glider Army, Dec. 1946 (1947 OBs).

—Possibly in West Siberian Military District, Sep. 1947 (48 OB).
—Suvorov *Inside the Soviet Army*, says this army will be formed in Baltic Military District in a future mobilization.
Units: Oct. 1944: 37, 38, 39 Guards Rifle Corps, 8, 11, 12, 14, 16 Guards Airborne Divisions, 13, 98, 99, 100 Guards Rifle Divisions.
Dec. 1944: 37, 38, 39 Guards Rifle Corps.
Feb. 1945: 37, 38, 39 Guards Rifle Corps; 98, 99, 100, 103, 104, 105, 107, 114 Guards Rifle Divisions.
Apr. 1945: 23 Tank Corps.

9 Reserve Army
—Formed in Gorki area, spring 1942.
—Became fourth formation of 24 Army, Aug. 1942.
—Reserve armies were RVGK.
Key Commanders: D. Kozlov, Aug. 1942.

10 Army
—Saved Tsaritsyn (Stalingrad) in civil war; Stalin Commissar, 1919.
—Western Special Military District as a covering army, 22 June 1941.
—Destroyed near Bialystok, June 1941.
—Zhukov lists as being activated near Ryazan, Nov. 1941.
—RVGK (MHJ), Dec. 1941.
—Stalinogorsk, Dec. 1941.
—Moscow counteroffensive, near Ryazan as main attack army, Dec. 1941.
—Germans identified a "new" 10 Army forming and moving to European Front, Sep. 1942.
—Kursk, July 1943.
—Kirov, Aug. 1943.
—Desna River, Sep. 1943.
—Smolensk Op. Sep. 1943.
Key Commanders: I.G. Zaharkina, 1939; F.I. Golikov, Nov. 1941.
Units: June 1941: 6 Mechanized Corps w/4, 7 Tank Divisions, 29 Motorized Division; 13 Mechanized Corps w/27, 31 Tank Divisions, 4 Motorized Division; 1 Rifle Corps w/1, 8 Rifle Divisions; 5 Rifle Corps w/86, 89 Rifle Divisions; 6 Cavalry Corps w/6 Cavalry Division; 13, 17, 24, 37, 113 Rifle Divisions.
Dec. 1941: 322, 330 Rifle Divisions.
July 1943: 139, 247, 330, 371, 385 Rifle Divisions.

10 Combat Engineer Army
—Voroshilovsk area, June 1942.

10 Guards Army
—Formed from 30 Army (NKVD troops), 16 Apr. 1943.

—Attacked Heeresgruppe Center at 4 Panzer/9 Army boundary, Aug. 1943.
—Roslavl, Aug. 1943.
—Smolensk, Sep. 1943.
—With 2 Baltic Front, Jan. 1944.
—Belorussia Op., June 1944.
—Opochka, July 1944.
—Southwest Leningrad Military District, 1946 (Feb. 1947 OB).
—Tallin, Baltic Military District, Apr. 1946, (Feb. 1948 OB and EUCOM Study).
Key Commanders: M.I. Kazakov, Feb. 1944.
Units: Dec. 1943: 7, 15, 19 Guards Rifle Corps.
    Apr. 1946: 7 Guards Rifle Corps w/7, 8 Guards Rifle Divisions; 8 Guards Rifle Corps w/7, 249 Rifle Divisions; 15 Guards Rifle Corps w/71 Guards Rifle, 182 Rifle Division.

10 Reserve Army
—Ryazan, Oct. 1941.
—Formed 10 Army, Nov. 1941.
—Reformed in Ivanovo area, spring 1942.
—Reserve armies were RVGK.
—Redesignated 5 Shock Army, Dec. 1942.
Key Commanders: Jan. 1942: M. Popov.

11 Army
—Activated North Caucasus Military District, Oct. 1918.
—Called "predecessor to Transcaucasus Military District" in Tbilisi (Tiflis) Press.
—Inactivated, Feb. 1919.
—Reactivated from Caspian-Caucasus Front in, Mar. 1919.
—Deactivated, June 1919.
—Reactivated on basis of the Astrakhan Group of Forces of the Western Front, Aug. 1919.
—Deactivated, became Independent Caucasus Red Banner Army, Aug. 1921.
—Reactivated in Belorussian Special Military District, Aug. 1939.
—Poland, Sep. 1939.
—West of Kaunus in Baltic Special Military District as covering army, 22 June 1941.
—Field Headquarters into RVGK; forces to 68 Army, Apr. 1943.
—RVGK, July 1943.
—Kursk offensive, 15 July 1943.
—Bryansk, Aug. 1943.

—Rogachev area, Sept. 1943.
—Deactivated; forces to 48/63 Armies, Dec. 1943.
Key Commanders: N.P. Medvaev, 1939-40; I. Fedyuniskiy, June 1943.
Units: June 1941: 3 Mechanzied Corps w/2, 5 Tank Divisions, 84 Motorized Division; 16 Rifle Corps w/5, 33 Rifle Divisions; 19 Lithuanian Rifle Corps w/179, 184 Rifle Divisions; 23, 126, 128, 188 Rifle Divisions.
July 1941: 70, 183, 202, 237 Rifle Divisions.
May 1943: 53 Rifle Corps, 4, 96, 260, 273, 323, 369 Rifle Divisions.

11 Guards Army
—Formed from 16 Army, 16 Apr. 1943.
—Orel offensive as main attack army at Bolkhov, July 1943.
—Vitebsk Orsha Op. as main attack army, June 1944.
—Vikavishkis, Aug. 1944.
—Vistula Oder Op., Jan. 1945.
—East Prussian Op.; in assault group of 3 Belorussian Front, Jan. 1945.
—Koenigsberg, Mar–Apr 1945.
—Field Headquarters used to form Headquarters East Prussian Special Military District, July, 1945.
—Baltic Military District in 1946, (Feb. 1947 OB).
Key Commanders: I.Kh. Bagramyan 1943; K.N. Galitskiy, 1943–45.
Units: May 1943: 8, 16, 36 Guards Rifle, 2 Guards Tank Corps, 152 Fortified Area.
July 1943: 1, 5, 8, 11, 16, 18, 26, 31, 36, 83, 84 Guards and 169 Rifle Divisions.
Dec. 1943: 8 Guards Rifle Corps w/26, 83 Guards Rifle Divisions; 16 Guards Rifle Corps w/1 Guards Motorized, 5, 16 Guards Rifle Divisions; 36 Guards Rifle Corps w/11, 31, 84 Guards Rifle Divisions; 83 Rifle Corps w/234, 235, 360 Rifle Divisions; 1 Tank Corps.

12 Army
—Activated, Nov. 1918 in North Caucasus Military District; deactivated Mar. 1919.
—Activated in the Ukraine, June 1919.
—Deactivated, Dec. 1920.
—Activated in Kiev Special Military District, Aug. 1939.
—Poland, Sep. 1939.
—Bukovina and Bessarabia, June 1940.
—Northwest of Chernovtsy as Kiev Special Military District covering army, 22 June 1941.

—Two rifle corps of 12 Army used to form 18 Army, June 1941.
—Zhitomir, July 1941.
—Destroyed in Uman pocket near Permovaisk, Aug. 1941.
—Deactivated, 10 Aug. 1941.
—Reactivated on basis of 17 Rifle Corps, Aug. 1941.
—Southern front; "relatively battleworthy" w/300–1200 men per division, July 1942.
—Kuban River, Caucasus, Aug. 1942.
—Headquarters transformed into Headquarters Tuapse Defensive Region, Sep. 1942.
—Third formation 12 Army activated in Southwest Front on basis of 5 Tank Army, Apr. 1943.
—Southwest Dnieper River, Sep. 1943.
—Forces absorbed into 18 Army, 29 Sep. 1943.
—Zaporozhye Bridgehead, Oct. 1943.
—Deactivated, Nov. 1943.
Key Commanders: Gen. A.A. Grechko July 1942.
Units: June 1941: 13, 17 Rifle, 16 Mechanized Corps; 44, 58, 60, 96, 164, 192 Rifle Divisions.
    Aug. 1941: 270, 274 Rifle, 11 Tank Division.
    Apr. 1943: 172, 203, 244, 333, 350 Rifle Divisions.
    Oct. 1943: 1 Guards Mechanized, 23 Tank, 66 Rifle Corps; 60 Guards, 203, 244, 304, 333 Rifle Divisions.

13 Army
—Activated from Group of Forces of Donetsk Axis, Mar. 1919.
—Deactivated, Nov. 1920.
—Formed from "Grendal's Special Detachment*," Finland, Nov. 1939.
—Deactivated, Mar. 1940.
—Reactivated in Western Special Military District, June 1941.
—Reserve Army, Minsk, June 1941.
—RVGK, June 1941.
—Smolensk July 1941.
—Moscow Sep. 1941.
—Destroyed in Bryansk Pocket, Oct. 1941.
—Counterattacked w/Bryansk Front at Yelets near Moscow, Dec. 1941.
—Voronezh, Jan. 1943.
—Near Kursk, Feb. 1943.
—Kursk (Ponyri), as main defensive army, July 1943.
—Dnieper River; first army to cross, Sep. 1943.
—Chernigov Pripyask Op., Sep. 1943.
—Crossed Dnieper at Chernigov, Oct. 1943.
—Kiev, Nov. 1943.

—Kiev Defensive Op., Dec. 1943.
—Zhitomir Berdichev Op. w/1 Ukrainian Front, Jan. 1944.
—Main attack army for Rovno-Lutsk Op., Jan. 1944.
—Shepetovka breakthrough, Mar. 1944.
—Attacked at Lutsk-Dubno; captured both, Mar. 1944.
—Lvov Sandomir Op., July 1944.
—Baranow Bridgehead, Aug. 1944.
—Vistula Oder Op., Jan. 1945 (Pilica River).
—Berlin Op., Apr. 1945.
—Karlovy Vary, Czechoslovakia, 8 May 1945.
—Carpathian Military District, March 1946 (EUCOM Study).
Key Commanders: N.P. Pukhov, 1944–45.
Units: Dec. 1939: 3, 15, 23 Rifle Corps; 31 Rifle Corps w/17, 24, 37 Rifle Divisions.
   June 1941: 17, 20 Mechanized Corps; 64, 100, 108, 161 Rifle, 36, 38 Tank, 210 Motorized Divisions.
   Sep. 1941: 6, 132, 137, 143, 148, 155, 160, 269, 282, 307 Rifle Divisions; 50 Tank, 21 Mountain and 52 Cavalry Divisions.
   Jan. 1943: 21, 23 Rifle Corps.
   May 1943: 17, 18 Guards Rifle, 15 and 29 Rifle Corps, 8, 15, 74, 81, 148, 307 Rifle Divisions..
   Sep. 1943: 17 Guards Rifle Corps w/2 Guards Airborne, 6, 70 Guards Rifle Divisions; also 15, 28 Rifle Corps; 74, 148, 181, 211 Rifle Divisions.
   Nov. 1943: 17, 18 Guards Rifle Corps.
   Jan. 1944: 24 Rifle Corps w/140, 149, 287 Rifle Divisions; 28 Rifle Corps w/4 Guards Airborne, 70 Guards, 246, 415 Rifle Divisions; 76 Rifle Corps w/6, 121 Guards, 112 Rifle Divisions; 77 Rifle Corps w/143, 181, 397 Rifle Divisions; 25 Tank Corps.
   Mar. 1944: 24, 28, 76 Rifle Corps.
   July 1944: 24, 27, 102 Rifle Corps.
*Served as prewar Chief of Main Artillery Directorate (GAU).

14 Army
—Activated, on the basis of the 2 Ukrainian Army, June 1919.
—Odessa, 1920.
—Deactivated, Jan. 1921.
—Created at Murmansk, Leningrad Military District, Oct. 1939.
—Finland Polar Region, Jan. 1940.
—Polar Region, Jan. 1941.
—Leningrad Military District as covering army, 22 June 1941.
—Defended Murmansk, summer 1941.
—Offensive operations, Murmansk area, Apr–May 1942.

—Petsamo Kirkenes Op. (Petsamo area), had 97,000 men, Sep. 1944.
—Kirkenes Offensive, Oct. 1944.
—Petrozavodsk, White Sea Military District, 1946–47 (Feb. 47 OB).
Units: June 1941: 14, 52, 88, 104, 122, 133, 186 Rifle, 23 Fortified Area, 1 Tank Divisions.
   Nov. 1942: 72 Rifle Brigade.
   Oct. 1944: 31, 99, 131 Rifle Corps; 126, 127 Light Rifle Corps; 10 Guards, 65, 83, 114, 367 Rifle Divisions.
   May 1946: 14, 24, 45, 368 Rifle Divisions.

15 Army
—Formed in Civil War from "Soviet Army of Latvia (Latvian Red Army)," 1919.
—Main attack army on Vilnius axis; V.I. Chuikov commanded a regiment in this army, May 1920.
—Inactivated, Dec. 1920.
—Reformed for Finnish War, 1940.
—Inactivated, Mar. 1940.
—Reformed at Birobidzhan from 2 Red Banner Army, June 1940.
—Birobidzhan, July 1941.
—In "Front Command Khabarovsk," Army headquarters at Birobidzhan, Apr. 1943.
—Manchurian Op., Aug. 1945.
—Amur River, Aug. 1945.
Key Commanders: Gen-Col P.A. Kurochkin, June 1940.
Units: Apr. 1943: 34, 39 Rifle Divisions, Novoye Fortified Area, 203 Tank Brigade.
   Aug. 1945: 34, 361, 388 Rifle Divisions, 171 Tank Brigade.

16 Army
—Formed in Civil war as the Western Army, Nov. 1918.
—Redesignated the Belorussian-Latvian Army, Mar. 1919.
—Redesignated 16 Army, June 1919.
—Berezina River, May 1920.
—Deactivated, May 1921.
—RVGK when reactivated at Borzya, Transbaikal Military District, July 1940.
—Transferred from Transbaikal Military District to Berdichev area, 13 May 1941.
—RVGK, July 1941.
—Shepetovka, July 1941.
—Destroyed in Smolensk Pocket, remnants used to form corps and rifle divs., July 1941.

—Yartsevo area, Sep. 1941.
—Reformed in Moscow area, Nov. 1941.
—Main attack army in Moscow counteroffensive, Dec. 1941.
—Lama River, Jan. 1942.
—Sukinichi, Feb. 1942.
—Redesignated 11 Guards Army, 16 Apr. 1943.
—Reactivated as part of Far East Front on Sakhalin Island, July 1943.
—Sakhalin Island Op., Aug. 1945.
Key Commanders: K.K. Rokossovskiy, 1940–41.
Units: May 1920: 8, 17 Rifle Divisions.
    July 1940: 5 Tank Corps w/13, 17 Tank, 109 Motorized Divisions.
    July 1941: 18, 46, 127, 132, 144, 152 Rifle Divisions, 13, 17, 57 Tank Divisions, 109, 213 Motorized Divisions.
    Sep. 1941: 1 Moscow Motorized, 38, 50, 64, 108, 129, 152, 158 Rifle Divisions; 101 Tank Division.
    Nov. 1941: 3 Guards, 78, 316 Rifle Divisions; 17, 50 Cavalry Divisions.
    Feb. 1942: 11 Guards, 322, 323, 324, 328 Rifle Divisions.
    Aug. 1945: 56 Rifle Corps, 79 Rifle Division.

17 Army
—Activated Transbaikal Military District, July 1940.
—Formed at Ulan Baator, Transbaikal Military District from 57th Independent Special Rifle Corps, 1940.
—Identified by Germans as equipping in Outer Mongolia with mobile formations; to be employed in that area, Sep. 1942.
—In "Front Command Chita," Apr. 1943.
—Manchurian Op., Aug. 1945.
Key Commanders: Gen-Major Korneyev, Apr. 1943.
Units: Apr. 1943: 10 Motorized, 36, 57 Rifle Divisions.
    Aug. 1945: 208, 278, 284 Rifle Divisions.

18 Army
—Activated on basis of Kharkov Military District, two rifle corps of 12 Army and forces of the Kiev Special Military District, June 1941.
—Yampol, Dniester, Bug area, July–Aug. 1941.
—Caught in Uman Pocket, Aug. 1941.
—Zaporozhye, Donets Basin, Oct. 1941.
—Southern Front; "relatively battleworthy" divisions of 300–1200 men, July 1942.
—Caucasus, Aug. 1942.
—Tuapse Defensive Op., 23 Sep–20 Dec 1942.

—Field Hedaquarters named 18 Landing Army by VGK, 11 Feb. 1943.
—Krasnodar, Feb. 1943.
—Reverted to combined arms army, 16 Mar. 1943.
—Novorossiysk area (Brezhnev political officer), Mar. 1943.
—Kuban Bridgehead (The Little Land), Apr. 1943.
—Absorbed 12 Army, 29 Sep. 1943.
—Assault landing on Kerch Peninsula, Nov. 1943.
—Radomysyl, Dec. 1943.
—RVGK, Dec. 1943.
—Kiev Defensive Op. from RVGK, Dec. 1943.
—Zhitomir Berdichev Op., one of main attack armies w/1 Ukrainian Front, Jan. 1944.
—RVGK (MHJ), June 1944.
—Lublin Brest Op. w/4 Ukrainian Front, July 1944.
—Mukachevo Uzhgorod Op., Sep. 1944.
—Carpathian Mountains near Czechoslovakia, Oct. 1944.
—Ruzemborok, Czechoslovakia, Apr. 1945.
—Olomouc, Czechoslovakia, May 1945.
—Absorbed into 52 Army, May 1945.
—Transcaucasus, June 1946 (EUCOM Study).
Key Commanders: Gen. E.P. Zhuravlev, July 1944.
Units: June 1941: 17 Rifle Corps w/60, 96 Mountain Divisions, 164 Rifle Division, 16 Mechanized Corps w/15, 39 Tank Divisions, 240 Motorized Division.
Dec. 1942: 32, 83 Guards, 31, 236, 353, 383, 395, 408 Rifle, 11, 12 Guards Cavalry Divisions.
Feb. 1943: 10 Guards, 16 Rifle Corps, 176, 318 Rifle Divisions.
Sep. 1943: 55 Guards (Shock Group), 76, 89, 318 Rifle Divisions.
Jan. 1944: 22 Rifle Corps w/129 Guards, 71, 317 Rifle Divisions; 52 Rifle Corps w/117 Guards, 24, 395 Rifle Divisions; 101 Rifle Corps w/161 Rifle Division; 17 Breakthrough Artillery Division.
May 1945: 8, 24 Rifle Divisions.

19 Army
—Formed in North Caucasus Military District, June 1941.
—Moved from North Caucasus Military District to Cherkassy-Belaya Tserkov area, 13 May 1941.
—RVGK, July 1941.
—Partly destroyed in Smolensk Pocket, July 1941.
—Reformed as 1 Shock Army, Nov. 1941.
—Second formation activated based on Kandalaksha Op. Group, Apr. 1942.

—Finnish Front, 1942–44.
—Kandalaksha area, Sep. 1944.
—RVGK, Nov. 1944
—East Pomeranian Op., Feb. 1945.
—Gdynia, Mar. 1945.
Key Commanders: I.S. Koniev, August 1941.
Units: July 1941: 25, 34 Rifle, 26 Mechanized Corps; 28, 38, 91, 129, 134, 158, 162, 171, 178, 214 Rifle, 1, 28 Mountain; 44, 48 Tank, 220 Motorized Divisions.
Oct. 1941: 50, 89, 91, 244 Rifle Divisions.
Mar. 1945: 31, 40, 132, 134 Rifle Corps, 10, 101, 102 Guards, 18, 27, 114, 177, 205, 272, 310, 313 Rifle Divisions.

20 Army
—RVGK when activated in Orel Military District, June 1941.
—RVGK, July 1941.
—Vitebsk-Orsha, 15 July 1941.
—Smolensk Pocket, partly destroyed, July 1941.
—Dorogobuzh area, Sep. 1941.
—Destroyed in Vyazma Pocket, Oct. 1941.
—Field Headquarters deactivated, Oct. 1941
—Reconstituted in RVGK from 1 Moscow Motorized Division and reserve troops at Lobnya, Moscow Military District, 29 Nov. 1941.
—Moscow; retook Solnechnogorsk; Stalin commended army, Nov–Dec 1941.
—RVGK (MHJ), Dec. 1941.
—Main attack army for Moscow counteroffensive, Dec. 1941.
—Lama River, Jan. 1942.
—Main attack army at Gzhahatsk, Jan. 1942.
—Rzhev Sychevka Op., July 1942.
—Pogorelo Gorodische Op., Aug. 1942.
—Nevel, Oct. 1943.
—RVGK, Nov. 1943.
—RVGK, Apr. 1944.
—Deactivated; Headquarters became Headquarters 3 Baltic Front, Apr. 1944.
Key Commanders: A.A. Vlasov, Dec. 1941; M.A. Reiter, Mar–Sep 1942; N.I. Gusev, Oct. 1943.
Units: June 1941: 61 Rifle Corps w/53, 110, 172 Rifle Divisions; 69 Rifle Corps, 7 Mechanized Corps w/1 Moscow Motorized, 14, 18 Tank Divisions; 18 Rifle Division.
Nov. 1941: 4 Guards, 20, 129, 173, 233, 312 Rifle Divisions; 24 Cavalry Division.

Dec. 1941: 331, 352 Rifle Divisions.
Aug. 1942: 82, 251, 312, 331, 354, 415 Rifle Divisions.

21 Army
—Activated Volga Military District (SME), May 1941.
—From Volga Military District to Chernigov-Konotop, 13 May 1941.
—RVGK, July 1941.
—Attacked at Rogachev, July 1941.
—Smolensk, absorbed 4 Army, July 1941.
—Destroyed in Kharkov sector near Kiev, Sep. 1941.
—Reactivated, Sep. 1941.
—Kharkov sector, Oct. 1941.
—Kharkov offensive, May 1942.
—Kletskaya, July 1942.
—Stalingrad offensive on main attack axis, Nov–Dec 1942.
—Designated 6 Guards Army, 16 Apr. 1943.
—RVGK when third formation raised from 3 Reserve Army, July 1943.
—Kursk, July 1943.
—Smolensk, Sep. 1943.
—Desna River to Gorki, Sep. 1943.
—RVGK; troops to 33 Army, Oct. 1943.
—RVGK to Leningrad front, Apr. 1944.
—Mannerheim Line, July 1944.
—Narva, Sep. 1944.
—Vistula Oder Op., Jan. 1945
—Opole, Poland, Jan. 1945.
—Czechoslovakia, May 1945.
—Eastern Leningrad Military District, June 1945 (EUCOM Study).
Key Commanders: Kuznetsov, Sep. 1941; I.M Chistyakov, Nov. 1942. D.N. Gusev, 1945.
Units: June 1941: 63 Rifle Corps w/61, 117, 167 Rifle Divisions; 66 Rifle Corps w/154, 232 Rifle Division; 25 Mechanized Corps w/ 50, 55 Tank, 219 Motorized Divisions.
July 1941: 53, 61, 102, 110, 117, 132, 148, 172, 187 Rifle, 50, 55 Tank, 219 Motorized Divisions.
Aug. 1941: 63, 66, 67 Rifle and 25 Mechanized Corps.
Nov. 1942: 3 Guards Cavalry; 4 Tank Corps; 63, 76, 96, 277, 293, 304, 333, 343 Rifle Divisions.
May 1943: 61, 69 Rifle Corps, 95, 174 Rifle Divisions.
Jul. 1943: 61 Rifle Corps w/51, 62, 119 Rifle Divisions; 63, 70, 76, 91, 95, 174 Rifle Divisions.
Nov. 1943: 99, 102 Rifle Corps. Apr. 1945: 120, 225, 229, 285 Rifle Divisions.

22 Army
—Activated in Ural Military District (SME), May 1941.
—Ural Military District to Velikiye Luki, 13 May 1941.
—RVGK, July 1941.
—Toropets, July 1941.
—Held up 3 Panzer Korps at Velikiye Luki, July 1941.
—Kalinin area, Dec. 1941.
—Leningrad, Dec. 1942.
—Northwest Front, July 1943.
—Belorussia Op., June 1944.
—South of Lake Luban, Aug. 1944.
—Riga, Oct. 1944.
—Courland, Apr. 1945.
—RVGK, Apr. 1945.
—Headquarters used to activate Headquarters Tauric (Crimea) Military District (SME), May 1945.
Units: June 1941: 51 Rifle Corps w/98, 112, 170 Rifle Division; 62 Rifle Corps w/174, 182 Rifle Divisions; 18, 117, 137, 138, 153, 154, 167, 170, 186, 232 Rifle Divisions, 14, 18, 42, 46 Tank Divisions, 1 Moscow and 185 Motorized Divisions.

23 Army
—Activated on the Karelian Isthmus, Leningrad Military District, May 1941.
—Leningrad Military District as covering army, Vipurii district, 22 June 1941.
—Karelian Isthmus, July 1941.
—Schlusselburg, Finnish Front, July–Aug. 1941.
—Trapped in Leningrad with 42 and 55 Armies, Sep. 1941.
—Leningrad, Dec. 1942.
—Vyborg Op., June 1944.
—Mannerheim Line, June–July 1944.
—Karelian Isthmus, May 1945.
Units: June 1941: 19, 50 Rifle, 10 Mechanized Corps; 14, 43, 115, 123, 142, 168, 177 Rifle Divisions.
June 1944: 97, 98, 115 Rifle Corps.

24 Army
—RVGK when activated in Siberia Military District, June 1941.
—RVGK, July 1941.
—First four Guards Rifle Divisions (100, 127, 153, 161 Rifle Divisions), from this army, 18 Sep. 1941.
—Yelnaya area with 13 divisions, Sep. 1941.

—Part of Reserve Front, Oct. 1941.
—Destroyed in Vyazma Pocket, Oct. 1941.
—Field Headquarters deactivated, Oct. 1941.
—Activated Moscow Military District in Moscow Defense Zone, Dec. 1941.
—RVGK, Jan. 1942.
—Renamed 1 Reserve Army, 1 May 1942.
—Reactivated in Southern Front on basis of an operational group of the front, July 1942.
—On Southern Front; only "Headquarters and special units left," diverted to rear to bring up to strength, probably in RVGK, July 1942.
—Forces to 12/37 Army; Headquarters to Grozny area, Aug. 1942.
—Fourth activation on basis of 9 Reserve Army, Aug. 1942.
—Stalingrad area, Sep. 1942.
—Stalingrad counteroffensive, Nov. 1942.
—RVGK, Jan. 1943.
—Became 4 Guards Army, 16 Apr. 1943.
—Not reformed after becoming guards.
—Some sources call it 24 Shock Army.
Key Commanders: D. Kozlov. 1942.
Units: June 1941: 52, 53 Rifle Corps.
  Sep. 1941: 19, 100, 120, 127, 133, 194, 248, 303, 309 Rifle Divisions; 103, 105, 106 Motorized, 102 Tank Divisions; 2, 6 People's Militia Divisions.
  Dec. 1941: 385 Rifle Division.
  May 1942: 73, 140, 228, 255 Rifle Divisions.
  Aug. 1942: 173, 207, 221, 292, 308 Rifle Divisions.
  Oct. 1942: 173, 207, 214, 221, 233, 258, 260, 273, 292, 298, 308 Rifle Divisions.
  Nov. 1942: 16 Tank Corps; 49, 84, 120, 173, 214, 233, 260, 273, 298 Rifle Divisions.

25 Army
—Formed in the Far East Military District from 1 Red Banner Army w/ Headquarters at Voroshilov (Ussuriysk), 18 Mar. 1941.
—In "Front Command Khabarovsk," Army headquarters at Razdolnoye, Apr. 1943.
—RVGK, Apr. 1945.
—Manchurian Campaign, Aug. 1945.
—North Korea, May 1946 (Feb. 1947 OB).
—Deactivated at Voroshilov, 1947 (Feb. 1948 OB).
Key Commanders: Gen-Lt Parussinov, Apr. 1943; I.M. Chistyakov, Aug. 1945.

Units: June 1941: 39, 105 Rifle Divisions.
Apr. 1943: 40, 119, 216 Rifle Divisions; 1, 4 Naval Rifle, 5 Rifle Brigades; 107 (Chansi), 108 (Possier), 110 (Kraskino), 111 (Schaffanski Rayon), 113 (Golubinia Utios), Slavyanka, Barabash Fortified Areas.
Apr. 1945: 393 Rifle Division.
Aug. 1945: 384, 395 Rifle Divisions.
May 1946: 1 Guards Airborne, 40, 105, 190, 238, 285 Rifle Divisions.

26 Army
—Activated in Kiev Special Military District, July 1940.
—Western Ukraine, Kiev Military District, 22 June 1941.
—Zhitomir area, July 1941.
—Destroyed on Kharkov sector with the Southwest Front, Sep. 1941.
—Field Headquarters deactivated, Sep. 1941.
—Reformed in Moscow Military District on basis of 1 Guards Rifle Corps, Oct. 1941.
—Referred to as "newly formed," Zusha River (Mozhaisk Line), Oct. 1941.
—Deactivated, 25 Oct. 1941.
—RVGK when reactivated in Volga Military District with 300 series Rifle Divisions, Nov. 1941.
—Leningrad, Nov. 1941.
—Used to form 2 Shock Army in RVGK, Dec. 1941.
—Fourth activation in Karelian Front on basis of Karelian operational group; in RVGK by Jan. 1942.
—Finnish Front, 1942–44.
—Finland, Sep. 1944.
—RVGK, Nov. 1944.
—Lake Balaton, took on main German attack w/4 Guards Army, Mar. 1945.
Units: June 1941: 8 Rifle and 8 Mechanized Corps, 99, 173 Rifle, 72 Mountain, 12, 34 Tank, 7 Motorized Divisions.
Oct. 1941: 6 Guards Rifle, 41 Cavalry Division, 5 Airborne Corps.
Nov. 1941: 327, 329, 344 Rifle, 73, 74 Cavalry Divisions.
Dec. 1941: 12, 133, 309, 340, 354, 365, 371 Rifle Divisions, 20, 44 Cavalry Divisions.
Mar. 1942: 23 Guards, 27, 54, 152, 186, 216 Rifle Divisions.

27 Army
—Activated on basis of Headquarters Baltic Special Military District, May 1941.

—Baltic Special Military District as second echelon army, 22 June 1941.
—Transformed into 4 Shock Army in Northwest Front, Dec. 1941.
—Velizh Demidov Op., Mar. 1942.
—Staraya Russa, Dec. 1942.
—Demyansk, Feb. 1943.
—RVGK in Steppe Military District, May 1943.
—From RVGK to Kursk, July 1943.
—Vorskla River in Belgorod Kharkov Op., Aug. 1943.
—Dnieper, in Fastov area, Oct. 1943.
—Kiev, Nov. 1943.
—Probably in Kiev Defensive Op., Dec. 1943.
—Zhitomir Berdichev Op. w/1 Ukrainian Front, Jan. 1944.
—Korsun Shevchenkovskiy Op.; stopped German breakout w/4 Guards Army, Jan. 1944.
—Uman Botosani Op., Mar. 1944.
—Crossed Prut River into Rumania (Ultra), 27 Mar. 1944.
—Targul Frumos, May 1944.
—Iasi Kishinev Op.; took command of 4 Rumanian Army, Aug. 1944.
—Sarviz Canal, Hungary, Mar. 1945.
—Focsani, Rumania, Dec. 1946 (Apr. 1947 OB).
Key Commanders: Gen-Col S.G. Trofimenko, Aug. 1944.
Units: June 1941: 22, 24 Rifle Corps, 16, 67, 180, 181, 182, 183, 184 Rifle Divisions.
May 1942: 87, 104, 188, 254, 384 Rifle Divisions.
Aug. 1943: 71, 147, 155, 166, 241 Rifle Divisions.
Jan. 1944: 47 Rifle Corps w/38, 136, 180 Rifle Divisions; 206, 309, 337 Rifle Divisions.
May 1944: 3 Guards Airborne Division, 35 Guards, 33, 47 Rifle Corps, 5 Mechanized Corps.

28 Army
—RVGK when activated in Archangelsk Military District, June 1941.
—RVGK, July 1941.
—Tried to relieve the Smolensk Pocket; destroyed, July 1941.
—Field Headquarters deactivated, 10 Aug. 1941.
—RVGK, second activation in Moscow Military District (SME), Nov. 1941.
—RVGK, Dec. 1941–May 1942.
—Second Kharkov Offensive; on main attack axis, May 1942.
—Field Headquartes reformed as 4 Tank Army, July 1942.
—Reactivated (third formation) on basis of Headquarters and forces of Stalingrad Military District, Aug. 1942.
—Stalingrad Counteroffensive, Nov. 1942.

—Kalmyk Steppes, Dec. 1942.
—Caucasus, at Rostov and Gulf of Taganrog, Jan–Feb 1943.
—Melitopol Op., Sep–Nov 1943.
—Mius River, Oct. 1943.
—Ukraine, Nov. 1943.
—South Russia with 4 Ukrainian Front, Jan. 1944.
—Kherson, Feb. 1944.
—Nikolayev, Apr. 1944.
—RVGK, May 1944.
—Belorussian Op.; cut Baranovichi-Slonim rail-line, June 1944.
—Berezina River, June 1944.
—Brest w/61 and 70 Armies, July 1944.
—RVGK, Sep–Oct 1944.
—Gumbinnen, Jan. 1945.
—East Prussian Op., Jan. 1945.
—Mariendorf, Apr. 1945.
—RVGK, Apr. 1945.
—Berlin Op., Apr. 1945.
—Czechoslovakia, May 1945.
—Grodno, Belorussia, May 1947 (Feb. 1948 OB).
—Records indicate this army was in the RVGK at least six times.
Key Commanders: D.I. Ryabishev, Mar–June 1942; Gen. A.A. Luchinskiy 1944–45.
Units: June 1941: 30, 33 Rifle Corps, 69 Motorized Division.
Nov. 1941: 359, 363, 367, 395 Rifle Divisions.
Sep. 1942: 34 Guards, 248 Rifle Divisions.
Nov. 1943: 130, 221, 248 Rifle Divisions.
Jan. 1944: 9 Rifle Corps w/230, 301 Rifle Divisions; 10 Guards Rifle Corps w/24, 109 Guards, 61, 77 Rifle Divisions; 320 Rifle Division.
June 1944: 3, 20 Guards, 8 Rifle Corps.
Jan. 1945: 65, 128 Rifle Corps, 54, 96 Guards and 152 Rifle Divisions.
Apr. 1945: 3 and 20 Guards Rifle Corps, 128 Rifle Corps; 61 Guards Rifle Division.

29 Army
—Activated in Moscow Military District on basis of 30 Rifle Division from NKVD troops, July 1941.
—RVGK, July 1941.
—Toropets area, Sep. 1941.
—Vyazma Pocket, Oct. 1941.
—Battle of Moscow, Kalinin area, Dec. 1941.

—Rzhev, Jan. 1942.
—Destroyed, Jan. 1942.
—South of Rzhev, Feb. 1942.
—Second formation at Rzhev, July 1942.
—Field Headquarters into RVGK, Feb. 1943.
—Formed Headquarters of 1 Tank Army, Apr. 1943.
—Not reformed.
Key Commanders: Gen-Lt Maslennikov, Dec. 1941.
Units: Sep. 1941: 243, 245, 253, 254, 256 Rifle Divisions.

30 Army
—RVGK when formed from NKVD troops (SME), July 1941.
—RVGK in Front of Reserve Armies, Olenino area, July 1941.
—Destroyed in Vyazma Pocket as part of Bryansk Front, Oct. 1941.
—Reformed in RVGK, Nov. 1941.
—Western Front from the RVGK, Nov. 1941.
—Moscow front, "grossly undermanned;" Nov. 1941.
—Moscow counterattack, Klin area; main attack army, Dec. 1941.
—Main attack on Rzhev, Jan. 1942; built up "to an assault army of pre-war organization," Jan. 1942.
—Rzhev front, Dec. 1942–May 1943.
—Redesignated 10 Guards Army, 16 Apr. 1943.
—Not reconstituted.
Units: July 1941: 119, 242, 243, 251 Rifle Divisions.
 Sep. 1941: 119, 242, 251 Rifle, 51 Tank Divisions.
 Nov. 1941: 5, 43, 101, 107 Motorized, 185, 242, 251, 256, 257, 316 Rifle Divisions, 18 Cavalry Division.

31 Army
—RVGK when activated in Moscow Military District from NKVD troops (SME), July 1941.
—RVGK, July 1941.
—RVGK, Sep. 1941.
—Counterattacked in Kalinin area, Dec. 1941.
—Main attack army for Rzhev-Sychevka Op., Aug. 1942.
—Rzhev, Dec. 1942.
—Baltic area, June 1943.
—Took Smolensk, 25 Sep. 1943.
—North of Orsha, Oct. 1943.
—Breakthrough army for Vitebsk-Orsha Op., June 1944.
—Masurian Lakes, Feb. 1945.
—RVGK, Apr. 1945.
—Berlin Op., Apr. 1945.

—Liberec, Czechoslovakia, May 1945.
Units: July 1941: 244, 246, 247, 249 Rifle Divisions.
    Sep. 1941: 119, 244, 246, 247, 249 Rifle Divisions.
    June 1944: 36, 71, 113 Rifle Corps.

32 Army
—RVGK when formed in Moscow Military District (SME), July 1941.
—Vyazma, Sep. 1941.
—Kharkov sector w/Southwest Front, Sep. 1941.
—RVGK as part of Reserve Front, Oct. 1941.
—Destroyed in the Vyazma Pocket, Oct. 1941.
—Forces sent to 16/19 Armies, Headquarters deactivated, Oct. 1941.
—Reactivated, Karelian Front from 2 operational groups, Mar. 1942.
—Karelia, 1943.
—Karelia, north of Lake Onega, June 1944.
—Sortavala, June 1944.
—Finland, July 1944; Finns wiped out 2 of its divisions at Ilomantsi, 19 Aug. 1944.
—Reported in White Sea Military District with Headquarters at Arkhangelsk, Dec. 1945 (Feb. 1947 OB).
Key Commanders: I.I. Fedyuninskiy, Sep. 1941; F.D. Gorelenko, June 1944.
Units: July 1941: 3, 7, 8, 13, 18 Militia Divisions.
    Sep. 1941: 3, 7, 8, 13, 18 Militia Divisions.
    Mar. 1942: 37, 71, 186, 263, 289, 313 Rifle Divisions, 64 Naval Rifle Brigade.

33 Army
—RVGK when activated in Moscow Military District (SME), July 1941.
—Forming, 14 July 1941.
—In the Reserve Front, 30 July 1941.
—RVGK, Sep. 1941.
—Reformed from reserve units at Naro Fominsk, Moscow Military District, Oct. 1941.
—Naro Fominsk, Nov. 1941.
—Mozhaisk, Jan. 1942.
—Destroyed, Mar. 1942.
—Reformed, secondary effort in Rzhev-Sychevka Op., July 1942.
—Vyazma, Dec. 1942.
—Desna River, Sep. 1943.
—Lenino, Oct. 1943.
—Kalinin area, Nov. 1943.
—Western Front, Jan. 1944.

—Belorussia w/2 Belorussian Front, May 1944.
—Kaunas area, July 1944.
—Vikavishkis, 17 Aug. 1944.
—RVGK, Sep. 1944.
—Breakthrough army for 1 Belorussian Front in the Vistula Oder Op., Jan. 1945.
—Furstenberg, Apr. 1945.
—Berlin, Apr. 1945.
Key Commanders: M.G. Yefremov, Oct. 1941–Feb. 1943; committed suicide.
Units: July 1941: 1, 5, 9, 17, 21 Militia Divisions.
Sep. 1941: 1, 5, 9, 17, 21 Militia Divisions.
Nov. 1941: 1 Moscow Motorized, 110, 113, 222 Rifle Divisions, 18 Independent Rifle Brigade.
Jan. 1942: 93, 110, 113, 160, 201, 222, 338 Rifle Divisions.
Oct. 1943: 42, 290 Rifle, 1 Polish Infantry Divisions.
May 1944: 69 Rifle Corps w/42, 222 Rifle Divisions; 72 Rifle Corps w/70, 157, 344 Rifle Divisions; 81 Rifle Corps w/32, 95, 153 Rifle Divisions.
Apr. 1945: 62 Rifle Corps.

34 Army
—Formed in Moscow Military District (SME), 14 July 1941.
—Rzhev/Vyazma area in Reserve Front, July 1941.
—Staraya Russa, Aug. 1941.
—Demyansk Pocket, Dec. 1941–Dec. 1942.
—Sent troops to 11/53 Armies; Headquarters to Staraya Russa Area where it took control of new troops, Mar. 1943.
—Sent its troops to 1 Shock Army; Field Headquarters and its Army regiments and brigades into the RVGK (SME), Nov. 1943.
—Renamed Headquarters 4 Army, Jan. 1944.
—The 34 Army was not reconstituted (SME).
Units: July 1941: 257, 259, 262 Rifle Divisions.
Mar. 1943: 26, 170, 254, 370 Rifle Divisions.

35 Army
—Activated at Iman, Far East Military District on basis of 18 Independent Rifle Corps, July 1941.
—Coastal defense mission, 1941–45.
—In "Front Command Khabarovsk," Army headquarters at Bikin, Apr. 1943.
—Part of Primorye Group of Forces which became 1 Far East Front, 1944–45.

—Manchurian Campaign, Aug. 1945.
—Maritime Military District, Jan. 1947 (EUCOM Study).
Units: July 1941: 35, 66, 78 Rifle Divisions.
      Apr. 1943: 35, 92 (?) Rifle Divisions, Iman Fortified Area.
      Aug. 1945: 66, 264, 363 Rifle Divisions.

36 Army
—Activated on basis of 12 Rifle Corps, Transbaikal Military District, July 1941.-Far East, 1941–44.
—In "Front Command Chita," Army headquarters at Borzya, Apr. 1943.
—Manchurian Campaign, Aug. 1945.
—Transbaikal Military District (EUCOM Study), Jan. 1947.
—Field Headquarters used to form Headquarters, Transbaikal Military District, 1953.
Units: July 1941: 65, 93, 94, 114 Rifle Divisions.
      Apr. 1943: 94, 211 Rifle Divisions, u/i Tank Corps.
      Aug. 1945: 2, 86 Rifle Corps, 293, 298 Rifle Divisions.

37 Army
—RVGK when activated in Southwest Front on basis of Kiev Fortified Region, Aug. 1941.
—Kiev Pocket, Aug. 1941.
—Deactivated, Sep. 1941.
—Reformed in Southwest Front as a shock formation (SME), Oct. 1941.
—Tatsinkaya, Oct. 1941.
—Reactivated in Southern Front, Nov. 1941.
—Rostov, Nov. 1941.
—First Kharkov offensive, Jan. 1942.
—Second Kharkov offensive, May 1942.
—Had divisions of 5–800 men, July 1942.
—Nalchik, Caucasus Mountains, July 1942.
—Grozny area, Sep. 1942.
—Caucasus, Jan. 1943.
—Krasnodar Op., Feb. 1943.
—Headquarters in RVGK, forces to 9/56 Armies, June 1943.
—RVGK, Sep. 1943.
—Reactivated in the Steppe Front, Sep. 1943.
—Dnieper River, 24-28 Sep. 1943.
—Krivoi Rog, Oct. 1943.
—With 2 Ukrainian Front, Jan. 1944.
—Distinguished itself in the liberation of Odessa Military District, Apr. 1944.
—Iasi Kishinev Op. as a main attack army, Aug. 1944.

—Tiraspol, Galati, Constanta, Aug. 1944.
—Varna, Bulgaria as 37 Independent Army, Aug. 1944.
—Southeast Yugoslavia (Ultra), mid-October 1944.
—Bulgaria; redesignated 10 Mechanized Army (EUCOM Study), 1946–47.
—"Suvorov" says army will be on northern front, Western theater of military operations, in a future war.
Key Commanders: Gen. A.A. Vlasov, Nov. 1941; M.N. Sharoldin, Aug. 1944.
Units: Aug. 1941: 147, 171, 175, 206, 284, 295 Rifle Divisions.
    Nov. 1941: 51, 96, 99, 216, 253, 295 Rifle Divisions.
    Aug–Nov 1942: 2 Guards, 11 NKVD, 275, 295, 392 Rifle Divisions.
    Jan. 1943: 2 Guards, 295, 351 Rifle Divisions.
    Sep. 1943: 57, 82 Rifle Corps, 53 Rifle Division.
    Oct. 1943: 57 Rifle Corps w/62, 92, 110 Guards Rifle Divisions; 82 Independent Rifle Corps w/1, 10 Guards Airborne Divisions, 5, 188 Rifle Divisions.
    Jan. 1944: 27 Guards Rifle Corps w/48, 58 Guards Rifle Divisions; 57 Rifle Corps w/15, 29 Guards, 228 Rifle Divisions; 82 RC w/10 Guards Airborne, 28 Guards, 188 Rifle Divisions; 1 Guards Airborne Division.
    Jul. 1944: 73 Rifle, 7 Mechanized Corps, 28, 92 Guards Rifle Divisions.
    Aug. 1944: 7 Mechanized Corps; 6 Guards, 66 Rifle Corps.

38 Army
—Activated in Southwest Front on basis of 8 Mechanized Corps, Aug. 1941.
—Battered at Lake Ilmen, Aug. 1941.
—Virtually destroyed in Kremenchug area (Kharkov sector), Sep. 1941.
—Referred to as "reactivated," Sep. 1941.
—Kremenchug, Sep. 1941.
—Kharkov sector, Oct. 1941.
—First Kharkov offensive, Jan. 1942.
—Belgorod, Apr. 1942.
—Second Kharkov offensive, May 1942.
—Headquarters used for Headquarters of 1 Tank Army; forces to 21 Army, 23 July 1942.
—Reactivated on Bryansk Front on basis of 4 Reserve Army, Aug. 1942.
—Moved to Kursk area, Feb. 1943.
—West of Oboyan, Kursk Op., July 1943.
—Captured Sumy, Sep. 1943.

—Operated mainly on main axes in the major offensive and defensive operations of the southwest sector (MHJ), Oct. 1943.
—Zhitomir, Nov. 1943.
—Lutezh Bridgehead near Kiev, Nov. 1943.
—Forced Dnieper on Kiev axis, Nov. 1943.
—Fastov, Nov–Dec 1943.
—Zhitomir Berdichev Op., one of main attack armies w/1 Ukrainian Front, Jan. 1944.
—Rolled up German 8 Army flank towards Vinnitsa; its infantry was 80% "Booty Ukrainians," Mar. 1944.
—Captured Vinnitsa, 20 Mar. 1944.
—Ternopol, June 1944.
—Lvov Sandomir Op.; took Lvov, July 1944.
—Czech Carpathian Mountains, Sep. 1944.
—Nowy Sacz, Poland, Jan. 1945.
—Prague, May 1945.
—Carpathian Military District, 1946-47 (EUCOM Study and Feb. 1947 OB).
Key Commanders: D.I. Ryabishev, June–Aug. 1941; Gen-Major V.V. Tsyganov, Sep. 1941; N. Chibisov, 1942; K.S. Moskalenko, 1943–45.
Units: Aug. 1941: 47 Tank, 169, 199, 300, 304 Rifle Divisions.
Sep. 1941: 166, 199, 226, 300, 304 Rifle, 34 Cavalry, 47 Tank Divisions, 10, 132 Tank Brigades; later, 47, 76 Mountain Rifle Divisions.
Oct. 1941: 47, 76, 169, 199, 226 300, 304 Rifle Divisions; 34 Cavalry, 47 Tank Divisions.
Aug. 1942: 167, 237, 240, 340 Rifle Divisions.
May 1943: 50 Rifle Corps w/167, 204, 240 Rifle Divisions.
Sep. 1943: 21, 23, 50, 51 Rifle Corps w/167, 180, 232, 240, 340 Rifle Divisions; 5 Guards Tank Corps.
Nov. 1943: 21, 23, 50, 51 Rifle Corps.
Jan. 1944: 17 Guards Rifle Corps w/68 Guards, 211, 241 Rifle Divisions; 21 Rifle Corps w/100, 135, 155 Rifle Divisions; 74 Rifle Corps w/107, 183, 305 Rifle Divisions; 13 Breakthrough Artillery Division.
July 1944: 52, 107 Rifle Corps.
Sep. 1944: 52, 67, 101 Rifle Corps, 70 Guards, 122, 140, 183, 211, 241, 304, 305, 340 Rifle Divisions; 1 Czechoslovakian Corps.

39 Army
—RVGK when activated, Archangelsk Military District, Oct. 1941.

—Seven of its ten divisions were from the Ural Military District, Dec. 1941.
—Rzhev, in RVGK, Dec. 1941.
—Torzitok, Jan. 1942.
—South of Rzhev, Feb. 1942.
—Destroyed, Feb. 1942.
—Headquarters deactivated, July 1942.
—Reactivated, Kalinin Front on basis of the second formation, 58 Army, Aug. 1942.
—Smolensk, Sep. 1943.
—Vitebsk area; main front strike force, Oct. 1943.
—Vitebsk Orsha Op.; broke through on Bobruysk axis, June 1944.
—Kaunos axis, Aug. 1944.
—East Prussia, Jan. 1945.
—Vistula Oder Op. w/1 Baltic Front, Jan. 1945.
—Koenigsberg, Mar–Apr 1945.
—Transferred to Far East, May–June 1945.
—Manchurian Op., Aug. 1945.
—Port Arthur, 1946, Feb. 1947 OB.
Units: Nov. 1941: 357, 361, 369, 371, 373, 377, 381 Rifle Divisions.
Dec. 1941: 355*, 357*, 359, 361, 363*, 369*, 373*, 375*, 379*, 381 Rifle Divisions. * divisions from Ural Military District.
Jan. 1942: 183, 220, 355, 361, 373 Rifle Divisions.
Aug. 1942: 158, 178, 348, 359 Rifle Divisions.
Jun. 1944: 5 Guards Rifle Corps w/17, 19, 91 Guards Rifle Divisions; 84 Rifle Corps w/158, 262 Rifle Divisions; 164, 215, 251 Rifle Divisions.

40 Army
—Activated on Southwest Front from 26 and 37 Armies, Aug. 1941.
—Kharkov, Aug. 1941.
—Konotop, Sep. 1941.
—Voronezh area, Jan. 1943.
—Main attack army, Voronezh Front, Jan–Nov 1943.
—Ostrogosh Rossosh Op., Jan. 1943.
—Kursk/Oboyan, Feb. 1943.
—Southwest of Kursk, July 1943.
—Belgorod Kharkov Op., Aug. 1943.
—First to reach Dnieper River w/3 Guards Tank Army, Sep. 1943.
—Kiev, Nov. 1943.
—Fastov, Dec. 1943.
—Zhitomir Berdichev Op. w/1 Ukrainian Front, Jan. 1944.
—Korsun Shevchenkovskiy Op., Jan. 1944.

Armies 57

—Targul Frumos, May 1944.
—Iasi Kishinev Op., Aug. 1944.
—Satu Mare, Hungary, Sep. 1944.
—Olomouc, Czechoslovakia, May 1945.
—Odessa Military District (EUCOM Study), Jan. 1946.
Key Commanders: K. Moskalenko, Jan. 1943; N. F. Vatutin, Sep. 1943.
Units: Aug. 1941: 2 Airborne Corps; 135, 293 Rifle Divisions; 10 Tank Division.
Sep. 1941: 2 Airborne Corps, 135, 293 Rifle Divisions; 10 Tank Division.
Jan. 1943: 25 Guards, 107, 140, 305, 340 Rifle Divisions.
May 1943: 47, 48 Rifle Corps; 309 Rifle Division.
Aug. 1943: 47 Rifle Corps.
Sep. 1943. 42, 68 Guards, 38, 161, 237, 253, 308, 337 Rifle Divisions.
Jan. 1944: 50 Rifle Corps w/74, 163, 240 Rifle Divisions; 51 Rifle Corps w/167, 232, 340 Rifle Divisions.
May 1944: 50, 51, 104 Rifle Corps, 135, 136 Rifle Divisions.

41 Army
—Activated on Kalinin Front on basis of two operational groups, May 1942.
—Bely, north of Smolensk, Dec. 1942.
—RVGK; Headquarters to RVGK, forces to 39/43 Armies, Mar. 1943.
—Headquarters formed basis of Headquarters Reserve Front, Apr. 1943.
—"Suvorov" says will be on central front of the western theater of military operations in a future war.
Units: May 1942: 17 Guards, 134, 135, 179, 239 Rifle Divisions.

42 Army
—Activated in Leningrad Front, 31 Aug. 1941.
—Trapped in Leningrad with 23 and 55 Armies, Sep. 1941.
—Leningrad Front, directly subordinate to Stavka VGK, Nov. 1941.
—Leningrad, Dec. 1942.
—Leningrad Offensive; took Krasnoye Selo, Jan. 1944.
—RVGK, July 1944.
—Pskov, July 1944.
Key Commanders: V.P. Sviridov, Mar. 1944–May 1945.
Units: Aug. 1941: 2, 3 Leningrad Militia Divisions; 291 Rifle Division.
Nov. 1941: 111, 259, 267, 288 Rifle Divisions.
Oct. 1942: 2, 3 Guards Rifle Divisions, Militia units.
Jan. 1944: 30 Guards Rifle Corps w/63 and 64 Guards Rifle Divisions.

43 Army
—RVGK when activated on basis of 33 Rifle Corps, July 1941.
—Part of Reserve Front in Rzhev-Vyazma area, July 1941.
—Yelnaya area, Sep. 1941.
—Roslavl, Oct. 1941.
—Vyazma Pocket, Oct. 1941.
—Referred to as "newly created," Oct. 1941.
—Maloyaroslavets, Mozhaysk Defense Line, Nov. 1941.
—RVGK, Sep. 1942.
—North of Smolensk, Dec. 1942.
—Smolensk, Sep. 1943.
—Vitebsk, Oct. 1943.
—Vitebsk Op., June 1944.
—Polotsk, July 1944.
—Kaunos axis, Aug. 1944.
—Memel, Oct. 1944.
—Tilsit, East Prussian Op.; in assault group of 3 Belorussian Front, Jan. 1945.
—Koenigsberg, Apr. 1945.
Units: Aug. 1941: 38, 53, 145, 149, 211, 217, 222, 279, 303 Rifle Divisions, 104 and 109 Tank Divisions.
Sep. 1941: 38, 53, 149, 211, 217, 222, 279, 303 Rifle Divisions; 109 Tank Division.
Nov. 1941: 5 Guards, 17, 53, 93, 194, 415 Rifle Divisions; 1, 2 Guards Cavalry Divisions.
June 1944: 1 Rifle Corps w/179, 306, 357 Rifle Divisions; 60 Rifle Corps w/156, 235, 334 Rifle Divisions; 92 Rifle Corps w/145, 209 Rifle Divisions; 55 Fortified Region; 56 and 252 Rifle Divisions.

44 Army
—Activated on basis of 40 Rifle Corps, Transcaucasus Military District, June 1941.
—On Iran border, July 1941.
—Amphibious landing, Kerch-Feodosiya, Dec. 1941.
—Kerch Peninsula, Dec 1941–Jan 1942.
—Crimea (Kerch), May 1942.
—Caucasus, Jan–Feb 1943.
—Rostov, Feb. 1943.
—Taganrog, May 1943.
—Mius River, Oct. 1943.
—Melitopol Op.; main attack army with 2 Guards and 5 Shock Armies, Sep–Nov 1943.

—Field Headquarters deactivated, Nov. 1943.
Units: Dec. 1941: 9, 63 Mountain., 157, 236 Rifle Divisions.
  May 1942: 223, 414, 416 Rifle Divisions.
  June 1942: 138, 156, 157, 236, 302 Rifle Divisions.
  Nov. 1942: 9 Rifle Corps, 223, 389, 402, 414 Rifle Divisions.
  Jan. 1943: 51, 223, 271, 320, 347, 414, 416 Rifle Divisions.
  May 1943: 37 Rifle Corps; 130, 151, 416 Rifle Divisions.

45 Army
—Activated in Transcaucasus Military District on basis of 23 Rifle Corps, July 1941.
—Covered Turkish border, 1941.
—Transcaucasus Front, July 1942.
—Iran, May 1943.
—Deactivated in Iran (SME), 1945.
—Yerevan, Transcaucasus Military District, Apr. 1946 (Aug. 1946 OB).
Units: July 1941: 138 Mountain, 31, 136 Rifle Divisions, 1 Mountain Cavalry Division.
  Apr. 1946: 13 Mountain Rifle Corps w/400 Rifle Division; 221, 402 Rifle Divisions.

46 Army
—Formed in Transcaucasus Military District on basis of 3 Rifle Corps, July 1941.
—Transcaucasus Front, July 1942.
—Caucasus Mountain passes, Sep. 1942.
—Caucasus, Jan. 1943.
—Took Krasnodar, Feb. 1943.
—RVGK, 29 Mar. 1943.
—RVGK w/Reserve Front, Apr. 1943.
—RVGK, July 1943.
—Dnieper River, Sep. 1943.
—Krivoi Rog Offensive, 23 Oct. 1943.
—South Russia w/3 Ukrainian Front, Jan. 1944.
—Galati, Aug. 1944.
—Iasi Kishinev Op.; trapped German 6 Army, Aug. 1944.
—On lower Danube River, Aug. 1944.
—Timiasora, Hungary, Sep. 1944.
—Tisa Bridgehead (Ultra), Oct. 1944.
—Yugoslavia, Oct. 1944.
—Budapest, Dec. 1944.
—Vienna, Apr. 1945.
—Odessa Military District (EUCOM Study), Jan. 1947.

Key Commanders: Gen. I.T. Schlemin, Aug. 1944.
Units: July 1941: 9, 47 Mountain, 4 Rifle Divisions.
Feb. 1943: 11 Guards Corps; 9 Guards, 31 Rifle Divisions.
Sep. 1943: 236 Rifle Division.
Jan. 1944: 6 Guards Rifle Corps w/20 Guards, 152, 353 Rifle Divisions; 34 Rifle Corps w/195, 236, 394 Rifle Divisions.
Oct. 1944: 10 and 31 Guards Rifle Corps.
Dec. 1944: 10 Guards Rifle, 18 Tank Corps.
Apr. 1945: 99 Rifle Division.

47 Army
—Activated in Transcaucasus Military District on basis of 28 Mechanized Corps, July 1941.
—North Caucasus Front, July 1942.
—Tuapse area, Aug. 1942.
—Taman Peninsula, Sep. 1942.
—Caucasus, Jan. 1943.
—Novorossiysk, Feb. 1943.
—Krasnodar, Feb. 1943.
—Units to 18/56 Armies; Headquarters to Reserve of North Caucasus Front, Mar. 1943.
—RVGK, Apr. 1943.
—RVGK when reformed in Reserve Front, 10 Apr. 1943.
—Into Steppe Military District, 15 Apr. 1943.
—Steppe Front, 9 July 1943.
—Kursk Op., July 1943.
—RVGK, Aug. 1943.
—RVGK to Voronezh Front (Akhtyrka), Aug. 1943.
—Khmelnistkiy area, Sep. 1943.
—RVGK, Oct. 1943.
—Kiev, early Nov. 1943.
—RVGK, Nov. 1943.
—Field Headquarters to 2 Belorussian Front, Jan. 1944.
—Korsun Shevchenkovskiy Op., Jan. 1944.
—Kovel, Feb. 1944.
—With 2 Belorussian Front, Mar. 1944.
—Lublin Brest Op.; made secondary attack, July 1944.
—Warsaw Bridgehead in Praga suburbs; replaced 2 Tank Army, Aug–Sep 1944.
—Vistula Oder Op. in Magnuszew Bridgehead, in 1 Belorussian Front, Jan. 1945.
—Stettin, Oder River, Mar. 1945.
—Berlin Op., Apr. 1945.

—Tbilisi Military District, Mar. 1946 (Mobilization Study).
Key Commanders: N.I. Gusev, July 1944.
Units: Feb. 1943: 3 Rifle Corps w/9, 60, 155 Rifle Brigades; 318 Mountain Rifle Division.
Jul. 1943: 23 and 52 Rifle Corps, 227 Rifle Division.
Mar. 1944: 77 Rifle Corps w/60, 143, 260 Rifle Divisions; 125 Rifle Corps w/76, 175, 328 Rifle Divisions.
Jan. 1945: 77, 125, 129 Rifle Corps, 129, 132, 143 Rifle Divisions.
Apr. 1945: 328 Rifle Division.

48 Army
—Activated in Northwest Front on the basis of the Novgorod Operational Group, July 1941.
—Leningrad; had only 6235 men, 31 artillery pieces and 5043 rifles, Aug. 1941.
—Field Headquarters deactivated; troops to 54 Army, Sep. 1941.
—Reformed in Mga area, Sep. 1941.
—Reactivated on basis of 28 Mechanized Corps (second formation), in the Bryansk Front, Apr. 1942.
—Orel axis, May 1942.
—East of Orel, Feb. 1943.
—Southwest of Kursk, Mar. 1943.
—Kursk, July 1943.
—Gomel Rechitsa Op., Oct. 1943.
—Rogachev, June 1944.
—Berezina River, 24 June 1944.
—Bobruysk, July 1944.
—Narew River, Poland, Sep. 1944.
—Vistula Oder Op., Jan. 1945.
—East Prussian Op., Mar. 1945
—Berlin Op., Narew River, Apr. 1945.
—Field Headquarters formed basis of Headquarters, Kazan Military District, Aug. 1945.
Key Commanders: P.D. Romanenko, Aug. 1944.
Units: July 1941: 70, 128, 237 Rifle Divisions.
Aug. 1941: 1 Militia, 70, 128, 237 Rifle Divisions, 21 Tank Division.
Sep. 1941: 128, 311 Rifle Divisions.
Apr. 1942: 1, 6 Guards, 8, 211, 284 Rifle Divisions.
May 1943: 73, 137, 143, 170, 399 Rifle Divisions.
July 1944: 42, 53 Rifle Corps, 122 Rifle Division.
Mar. 1945: 17, 73, 137, 170 Rifle Divisions, 16 Light Rifle Division.

49 Army
—Activated in Moscow Military District, Aug. 1941.
—RVGK, Sep. 1941.
—Mozhaysk Defense Line (Kaluga), Nov. 1941.
—Left wing of Western Front, Dec. 1941.
—Vyazma, Dec. 1942.
—Smolensk, Sep. 1943.
—Desna River to Gorki, Sep. 1943.
—Novgorod, Jan. 1944.
—Belorussia w/2 Belorussian Front, May 1944.
—Mogilev sector; secondary attack, June 1944.
—With 2 Belorussian Front, Nov. 1944.
—East Prussian Op., Jan. 1945.
—Pomeranian Op., Feb. 1945.
—Berlin Op., Apr. 1945.
Key Commanders: I. G. Zakharkin, Nov. 1941.
Units: Aug. 1941: 194 Mountain, 220 Motorized, 248, 298, 4 Militia Rifle Divisions.
Sep. 1941: 194 Mountain, 220 Motorized, 248 Rifle, 4 Militia Divisions.
Oct. 1941: 7 Guards, 198 Motorized, 238, 258, 290, 330 Rifle Divisions; 31, 108 Cavalry Divisions.
Dec. 1941: 5 Guards, 60, 194, 415 Rifle Divisions.
June 1944: 69, 70, 81 Rifle Corps; 32, 42, 49, 64, 95, 153, 199, 222, 290, 330, 369 Rifle Divisions.
Mar. 1945: 70, 121 Rifle Corps, 42, 139, 199, 238, 380, 385 Rifle Divisions, 15 Breakthrough Artillery Division.

50 Army
—Formed in Bryansk Front on basis of 2 Rifle Corps, Aug. 1941.
—In front of Moscow, Sep. 1941.
—Bryansk Pocket, Oct. 1941.
—Tula, Nov. 1941.
—Kashira, Nov. 1941.
—Popov Mobile Group formed from 50 Army, Dec. 1941.
—Kursk, July 1943.
—Roslavl, Aug. 1943.
—Smolensk, Sep. 1943.
—East of Mogilev, Oct. 1943.
—Belorussia w/2 Belorussian Front, May 1944.
—Mogilev Op., June 1944.
—Grodno, July 1944.
—Bialystok, Dec. 1944.

—East Prussia Op., Jan–Apr 1945.
—Koenigsberg, Apr. 1945.
—Field Headquarters became Headquarters, East Siberian Military District, Oct., 1945.
Key Commanders: Gen. Petrov (KIA, Oct. 1941 as commander, Bryansk Front).
Units: Aug. 1941: 217, 258, 269, 278, 279, 280, 290 Rifle Divisions, 55 Cavalry Division.
Sep. 1941: 217, 258, 260, 269, 278, 279, 280, 290 Rifle Divisions; 55 Cavalry Division.
Oct. 1941: 154, 217, 258, 260, 278, 279, 290 Rifle Divisions.
Dec. 1941: 6 Guards, 154, 239, 260, 299, 413 Rifle Divisions; 41 Cavalry Division.
Nov. 1941: 173, 340 Rifle Divisions; 1 Guards Cavalry Corps, 112 Tank Division.
May 1943: 38 Rifle Corps, 1 Guards, 49, 212, 324, 325 Rifle Divisions.

51 Army
—Formed as an Independent Army in the Crimea on the basis of 9 Independent Rifle Corps, Aug. 1941.
—Evacuated to Taman Peninsula, 16 Nov. 1941.
—In Kerch-Feodosiya assault landing w/44 Army, Dec. 1941.
—RVGK at Kerch, May 1942.
—Stalingrad Counteroffensive, Nov. 1942.
—Kotelnikovo and Mushkova River, Dec. 1942.
—Rostov, Jan. 1943.
—Caucasus, Feb. 1943.
—Manstein calls it "51 Shock Army," 1943.
—Trapped German 29 Corps near Sea of Azov, Aug. 1943.
—Took Melitopol, Oct. 1943.
—With 4 Ukrainian Front, Jan. 1944.
—Perekop Isthmus, Apr. 1944.
—Crimea and Sevastopol, May 1944.
—Regrouped via RVGK to Belorussia, May 1944.
—Strategic reserve army for Belorussian Op., June 1944.
—Polotsk, in 1 Baltic Front, July 1944.
—Jelgava, 30 July 1944.
—Riga area, Aug. 1944.
—Riga, Oct. 1944.
—Lithuania, Dec. 1945 (EUCOM Study).
Key Commanders: N. Trufanov, Nov. 1942; Gen-lt Ya.G. Kreyzer, 1943-44.

Units: Aug. 1941: 106, 156, 271, 276 Rifle Divisions, 40, 42, 48 Cavalry, 1, 2, 3, 4 Militia Divisions.
Jul. 1942: 91, 138, 157, 302 Rifle, 110, 115 Cavalry Divisions.
Oct–Nov 1942: 4, 13 Mechanized, 13 Tank Corps, 15 Guards, 91, 126, 302 Rifle Divisions, 4 Guards Cavalry Corps.
Dec. 1942: 4 Cavalry, 13 Tank Corps, 38, 91, 96, 126, 302 Rifle Divisions, 76 Fortified Area.
Jan. 1944: 10 Rifle Corps w/216, 257, 263, 346 Rifle Divisions; 54 Rifle Corps w/91, 126, 315 Rifle Divisions; 55 Rifle Corps w/87, 347, 387 Rifle Divisions; 2 Guards Breakthrough Artillery Division.
Apr. 1944: 1 Guards Rifle Corps w/33 Guards, 91, 346 Rifle Divisions; 10 Rifle Corps w/216, 257, 279 Rifle Divisions; 63 Rifle Corps w/263, 267, 417 Rifle Divisions; 77 Rifle Division.
July 1944: 1 Guards Rifle Corps; 267, 417 Rifle Divisions.
Oct. 1944: 1 Guards Rifle Corps; 10 Rifle Corps w/77, 257 Rifle Divisions, 83 Rifle Corps w/267, 417 Rifle Divisions.
Aug. 1944: 25, 77, 91, 279 Rifle Divisions.

52 Army
—RVGK when formed in Southwest Front on basis of 25 Independent Rifle Corps, Aug. 1941.
—Kerch/Feodosiya landing, Jan. 1942.
—Volkhov Op., Jan. 1942.
—Voronezh Front, Sep. 1943.
—Assault crossing of Dnieper, Nov. 1943.
—Korsun Shevchenkovskiy Op. w/2 Ukrainian Front, Jan. 1944.
—Uman, Mar. 1944.
—On Dniester, south of Balta (Ultra), 29 Mar. 1944.
—Targul Frumos, May 1944.
—Iasi Kishinev Op., Aug. 1944.
—Vistula Oder Op., at Czestochowa, Jan. 1945.
—Wroclaw, Jan. 1945.
—Berlin Op., Apr. 1945.
—Spree River, Apr. 1945.
—Prague, May 1945.
—Absorbed 18 Army, May 1945.
—Ukraine to suppress guerillas, 1946–47.
—Grigorenko stated that, had he accepted command of a division in this army, his "career would have been assured," Dec. 1945.
Key Commanders: K.A. Koroteyev, Aug. 1944–May 1945.
Units: Aug. 1941: 267, 285, 288, 292, 312, 314, 316 Rifle Divisions.
Nov. 1943: 62, 92 Rifle Divisions.

Jan. 1944: 73 Rifle Corps w/7 Guards Airborne, 62 Guards Rifle Divisions; 78 Rifle Corps; w/254, 373 Rifle Divisions; 294 Rifle Division.
Apr. 1945: 48 Rifle Corps.

53 Army
—Formed in North Caucasus Military District to cover southeast border and prepare regiments and divisions for the active army, Aug. 1941.
—Deactivated, Dec. 1941.
—Reformed on basis of Southern Group of Forces of 34 Army, Apr. 1942.
—Iran, 1941–42.
—Demyansk Pocket, Dec. 1942.
—Kursk, July 1943.
—Main attack army for Belgorod Kharkov Op., Aug. 1943.
—Vorskla River, Sep. 1943.
—Poltava area, 21 Sep. 1943.
—Kremenchug, 28 Sep. 1943.
—Korsun Shevchenkovskiy Op., main attack army w/2 Ukrainian Front, Jan. 1944.
—Iasi Kishinev Op., took command of 1 Rumanian Army, Aug. 1944.
—Bucharest, Aug. 1944.
—Arad, Hungary, Sep. 1944.
—Zvolen, Czechoslovakia, Apr. 1945.
—Brno, Cz. May 1945.
—To Choybalsan, June 1945.
—Manchurian campaign, Aug. 1945.
—Transcaucasus Military District, Nov. 1947 (EUCOM study).
Key Commanders: I.V. Galinin, Jan. 1944; Gen. I.M. Managarov, Aug. 1944.
Units: Apr. 1942: 22 Guards, 23, 130, 166, 235, 241, 250, 375 Rifle Divisions.
Jun. 1943: 49, 75 Rifle Corps, 84, 252, 256 Rifle Divisions.
Sep. 1943: 48 Rifle Corps; 84, 116, 214, 233, 299, 375 Rifle Divisions.
Jan. 1944: 48 Rifle Corps w/14 Guards, 252, 299 Rifle Divisions; 75 Rifle Corps w/116, 213, 233 Rifle Divisions; 16 Breakthrough Artillery Division.

54 Army
—RVGK, Moscow Military District, formed on basis of 44 Rifle Corps, Aug. 1941.
—RVGK, Sep. 1941.

—Tikhvin, Nov–Dec 1941.
—Leningrad, Dec. 1941.
—Volkhov, Jan. 1942.
—Leningrad, Dec. 1942.
—Leningrad Novgorod Op., Jan. 1944.
—Units sent to 1 Shock and 61 Army, Oct. 1944.
—Army Headquarters to Front Reserve then RVGK, Oct. 1944.
—Deactivated, Dec. 1944.
Key Commanders: MSU G.I. Kulik, Sep. 1941; I.I. Fedyuninskiy, Dec. 1941.
Units: Aug. 1941: 285, 286, 310, 314 Rifle Divisions.
　　　Sep. 1941: 4, 5 Airborne Corps; 285, 286, 310, 314 Rifle, 27 Cavalry Divisions.
　　　Oct. 1941: 2, 4 Guards Rifle, 128, 286, 294, 310 Rifle Divisions, 21 Tank Division.
　　　Jan. 1944: 111, 115, 199 Rifle Divisions.

55 Army
—Formed on Leningrad Front, 31 Aug. 1941.
—Kolpino, near Leningrad, Aug. 1941.
—Trapped in Leningrad with 23 and 42 Armies, 1941–43.
—Leningrad, Dec. 1942.
—Combined w/67 Army, Dec. 1943.
Key Commanders: V.P. Sviridov, Nov. 1941–Dec. 1943.
Units: Aug. 1941: 70, 90, 168, 237, 291 Rifle, 1, 4 Militia Divisions.

56 Army
—Formed as Independent Army at Rostov on basis of Headquarters, North Caucasus Military District, Oct. 1941.
—Independent Army, Rostov, Oct–Nov 1941.
—Rostov, in Southern Front, Nov. 1941.
—Mius River, Feb. 1942.
—Taganrog Op., Mar. 1942.
—Caucasus Front, June 1942.
—Had only Headquarters and special units left on southern front, July 1942.
—Krasnodar, Jan–Feb 1943.
—Kuban, Mar–Apr 1943.
—Failed twice to break German defense at Krymskaya, Apr. 1943.
—Renamed Independent Coastal Army, Nov. 1943.
—Field Headquarters of Independent Coastal Army named Headquarters of Tauric Military District, July 1945.
Key Commanders: A.I. Ryzhov Aug. 1942; A. Grechko, Jan. 1943.

Units: Oct. 1941: 31, 317, 343, 347, 353 Rifle, 302 Mountain Rifle Divisions.
    Jan. 1942: 106, 339 Rifle Divisions.
    Mar. 1942: 68, 76, 78, 81 Naval Rifle Brigades.
    June 1942: 3 Guards Rifle Corps, 30, 31, 339 Rifle Divisions, 16 Rifle Brigade.
    Sep. 1942: 11 NKVD, 242 Mountain Rifle Divisions, 63 Cavalry Division.
    Jan. 1943: 32, 55 Guards, 61 Rifle, 20, 83 Mountain Rifle Divisions.
    Mar. 1943: 20, 55 Guards., 61, 83 Mountain, 339, 353, 383, 394 Rifle Divisions.

57 Army
—RVGK when formed as Independent Army at Stalingrad, North Caucasus Military District, Oct. 1941.
—Kharkov offensive, Jan. 1942.
—Destroyed in Barvenkovo salient, Second Kharkov offensive, May 1942.
—Hit Rumanians in Stalingrad counteroffensive, Nov. 1942.
—Stalingrad, Jan. 1943.
—Kuban bridgehead, Apr. 1943.
—Kursk, July 1943.
—Fourth battle of Kharkov, Aug. 1943.
—Donets, Aug. 1943.
—With 2 Ukrainian Front, Jan. 1944.
—Iasi Kishinev Op. at Galati, Aug. 1944.
—Sofia, Bulgaria, Sep. 1944.
—Southeast Yugoslavia (Ultra), Oct. 1944.
—Belgrade, 20 Oct. 1944.
—Hungary, Nov. 1944.
—Kapsovar, Hungary, Mar. 1945.
—Lake Balaton, Mar. 1945.
Key Commanders: D.I. Ryabishev, Oct. 1941–Mar. 1942; F.I. Tolbukhin, Nov. 1942; Gen. N.A. Gagen, Aug. 1944.
Units: Oct. 1941: 333, 335, 337, 341, 349, 351 Rifle, 79 Cavalry Divisions.
    Nov. 1942: 13 Tank Corps, 169, 422 Rifle Divisions.
    July 1943: 64, 68 Rifle Corps, 303 Rifle Division.
    Jan. 1944: 49 Rifle Corps w/19, 233 Rifle Divisions; 64 Rifle Corps w/73, 78 Guards, 52 Rifle Divisions; 68 Rifle Corps w/ 80 Guards, 93, 113 Rifle Divisions; 53 Rifle Division.
    Oct. 1944: 64, 68, 75 Rifle Corps, 1 Guards Fortified Area, 236 Rifle Division.

58 Army
—RVGK when formed in Siberia Military District (SME), Nov. 1941.
—To Archangelsk Military District from Siberia Military District, Dec. 1941.
—Formed Makhachkala, Trans., Aug. 1942.
—FHO calls it 58 Reserve Army, Aug. 1942.
—Caucasus, Voroshilovsk, Jan. 1943.
—Mozdok, Jan. 1943.
—Slavyanskaya, Caucasus, Feb. 1943.
—North Caucasus Front, May 1943.
—RVGK, Sep. 1943.
—Deactivated, end-Oct. 1943.
—Field Headquarters transformed into the directorate of Volga Military District (SME), Nov. 1943.
Units: Nov. 1941: 362, 364, 368, 370, 382, 384 Rifle, 77 Cavalry Divisions.
　　　Aug. 1942: 317, 328, 337 Rifle Divisions.
　　　Nov. 1942: 271, 319, 416 Rifle Divisions.
　　　Jan. 1943: 89, 317, 337, 417 Rifle Divisions.

59 Army
—RVGK when formed in Siberia Military District, Nov. 1941.
—To Archangelsk Military District, Nov. 1941.
—Leningrad, Dec. 1941.
—Volkhov Op., Jan. 1942.
—Volkhov Front, 1942–44.
—Novgorod Luga Op., Jan. 1944.
—Luga, Feb. 1944.
—Took Vyborg, 21 June 1944.
—Mannerheim Line, July 1944.
—Leningrad to 1 Ukrainian Front, Dec. 1944.
—Vistula Oder Op., Krakow, Jan. 1945.
—Jaromer, Czechoslovakia, May, 1945.
—Headquarters formed Headquarters, Stavropol Military District, w/ Headquarters of 1 Guards Cavalry-Mechanized Group (Group Pliyev), July 1945.
Key Commanders:　T.F. Shtykov, Jan. 1944.
Units: Nov. 1941: 366, 372, 374, 376, 378, 382 Rifle, 78, 87 Cavalry Divisions.
　　　Jan. 1944: 6, 14, 112 Rifle Corps; 2, 65, 191, 225, 239, 255, 310, 377, 378 Rifle Divisions, 150 Fortified Area.

60 Army
—RVGK when activated Moscow Military District w/300-series divisions, Aug. 1941.
—Redesignated 3 Shock Army, Dec. 1941.
—The 3 Reserve Army, spring 1942; redesignated 60 Army in RVGK, July 1942.
—Took Voronezh, Jan. 1943.
—Kursk, July 1943.
—Attacking towards Kiev (Ssevsk), Aug. 1943.
—Dnieper Offensive, Sep. 1943.
—Yasnogorodkha Bridgehead, Nov. 1943.
—Kiev, Nov. 1943.
—Took Korosten, 7 Nov. 1943.
—Headquarters and army overrun by German 48 Panzer Corps near Korosten, Radomysl, Zhitomir, 6–15 Dec. 1943.
—Zhitomir Berdichev Op. w/1 Ukrainian Front at Shepetovka, Jan. 1944.
—Rovno Lutsk Op., Jan–Feb 1944.
—Proskurov Chernovtsy Op., Mar. 1944.
—Ternopol, Mar. 1944.
—Lvov Sandomir Op., July 1944.
—Krakow w/1 Ukrainian Front, Jan. 1945.
—Olomouc, Czechoslovakia, May 1945.
Key Commanders: M. Antonyuk, 1942; I. Chernyakhovskiy, Jan. 1944; P. Kurochkin, Jul. 1944.
Units: Nov. 1941: 348, 352, 358, 360 Rifle Divisions.
Jan. 1943: 141, 232, 303, 322 Rifle, 10 Artillery Divisions.
May 1943: 24 and 30 Rifle Corps.
Sep. 1943: 7 Guards Mechanized Corps, 132 Rifle Division.
Nov. 1943: 24, 30, 77 Rifle Corps, 75 Guards, 112, 121, 141, 226 Rifle Divisions.
Jan. 1944: 15 Rifle Corps w/322, 336 Rifle Divisions; 18 Guards Rifle Corps w/148, 280, 351 Rifle Divisions; 23 Rifle Corps w/ 8, 147, 226 Rifle Divisions; 30 Rifle Corps w/121, 141 Rifle Divisions.
Jul. 1944: 15, 23, 28 Rifle Corps, 148 Rifle Division.

61 Army
—RVGK when activated in Volga Military District w/300-series divisions, Nov. 1941.
—Orel area; 4 of 6 divisions from Volga Military District, Dec. 1941.
—Rzhask area w/Southwest Front, Dec. 1941.
—Main attack army for Bolkhov Op., July 1942.

—Kursk Offensive, Bolkhov area, July 1943.
—Dnieper River, Sep. 1943.
—Chernigov, Sep. 1943.
—Udalevka, Belorussia, Oct. 1943.
—East of Pinsk, Jan. 1944.
—Belorussia w/2 Belorussian Front, Mar. 1944.
—Took Brest with 28 and 70 Armies, 28 July 1944.
—RVGK, Aug. 1944.
—To Riga axis, Oct. 1944.
—Vistula Oder Op.in 1 Belorussian Front, Jan. 1945.
—Stettin, Jan. 1945.
—Berlin Op., Apr. 1945.
Key Commanders: F.I. Kuznetsov Dec. 1941; M.M. Popov, June 1942; P.A. Belov June 1942–May 1945.
Units: Nov. 1941: 342, 346, 350, 356, 385, 387, 391 Rifle Divisions.
Dec. 1941: 287, 342*, 346*, 350*, 356*, 387 Rifle Divisions.
*division from Volga Military District.
Sep. 1943: 7 Guards Independent, 15 Rifle Corps.
Mar. 1944: 9 Guards Rifle Corps w/12, 76, 77 Guards Rifle Divisions; 89 Rifle Corps w/15, 356, 415 Rifle Divisions; 23, 55 Rifle Divisions.
Jan. 1945: 9 Guards, 80, 89 Rifle Corps, 2 Guards Cavalry Corps; 119 Fortified Area.

62 Army
—Formed as 7 Reserve Army, 28 May 1942.
—Redesignated 62 Army, 10 July 1942.
—Kletskaya, July 1942.
—Stalingrad, July 1942–Feb. 1943.
—RVGK, Mar 1943.
—Designated 8 Guards Army, 16 Apr. 1943.
—Not reconstituted.
Key Commanders: V. Kolpakchi, 1942; Gen. V. Chuikov, 1942–43.
Units: July 1942: 33 Guards, 147, 181, 184, 192, 196 Rifle Divisions.
Nov. 1942: 13, 37, 39 Guards, 45, 95, 112, 138, 193, 284, 308 Rifle Divisions, 92 Naval Rifle Brigade.

63 Army
—Formed as 5 Reserve Army, 28 May 1942.
—Redesignated 63 Army, 10 July 1942.
—RVGK, July 1942.
—Stalingrad summer-fall 1942.
—Reformed as 1 Guards Army, Nov. 1942.

—Reformed from 2 Reserve Army, Mar. 1943.
—Kursk, July 1943.
—Orel, Aug. 1943.
—Gomel, Oct. 1943.
—Deactivated, Feb. 1944.
Key Commanders: V.I. Kuznetsov, Nov. 1942.
Units: July 1942: 14 Guards, 1, 127, 153, 197 Rifle Divisions.
    Mar. 1943: 129, 235, 250, 348, 380, 397 Rifle Divisions.
    May 1943: 40 Rifle Corps, 41, 271, 348, 397 Rifle Divisions.

64 Army
—Formed as 1 Reserve Army, 28 May 1942.
—Redesignated 64 Army, 10 July 1942.
—RVGK, July 1942.
—Stalingrad area, summer-fall 1942.
—Rushed to Kharkov area, Feb. 1943.
—Became 7 Guards Army, 16 Apr. 1943.
—Not reconstituted.
Key Commanders: V.I. Chuikov, 1942.
Units: July 1942: 18, 29, 112, 131, 214, 229 Rifle Divisions.
    Nov. 1942: 7 Rifle Corps; 36 Guards, 29, 38, 157, 204 Rifle Divisions, 66, 154 Independent Naval Rifle Brigades.

65 Army
—Formed from remnants of 4 Tank Army, Oct. 1942.
—Stalingrad area, Nov 1942–Jan 1943.
—RVGK, Northwest of Kursk, Feb. 1943.
—Kursk, July 1943.
—Dnieper, Sep. 1943.
—Gomel Rechitsa Op., Oct. 1943.
—Belorussian Op. June 1944.
—S of Bobruysk, July 1944.
—East Prussia; assault group of 2 Belorussian Front, Jan. 1945.
—Bydgoszcz, Jan. 1945.
—Czarne, Vistula Oder Op., Feb. 1945.
—Danzig, Mar. 1945.
—Berlin Op., Apr. 1945.
—Waldenburg, Poland as 7 Mechanized Army, Oct. 1947 (Feb. 1948 OB).
Key Commanders: P.I. Batov, 1942–45.
Units: Oct. 1942: 23, 24, 304, 321 Rifle Divisions.
    Nov. 1942: 4, 27, 40 Guards, 24, 252, 258, 304, 321 Rifle Divisions.

Aug. 1943: 60 Rifle Division.
Mar. 1945: 18, 46, 105 Rifle Corps, 37, 44 Guards, 15, 69, 108, 186, 191, 193, 354, 413 Rifle Divisions.
Feb. 1947: 105 Rifle Corps; 18, 20 Tank Divisions; 18 Rifle Division; 44 Mechanized Division.

66 Army
—Activated at Saratov, Volga Military District from 8 Reserve Army, Aug. 1942.
—RVGK, Aug. 1942.
—Stalingrad area, summer-fall 1942.
—Stalingrad counteroffensive, Nov. 1942.
—Redesignated 5 Guards Army, 16 Apr. 1943.
—Not reconstituted.
Key Commanders: R.Ya. Malinovskiy, 1942; A.S. Zhadov 1942–43.
Units: Aug. 1942: 42, 49, 99, 120, 231, 299, 316 Rifle Divisions.
Nov. 1942: 64, 99, 116, 226, 299, 343 Rifle Divisions.

67 Army
—Activated on basis of Nevsk Operational Group, Oct. 1942.
—Leningrad, Dec. 1942.
—Leningrad offensive, Jan. 1943.
—Combined w/55 Army; Headquarters 55 Army became Headquarters 67 Army, Dec. 1943.
—Leningrad offensive, Jan. 1944.
—Pechory, Aug. 1944.
—Latvia, Oct. 1944.
—Plaskow, Poland, Jan. 1945.
Key Commanders: Gen-Maj M.P. Dukhanov, Jan. 1943; V.P. Sviridov, Dec. 1943–Mar. 1944.
Units: Nov. 1942: 45, 46, 86 Rifle Divisions.
Jan. 1943: 45 Guards, 13, 86, 123, 136, 268 Rifle Divisions, 16 Fortified Area.

68 Army
—RVGK when activated on basis of Field Headquarters, 57 Army (SME), Feb. 1943.
—Special assault army for Demyansk, Feb. 1943.
—Vyazma, Aug. 1943.
—Smolensk Op. as main attack army; took city, Sep. 1943.
—East of Orsha, Oct. 1943.
—Deactivated, Nov. 1943.
Units: Feb. 1943: 1, 5, 7, 8, 10 Guards Airborne Divisions.

69 Army
—Activated on basis of 18 Independent Rifle Corps on the Voronezh Front, Feb. 1943.
—Badly shot up at Kharkov; commander stated "no operational units or a single tank left," Feb. 1943.
—Belgorod Kharkov Op.; assaulted Kharkov, Aug. 1943.
—RVGK, Nov. 1943.
—Kovel, June 1944.
—Lvov Sandomir Op., July 1944.
—Vistula Oder Op. w/1 Belorussian Front (Pulawy Bridgehead), Jan. 1945.
—Liberated Auschwitz, Jan. 1945.
—Berlin Op., Apr. 1945.
Key Commanders: V.Ya. Kolpakchi, June–Aug. 1944.
Units: Feb. 1943: 161, 180, 270 Rifle Divisions.
May 1943: 107, 111, 183, 270, 305 Rifle Divisions.
Jan. 1945: 25, 61, 91 Rifle Corps, 11 Tank Corps; 77 Guards, 4, 117, 134, 214, 247, 274, 312, 364, 370 Rifle Divisions.
Apr. 1945: 25, 61, 91 Rifle Corps; 77 Guards, 4, 117, 134, 247, 274, 312, 364, 370 Rifle Divisions.

70 Army
—RVGK when activated over a four month period based on the personnel of the border and interior forces of the NKVD (SME), Oct. 1942–Feb. 1943.

—Formed from NKVD troops from Far East, Central Asia and Transbaikal Military Districts (FHO), in Sverdlovsk, Urals Military District, Oct. 1942.
—Deployed to Central Front, Kursk area, Feb. 1943.
—Kursk, July 1943.
—Kursk counteroffensive, 15 July 1943.
—RVGK, Nov. 1943.
—To 2 Belorussian Front, Feb. 1944.
—Kovel, Feb. 1944.
—Belorussia w/2 Belorussian Front, Mar. 1944.
—Pinsk, June 1944.
—Took Brest with 28 and 61 Armies, July 1944.
—RVGK, July 1944.
—RVGK to Warsaw area, Aug–Sep 1944.
—Reserve of 1 Belorussian Front, 29 Oct. 1944.
—Reserve of 2 Belorussian Front, 19 Nov. 1944.
—East Prussia, Jan. 1945.

—Torun, Poland, Jan. 1945.
—Vistula River, Feb. 1945.
—Gdynia, Pomeranian Op., Mar. 1945.
—Assault army for Oder Op., Mar. 1945.
—Berlin Op., Apr. 1945.
—Koslin, Poland, Oct. 1947 (Feb. 1948 OB).
Key Commanders: I.V. Galinin, July 1943; V.S. Popov, July 1944–March 1945.
Units: Feb. 1943: 102, 106, 140, 162, 175, 181 Rifle Divisions.
Nov. 1943: 135, 202 Rifle Divisions.
Mar. 1944: 114 Rifle Corps w/38 Guards, 160 Rifle Divisions; 96 Rifle Corps w/185 Rifle Division; 212, 397 Rifle Divisions.
Sep. 1944: 38 Guards, 36 and 160 Rifle Divisions.
Mar. 1945: 2, 47, 96, 114 Rifle Corps; 38, 76 Guards, 1, 71, 136, 160, 162, 165, 200, 330, 369 Rifle Divisions.
Oct. 1947: 22 Tank, 26, 27 Guards Rifle Divisions.

CHAPTER TWO

Honorifics for Corps and Divisions

As of 20 Oct. 1984

Honorifics were awarded by the Soviet government to units which had singularly distinguished themselves in combat at, or in the liberation of, particular locations. For example, the 50th Guards Rifle Division distinguished itself in the liberation of Baranovichi. The division was awarded the honorific "Baranovichi" which then became part of its official title. Some units were awarded an honorific based on the location in which they were formed or as a recognition of their special status or ethnic composition. For example, the 4th "Kuban Cossack" Cavalry Corps (ethnicity), and the 1st Moscow "Proletarian" Motorized Division (location formed and special status). Like battle honorifics, these became part of the official unit designation. Honorifics, where known, are identified in quotes at the end of the chronological history of that unit along with any battle decorations awarded. Honorifics were awarded for offensive operations only.

Alexandrija—8 MC, 110 GRD, 111, 214 RD.
Amur Reserve—12 RD.
Anapa—414 RD.
Armansk—51 GRD.
Armenian—89, 261, 446 RD.
Artemovsk—259, 266 RD.
Azerbaijan—416 RD.

Bachmach—75 GRD, 132 RD.
Balashov—61 RD.
Baltiysk—See Memel.
Baranovichi—44, 50, 54, 75 GRD, 9, 10 GCD, 30 CD, 61, 130, 193, 354 RD.
Barvenkovo—39 GRD.

Bashkir—16 GCD, 112 CD.
Batum—9 RD.
Belgorod—89 GRD, 305, 375 RD.
Belorussia—2 RD.
Belorussian SSR (in the name of the)—120 GRD.
Berdichev—117 GRD, 24, 389 RD.
Berislav—86 GRD.
Berlin—8 GMC, 6, 7 GTC, 9 TC, 11TC/TD.
Beshiza—4, 273 RD.
Bialystok—120 GRD, 5, 129, 250, 269, 283, 348 RD.
Blinov (in the name of M.F.)—1 GCD.
Bobruysk—9 TC, 75 GRD, 17, 102, 137, 217, 250, 348, 354 RD.
Bogashev—(Bogucharsk), 40 RD.
Bolgrad—71, 72 GRD.
Borislav—72, 109 GRD, 155 RD.
Borisov—19 GRD, 174, 200, 277, 331, 371 RD.
Brandenburg—7 GCC, 77 GRD, 134, 247, 307, 383 RD.
Brest—9 GRC, 76 GRD, 9 GCD, 30 CD, 1, 130, 186, 413 RD.
Bryansk—197, 323, 331 RD.
Bucharest—5 GCC, 74, 203, 375 RD.
Budapest—2 GMC, 18 GRC, 1 GARD, 4, 25, 32, 41, 49, 59, 62, 66, 86, 108 GRD, 84, 151, 155, 297, 337, 353 RD.
Budenny (in the name of S.)—6 CD.

Carpathian—8 GMC, 11 GTC, 2 GARD, 66, 128 GRD, 8, 24, 30, 99, 138, 141, 151, 167, 240 271, RD.
Chelyabinsk—85 RD.
Central Asia—162 RD.
Cherkassy—(Korsun), 7 GARD, 12 GCD, 63 CD, 27, 41 GRD, 202, 206, 254, 294, 373 RD.
Chernigov—76, 77 GRD, 16 GCD, 7, 148, 157, 173, 212 RD.
Cholm—33, 81, 115, 145, 312 RD.
Chongar—6 CD.
Comintern—7 GRD.
Communist—234 RD.
Constanza—394 RD.
Cossack—6, 17 CC, 6, 29 CD.
Crimean—2 GRD, 3 RD.
Czechoslovakia—24 RD.
Czechoslovakian Proletariat (in the name of)—5 RD.
Czestochowa—127, 254 RD.

Daghestan—13 RD.

Danube—20, 73, 92 GRD.
Debica—148, 162, 226, 302 RD.
Debolzewo—346 RD.
Debrecen—78, 337 RD.
Demidov—262, 270 RD.
Dnepropetrovsk—60 GRD, 152, 236 RD.
Dneprovsk—36 GRD, 110, 303 RD.
Dneprozherzhinsk—(See Lower Dniester).
Dnieper—70, 106, 193, 240 RD.
Dno—23 GRD.
Dombova—225 RD.
Don—1 GTC, 38 RD.
Donbas—80 RD.
Don Cossack—5 GCC, 5, 11 GCD, 4, 13, 15, 16 CD.
Donetsk—50 GRD.
Dorpat—86, 282, 288 RD.
Drohobycz—141, 155, 276 RD.
Duchovschtschina (Dukhov)—21 AD, 17, 91 GRD, 184 RD.
Dzerzhinskiy (in the name of F.)—160 RD, 1 NKVD.

East Siberian—26 GRD, 93 RD.
Elblag—321, 381 RD.
Estonian—8 GRC, 8 RC, 8 RD, 249 RD.

Fabritsiusa, Jana (in the name of)—14 GRD, 96 RD.
Far East—102 RD.
Feodosiya—32, 128 GRD, 227 RD.
Focsani—163 RD.
Frunze—113 RD.

Gatchina—18, 23 AD, 86, 120, 125, 196, 201, 224, 291 RD.
Georgian SSR—9 RD.
German Proletariat (in the name of)—4 RD.
Glukhov—1 GAD, 70 GRD, 226 RD.
Gomel—22 AD, 121 GRD, 96, 179, 250, 283 RD.
Gorkhovsk—17 RD.
Gorki—17 RD.
Gorlovka—126, 271 RD.
Gorodok—2 GMD, 5, 11, 26, 83 GRD.
Gorskaya—28 RD.
Grodno—5, 6 GCD, 42, 220 RD.
Grosswardein—337 RD.
Grunische—47, 52, 414 RD.

Gumbinnen—48, 50, 54, 96 GRD, 130, 184 RD.

Hungarian—151, 167 RD.

Iasi—See Jassy.
Idritsk—150 RD.
Ilovaysk—96 GRD.
Insterburg—26, 50, 96 GRD, 144, 157, 159, 170 RD.
Irkutsk—55 GRD, 30 RD.
Iron—24 RD.
Ivanovo—332 RD.
Izmail—353 RD.
Izyaslav—109 GRD.

Jarzevo—82 GRD, 82, 274, 320, 359 RD.
Jassy—6 GARD, 62, 69, 81 GRD, 233, 254, 303 RD.
Jelnaya—see Yelnaya.
Jenakijevo—34, 40 GRD, 320 RD.

Kalinin (in the name of M.I.)—2 GRD, 43, 48 RD.
Kalinkovichi—77 GRD, 81, 253, 354, 356 RD.
Kaluga—81 RD.
Kamenets Podolsk—6 GMC.
Kantemirov—4 GTC, 17 TC.
Karatschew (Karachev)—16, 84 GRD, 238, 369, 385 RD.
Kashino—48 RD.
Kattowice—128 GRD, 80, 107, 128, 135, 225, 245, 246, 285, 286, 291, 322, 336 RD.
Kavkas—9, 20 RD.
Kaunas—See Kovno.
Kharkov—15, 28, 71, 89, 93 GRD, 23, 84, 116, 183, 252, 299, 375 RD.
Kherson—86 GRD, 295, 297 RD.
Khingan—19, 91, 110 GRD, 262 RD.
Kielce—117, 121 GRD, 127, 172, 287, 389 RD.
Kiev—9 MC, 5, 6, 7 GTC, 3 GMD, 13, 17 AD, 23, 30, 44, 74, 121, 136, 141, 163, 180, 218, 226, 232, 240, 340 RD.
Kikvidze (in the name of)—16 RD.
Kingisepp—98, 125, 189, 314 RD.
Kirkenes—10, 99 GRD, 14, 368 RD.
Kirov—139 RD.
Kirovograd—11, 16 AD, 50, 297, 409 RD.
Kishinev—41 GRD, 31, 84, 233, 266, 303, 416 RD.

Konotop—143, 280 RD.
Korosten—112, 143, 280 RD.
Korsun—See Cherkassy.
Kostroma Proletariat—49 RD.
Kotelnikovo—3 GTC.
Kovel—76, 143, 280 RD.
Kovno (Kaunos)—7 GMD, 11, 17 GRD, 63, 144, 277, 371 RD.
Krakow—107, 246, 302, 322 RD.
Kramatorsk—59 GRD.
Krasnodar—9, 22, 106 RD.
Krasnograd—1 MC, 58, 71, 81 GRD.
Krasnogvardeysk—86, 120, 125, 196 RD.
Krasnosel'sk—63 GRD.
Krasnoyarsk—94 RD.
Krasnoye Selo—125 RD.
Kremenchug—6 GARD, 214, 233 RD.
Kremjanez—107 RD.
Krichev—212, 385 RD.
Krivoi Rog—20, 48 GRD, 41 RD.
Kuban Cossacks—4 GCC, 17 CC, 4, 9, 10 GCD, 6, 12, 13 CD.
Kulagino—178 RD.
Kursk— 55 RD.
Kuzbas—71, 376 RD.

Latvian—43, 130 RC, 43 GRD, 129, 181, 201, 308 RD.
Lebedin—139 RD.
Lemberg—See Lvov.
Lenin—60 RD.
Leningrad—63 GRD, 11, 67, 85, 286 RD, 4 CD.
Leszno—157, 158 RD.
Lida—6 GCD, 32 CD.
Lissitschansk—279 RD.
Lithuanian—16, 181 RD.
Lombrova—245 RD.
Lomza—238, 380, 385 RD.
Losovaya—35, 38 GRD.
Lower Dniester—20, 59, 61 GRD, 93, 113, 333, 353 RD.
Lublin—28 GRC, 79 GRD, 14, 15, 16 GCD.
Lubny—337 RD.
Luga—123, 181 RD.
Luminets—54 GRD, 9 GCD, 30 CD, 61, 69, 73, 96, 194, 354 RD.
Lumonosovvo—231 RD.
Lunaburg—154 RD.

Lutsk—61 GRD, 46 RD.
Lvov—6 GMC, 10 GTC, 69, 70, 129 GRD, 140, 148, 183, 302 RD.
Lyuban—80, 177, 281, 374 RD.

Makeyevka—54 GRD.
Malinovskiy (in the name of R.Ya.), 10 GTC/GTD.
Mariupol—221 RD.
Masurian—62, 88, 174, 331, 362 RD.
Melitopol—91, 118, 126, 315, 347 RD.
Memel—(Baltiysk), 84 GRD, 16, 179, 344 RD.
Mga—124, 268 RD.
Minsk—1, 120 GRD, 8, 220, 331 RD.
Mirgorod—93, 373 RD.
Mitau—279 RD.
Mogilev—238, 290 RD.
Moldavia—95 RD.
Molodechno—83 GRD, 6 GCD.
Mongolian Far East—1, 5, 6, 7, 8 CD.
Morosova Cossacks—8 GCD.
Moscow—1 GRD, 17 RD.
Mountain Workers—395 RD.
Mozyr—55, 415 RD.

Narva—120, 131, 191 RD.
Neman—16, 84 GRD, 124, 157, 331, 338 RD.
Nevel—21 GRD, 28, 47, 72, 360 RD.
Nikolayev—86 GRD, 25, 295 RD.
Nikopol—2 GMC, 50, 59, 74, 79 GRD.
Novgorod—102 GRD, 65, 102, 140, 162, 191, 225, 301, 372, 378, 382 RD.
Novocherkassk—37 RD.
Novograd Volynskiy—149, 287 RD.
Novomoskovsk—164, 195 RD.
Novorossiysk—318 RD.
Novosybkov—73, 308, 399 RD.
Novobug—4 GCC, 27 GRD.

Oder—78, 95 GRD, 31, 58, 125, 128, 172, 197, 213, 225, 285, 309, 350, 359, 389 RD.
Omsk—27 GRD, 27, 73 RD.
Ordzhonikidze—77, 123 RD.
Orel—84 GRD, 5, 6, 129, 380 RD.
Orlov—(See Orel).

Orsha—16, 84 GRD, 220, 331 RD.
Osowiec—110, 139, 238, 290, 362, 385 RD.
Ostralenka—269 RD.
Ostrov—288 RD.
Ovruch—4 GARD.

Pacific—39 RD.
Panfilov (in the name of)—8 GRD, 12, 316 RD.
Pankratovo—185 RD.
Parkhemenko (in the name of S.)—6 GCD.
Pavlograd—60 GRD, 172 RD.
Pavlovsk—72, 85 RD.
Pechenga—See Petsamo.
Perekop—19 RC, 51 RD.
Perm—21, 46, 90 RD.
Pervomaysk—8 GARD.
Petrikov—117 GRD.
Petrozavodsk—272, 368 RD.
Petsamo—10, 99, 101 GRD, 14 RD.
Pinsk—55 GRD, 397 RD.
Piryatin—237, 309 RD.
Plaskov—128, 291, 376 RD.
Plastun—9 RD.
Polar—186 RD.
Polotsk—5, 21, 51 GRD, 51, 270, 332, 360 RD.
Poltava—9 GARD, 13, 66, 95, 97 GRD.
Pomerania—94, 102 GRD, 89, 150, 248, 266, 397 RD.
Ponowiek—33 GRD, 417 RD.
Posen (Poznan)—27 GRD, 117, 312 RD.
Praga—60, 76, 143, 234 RD.
Prague—15, 58, 93 GRD.
Pressburg—4, 6 GARD, 72, 81, 93 GRD, 1, 41, 252, 375 RD.
Prettwitz—409 RD.
Pri Amur—42 RD.
Priluki—42 GRD.
Proletarian—1 GRD, 19, 49, 71, 331 RD.
Proskurov—68 GRD.
Prut—42 GRD.
Pskov—376 RD.
Pugachev—53 RD.
Pushkin—56 RD.

Radom—11 TC/TD, 76, 77 GRD, 247, 274 RD.

Rechitsa—8, 37 GRD, 170, 194 RD.
Rezkaja—17 RD.
Ribschevo—306 RD.
Riga—29, 30, 33, 52, 53, 65, 75 GRD, 23, 44, 56, 356, 376, 379, 391 RD.
Rilsk—112. 121 RD.
Rogachev—120, 121 GRD, 186, 269 RD.
Roman—6 GARD, 62, 69, 72, 81 GRD, 6, 254 RD.
Romodan—218 RD.
Romny—163 RD.
Ropsha—48, 98, 131 RD.
Rosslau—326 RD.
Roslavl—49, 139, 247, 277, 344 RD.
Rotthammer—242 RD.
Rovno—6 GRD.
RSFSR (in the name of Supreme Soviet of the)—55 GRD.
Rudjna (Rudna)—19 GRD.
Rzhev—8 GRD.

Samara—24, 33 RD, 7 CD.
Sevastopol—32, 33, 128 GRD.
Shauliai—33 GRD, 417 RD.
Shepetovka—56 GRD, 148, 280, 351 RD.
Shlobin—73, 217 RD.
Shumilov (Shumlin)—19 RD.
Shumsk—148 RD.
Siberian—70, 89, 140 RD.
Siberian Revolutionary Committee (in the name of the)—12 RD.
Siberian Sharpshooter—11 RD.
Sibirsk—35 RD.
Silesia—13, 33 GRD.
Simbirsk—See Ul'yanovsk.
Simferopol—77 RD.
Simovniki—(See Ziminovskiy).
Sinelnikovo—25 GRD, 333 RD.
Sivash—15, 263, 267, 417 RD.
Siverebkoma—12 RD.
Slonim—54 GRD, 9 GCD, 30 CD, 61, 69, 73, 96, 194, 354 RD.
Smolensk—4 GAD, 42, 56 GRD, 32 CD, 4, 42, 133, 153, 199, 215, 222, 312, 331 RD.
Snamenka—See Znamenka.
Solnechnogorsk—50 RD.
Sslavjarsk—61 GRD, 297 RD.

Slutsk—10 GCD, 85 RD.
Ssumy—167, 232, 340 RD.
Ssvesk—1 GAD, 55, 60, 69, 102, 140, 162, 417 RD.
Stalin—6, 14 RC, 26, 150 RD.
Stalina—See Donetsk.
Stalingrad—3, 4 GMC, 4 TC, 5 GTC, 5 TC, 5 GAD, 31, 73, 92 GRD, 31, 181 RD.
Stalino—50 GRD, 230, 301 RD.
Stanislav—18 GRC, 141, 151, 161, 309, 395 RD.
Stavropol—1 GCD, 10 CD.
Stepina—60 RD.
Stettin—15 RD.
Stryy—30, 155, 276 RD.
Sverdlovsk—75 RD.
Svenigorod—See Zvenigorod.
Svir—98, 99, 100 GRD, 272 RD.

Taganrog—2 GAD, 130, 415 RD.
Tadjik SSR (in the name of the)—68 RD.
Taman—2, 32 GRD, 74, 89, 242, 339, 395 RD.
Tambov—10 RD.
Tannenburg—5, 169, 170, 194, 217, 283, 399 RD.
Tarnopol—302 RD.
Tartu—86, 189, 191, 288 RD.
Tatsin—2 GTC.
Temruk—56, 227, 276, 316 RD.
Tersk—6, 10 CD.
Tilsit—(Sovetsk) 26, 262 RD.
Tolbulkhin (in the name of MSU)—6 RD.
Tomsk—78 RD.
Torun—76, 77 GRD, 1, 160, 162, 165 RD.
Tossno—364 RD.
Transbaikal—36 Mtz, 106 RD.
Transylvania—3 GARD, 13 GRD, 133, 163, 180, 232, 240 RD.
Tschodovo—(Tschudowo) 44, 321 RD.
Tudor Vladimeriscu (in the name of)—1 Rumanian RD.
Turkmen—83 RD.
Turkestan—128 GRD.
Tyumen—65 RD.

Ukrainian SSR (in the name of)—2 GCD.
Ul'yanovsk (Simbirsk)—16, 24 RD.
Uman—9 GTC, 3, 16 TC, 3 GARD, 16 AD, 80 GRD, 53 RD.

Unetschka—217 RD.
Ungvar—(Hungary) 66 GRD, 151, 167 RD.
Ural—57, 175, 377 RD.
Ural Volunteer—10 GTC, 30 TC.

Verchnedneprovsk—36 GRD, 110, 303 RD.
Verdino—134 RD.
Vilna—(Vilnius) 63, 144, 277, 371 RD.
Vinnitsa—14 GRD, 241 RD.
Vitebsk—3 GAD, 17, 31, 44, 51, 67, 83, 90 GRD, 5, 23, 51, 63, 88, 97, 144, 158, 159, 164, 179, 204, 251, 262, 277, 306, 334, 371 RD.
Volgograd—(See Stalingrad).
Volkhov—5, 129 RD.
Voronezh—1 GMC, 19 RD.
Voroshilov (in the name of K.)—4 CD.
Vyborg—64 GRD, 265, 372 RD.

Walcz—23, 52 GRD, 44, 56, 283, 376 RD.
Warsaw—60, 76, 143, 328 RD.
Wolnowacha—3 GRD, 11 GCD.

Yalta—128 GRD, 227 RD.
Yampol—8 RD.
Yaroslavl—109 GRD, 18 RD.
Yelnaya—29 GRD, 76 RD.
Yerevan—261 RD.
Yevpatoriya—19 TC, 3, 24 GRD.

Zaporozhye—7, 9 AD, 50, 78, 79, 82, 88 GRD, 50, 203, 244 RD.
Zhadanov (in the name of A.A.)—45 GRD.
Zhemerinka—151 RD.
Zhitomir—9 MC, 3, 17 AD, 23, 30, 99 129 GRD, 1, 2, 7 GCD, 218, 304, 322, 336, 350 RD.
Ziminovskiy—(Simovniki) 5 GMC.
Zlatovsk—26 RD.
Znamenka—6 GARD, 95, 110 GRD, 214, 233 RD.
Zvenigorod—1, 5 GARD, 62 GRD, 136 RD.

ABBREVIATIONS

AD—Artillery Division.
CC—Cavalry Corps.
CD—Cavalry Division.
GAD—Guards Artillery Division.

GARD—Guards Airborne Division.
GCC—Guards Cavalry Corps.
GCD—Guards Cavalry Division.
GMC—Guards Mechanized Corps.
GMD—Guards Mortar Division.
GRC—Guards Rifle Corps.
GRD—Guards Rifle Division.
GTC—Guards Tank Corps.
GTD—Guards Tank Division.
MC—Mechanized Corps.
MTZ—Motorized
RC—Rifle Corps.
RD—Rifle Division.
TC—Tank Corps.

CHAPTER THREE

Corps

Two general types of corps, the mobile and the operational control corps, were found in the Red Army in the Great Patriotic War. Artillery and rifle corps functioned as operational control corps, while cavalry, mechanized, and tank corps were mobile formations.

The artillery corps, usually identified as the breakthrough artillery corps, controlled two or more artillery divisions with other units of the RVGK being assigned as required by the mission. There was considerable variation between these corps due to task organizing. Ten of these corps have been identified as existing in postwar writings although the Germans only identified four. Rifle corps were operational tactical formations that consisted of a headquarters and attached support controlling three or four rifle divisions. The main headquarters echelon contained operations, signals, intelligence, and penal sections, and artillery, engineer, and chemical warfare staffs. The rear echelon was a skeleton organization which handled reports and requisitions from subordinate units and which could reinforce those subordinates in an emergency. Attached corps troops normally included a howitzer regiment, a tank destroyer regiment, a signal battalion and an engineer construction unit.

Cavalry corps consisted of three cavalry divisions, 2–4 independent tank regiments, a self-propelled artillery regiment and a motorized heavy mortar regiment. They had a basic complement of supporting combat and combat service support arms tailored to their basic needs and mission. While seemingly outdated, these units were highly mobile, became increasingly mechanized, and performed with great distinction. Mechanized Corps were the most powerful individual corps in the Red Army. They were comparatively few in number, highly mechanized and motorized, and actually had more tanks than a tank corps. These corps constituted an asset of the RVGK assigned to a front or army commander. The primary mission of the corps was to conduct exploitation of breakthroughs, pursuit, or counterattack. Its composition included three mechanized brigades, a tank brigade, six artillery regiments, and supporting arms and services. The tank corps usually formed a part of the mobile strike force of the army or front commander. Tank corps could be part of a tank army or independent; many were assets of the VGK. They were used to deliver the decisive blow on a narrow sector or to exploit a breakthrough with other arms. A tank corps was composed of three tank brigades, a motorized rifle brigade, six artillery regiments, and supporting arms and services. Self-propelled artillery regiments assigned to the corps varied from one to four depending on the mission.

Rifle Corps were commonly found in the composition of armies at the beginning of the war. Casualties in the summer and fall of 1941 were so heavy, however, that most corps were disbanded by the end of the year. They were reconstituted in early 1943 and came into general use for the duration of the war.

The units listed as subordinate are not necessarily all inclusive but are those that can be confirmed as subordinate to the corps headquarters for the time and place indicated. Honorifics are listed in quotes at the end of the chronological history of the unit followed by all identified decorations.

Guards Artillery, Cavalry, Mechanized, Tank, and Rifle Corps

1 Guards Cavalry Corps
—Formed from 2 Cavalry Corps, 26 Nov. 1941.
—Kashira w/50 Army, Nov. 1941.
—Stalinogorsk, Dec. 1941.
—Lozovaya area w/6 Army, Feb. 1943.
—Reserve, Kupyansk-Svyatovo, Apr. 1943.
—Belgorod Kharkov Op., Aug. 1943.
—Lutezh Bridgehead, Dnieper, as Central Front mobile group, Sep. 1943.
—RVGK, Sep. 1943.
—Voronezh Front, Sep. 1943.
—North of Kiev w/3 Guards Tank Army, Oct. 1943.
—Kiev, Nov. 1943.
—Brusilov, Kiev area; badly beaten by German 48 Panzer Corps, Nov. 1943.
—Rovno Lutsk Op. w/1 Ukrainian Front, Jan. 1944.
—In cavalry mechanized group of 1 Ukrainian Front w/25 Tank Corps, July 1944.
—Yaroslav Przemysl Op.; worked with 1 Tank Army, July 1944.
—Carpathian Duklinskiy Op. w/38 Army; cut off and nearly destroyed, Sep. 1944.
—Vistula Oder Op., Jan. 1945.
—Silesia, Feb. 1945.
—Berlin Op., Apr. 1945.
—Pomerania, Poland, Mar. 1946 (Feb. 1947 OB).

Key Commanders: Gen. Baranov, July 1944.
Units: Jan. 1944: 1, 2, 7 Guards Cavalry Divisions, 61, 87 Tank Regiments.
Mar. 1946: 4 Tank Division, 4 Guards Cavalry Division.

1 Guards Mechanized Corps
—Formed on basis of 1 Guards Rifle Division "Lenin," Tambov, Nov. 1942.
—RVGK, Dec. 1941.
—Stalingrad axis, Sep. 1942.
—Don River w/3 Guards Army, Dec. 1942.
—Don basin, Jan–Feb 1943.
—In reserve North of Voroshilovgrad w/Steppe Front, Apr. 1943.
—Kursk w/5 Guards Tank Army, July 1943.
—Zaporozhye axis, Sep. 1943.
—Donets, broke through German 1 Panzer Army; nearly destroyed, Sep. 1943.
—RVGK, Oct. 1943.
—Dnieper River w/12 Army, Oct. 1943.
—Zaporozyhe w/8 Guards Army, Oct. 1943.
—Budapest, Dec. 1944.
—Budapest area, Jan. 1945.
—Lake Balaton, Mar. 1945.
—Vienna, Mar–Apr 1945.
—Berlin Op., Apr. 1945.
—Austrian Alps, May 1945.
—Tbilisi as 1 Guards Mechanized Division, Mar. 1946 (Feb. 1947 OB).
—"Vienna, Voronezh," Orders of Lenin, Kutuzov.
Units: Oct. 1943: 1, 2, 3 Guards Mechanized Brigades, 9, 16, 17 Guards Tank Regiments.

1 Guards Rifle Corps
—Formed Oct. 1941.
—Airlifted to Orel-Tula area, Oct. 1941.
—Basis for reactivation of 5 Army at Mozhaisk, Oct. 1941.
—Reformed, at Mtsenk in Moscow area, Dec. 1941.
—Basis for second formation, 26 Army (SME), Dec. 1941.
—Reformed, at Staraya Russa w/11 Army, Jan. 1942.
—Staraya Russa w/1 Shock Army, Feb. 1942.
—Demyansk, Feb. 1942.
—Stalingrad w/2 Guards Army, Dec. 1942.
—Taganrog w/2 Guards Army, Jan. 1943.
—With Southern Front, May 1943.

—With 4 Ukrainian Front, Jan. 1944.
—Perekop Isthmus w/51 Army, Apr. 1944.
—Crimea w/2 Guards Army, May 1944.
—Shauliai w/51 Army, July 1944.
—Tukums w/51 Army, Aug. 1944.
—Riga, w/51 Army, Oct. 1944.
—Memel, Oct. 1944.
Units: Oct. 1941: 5, 6 Guards Rifle Divisions, 4, 11 Independent Tank Regiments.
Feb. 1942: 74 Naval Rifle Brigade.
Jan. 1944: 33, 86 Guards Rifle Divisions.
Apr. 1944: 33 Guards, 91, 346 Rifle Divisions.
Oct. 1944: 257, 267, 346 Rifle Divisions.

1 Guards Tank Corps
—Formed Moscow area as 26 Tank Corps, July 1942.
—Don River, Nov. 1942.
—Guards, Dec. 1942.
—Kharkov w/6 Army mobile group, Feb. 1943.
—Badly beaten by Germans near Pavlograd, Mar. 1943.
—Reserve, Voroshilovgrad area, Apr. 1943.
—Orel, July 1943.
—Bryansk Front, Aug. 1943.
—Belorussia, Oct. 1943.
—Rechitsa, Nov. 1943.
—RVGK, June 1944.
—RVGK to 1 Belorussian Front, June 1944.
—Belorussian Op. as mobile group of 65 Army, June 1944.
—Minsk, July 1944.
—Poland, Nov. 1944.
—Vistula Oder Op., Jan. 1945.
—Inster River w/11 Guards Army as an independent corps of 1 Belorussian Front (captured German SIGINT document), 7 Jan. 1945.
—Danzig, Mar. 1945.
—Oder River; had 47 "JS" tanks and 23 self-propelled guns, Apr. 1945.
—Berlin, Apr. 1945.
—Rostock, May 1945.
—Probably an independent corps.
—"Don," Orders of Lenin, Red Banner, Suvorov.
Key Commanders: Gen. Panov, Dec. 1943.
Units: Jan. 1945: 15, 16, 17 Guards Tank Brigades, 1 Guards Motorized Rifle Brigade.

2 Guards Cavalry Corps
—Guards from 3 Cavalry Corps, 26 Nov. 1941.
—Moscow offensive as mobile group, Dec. 1941.
—Istra, Dec. 1941.
—Moscow, Lama River; in mobile group of 5 Army, Jan. 1942.
—Mobile group of 20 Army at Rzhev, Jan. 1942.
—Pogorole Gorodistche Op.; in front mobile group; had three divisions and 6,000 men, Aug. 1942.
—Bryansk area, Feb. 1943.
—RVGK, June 1943.
—Western Front reserve, Kursk, July 1943.
—Kursk counteroffensive, Aug. 1943.
—RVGK, June 1944.
—To 1 Belorussian Front, June 1944.
—Mobile group of 1 Belorussian Front w/11 Tank, 7 Guards Cavalry Corps, July 1944.
—Poland, July 1944.
—Brest/Warsaw area, Aug. 1944.
—RVGK, Jan. 1945.
—Vistula Oder Op.; w/61 Army as mobile group of 1 Belorussian Front (captured German SIGINT document), 12 Jan. 1945.
—East Pomerania, Mar. 1945.
—Berlin Op., Apr. 1945.
—Order of Red Banner.
Key Commanders: Gen-Maj Pliyev, Feb. 1942; Gen. Kryukov, July 1944.
Units: June 1944: 3, 4, 17 Guards Cavalry Divisions, 184, 189 Tank Regiments.
Jan. 1945: 3, 4, 17 Guards Cavalry Divisions, w/160, 184, 189 Tank Regiments respectively.

2 Guards Mechanized Corps
—Formed Tambov on basis 22 Guards Rifle Division, Nov. 1942.
—Stalingrad w/2 Guards Army, Dec. 1942.
—Rostov axis w/2 Guards Army, Jan. 1943.
—Mius River, Feb. 1943.
—Don Basin, Aug. 1943.
—Broke through to Taganrog, Aug. 1943.
—Melitopol Op. as mobile group, Sep. 1943.
—Reserve, 4 Ukrainian Front, Jan. 1944.
—Nikopol w/5 Shock Army, Jan. 1944.
—Nikolayev, Mar. 1944.
—Odessa, Apr. 1944.

—RVGK, May–Sep 1944.
—Tisa River w/46 Army, Sep. 1944.
—Kecskemet, Oct. 1944.
—Budapest w/46 Army, Dec. 1944.
—Vienna, Mar. 1945.
—Esztergom w/46 Army, Apr. 1945.
—South of Vienna w/1 Guards Mechanized and 23 Tank Corps, Apr. 1945.
—Prague w/6 Guards Tank Army, May 1945.
—Independent Corps.
—"Nikopol, Budapest," Orders of Red Banner, Suvorov.
Units: Nov. 1942: 4, 5, 6 Guards Mechanized, 21, 22, 23, 24, 25 Guards Tank Regiments.
Jan. 1944: 4, 5, 6 Guards Mechanized, 37 Guards Tank Brigade.

2 Guards Rifle Corps
—Moscow, Dec. 1941.
—Staraya Russa w/11 Army, Jan. 1942.
—Staraya Russa w/1 Shock Army, Feb. 1942.
—Demyansk Pocket, Feb. 1942.
—Kalinin Front, Aug. 1943.
—Nevel Gorodok Op. w/6 Guards Army, Feb. 1944.
—Vitebsk Orsha Op. w/6 Guards Army, June 1944.
—Baltic Military District w/6 Guards Army, Oct. 1946, (Apr. 1947 OB).
Units: Aug. 1942: 75 Naval Rifle Brigade.
Nov. 1944: 71 Guards, 166 Rifle Divisions.

2 Guards Independent Tank Corps
—Formed on Southwest Front, near Voroshilovgrad, Apr. 1942.
—RVGK as 24 Tank Corps, Oct. 1942.
—Reformed as Guards from 24 Tank Corps, 26 Dec. 1942.
—Donbass, Dec. 1942.
—Voroshilovgrad axis, Feb. 1943.
—Kharkov, Mar. 1943.
—Voronezh Front, Ostrogosh region, Mar–Apr 1943.
—Kursk, as Voronezh Front reserve, June 1943.
—Kursk w/1 Tank and 5 Guards Tank Armies (Prokhorovka), July 1943.
—Belgorod Kharkov Op. w/5 Guards Tank Army, Aug. 1943.
—RVGK, Aug–Sep 1943.
—To 31 Army and 5 Army, Smolensk Op., Sep. 1943.
—Western Front on Vitebsk-Orsha axis w/31 Army, Oct. 1943.
—Zhitomir Berdichev area, Dec. 1943.

—RVGK, Apr. 1944.
—To 3 Belorussian Front, June 1944.
—Belorussian Op., at Orsha w/11 Guards Army mobile group, June 1944.
—Minsk, July 1944.
—Minsk, July 1944.
—Neman River, July 1944.
—Mariumpol, Aug. 1944.
—Gumbinnen, Oct. 1944.
—Insterburg, Oct. 1944.
—Inster River w/11 Guards Army, 33 Army, Jan. 1945.
—Vistula Oder Op. in 5 Army zone, Jan. 1945.
—Koenigsberg Op. (Insterberg-Gumbinnen axis), Apr. 1945.
—Berlin Op., Apr. 1945.
—Riga, as 2 Guards Tank Division, Nov. 1946 (Feb. 1947 OB).
—All Brigades had Order of Red Banner; 4 and 25 Guards Tank Brigades may be "Yelnaya."
—"Tatsin," Orders of Lenin, Red Banner, Suvorov.
Key Commanders: Gen-Lt V.M. Badanov, Dec. 1942–June 1943; Gen-Lt A.S. Burdenii June 1943–May 1945.
Units: July 1943: 4, 25, 26 Guards Tank Brigades, 47 Guards Breakthrough Tank Regiment, and 4 Guards Motorized Rifle Brigade.

3 Guards Cavalry Corps
—Formed from 5 Cavalry Corps, 25 Dec. 1941.
—Kharkov Offensive as Mobile group of 28 Army, May 1942.
—Kalach area, July 1942.
—Stalingrad offensive w/21 Army, Nov. 1942.
—Stalingrad Front w/5 Shock Army, Dec. 1942.
—Novocherkassk area in reserve, Apr. 1943.
—RVGK w/Steppe Front, June 1943.
—With Southwest Front, Aug. 1943.
—Smolensk, Sep. 1943.
—Vitebsk Orsha Op., June 1944.
—Grodno, July 1944.
—Allenstein, as independent corps of 1 Belorussian Front (captured German SIGINT document), 7 Jan. 1945.
—East Prussian Op., Mar. 1945.
—Berlin Op. as mobile group w/5 Guards Tank Army, Apr. 1945.
—Independent corps.
Key Commanders: Gen. Pliyev, Dec. 1942.
Units: Dec. 1942: 5, 6 Guards, 32 Cavalry Divisions, 198 Tank Regiment.

3 Guards Mechanized Corps
—Former 4 Mechanized Corps, Nov. 1942.
—Guards, 18 Dec. 1942.
—Kotelnikovo versus 4 Panzer Army, Dec. 1942.
—Stalingrad, Dec. 1942.
—Mius River, Feb. 1943.
—Reserve north of Rovenki, Apr. 1943.
—RVGK, June 1943.
—Kursk w/47 Army, July 1943.
—Kursk counteroffensive w/Voronezh Front, July–Aug. 1943.
—Voronezh Front, Sep. 1943.
—Proskurov Chernovtsy Op., Mar. 1944.
—Vitebsk Orsha Op., in cavalry-mechanized group of 3 Belorussian Front, June 1944.
—Shauliai, July 1944.
—Vilnius Op., July 1944.
—Riga axis, Aug. 1944.
—Memel Op., Oct. 1944.
—Independent Corps.
—"Stalingrad."
Units: June 1944: 7, 8, 9 Guards Mechanized Brigades, 35, 42 Guards Tank Regiments.

3 Guards Rifle Corps
—Formed from naval rifle/infantry brigades, late-1941.
—Matveyev Kurgan w/56 Independent Army, Jan. 1942.
—Rostov w/56 Independent Army, Mar. 1942.
—Southern Front w/56 Independent Army, June 1942.
—With Southern Front, May 1943.
—South Russia w/5 Shock Army, 3 Ukrainian Front, Jan. 1944.
—Crimea w/Independent Coastal Army, Apr. 1944.
—Belorussia Op. w/28 Army (Tremlya River), June 1944.
—Gumbinnen Op. w/28 Army, Jan. 1945.
—Koenigsberg area, Apr. 1945.
—Berlin Op. w/28 Army, Apr. 1945.
—RVGK w/28 Army, Apr. 1945 (SME).
—Baranovichi w/28 Army, May 1947 (Feb. 1948 OB).
—Independent Corps.
Units: Jan. 1942: 68, 76 Naval Rifle/Infantry Brigades.
      Jan. 1944: 50, 54, 96 Guards Rifle Divisions.
      June 1944: 50, 96 Guards Rifle Divisions.
      Nov. 1944: 50, 54 Guards Rifle Divisions.

3 Guards Tank Corps
—Formed in Kalinin area as 7 Tank Corps, before June 1942.
—Guards, Jan. 1943.
—Stalingrad, winter 1942–43.
—Voronezh w/5 Tank Army, Jan. 1943.
—Reserve, Novy Oskol area, Apr. 1943.
—RVGK, June 1943.
—Kursk counteroffensive w/4 Guards Army, July–Aug. 1943.
—Voronezh Front, Aug. 1943.
—Vitebsk Orsha Op. w/5 Guards Tank Army, June 1944.
—Minsk w/5 Guards Tank Army, July 1944.
—Kaunus, Sep. 1944.
—East Prussian Op., Jan. 1945.
—east Pomeranian Op., Feb. 1945.
—Koszalin, Pomerania w/19 Army, Feb. 1945.
—Berlin Op., Apr. 1945.
—The 3rd, 18th "Minsk," and 19th Guards Tank Brigades, 2 Guards Motorized Rifle Brigade "Minsk;" all have Order of Lenin.
—"Kotelnikovo," Orders of Red Banner, Suvorov.
Key Commanders: P.A. Rotmistrov, Jan. 1943; LTG A. P. Panfilov, 1945.
Units: June 1944: 3, 18, 19 Guards Tank Brigades, 2 Guards Motorized Rifle Brigade.

4 Guards Cavalry Corps
—Activated Krasnodar as 17 Cavalry Corps, Jan–Apr 1942.
—Guards, "Kuban Cossacks," Aug. 1942.
—Tuapse, Sep. 1942.
—Central Asia to Stalingrad area, Oct. 1942.
—RVGK Corps, Oct. 1942.
—Staro Shchedrinskaya, Oct. 1942.
—North Caucasus, Jan. 1943.
—Stavropol axis, Feb. 1943.
—Reserve west of Starobelsk, Apr. 1943.
—Mius River w/5 Shock Army, Aug. 1943.
—Taganrog, Aug–Sep 1943.
—Melitopol Op. w/51 Army, Oct. 1943.
—South Russia w/3 Ukrainian Front, Jan. 1944.
—Perekop, Sea of Azov, Feb. 1944.
—Novy Bug (Snigirov Op.), Mar. 1944.
—Odessa, Apr. 1944.
—Novy Bug, Apr. 1944.

—RVGK, June 1944.
—To 1 Belorussian Front, June 1944.
—Belorussia, as part of Cavalry-Mechanized Group Pliyev, June 1944.
—Lublin axis w/11 Tank Corps, July 1944.
—Vistula, Southeast of Warsaw, Aug. 1944.
—Rumania w/1 Guards Cavalry-Mechanized Group, 2 Ukrainian Front, Aug. 1944.
—Budapest, Oct. 1944–Feb. 1945.
—Lake Balaton axis, Feb. 1945.
—Bratislava, Mar–Apr 1945.
—Prague Op., May 1945.
—Stalingrad, North Caucasus Military District, Apr. 1946 (Feb. 1947 OB).
—"Kuban Cossacks, Novy Bug," Orders of Lenin, Red Banner, Kutuzov, Suvorov.
Units: Sep. 1942: 9, 10 Guards, 30, 110 Cavalry Divisions.
    Aug. 1944: 9, 10 Guards, 30 Cavalry Divisions, 128, 134, 151 Tank Regiments.
    Apr. 1946: 8, 9, 10 Guards Cavalry Divisions.

4 Guards Mechanized Corps
—Reformed from 13 Tank Corps, Jan. 1943.
—Stalingrad, winter 1942–43.
—Mius front; nearly wiped out at Matveyev Kurgan, Feb. 1943.
—With Southern Front, May 1943.
—Kursk, July 1943.
—Broke through Mius river w/5 Shock Army, Aug. 1943.
—Melitopol area, Sep–Nov 1943.
—Nikopol Bridgehead w/8 Guards Army, Jan–Feb 1944.
—Snigerevka w/8 Guards Army, Mar. 1944.
—Broke through Ingul River to Novy Bug, Mar. 1944.
—Odessa w/Cavalry Mechanized Group Pliyev, Apr. 1944.
—Iasi Kishinev Op. as mobile group w/7 Mechanized and 18 Tank Corps, Aug. 1944.
—Bulgaria, Sep. 1944.
—Morava River, Yugoslavia, 10 Oct. 1944.
—Belgrade w/57 Army; 14, 15 Guards Mechanized Brigades distinguished themselves, 20 Oct. 1944.
—Kraljevo, Yugoslavia (Ultra), 26 Oct. 1944.
—Budapest, w/46 Army, Nov. 1944.
—Hungary w/6 Guards Tank Army, Dec. 1944.
—Hungary w/7 Guards Army; reduced to 5,200 men, 14 tanks, 96 guns and mortars, Jan. 1945.

—RVGK (SME), Apr. 1945.
—Sliven, Bulgaria, Jan. 1946 (Feb. 1947 OB).
—"Stalingrad," Orders of Red Banner, Suvorov, Kutuzov.
Key Commanders: Gen-Lt V.I. Zhdanov, Oct. 1944.
Units: Jan. 1944: 13, 14, 15 Guards Mechanized Brigades, 38 Guards Tank Brigade, 37 Guards Tank and 68 Guards Heavy Tank Regiments.
   Jan. 1946: 13, 14, 15 Guards Mechanized Regiments/Brigades.

4 Guards Rifle Corps
—Lyuban axis w/2 Shock Army, Feb. 1942.
—Lyuban Op. w/54 Army, Mar–May 1942.
—Neva River, Leningrad Front w/2 Shock Army, Oct. 1942.
—Pavlograd w/12 Army, Feb. 1943.
—Lozovaya w/6 Army, Feb. 1943.
—Kursk w/1 Guards Army, July 1943.
—Kirovograd area w/8 Guards Army, 1 Ukrainian Front, Jan. 1944.
—Vistula River w/8 Guards Army, Aug. 1944.
—Poznan w/8 Guards Army, Feb. 1945.
—Crossed Oder River, Feb. 1945.
—Berlin Op.; main assault corps w/8 Guards Army, Apr. 1945.
—Gera, Germany, Aug. 1946 (Feb. 1947 OB).
Units: Mar. 1942: 140 Independent Rifle Brigade.
   Jan. 1944: 35, 47, 57 Guards Rifle Divisions.
   Nov. 1944: 35, 47 Guards Rifle Divisions.
   Aug. 1946: 20 Guards Mechanized, 39 Guards Rifle Divisions.

4 Guards Tank Corps
—Formed Voronezh as 17 Tank Corps, Spring, 1942.
—Guards, 2 Jan. 1943.
—Stalingrad, Winter 1942–43.
—Voronezh, Jan. 1943.
—With Popov's Front mobile group, Feb. 1943.
—Krasnoarmeskoye, Feb. 1943.
—Badly beaten by Germans near Pavlograd, Mar. 1943.
—RVGK w/Steppe Front, Apr. 1943.
—With Southern Front, May 1943.
—Kursk as Voronezh Front reserve, June 1943.
—Oboyan, Kursk w/27 Army, July 1943.
—Belgorod Kharkov Op. (Akhtyrka), Aug. 1943.
—RVGK, Nov. 1943.
—From RVGK to Kiev Defensive axis, Dec. 1943.
—Zhitomir Berdichev Op. w/1 Ukrainian Front, Dec. 1943–Jan. 1944.

—Ukraine w/1 Ukrainian Front, Jan. 1944.
—Ternopol, Mar. 1944.
—Poland, July 1944.
—Lvov Sandomir Op. (Kolthov Corridor), July 1944.
—Lvov, July 1944.
—Carpathian Duklinskiy Op. w/38 Army; had 45 tanks, 18 self propelled guns, Sep. 1944.
—Vistula Oder Op. w/5 Guards Army; had 178 tanks, 61 self propelled guns, Jan. 1945.
—Krakow, Jan. 1945.
—Berlin Op.on Dresden axis; had 110 tanks and self propelled guns, Apr. 1945.
—Prague, May 1945.
—Moscow as 4 Guards Tank Division, Nov. 1946 (Feb. 1947 OB).
—Independent Corps.
—The 12 Guards Tank Brigade "Shepetovka," Orders of Red Banner, Suvorov, Kutuzov; 13 Guards Tank Brigade "Shepetovka," Orders of Red Banner, Suvorov, Kutuzov; 14 Guards Tank Brigade "Zhitomir, Shepetovka," Orders of Red Banner, Suvorov, Kutuzov; 3 Guards Motorized Rifle Brigade "Yampol," Orders of Red Banner, Suvorov, Kutuzov. The 61 Guards Tank Brigade "Sverdlovsk, Lvov," associated with the corps.
—"Kantemirov," Orders of Lenin, Red Banner.
Key Commanders: Gen-Lt P.P. Poluboyarov 1942–46.
Units: Dec. 1943: 12, 13, 14 Guards Tank Brigades, 3 Guards Motorized Rifle Brigade.

5 Guards Cavalry Corps
—Former 10 Cavalry Corps (FHO), 1942.
—Activated as Guards Cavalry Corps (SME), Nov. 1942.
—Kizylar, North Caucasus Military District, Nov. 1942.
—Tuapse Defensive Op. w/18 Army, Dec. 1942.
—North Caucasus, Jan. 1943.
—Novocherkassk area as reserve, Apr. 1943.
—RVGK, June 1943.
—To Southern Front, Sep. 1943.
—Mius River, Sep. 1943.
—Melitopol Op., Oct. 1943.
—Kirovograd area, Jan. 1944.
—Korsun Shevchenkovskiy Op. w/4 Guards Army, Jan. 1944.
—Uman Botosani Op., Mar. 1944.
—Targul Frumos, May 1944.
—Iasi Kishinev Op. as part of cavalry-mechanized group w/23 Tank Corps, Aug. 1944.

—Debrecen Op., Oct. 1944.
—Budapest, Dec. 1944.
—Budapest area, Jan. 1945.
—Lake Balaton Op., Mar. 1945.
—Vienna, Mar. 1945.
—Independent Corps.
—Corps reduced to 5 Guards Cavalry Division, North Caucasus Military District, Apr. 1946 (Feb. 1947 OB).
—"Budapest, Don Cossacks," Order of Red Banner.
Units: May 1944: 11, 12 Guards and 63 Cavalry Divisions, 60, 64, 71, 119 Tank Regiments.

5 Guards Mechanized Corps
—Formed as 14 Tank Corps, then 6 Mechanized Corps, Nov. 1942.
—Guards, Jan. 1943.
—Kotelnikov/Zimovniki area, Dec. 1942.
—Kharkov w/5 Guards Tank Army, Feb. 1943.
—Novocherkassk area in reserve w/Steppe Front, Apr. 1943.
—Kursk w/5 Guards Tank Army, July 1943.
—Orel, July 1943.
—Belgorod Kharkov Op., Aug. 1943.
—RVGK, Jan. 1944.
—Kirovograd w/53 Army, Jan. 1944.
—Targul Frumos w/5 Guards Tank Army, May 1944.
—Moravka Ostrava, Czechoslovakia, Mar. 1945.
—Luckenwalde, Apr. 1945.
—Berlin Op.; had 12,135 men, 64 T-34 tanks, 22 SU-122 self propelled guns, 30 SU-76 self propelled guns, Apr. 1945.
—Jaromer, Czechoslovakia, May 1945.
—Prague w/4 Guards Tank Army, May 1945.
—To Central Asia, May 1945.
—The 10 Guards Mechanized Brigade "Prague," Order of Kutuzov; 12 Guards Mechanized Brigade, Orders of Red Banner, Kutuzov, Bogdan Khmelnitskiy; 24 Guards Tank Brigade "Prague," Orders of Suvorov, Bogdan Khmelnitskiy.
—"Ziminovskiy (Simovniki)," Order of Kutuzov.
Units: May 1945: 10, 11, 12 Guards Mechanized, 24 Guards Tank Brigade, 51 Guards Tank Regiment.

5 Guards Rifle Corps:
—Velikiye Luki w/3 Shock Army, Jan. 1943.
—Nevel Op., Feb. 1943.
—Kalinin Front, Aug. 1943.

—Bogushev axis, Belorussian Op.; main attack corps of 3 Belorussian Front w/39 Army, June 1944.
—Port Arthur w/39 Army, June 1946 (Feb. 1947 OB).
Units: June 1944: 17, 19, 91 Guards Rifle Divisions.
June 1946: 17, 91 Guards, 358 Rifle Divisions.

5 Guards Tank Corps:
—Activated as 4 Tank Corps, Voronezh area, before June 1942.
—Guards, 7 Feb. 1943.
—Voronezh Front, Jan. 1943.
—Liberated Kharkov, Feb. 1943.
—Reserve, Ostrogosk area, Apr. 1943.
—Kursk w/1 Tank Army, July 1943.
—Bolkhov Op., July 1943.
—Akhtyrka, Belgorod Kharkov Op., Aug. 1943.
—RVGK w/37 Army, Sep. 1943.
—Dnieper (Svarem'ye area) w/38 Army, Oct. 1943.
—Shevchenko, Kiev area w/38 Army, Nov. 1943.
—Kiev w/38 Army, Nov. 1943.
—Badly beaten by German 48 Panzer Korps near Brusilov, Nov. 1943.
—Kiev Defensive Op., Dec. 1943.
—Zhitomir Berdichev Op. Jan. 1944.
—Basis, w/5 Mechanized Corps, for forming 6 Tank Army in RVGK, Jan. 1944.
—Reconstituted; at Korsun Shevchenkovskiy Op. w/1 Ukrainian Front, Jan. 1944.
—Uman Botosani Op., Mar. 1944.
—Targul Frumos, May 1944.
—Iasi Kishinev Op. w/6 Tank Army, Aug. 1944.
—Debrecen Op., Hungary w/6 Guards Tank Army (rest of war), Oct. 1944.
—Budapest, Dec. 1944.
—Budapest, Jan. 1945.
—Vienna, Mar. 1945.
—Berlin Op., Apr. 1945.
—Prague, May 1945.
—To Far East, July 1945.
—Manchurian Op. w/6 Guards Tank Army, Aug. 1945.
—Independent Corps.
—The 20 Guards Tank Brigade "Mukden;" 21 Guards Tank Brigade "Zhitomir, Vienna," Twice Order of Red Banner, Orders of Suvorov, Kutuzov; 22 Guards Tank Brigade "Port Arthur," Orders of Red Banner, Bogdan Khmelnitskiy; 6 Guards Motorized Rifle Brigade "Vienna, Mukden," Orders of Red Banner, Suvorov, Bogdan Khmelnitskiy.

—"Stalingrad, Kiev," Orders of Lenin, Red Banner, Suvorov, Kutuzov.
Units: May 1944: 20, 21, 22 Guards Tank Brigades, 6 Guards Motorized Rifle Brigade, 48 Guards Heavy Tank Breakthrough Regiment.

6 Guards Cavalry Corps
—Former 7 Cavalry Corps.
—Northern Donets, Feb. 1943.
—Reserve in Novy Oskol area, Apr. 1943.
—With Western Front, Aug. 1943.
—Lenino, near Mogilev, as mobile group, Oct. 1943.
—Korsun Shevchenkovskiy Op., Jan. 1944.
—Rovno Lutsk Op., Jan. 1944.
—Southwest Ukraine, W/1 Ukrainian Front, Feb. 1944.
—With 1 Ukrainian Front as cavalry-mechanized group w/31 Tank Corps and 3 Guards Army, July 1944.
Key Commanders: Gen. Sokolov, July 1944.
Units: Jan. 1944: 8, 13 Guards, 8 Cavalry Divisions, 136, 154, 250 Tank Regiments.

6 Guards Mechanized Corps
—History from 82 Rifle Division, formed at Perm, Ural Military District, 1932.
—Became 82 Motorized Rifle Division by 1939.
—Reformed as 3 Guards Motorized Rifle Division, 17 Mar. 1942.
—Reformed as 6 Guards Mechanized Corps on basis of 3 Guards Motorized Rifle Division and 49 Mechanized Brigade, June 1943.
—Orel axis w/4 Tank Army (rest of war), July 1943.
—Karachev, July–Aug. 1943.
—RVGK, Aug. 1943–Jan. 1944.
—Proskurov Chernovtsy Op., Mar. 1944.
—Kamenets Podolsk, Mar. 1944.
—Lvov Sandomir Op., July 1944.
—Lvov, July 1944.
—Kielce, Vistula Oder Op., Jan. 1945.
—Lower Silesia Op., Feb. 1945.
—Berlin Op. (Brandenburg), Apr. 1945.
—Prague, May 1945.
—Berlin w/4 Guards Tank Army, Oct. 1946 (Feb. 1947 OB).
—"Lvov" honorific to 16 Guards Mechanized Brigade, 1 Guards Self Propelled Artillery Regiment, 396 Anti Aircraft Artillery Regiment.
—"Lvov, Kamenets Podolsk," Orders of Lenin, Red Banner, Suvorov.
Commanders: Gen. Lelyushenko, Apr. 1945.
Units: Mar. 1944: 16, 17 Guards Mechanized, 49 Mechanized Brigades, 29, 56 Tank Regiments.

6 Guards Rifle Corps
—Formed on basis of 4 Guards Rifle Division, Feb. 1942.
—Lyuban, possibly w/2 Shock Army, Feb. 1942.
—Leningrad Front, possibly w/2 Shock Army, Apr. 1942.
—Kursk w/1 Guards Army, July 1943.
—South Russia w/46 Army, 3 Ukrainian Front, Jan. 1944.
—Iasi Kishinev Op. w/37 Army, Aug. 1944.
—Yugoslavia, attacked by US aircraft; corps commander killed, Nov. 1944.
—Braila, Rumania, 1946 (Sep. 1947 OB).
Key Commanders: Gen-Lt G.P. Kotov, Nov. 1944 (killed in action).
Units: Jan. 1944: 20 Guards, 152, 353 Rifle Divisions.
     Aug. 1944: 20 Guards Rifle Division.
     Nov. 1944: 195 Rifle Division.

6 Guards Tank Corps
—Activated as 12 Tank Corps, Moscow, May 1942.
—Guards, 26 July 1943.
—With Bryansk Front, Aug. 1943.
—Dnieper River w/Voronezh Front, Sep. 1943.
—Kiev Op. w/3 Guards Tank Army (Rest of War), Nov. 1943.
—Fastov, Nov. 1943.
—Kiev Defensive Op., Dec. 1943.
—Zhitomir Berdichev Op., Jan. 1944.
—Proskurov Chernovtsy Op., Mar. 1944.
—Ternopol, Apr. 1944.
—Lvov Sandomir Op., July 1944.
—Lvov, July 1944.
—Sandomir Silesia Op., Jan. 1945.
—Berlin Op., Apr. 1945.
—Zossen, Apr. 1945.
—Prague, May 1945.
—Germany as 6 Guards Tank Division, 3 Guards Tank Army, June 1946 (Feb. 1947 OB).
—The 51 Guards Tank Brigade "Fastov," Orders of Red Banner, Bogdan Khmelnitskiy; 53 Guards Tank Brigade "Fastov," Orders of Lenin, Red Banner, Suvorov.
—"Kiev, Berlin," Orders of Lenin, Red Banner, Suvorov, Bogdan Khmelnitskiy.
Units: Jan. 1944: 51, 52, 53 Guards Tank, 22 Guards Motorized Rifle Brigades.

7 Guards Cavalry Corps
—Activated at Orel-Tula, Moscow Military District as 8 Cavalry Corps, Jan-June 1942.

—Guards, 14 Feb. 1943.
—Reserve, area west of Starobelsk, Apr. 1943.
—RVGK, June 1943.
—Kursk, July 1943.
—Chernigov, Sep. 1943.
—Mozyr w/61 Army, Jan. 1944.
—RVGK, June 1944.
—Lublin Brest Op., July 1944.
—Captured Lublin w/2 Tank Army, July 1944.
—Mobile Group of 1 Belorussian Front w/2 Guards Cavalry Corps, 1 Tank Corps, July 1944.
—RVGK (MHJ), Jan. 1945.
—Vistula Oder Op. (Pulawy Bridgehead) as an independent corps of 1 Belorussian Front (captured German SIGINT document), Jan. 1945.
—Radom Lodz Op., Jan. 1945.
—Kustrin Bridgehead, Feb. 1945.
—East Pomerania, Feb. 1945.
—Berlin Op., Apr. 1945.
—Brandenburg, Apr. 1945.
—Independent corps.
—"Brandenburg," Orders of Lenin, Red Banner, Suvorov.
Key Commanders: Gen. M.P. Konstantinov, June-July 1944.
Units: Jan. 1942: 21 Mountain, 55, 112 Cavalry Divisions.
      July 1944: 14, 16 Guards Cavalry Divisions.

7 Guards Mechanized Corps
—Former 2 Mechanized Corps.
—RVGK, Apr. 1943.
—With Bryansk Front, Aug. 1943.
—Desna River w/2 Tank Army, Sep. 1943.
—Dnieper River w/Central Front, Sep. 1943.
—RVGK, Chernigov area, Aug. 1944.
—RVGK, Jan. 1945.
—Vistula Oder Op., as 1 Ukrainian Front Reserve, Jan. 1945.
—Berlin Op., Apr. 1945.
—Manchurian Op. w/6 Guards Tank Army, Aug. 1945.
Units: Jan. 1945: 24, 25, 26 Guards Mechanized, 57 Guards Tank Brigades; 176 Tank Regiment.

7 Guards Independent Rifle Corps
—With Western Front, Aug. 1943.
—Chernigov w/61 Army, Sep. 1943.
—Baltic area w/10 Guards Army, Dec. 1943.
—Leningrad Military District w/10 Guards Army, Apr. 1946 (Feb. 1947 OB).

Units: Nov. 1944: 7, 8 Guards Rifle Divisions.
Apr. 1946: 7, 8 Guards Rifle Divisions.

7 Guards Tank Corps
—Activated as 15 Tank Corps, Stalingrad, Apr-May 1942.
—Guards, 26 July 1943.
—With Bryansk Front, Aug. 1943.
—Bukrin and Lutezh Bridgeheads w/3 Guards Tank Army (rest of war), Oct. 1943.
—Kiev axis, Oct. 1943.
—Kiev Op., Nov. 1943.
—Fastov, Nov. 1943.
—Kiev Defensive Op., Dec. 1943.
—Zhitomir Berdichev Op., Jan. 1944.
—Proskurov Chernovtsy Op., Mar. 1944.
—Lvov Sandomir Op., July 1944.
—Teltow Canal, Berlin Op., Apr. 1945.
—Prague, May 1945.
—Wunsdorf, Germany as 7 Guards Tank Division, w/3 Guards Tank Army, 1946 (Feb. 1947 OB).
—"Kiev, Berlin," Orders of Lenin, Twice Red Banner, Suvorov.
Units: Jan. 1944: 54, 55, 56 Guards Tank, 23 Guards Motorized Rifle Brigades.

8 Guards Mechanized Corps
—Former 3 Mechanized Corps; formed from 1 Tank Corps, Sep. 1942.
—Kursk, July 1943.
—Dnieper River, Sep. 1943.
—Guards, Oct. 1943.
—Kiev Defensive Op.; meeting engagement w/German 20 Motorized Division at Chernorudok, 27 Dec. 1943.
—Zhitomir Berdichev Op., Jan. 1944.
—Zhmerinka w/1 Guards Tank Army (rest of war), Jan. 1944.
—Proskurov Chernovtsy Op., Mar. 1944.
—Chortkov, Mar. 1944.
—Lvov Sandomir Op., July 1944.
—Reached Gulf of Riga cutting off Heeresgruppe North, 27 July 1944.
—Vistula Oder Op., Jan. 1945.
—East Pomeranian Op., Feb. 1945.
—Berlin Op., Apr. 1945.
—Grimma, Germany as 8 Guards Mechanized Division, Sep. 1946 (Feb. 1947 OB).
—The 20 Guards Mechanized Brigade "Zaleschitski," Orders of Lenin,

Red Banner, Suvorov, Bogdan Khmelnitskiy; 1 Guards Tank Brigade "Chortkov," Twice Order of Lenin, Orders of Red Banner, Suvorov, Kutuzov, Bogdan Khmelnitskiy, in the name of Marshal of Tank Troops Katukov.
—"Carpathian, Berlin," Order of Suvorov.
Units: Mar. 1944: 19, 20, 21 Guards Mechanized, 1, 64 Guards Tank Brigades.

8 Guards Rifle Corps
—Pogorole Gorodische Op. w/20 Army, Aug. 1942.
—Bolhov, Kursk Op., w/11 Guards Army, July 1943.
—Main attack corps of 11 Guards Army at Orel, July 1943.
—With Bryansk Front, Aug. 1943.
—Leningrad Military District w/10 Guards Army, Apr. 1946 (Feb. 1947 OB).
—"Estonian."
Units: July 1943: 11, 26, 83 Guards Rifle Divisions.
Dec. 1943: 26, 83 Guards Rifle Divisions.
Nov. 1944: 5, 26, 37, 83 Guards Rifle Divisions.
Apr. 1946: 7, 249 Rifle Divisions.

8 Guards Tank Corps
—Former 2 Tank Corps.
—Kiev, Nov. 1943.
—Badly beaten by German 48 Panzer Korps at Brusilov, Nov. 1943.
—Kiev Defensive Op., Dec. 1943.
—Lublin Brest Op. w/2 Guards Tank Army, July 1944.
—Vistula Oder Op. w/2 Guards Tank Army, Jan. 1945.
—East Pomeranian Op. w/1 Guards Tank Army, Feb. 1945.
—East Prussian Op. w/48 Army, Mar. 1945.
—Bad, Frienwalde, Germany as 8 Guards Tank Division, 2 Guards Mechanized Army, July 1946 (Feb. 1947 OB).
—Independent Corps.
Units: July 1944: 26, 99, 169 Tank, 56 Motorized Rifle Brigades, 15 Guards Heavy Tank Regiment.

9 Guards Mechanized Corps
—Lvov Sandomir Op., July 1944.
—Budapest, Dec. 1944.
—Berlin Op. w/6 Guards Tank Army (rest of war), Apr. 1945.
—Prague Op., May 1945.
—Manchurian Op., Aug. 1945.

9 Guards Rifle Corps
—Activated at Kaluga on basis of 12 Guards Rifle Division, June 1942.
—Volkhov w/61 Army (rest of war), July 1942.
—Kursk as a main attack corps, July 1943.
—Orel, July 1943.
—With Bryansk Front, Aug. 1943.
—Desna River, Sep. 1943.
—Dnieper River, Sep. 1943.
—Chernigov, Sep. 1943.
—Belorussia, Oct. 1943.
—East of Pinsk, Jan. 1944.
—With 61 Army, 2 Belorussian Front, Mar. 1944.
—Belorussian Op., June 1944.
—Brest, July 1944.
—Riga, Oct. 1944.
—Vistula Oder Op. w/61 Army, Jan. 1945.
—Berlin Op. w/5 Shock Army, Apr. 1945.
—Reorganized and unified w/Headquarters 20 Rifle Corps Red Banner, May 1945.
—"Brest," Orders of Red Banner, Kutuzov.
Units: June 1942: 12 Guards, 105, 108, 110, 257 Rifle Divisions.
  Mar. 1944: 12, 76, 77 Guards Rifle Divisions.

9 Guards Tank Corps
—Raised as 3 Tank Corps near Tula, Apr. 1942.
—Uman as 3 Tank Corps, Mar. 1944.
—Gds, Nov. 1944.
—Warsaw, Jan. 1945.
—Vistula Oder Op. w/2 Guards Tank Army, Jan. 1945.
—East Pomeranian Op. w/2 Guards Tank Army, Feb. 1945.
—Berlin Op. w/2 Guards Tank Army, Apr. 1945.
—Prague Op. w/6 Guards Tank Army, Apr. 1945.
—Neustrelitz, Germany as 9 Guards Tank Division w/2 Guards Mechanized Army, Aug. 1946 (Feb. 1947 OB).
—"Uman," Orders of Lenin, Red Banner, Suvorov.
Units: Jan. 1945: 47 Guards Tank Brigade.

10 Guards Rifle Corps
—Formed from Guards Airborne Brigades in the Moscow area in the RVGK, summer 1942.
—To the Caucasus, Aug. 1942.
—Astrakhan, Aug. 1942.
—Makhachkala, Sep. 1942.

—Ordzhonikidze axis, Oct. 1942.
—Ordzhonikidze, Nov. 1942.
—Maikop area, Dec. 1942.
—Novorossiysk w/18 Assault Army, Feb. 1943.
—North Caucasus, May 1943.
—With 28 Army, 3 Ukrainian Front, Jan. 1944.
—Iasi Kishinev Op. as front reserve, Aug. 1944.
—Belgrade Op. w/46 Army, Oct. 1944.
—Hungary w/46 Army, Nov. 1944.
—Budapest w/46 Army, Dec. 1944.
—Probably an independent corps.
Units: Oct. 1942: 4, 5, 6, 7 Guards Airborne Brigades.
Jan. 1944: 24, 109 Guards, 61, 77 Rifle Divisions.
Nov. 1944: 49, 109 Guards Rifle Divisions.
Mar. 1945: 83 Naval Infantry Brigade.

10 Guards Tank Corps
—Activated on initiative of the workers of the Urals as the 30th Tank Corps, "Ural Volunteers," w/197, 243, 244 Tank Brigades and 30 Motorized Rifle Brigades, Feb–Mar 1943.
—With 4 Tank, later 4 Guards Tank Army, 1942–45.
—Orel Op., July 1943.
—Orel Bryansk Op., Aug. 1943.
—Guards, 23 Oct. 1943.
—RVGK, Sep. 1943–Feb. 1944.
—Proskurov Chernovtsy Op., Mar. 1944.
—Lvov area, July 1944.
—Vistula Oder Op., Jan. 1945.
—Lower Silesian Op., Feb. 1945.
—Nysa, Poland, Mar. 1945.
—Berlin Op., Apr. 1945.
—Prague, May 1945.
—Oranienburg, Germany as 10 Guards Tank Division w/4 Guards Mechanized Army, Sep. 1946 (Feb. 1947 OB).
—The 61 Guards Tank Brigade "Sverdlovsk, Lvov" 62 and 63 Guards Tank Brigade "Chelyabinsk," 29 Guards Motorized Brigade "Unetchsk."
—"Ural Volunteers, Lvov," Orders of Red Banner, Suvorov, Kutuzov.
Units: July 1944: 61, 62, 63 Guards Tank, 29 Guards Motorized Rifle Brigades.

11 Guards Rifle Corps
—Formed in the Moscow area in the RVGK from rifle brigades, summer 1942.

—Astrakhan, Aug. 1942.
—Makhachkala, Sep. 1942.
—Ordzhonikidze as Transcaucasus Front Reserve, Oct. 1942.
—Ordzhonikidze w/9 Independent Army, Nov. 1942.
—North Caucasus, May 1943.
—Kerch Landing, Nov. 1943.
—Kerch w/Independent Coastal Army, Jan. 1944.
—Crimea w/Independent Coastal Army, Apr. 1944.
—Sevastopol (Sapun Heights), w/Independent Coastal Army, Apr. 1944.
—Schniedemuhl w/3 Shock Army, Jan. 1945.
—Magdeburg area w/3 Shock Army, 1945 (Feb. 1947 OB)
—In Baltic Military District, Dec. 1946 (Feb. 1948 OB).
—Independent Corps.
Units: Oct. 1942: 10 Guards, 34, 67 Rifle Brigades.
Nov. 1943: 2, 32, 55 Guards Rifle Divisions.
Jan. 1944: 2, 32 Guards, 414 Rifle Divisions.

11 Guards Tank Corps
—Formed at Kalinin as 6 Tank Corps, Apr. 1942.
—Guards, July 1943.
—Belgorod Kharkov Op., Aug. 1943.
—Kiev Defensive Op., Dec. 1943.
—Zhitomir Berdichev Op., Jan. 1944.
—Proskurov Chernovtsy Op. w/1 Guards Tank Army (rest of war), Mar. 1943.
—Heavy losses in breakout of 1 Panzer Army from Bucach, Apr. 1944.
—Belorussian Op. as mobile group, June 1944.
—Berdichev, June 1944.
—Lvov Sandomir Op., July 1944.
—Lodz, Aug. 1944.
—Vistula Oder Op., Jan. 1945.
—Poznan, Feb. 1945.
—Berlin Op., Apr. 1945.
—Glauchau, Germany as 11 Guards Tank Division, 1 Guards Mechanized Army, June 1946 (Feb. 1947 OB).
—The 40 Guards Tank Brigade "Chortkov," Orders of Lenin, Red Banner, Suvorov, Bogdan Khmelnitskiy, Red Star; 44 Guards Tank Brigade "Berdichev," Orders of Lenin, Red Banner, Suvorov, Kutuzov, Red Star, Bogdan Khmelnitskiy, Mongolian Order of the Red Combat Star; 45 Guards Tank Brigade "Gusyatin," Orders of Lenin, Red Banner, Suvorov, Bogdan Khmelnitskiy; 27 Guards Motorized Rifle Brigade "Chernovtsy," Orders of Red Banner, Suvorov, Kutuzov.
—"Carpathian, Berlin" Orders of Red Banner, Suvorov.

Commanders: Gen-Lt A.I. Getman, 1944; Col. A. Kh. Babadzhanyan, 1945.
Units: Jan. 1944: 40, 44, 45 Guards Tank, 27 Guards Motorized Rifle Brigades.

12 Guards Rifle Corps
—Staraya Russa w/34 Army, Mar. 1943.
—With Kalinin Front, Aug. 1943.
—Seelow Heights, Apr. 1945.
—Bernburg, Germany w/3 Mechanized Army, Nov. 1946 (Feb. 1947 OB).
Units: Nov. 1946: 22 Motorized Rifle, 23 Guards Rifle, 33 Rifle Divisions.

12 Guards Tank Corps
—Former 16 Tank Corps of 2 Tank Army.
—Vistula Oder Op. w/2 Guards Tank Army, Jan. 1945.
—East Pomeranian Op. w/2 Guards Tank Army, Feb. 1945.
—Berlin Op. w/2 Guards Tank Army, Apr. 1945.
—Germany as 12 Guards Tank Division w/2 Guards Mechanized Army, Dec. 1946 (Feb. 1947 OB).

13 Guards Rifle Corps
—Stalingrad w/2 Guards Army, Dec. 1942.
—Nevel Op., Feb. 1943.
—With Southern Front, May 1943.
—Gorodok, Dec. 1943.
—South Russia w/2 Guards Army, 4 Ukrainian Front, Jan. 1944.
—Crimea w/2 Guards Army, Apr. 1944.
—Latvia, Nov. 1944.
—Koenigsberg w/43 Army, Apr. 1945.
Units: Jan. 1944: 3, 49, 87 Guards, 295 Rifle Divisions.
   Apr. 1944: 3, 24, 87 Guards Rifle Divisions.
   Nov. 1944: 3 Guards Rifle Division.
   Apr. 1945: 260 Naval Infantry Brigade.

14 Guards Rifle Corps
—Northwest Front Reserve, July 1943.
—With Southwest Front, Aug. 1943.
—Latvia, Nov. 1944.
Units: July 1943: 43, 53 Guards, 7 Rifle Divisions.
   Nov. 1944: 23, 52, 53 Guards Rifle Divisions.

15 Guards Rifle Corps
—With Southwest Front, Aug. 1943.
—West of Smolensk w/10 Guards Army, Dec. 1943.
—Southwest Leningrad Military District w/10 Guards Army, Apr. 1946 (Feb. 1947 OB).
Units: Apr. 1946: 71 Guards Rifle, 182 Rifle Divisions.

16 Guards Rifle Corps
—Breakthrough corps w/11 Guards Army at Orel, July 1943.
—With Bryansk Front, Aug. 1943.
—Breakthrough corps, Orsha axis w/11 Guards Army, June 1944.
—Neman River, July 1944.
—Baltic Military District, Jan. 1947 (Feb. 1947 OB).
Units: Dec. 1943: 1 Guards Motorized, 5, 16 Guards Rifle Divisions.

17 Guards Rifle Corps
—Conspicuous gallantry displayed at Kursk w/13 Army, July 1943.
—Kiev axis (Sevsk-Mikhalovsky Farm), Aug. 1943.
—Belgorod Kharkov Op. w/60 Army, Aug. 1943.
—Dnieper River, Sep. 1943.
—Chernigov Pripyask Op. w/13 Army, Sep. 1943.
—Ukraine w/38 Army, 1 Ukrainian Front, Jan. 1944.
—Mukachevo, Carpathian Mountains, Sep. 1944.
Units: July 1943: 6, 70, 75 Guards Rifle Divisions.
      Sep. 1943: 2 Guards Airborne, 6, 70 Guards Rifle Divisions.
      Jan. 1944: 68 Guards, 211, 241 Rifle Divisions.
      Nov. 1944: 2 Guards Airborne Rifle Division.

18 Guards Independent Rifle Corps
—Activated in the RVGK, Moscow w/2, 3, 4 Guards Airborne Rifle Divisions, Apr. 1943.
—Headquarters created from 27 Rifle Corps of the RVGK, Apr. 1943.
—Kursk area w/13 Army, May, 1943.
—Kursk w/13 Army, July 1943.
—Ponyri (Kursk) w/13 Army, July 1943.
—Central Front Reserve, July 1943.
—Belgorod Kharkov Op., Aug. 1943.
—Konotop w/60 Army, Sep. 1943.
—North of Kiev, Oct. 1943.
—Kiev Op. at Ovruch, Nov. 1943.
—Kiev Defensive Op., Dec. 1943.
—Zhitomir Berdichev Op. w/60 Army, 1 Ukrainian Front, Jan. 1944.
—Rovno Lutsk Op. at Shepetovka, Feb. 1944.
—Proskurov Chernovtsy Op. at Izyaslav, Mar. 1944.

—Kamenets Podolsk w/60 Army, Mar. 1944.
—Bucach, Apr. 1944.
—Lvov Sandomir Op., July 1944.
—Stanislav, Aug. 1944.
—Carpathian Uzhgorod Op. w/1 Guards and 18 Armies, Sep. 1944.
—Subordinated to 2 Ukrainian Front, Nov. 1944.
—Budapest, Dec. 1944.
—Budapest, Jan. 1945.
—Hron Bridgehead, Feb. 1945.
—Vienna w/46 Army, Mar–Apr 1945.
—Bratislava Brno Op. w/53 Army, Apr–May 1945.
—Prague Op. May 1945.
—To Far East w/53 Army, May 1945.
—Manchurian Op., Aug. 1945.
—Germany, 1946 (Feb. 1947 OB).
—"Stanislav, Budapest," Order of Red Banner.
Units: Apr. 1943: 2, 3, 4 Guards Airborne Rifle Divisions.
July 1943: 2, 3, 4 Guards Airborne, 8, 148, 254 Rifle Divisions.
Jan. 1944: 148, 240, 351 Rifle Divisions.
Apr. 1944: 226, 260 Rifle Divisions.
Sep. 1944: 151, 161 Rifle Divisions.
Nov. 1944: 15, 69 Rifle Divisions.

19 Guards Rifle Corps
—With Western Front, Aug. 1943.
—Belorussia w/10 Guards Army, Dec. 1943.
Units: Nov. 1944: 22 Guards Rifle Division.

20 Guards Airborne Rifle Corps
—With Western Front, May 1943.
—Kursk w/4 Guards Army, July 1943.
—Akhtyrka, Aug. 1943.
—Korsun Shevchenkovskiy Op. w/4 Guards Army, Jan. 1944.
—Hungary w/4 Guards Army, Nov. 1944.
—Budapest w/4 Guards Army, Jan. 1945.
—Vienna, Mar–Apr 1945.
—Berlin Op. w/28 Army, Apr. 1945.
—RVGK w/28 Army, Apr. 1945.
—Belorussia, July 1946 (EUCOM Study).
Units: Jan. 1944: 5 Guards Airborne, 66 Guards, 375 Rifle Divisions.
Nov. 1944: 6, 7, 8 Guards Airborne Rifle Divisions.

21 Guards Rifle Corps
—With Voronezh Front, Aug. 1943.

—Korsun Shevchenkovskiy Op. w/4 Guards Army, Jan. 1944.
—Kursk w/4 Guards Army, July 1944.
—Hungary, Nov. 1944.
—Szeksferhervar, Dec. 1944.
—Hungary w/4 Guards Army, Jan. 1945.
Units: Jan. 1944: 69 Guards, 138 Rifle Divisions.
　　　　Nov. 1944: 40, 41, 62, 69 Guards Rifle Divisions.

22 Guards Rifle Corps
—Kursk w/6 Guards Army, July 1943.
—With Voronezh Front, Aug. 1943.
—Belorussia Op. w/6 Guards Army, June 1944.
Units: July 1943: 67, 71 Guards Rifle Divisions.

23 Guards Independent Rifle Corps
—Kursk w/6 Guards Army, July 1943.
—With Voronezh Front, Aug. 1943.
—Vitebsk Orsha Op. w/6 Guards Army, June 1944.
—Budapest axis, Oct. 1944.
Units: July 1943: 52 Guards, 375 Rifle Divisions.

24 Guards Rifle Corps
—Kursk w/7 Guards Army, July 1943.
—Dnieper River w/7 Guards Army, Sep. 1943.
—Kirovograd w/7 Guards Army, 2 Ukrainian Front, Jan. 1944.
—Targul Frumos w/7 Guards Army, May 1944.
—Hron Bridgehead w/7 Guards Army, Feb. 1945.
—Bratislava, Apr. 1945.
Units: Jan. 1944: 8 Guards Airborne, 36, 41 Guards Rifle Divisions.
　　　　Sep. 1943: 73, 78 Guards, 19 Rifle Divisions.

25 Guards Rifle Corps
—Kursk w/7 Guards Army, July 1943.
—Dnieper River w/7 Guards Army, Sep. 1943.
—Kirovograd w/7 Guards Army, 2 UK Front, Jan. 1944.
—Targul Frumos w/7 Guards Army, May 1944.
—Hron Bridgehead w/7 Guards Army, Feb. 1945.
—Bratislava, Apr. 1945.
Units: July 1943: 73, 78, 81 Guards Rifle Divisions.
　　　　Sep. 1943: 72, 81 Guards, 53 Rifle Divisions.
　　　　Jan. 1944: 41, 72, 81 Guards, 409 Rifle Divisions.
　　　　Nov. 1944: 53 Rifle Division.
　　　　Apr. 1945: 4 Guards Airborne, 409 Rifle Divisions.

26 Guards Rifle Corps
—Kursk w/27 Army, July 1943.
—With Voronezh Front, Aug. 1943.
—Southwest Ukraine with 2 Ukrainian Front as an Independent Corps, Jan. 1944.
—Iasi, Apr. 1944.
—Targul Frumos, May 1944.
—Kustrin Bridgehead w/5 Shock Army, Feb. 1945.
—Probably an independent corps.
Units: July 1943: 71, 155, 166, 241 Rifle Divisions.
     Jan. 1944: 25 Guards, 6, 31 Rifle Divisions.
     May 1944: 25, 89, 110 Guards, 375 Rifle Divisions.
     Nov. 1944: 25 Guards Rifle Division.

27 Guards Rifle Corps
—Southwest Ukraine w/37 Army, 2 Ukrainian Front, Jan. 1944.
—Vistula River w/8 Guards Army, July 1944.
—Iasi Kishinev Op. as 2 Ukrainian Front Reserve, Aug. 1944.
—Carpathian Mountains w/4 Ukrainian Front, Sep. 1944.
—Uzhgorod Mukachevo Op., Oct. 1944.
—Poprad, Czechoslovakia w/18 Army, Jan. 1945.
—Independent Corps.
Units: Jan. 1944: 48, 58 Guards Rifle Divisions.
     Jan. 1945: 8, 137 Rifle Divisions.

28 Guards Rifle Corps
—Activated at Voronezh as 15 Rifle Corps (second formation), Nov. 1942.
—Headquarters renamed Guards, divisions to 34 Rifle Corps, Apr. 1943.
—Assigned 39, 79, 88 Guards Rifle Divisions for rest of war and subordinated to 8 Guards Army for rest of war, May 1943.
—Izyum, July 1943.
—Zaporozhye Bridgehead, Oct. 1943.
—South Russia w/8 Guards Army, 3 Ukrainian Front, Jan. 1944.
—Odessa, Apr. 1944.
—Lublin Brest Op., July 1944.
—Vistula River, Aug. 1944.
—Magnuszew Bridgehead, Aug. 1944–Jan. 1945.
—Poznan, Feb. 1945.
—Kustrin Heights, Feb. 1945.
—Seelow Heights, Apr. 1945.
—Berlin Op., Apr. 1945.
—Gera, Germany w/8 Guards Mechanized Army, Aug. 1946 (Feb. 1947 OB).

—"Lublin," Orders of Red Banner, Suvorov.
Units: May 1943–May 1945: 39, 79, 88 Guards Rifle Divisions.
　　　Aug. 1946: 19 Guards Mechanized, 57, 88 Guards Rifle Divisions.

29 Guards Rifle Corps
—With Southwest Front, Aug. 1943.
—Zaporozhye Bridgehead w/8 Guards Army (rest of war), Oct. 1943.
—South Russia w/3 Ukrainian Front, Jan. 1944.
—Vistula River, Aug. 1944.
—Magnuszew Bridgehead, Aug. 1944–Jan. 1945.
—Vistula Oder Op., Jan. 1945.
—Poznan, Feb. 1945.
—Seelow Heights, Apr. 1945.
—Erfurt area w/8 Guards Mechanized Army, Aug. 1946 (Feb. 1947 OB).
Units: Jan. 1944: 24, 74, 82 Guards Rifle Divisions.
　　　Nov. 1944: 74 Guards Rifle Division.
　　　Aug. 1946: 21 Guards Mechanized, 82, 102 Guards Rifle Divisions.

30 Guards Rifle Corps
—Leningrad area, Jan. 1943.
—Leningrad area, Jan. 1944.
—Krasnogvardeysk, Jan. 1944.
—RVGK w/2 Shock Army, Sep. 1944.
—Ema Igi River w/2 Shock Army, Sep. 1944.
—Tallinn area w/2 Shock Army, Sep. 1944.
—Courland, Apr. 1945.
Units: Sep. 1944: 45, 64 Guards, 372 Rifle Divisions.
　　　Nov. 1944: 45, 63 Guards Rifle Divisions.

31 Guards Rifle Corps
—With Southern Front, May 1943.
—Kursk w/4 Guards Army, July 1943.
—Mius River w/5 Shock Army, Aug. 1943.
—RVGK, Dec. 1943.
—Nikopol, Jan. 1944.
—Hungary, Nov. 1944.
—Hungary w/4 Guards Army, Dec. 1944.
—Budapest Op. (Bicske), Jan. 1945.
—Szombathely, Hungary w/5 Guards Army, Sep. 1946 (Feb. 1947 OB).
—Probably an Independent Corps.
Units: Aug. 1943: 4, 34, 40 Guards Rifle Divisions.

Nov. 1944: 4, 34, 40 Guards Rifle Divisions.
Sep. 1946: 14, 62 Guards Rifle, 309 Motorized Rifle Divisions.

32 Guards Rifle Corps
—Kursk, w/5 Guards Army (to end of war), July 1943.
—Kirovograd, Jan. 1944.
—Lvov Sandomir Op., July 1944.
—Sandomir Bridgehead, Jan. 1945.
—Main attack corps for Vistula Oder Op., Jan. 1945.
—Czestochowa, Jan. 1945.
—Niessa River, Apr. 1945.
—Berlin Op., main attack corps, Apr. 1945.
—St. Polten, Austria w/5 Guards Army, Nov. 1946 (Feb. 1947 OB).
—Carpathian Military District w/5 Guards Army, 1947 (July 1947 OB).
Units: Jan. 1944: 6 Guards Airborne, 95, 97, 110 Guards, 214 Rifle Divisions.
Jan. 1945: 13, 95, 97 Guards Rifle Divisions.
Nov. 1946: 4, 95 Guards, 13 Guards Motorized Rifle Divisions.

33 Guards Rifle Corps
—Kursk w/5 Guards Army (rest of war), July 1943.
—Kirovograd, Jan. 1944.
—Lvov Sandomir Op., July 1944.
—Sandomir Bridgehead, Jan. 1945.
—Vistula Oder Op., Jan. 1945.
—Niessa River, Apr. 1945.
—Berlin Op., Apr. 1945.
—Prague, May 1945.
Units: Jan. 1944: 9 Guards Airborne, 13 Guards, 111 Rifle Divisions.
July 1944: 9 Guards Airborne, 14, 78 Guards Rifle Divisions.

34 Guards Rifle Corps
—With Southwest Front, Aug. 1943.
—South Russia w/3 Guards Army, 3 Ukrainian Front, Jan. 1944.
—Lvov Sandomir Op. w/5 Guards Army, July 1944.
—Sandomir Bridgehead, Jan. 1945.
—Vistula Oder Op. w/5 Guards Army, Jan. 1945.
—Niessa River w/5 Guards Army, Apr. 1945.
—Berlin Op., Apr. 1945.
Key Commanders: D.I. Ryabishev, 1943.
Units: Jan. 1944: 59, 61 Guards, 243 Rifle Divisions.
July 1944: 15, 58 Guards Rifle Divisions.

35 Guards Rifle Corps
—Formed from 7 Rifle Corps, Apr. 1943.
—Kursk w/7 Guards Army, July 1943.
—Kirovograd w/5 Guards Army, 2 Ukrainian Front, Jan. 1944.
—Targul Frumos w/27 Army, May 1944.
—Iasi Kishinev Op. w/27 Army, Aug. 1944.
—Lake Balaton Op., Mar. 1945.
—Berlin Op., Apr. 1945.
—Probably an Independent Corps.
Units: Jan. 1944: 93, 94 Guards, 78, 84 Rifle Divisions. 36 Guards Rifle Corps

36 Guards Rifle Corps
—Bolkhov as main attack corps for 11 Guards Army, July 1943.
—Vitebsk Orsha Op. as main attack corps for 11 Guards Army, June 1944.
—East Prussia, Nov. 1944.
—Koenigsberg, Apr. 1945.
Units: July 1943: 5, 18, 84 Guards Rifle Divisions. Dec. 1943: 11, 31, 84 Guards Rifle Divisions.
Nov. 1944: 16, 18, 84 Guards Rifle Divisions.

37 Guards Rifle Corps
—RVGK when formed from 13, 14, 15 Guards Airborne Divisions., Jan. 1944.
—Karelian Front, May 1944.
—Svir River w/7 Independent Army, June 1944.
—Redesignated Guards Airborne Corps, Nov. 1944.
—RVGK w/Independent Airborne Army, Nov. 1944.
—Independent Airborne Army (redesignated 9 Guards Army), Dec. 1944.
—Hungary w/9 Guards Army, Mar. 1945.
—Vienna, Apr. 1945.
—Prague, May 1945.
—Possibly in West Siberian Military District, Sep. 1947 (EUCOM Study).
Units: May 1944: 98, 99, 100 Guards Rifle Divisions, 69 Naval Rifle Brigade.
Oct. 1944: 13, 14, 16 Guards Airborne Rifle Divisions.
Dec. 1944: 98, 99, 103 Guards Rifle Divisions (to end of war).

38 Guards Rifle Corps
—Created as Guards Airborne Corps in RVGK, Aug. 1944.
—RVGK w/Independent Airborne Army, Nov. 1944.
—Independent Airborne Army (redesignated 9 Guards Army), Dec. 1944.

—Hungary w/9 Guards Army, Jan. 1945.
—Southeast of Budapest, Feb. 1945.
—Vienna, Apr. 1945.
—Prague Op., May 1945.
Units: Oct. 1944: 11, 12, 16 Guards Airborne Rifle Divisions.
	Dec. 1944: 104, 105, 106 Guards Rifle Divisions (rest of war).

39 Guards Rifle Corps
—Created as a Guards Airborne Corps, Aug. 1944.
—RVGK w/Independent Airborne Army, Nov. 1944.
—Independent Airborne Army (redesignated 9 Guards Army), Dec. 1944.
—Southeast of Budapest, Feb. 1945.
—Vienna, Apr. 1945.
—Prague Op., May 1945.
Units: Oct. 1944: 8, 14 Guards Airborne, 100 Guards Rifle Divisions.
	Dec. 1944: 100, 107, 114 Guards Rifle Divisions (rest of war).

40 Guards Rifle Corps
—Pomeranian Op. w/19 Army, Mar. 1945.
—Rugen Island, Apr. 1945.

Airborne, Artillery, Cavalry, Mechanized, Rifle, Tank Corps

1 Airborne Corps
—Formed 37 Guards Rifle Division, July 1942.
—Headquarters second formation became 4 Guards Airborne Division, Dec. 1942.
Units: June 1941: 1, 204, 211 Airborne Brigades.
	June 1942: 1, 2, 5 Airborne Brigades.

1 Cavalry Corps
—Stalinogorsk, Dec. 1941.
—Vyazma, Jan. 1942.
—First Kharkov Offensive, Jan. 1942.
—Targul Frumos, May 1944.
Key Commanders: P.A. Belov, Jan. 1942.

1 Mechanized Corps
—Possibly formed in Minsk, Nov. 1936.
—Possibly at Smolensk, Sep. 1937.
—Formed (reformed?) in Moscow, July 1940.
—Baltic Military District, June 1941.
—Probably in Novgorod, July 1941.

—Raised Gorki, Moscow Military District w/2 Tank Army, Aug. 1942.
—Rzhev in 41 Army zone, Jan. 1943.
—Orel Op. w/11 Guards Army, July 1943.
—Belgorod Kharkov Op. w/53 Army as mobile group, Aug. 1943.
—Krasnograd, Sep. 1943.
—Zaporozhye Bridgehead, Oct. 1943.
—Southwest Ukraine w/2 Ukrainian Front, Jan. 1944.
—To 1 Belorussian Front, June 1944.
—Belorussian Op. w/4 Guards Cavalry Corps in cavalry-mechanized group, June 1944.
—Kustrin Bridgehead w/5 Shock Army, Jan. 1945.
—Berlin Op. w/2 Guards Tank Army; had many M4A2 US tanks, Apr. 1945.
—Independent corps.
—"Krasnograd."
Key Commanders: Gen-Lt P. Romanenko, July 1940.
Units: Sep. 1937: 21 Mechanized Brigade.
    June 1941: 1, 3 Tank Division, 25, 30 Cavalry Divisions, 163 Motorized Division.
    Aug. 1942: 19, 35, 37 Mechanized, 219 Tank Brigades.
    Jan. 1944: 19, 35, 37 Mechanized, 219 Tank Brigades.

1 Independent Rifle Corps
—North of Lake Ladoga w/8 Army, Feb. 1940.
—Possibly reactivated in North Caucasus Military District, 1941.
—Osovets area w/10 Army, Western Special Military District, June 1941.
—Novgorod, July 1941.
—North Caucasus Front, July 1942.
—Sea of Azov, July 1942.
—Krasnodar, Aug. 1942.
—Dvina River, Vitebsk Op. w/43 Army; main attack corps, June 1944.
Units: June 1941: 1, 8 Rifle Divisions.
    June 1944: 179, 306, 357 Rifle Divisions.

1 Special Corps
—Mstensk, Southwest of Moscow, Oct. 1941.

1 Tank Corps
—Raised at Voronezh, Apr–May 1942.
—Kharkov, May 1942.
—Stalingrad axis, June 1942.
—Stalingrad offensive w/5 Tank Army, Nov. 1942.
—Kursk w/11 Guards Army, July 1943.

—Orel, July 1943.
—Belgorod Kharkov Op., Aug. 1943.
—To 1 Baltic Front, June 1944.
—Vitebsk Op. w/43 Army, June 1944.
—To 1 Baltic Front reserve, Aug. 1944.
—Dvinsk, Aug. 1944.
—Memel Op., Oct. 1944.
—Vistula Oder Op. w/39 Army, Jan. 1945.
—East Prussia Op., w/5 Guards Tank Army mobile group, Jan. 1945.
—Berlin Op. w/1 Belorussian Front, Apr. 1945.
Key Commanders: M.Ye. Katukov, May 1942.
Units: Nov. 1942: 89, 117, 159 Tank Brigades, 44 Motorized Rifle Brigade; 159 Rifle Division.
    Apr. 1945: 1 Polish Armored Corps.

2 Airborne Corps
—Kiev, July 1941.
—Southwest Front w/40 Army, Aug–Sep 1941.
—Formed 32 Guards Rifle Division, May 1942.
—Second formation probably formed Guards Airborne Division, Dec. 1942.
Units: June 1941: 2, 3, 4 Airborne Brigades.

2 Breakthrough Artillery Corps
—RVGK.
—Kursk w/63 Army, July 1943.

2 Cavalry Corps.
—Formed from 2 Cavalry Army, 6 Dec. 1920.
—Eastern Poland, Sep. 1939.
—Odessa Military District w/9 Indepedent Army, June 1941.
—Mogilev Podolsk in shock group w/2 Mechanized and 48 Rifle Corps, July 1941.
—Ingulets River w/9 and 18 Armies, Aug. 1941.
—RVGK (MHJ), Nov. 1941.
—Moscow, on Kashira axis, Nov. 1941.
—Reformed as 1 Guards Cavalry Corps, 26 Nov. 1941.
—Volokolamsk, Jan. 1942.
—Kharkov Offensive as Southwest Front reserve, May 1942.
Commanders: Gen-Maj P.A. Belov, Nov. 1941.
Units: June 1941: 9, 5, 72 Cavalry Divisions, 15 Motorized Rifle Division.
    Nov. 1941: 5, 9 Cavalry Divisions.
    Jan. 1942: 62, 64, 70 Cavalry Divisions.

2 Mechanized Corps
—Odessa Military District w/9 Independent Army, June 1941.
—Mogilev Podolsk in shock group w/2 Cavalry and 48 Rifle Corps, July 1941.
—Reformed, Sep. 1942.
—Manych River w/Rotmistrov's mobile group, Jan. 1943.
—Kursk w/3 Guards Tank Army, July 1943.
—Orel, July 1943.
—Reformed as 7 Guards Mechanized Corps, 1943.
Units: June 1941: 11, 16 Tank, 15 Motorized Divisions.

2 Rifle Corps.
—Headquarters at Minsk w/13 Army, June 1941.
—With Western Front, July 1941.
—Borisov area, July 1941.
—Basis of 50 Army, Bryansk Front, Aug. 1941.
—Oder River, Mar. 1945.
—Transbaikal Military District w/36 Army, Aug. 1945.
Units: June 1941: 100, 161 Rifle Divisions.

2 Tank Corps
—Formed Apr–May 1942.
—Kharkov w/5 Tank Army, May 1942.
—Stalingrad axis w/5 Tank Army, July 1942.
—Northern Donets, Dec. 1942.
—In reserve, Kupyansk-Svyatovo area, Apr. 1943.
—Kursk w/5 Guards Tank Army, July 1943.
—Kursk counteroffensive w/Voronezh Front, Aug. 1943.
—Voronezh Front, Sep. 1943.
—Became 8 Guards Tank Corps, by Nov. 1943.

3 Airborne Corps
—Formed Apr. 1941; RVGK Aug. 1941.
—Odessa Military District w/9 Independent Army, June 1941.
—Odessa, Aug. 1941.
—Kiev, incorporated into 40 Army, Sep. 1941.
—Redesignated 87 Rifle Division, Fall 1941.
—Corps reformed by 1942.
—Became 33 Guards Rifle Division, June 1942.
—Third formation probably became a Guards Airborne Division, Dec. 1942.
Units: June 1941: 5, 6, 212 Airborne Brigades.

3 Breakthrough Artillery Corps
—RVGK.
—Activated as 3 Counterbattery Artillery Corps, Leningrad, 1943.
—Leningrad Front 1943–44.
—Reformed into 3 Breakthrough Artillery Corps, Jan. 1944.
—Berlin Op., Apr. 1945.

3 Cavalry Corps
—Belorussian Maneuvers, Sep. 1936.
—Apparently had all elite formations, May 1937.
—Minsk, Oct. 1938.
—Became 2 Guards Cavalry Corps, 26 Nov. 1941.
—Second formation in Stalingrad offensive; had 45% casualties, Nov. 1942.
—Steppe Front, Apr. 1943.
—In cavalry-mechanized group of 3 Belorussian Front, June 1944.
Key Commanders: G.K. Zhukov, 1937; Gen-Maj L.M. Dovator, Nov. 1941.
Units: Sep. 1936: 4, 7 Cavalry Divisions, 10 Motor-Mechanized Brigade; 21 Mechanized Brigade (B.T. Tanks).
May. 1937: 7, 11 Cavalry Divisions.
Nov. 1941: 50, 53 Cavalry Divisions.

3 Mechanized Corps
—Formed in Vilno-Alitus-Ukmerge area, possibly from 3 Cavalry Corps, July 1940.
—Baltic Special Military District w/11 Army, June 1941.
—Counterattacks in Baltic area failed, July 1941.
—Formed from 1 Tank Corps, Sep. 1942.
—Kalinin Front, Dec. 1942.
—Rzhev in 22 Army zone, Jan. 1943.
—Kursk w/1 Tank Army, July 1943.
—Belgorod Kharkov Op. w/1 Tank Army, Aug. 1943.
—Reformed as 8 Guards Mechanized Corps, Oct. 1943.
—Riga w/51 Army, July 1944.
Key Commanders: Gen-Lt Y. Yeremenko, July 1940; P.A. Rotmistrov, Chief of Staff, June 1941; M.Ye. Katukov, Dec. 1941.
Units: July 1940: 2, 5 Tank, 84 Motorized Divisions.
June 1941: 2, 5 Tank, 84 Motorized Divisions.
Aug. 1943: 1, 3, 10 Mechanized, 32, 49 Tank Brigades.

3 Mountain Rifle Corps
—Formed Transcaucasus Military District, 1940.

—Krasnodar area w/47 Army, Feb. 1943.
—North Caucasus, May 1943.
—Crimea w/4 Ukrainian Front, Apr. 1944.
—Carpathian Uzhgorod Op., Sep. 1944.
—Carpathian Military District, Aug. 1947 (EUCOM Study).
—See 3 Rifle Corps.
Units: Feb. 1943: 9, 60, 155 Rifle Brigades.
       Apr. 1944: 128 Guards, 242, 318 Mountain Rifle Divisions.
       Aug. 1947: 128 Guards, 318 Mountain Rifle Divisions.

3 Rifle Corps
—Finland w/13 Army, Dec. 1939.
—Basis for forming 46 Army, Transcaucasus Military District, July 1941.
—Ordzhonikidze, Oct. 1942.
—Maikop area, Dec. 1942.
—Kerch w/Independent Coastal Army, Jan. 1944.
—May be same as 3 Mountain Rifle Corps.
Units: Oct. 1942: 9, 57, 60 Rifle Brigades.

3 Tank Corps
—Formed Tula, Moscow Military District, Apr. 1942.
—Volkhov w/61 Army, July 1942.
—Southwest Front w/3 Tank Army, Aug. 1942.
—RVGK (SME), Sep 1942–Jan 1943.
—With Popov's front mobile group, Feb–Mar 1943.
—Don Basin, Jan. 1943.
—Severely defeated by Germans near Pavlograd, Mar. 1943.
—RVGK, Mar–Apr 1943.
—Kursk (Ponyri); w/2 Tank Army (to end of war), July 1943.
—Bolkhov, July 1943.
—Orel, July 1943.
—Bogodukhov, had 360 tanks in Belgorod Kharkov Op., Aug. 1943.
—RVGK, Sep 1943–Jan 1944.
—Vinnitsa axis, Feb. 1944.
—Uman Botosani Op., Mar. 1944.
—Targul Frumos; had Valentine tanks, May 1944.
—Belorussia Op., June 1944.
—Lublin; took city, July 1944.
—Destroyed near Warsaw, Aug. 1944.
—Became 9 Guards Tank Corps, Nov. 1944.
—"Uman," Order of Suvorov.
Units: Jul. 1943: 50, 51, 103 Tank, 3 Motorized Rifle Brigades.

4 Airborne Corps
—Headquarters at Marina Gorka, Western Special Military District, June 1941.
—Berezina and Krichev Ops., June 1941.
—Belorussia, July 1941.
—RVGK in Moscow area w/54 Army, Sep. 1941.
—Vyazma; paradropped, Jan. 1942.
—Fought behind German lines for 6 months, Jan–June 1942.
—Became 38 Guards Rifle Division, July 1942.
—Second formation named 1 Guards Airborne Division, Dec. 1942.
Key Commanders: Gen-Maj Levashov, Jan. 1942.
Units: June 1941: 7, 8, 9, 214 Airborne Brigades.
    Dec. 1942: 7, 8, 9, 214 Airborne Brigades.

4 Breakthrough Artillery Corps
—RVGK (SME).
—Kursk, as RVGK formation w/13 Army, July 1943.
—Kursk, had 484 guns, 216 mortars, 432 rocket launchers, July 1943.
—Belorussian Op. w/1 Belorussian Front, June 1944.
—Berlin Op., Apr. 1945.
—Rathenow, Germany, Dec. 1946 (Feb. 1948 OB).
Units: July 1943: 5, 12 Breakthrough Artillery Divisions, 5 Guards Rocket Barrage Division.
    Dec. 1946: 6, 34 Artillery Divisions.

4 Cavalry Corps
—Eastern Poland, Sep. 1939.
—Krasnovodsk, Sep. 1942.
—Southwest Front, Oct. 1942.
—RVGK, Nov. 1942.
—Stalingrad offensive w/51 Army, Nov. 1942.
—Badly mauled by Germans at Kotelnikovo, Dec. 1942.
—Reserve near Voroshilovgrad, Apr. 1943.
—RVGK, July 1943.
—Belgorod Kharkov Op., Aug. 1943.
Units: Nov. 1942: 61, 81, 115 Cavalry Divisions.

4 Mechanized Corps
—Kiev Special Military District, Aug. 1940.
—Lvov w/6 Army; one of four corps w/some T-34 and KV tanks, June 1941.
—Reformed from 28 Tank Corps, Oct. 1942.

—RVGK to 51 Army, Oct. 1942.
—Stalingrad offensive w/51 Army as mobile group, Nov. 1942.
—RVGK w/5 Shock Army, Dec. 1942.
—Nizhne Cherkaya, 1 Dec. 1942.
—Named 3 Guards Mechanized Corps, 18 Dec. 1942.
—Second formation at Kursk, July 1943.
—RVGK, Aug. 1943.
—RVGK to Akhtyrka, Aug. 1943.
—Belgorod Kharkov Op., Aug. 1943.
Key Commanders: Gen-Maj A.A. Vlasov, June 1941; Gen-Maj V.T. Volsky, Nov. 1942.
Units: Aug. 1940: 8, 10 Tank, 81 Motorized Divisions.
June 1941: 8, 32 Tank, 81 Motorized Divisions.
Nov. 1942: 36, 59, 60 Mechanized Brigades, 55, 158 Tank Regiments.

4 Independent Rifle Corps
—Vitebsk, Belorussia Military District, June 1934.
—Western Special Military District w/3 Army, June 1941.
—Commander captured by Germans, July 1941.
—Destroyed near Kharkov, Feb. 1943.
—Karelian Front, Aug. 1943.
—Svir River, Karelia w/7 Independent Army, June 1944.
Units: June 1941: 27, 56, 85 Rifle Divisions.
June 1944: 70 Independent Naval Rifle Brigade.

4 Tank Corps
—Formed Voronezh, Apr. 1942.
—Kharkov, May 1942.
—Voronezh, June 1942.
—Stalingrad axis, July 1942.
—Stalingrad, Aug. 1942.
—Volga Corridor, Stalingrad axis w/1 Guards Army, Sep. 1942.
—RVGK, Nov. 1942.
—Sovetsky pocket w/21 Army during Stalingrad offensive, Nov. 1942.
—Ostrogosh Rossosh Op. w/40 Army, Jan. 1943.
—Named 5 Guards Tank Corps, 7 Feb. 1943; 4 Tank Corps reformed.
—Northwest Poland as 4 Tank Division w/1 Guards Cavalry Corps, Mar. 1946, (Feb. 1947 OB).
—Probably Independent Corps.
—"Stalingrad."
Key Commanders: Gen-Lt V. Volsky, Nov. 1942
Units: Apr. 1942: 45, 47, 102 Tank, 4 Motorized Rifle Brigades.

Nov. 1942: 45, 69, 102 Tank, 4 Motorized Rifle Brigades; 277, 343 Rifle Divisions.

5 Airborne Corps.
—Baltic Special Military District, June 1941.
—RVGK w/54 Army in Moscow area, Sep. 1941.
—Orel, Oct. 1941.
—Moscow area w/26 Army, Oct. 1941.
—Reformed as 39 Guards Rifle Division, Aug. 1942.
—Second formation in Orel-Bryansk Op., Oct. 1942.
—Probably formed a Guards Airborne Division, Dec. 1942.
Units: June 1941: 9, 10, 201 Airborne Brigades.

5 Breakthrough Artillery Corps
—RVGK (FHO and SME).
—Belorussian Op. w/3 Belorussian and 1 Baltic Front, June 1944.
—Vitebsk Orsha Op., June 1944.
Units: May 1944: 3, 5, 7 Artillery Divisions.
June 1944: 3, 4, 5 Guards Artillery Divisions, 95 Heavy Howitzer Brigade, 99 Artillery Brigade, 43 Rocket Barrage Brigade.

5 Cavalry Corps
—Possibly in Belorussia Military District, Oct. 1936.
—Eastern Poland, Sep. 1939.
—Kharkov sector, between 21 and 38 Armies, Sep. 1941.
—Moscow Offensive, Dec. 1941.
—Reformed as 3 Guards Cavalry Corps, 25 Dec. 1941.
—Second formation at Kharkov, Jan. 1942.
—Kharkov Op., May 1942.
Key Commanders: K.K. Rokossovski, Oct. 1936.
Units: Sep. 1941: 3, 14 Cavalry; 117, 154 Rifle Divisions.

5 Mechanized Corps
—Transbaikal Military District w/16 Army as 5 Tank Corps, July 1940.
—Converted to 5 Mechanized Corps, 1941.
—Transferred to West, in RVGK w/16 Army, May 1941.
—Bobruysk, Western Special Military District w/16 Army, June 1941.
—Smolensk w/16 Army, July 1941.
—Senno w/20 Army, July 1941.
—Dnieper River, Aug. 1941.
—Solovev w/16 Army, Aug. 1941.
—RVGK, Surovikino (Stalingrad); had 193 Tanks w/5 Tank Army, Oct. 1942.

—Chir River, Rostov Oblast, Dec. 1942.
—In reserve North of Voroshilovgrad, Apr. 1943.
—Smolensk, Sep. 1943.
—Lenino (near Mogilev), as mobile group of 33 Army, Oct. 1943.
—Korsun Shevchenkovskiy Op. w/5 Guards Tank Army, Jan. 1944.
—Basis for forming 6 Tank Army w/5 Guards Tank Corps in the RVGK, Jan. 1944.
—Uman Botosani Op. w/6 Tank Army, Mar. 1944.
—Targul Frumos w/27 Army, May 1944.
—Iasi Kishinev Op. w/6 Tank Army, Aug. 1944.
—With 60 Army, 1 Ukrainian Front, Mar. 1945.
—Deployment patterns suggest it is an independent corps.
Key Commanders: Gen-Maj M.V. Volkhov, Nov. 1942.
Units: June 1941: 13, 17 Tank, 109 Motorized Rifle Divisions.
Nov. 1942: 45, 49, 50 Mechanized Brigades, 168, 188 Tank Regiments, 119, 321 Rifle Divisions.
Nov. 1944: 2, 9, 45 Mechanized Brigades, 233 Tank Brigade, 252 Tank Regiment.

5 Independent Rifle Corps
—Belorussia Military District, 1934.
—Belorussian Maneuvers, Sep. 1936.
—Northeast Poland w/10 Army, 21 June 1941.
—Ussuriysk, Far East Military District, Aug. 1945.
Units: Sep. 1936: 4, 8 Rifle Divisions; 3, 4 Mechanized Brigades (T-26 Tanks).

5 Tank Corps
—Transbaikal w/16 Army, July 1940.
—Converted to 5 Mechanized Corps, 1941.
—Reformed, Apr–May 1942.
—Second formation on Don River, Nov. 1942.
—Bolkhov w/11 Guards Army (Kursk), July 1943.
—Orel w/11 Guards Army, 20 July 1943.
—Bryansk Front, Aug. 1943.
—Dnieper River w/38 Army, Sep. 1943.
—Iasi Kishinev Op.; commander killed, Aug. 1944.
—Ploesti, Aug. 1944.
—Bialystok as 5 Tank Division, Mar. 1946 (Feb. 1947 OB).
Units: July 1940: 17, 19 Tank, 109 Motorized Rifle Division.
July 1943: 24 Tank Brigade.

6 Airborne Corps
—Named 40 Guards Rifle Division, July 1942.
—Second formation probably formed Guards Airborne Division, Dec. 1942.

6 Breakthrough Artillery Corps
—RVGK (SME).
—Berlin Op., Apr. 1945.

6 Cavalry Corps
—Bobruysk, Belorussian Military District 1937–38.
—Kaunus, June 1940.
—Suwalki Bulge w/10 Army, in mechanized group under I.V. Boldin, Deputy Commander of the Western Front, 23 June 1941.
—Rarev River, June 1941.
—First Kharkov Offensive, Jan. 1942.
—Second Kharkov Offensive, May 1942.
—"Cossack, Stalin."
Key Commanders: G.K. Zhukov, 1937–38; Gen. Y. Yeremenko, June 1940. N.S. Nikitin, June 1941 (may have been division commander in corps).
Units: May 1937: 4 "Don Cossack," 6 "Chongar," 29 Cavalry Divisions.
June 1941: 6, 36 Cavalry Divisions.
June 1944: 26, 28, 49 Cavalry Divisions.

6 Mechanized Corps
—Grodno, Western Special Military District w/10 Army, June 1941.
—Destroyed, in mechanized group under I.V. Boldin, Deputy Commander of the Western Front, 23 June 1941.
—Reformed from 14 Tank Corps in North Caucasus, Nov. 1942.
—RVGK, Dec. 1942.
—Kotelnikovo, Dec. 1942.
—Manych River w/Rotmistrov's mobile group, Jan. 1943.
—Reformed as 5 Guards Mechanized Corps, Jan. 1943.
—Second Formation in Bryansk Front, Aug. 1943.
Key Commanders: M.G. Khatskilevich, 1941; S.I. Bogdanov 1942.
Units: June 1941: 4, 7 Tank, 29 Mechanized Divisions.
Dec. 1942: 51, 54, 55 Mechanized Brigades, 76, 80 Tank Regiments.

6 Rifle Corps
—Kiev Special Military District, Aug. 1940.

—Kiev Special Military District w/6 Army, June 1941.
—Kharkov w/6 Army, May 1942.
—Bely, Nov. 1942.
—Rzhev salient, Dec. 1942.
—Chernuski (Alexander Matrosov, Hero of the Soviet Union here w/56 Guards Rifle Division) w/3 Shock Army, Feb. 1943.
—Kalinin Front, Aug. 1943.
—Novgorod Luga Op. w/59 Army; main attack corps, Jan. 1944.
—Probably an independent corps.
—"Stalin."
Key Commanders: Gen-Lt Povetkin, Aug. 1943.
Units: Oct. 1940: 97, 159 Rifle Divisions.
  Feb. 1943: 56 Guards Rifle Division.
  Jan. 1944: 65, 239, 310 Rifle Divisions.

6 Tank Corps
—Formed Kalinin area, Apr. 1942.
—Pogorelo Gorodische Op.; in front mobile group with 24 KV, 46 T-34, 30 T-70, 69 T-60 tanks, Aug. 1942.
—Rzhev, Aug. 1942.
—Rzhev Sychevka rail line w/2 Guards Army, Dec. 1942.
—The 100 Tank Brigade to 31 Tank Corps; gained 112 Tank Brigade; former 112 Tank Division, Mar. 1943.
—Kursk w/1 Tank Army, July 1943.
—Belgorod Kharkov Op. w/1 Tank Army, Aug. 1943.
—Became 11 Guards Tank Corps, Oct. 1943.
—Second formation at Kiev, Nov. 1943.
Key Commanders: A.I. Getman, 1942–44.
Units: Dec. 1942: 22, 100, 200 Tank, 6 Motorized Rifle Brigades.
  July 1943: 22, 112, 200 Tank, 6 Motorized Rifle Brigades.

7 Airborne Corps
—Became 34 Guards Rifle Division, 1942.
—Second formation probably became Guards Airborne Division, Dec. 1942.

7 Breakthrough Artillery Corps
—Kursk w/61 Army, July 1943.
—Bryansk, Aug. 1943.
—Bukrin Bridgehead, Oct. 1943.
—Kiev in support of 38 Army, Nov. 1943.
—From Bukrin to Lutezh Bridgehead, Nov. 1943.
—With 1 Ukrainian Front, June 1944.

—Berlin Op., Apr. 1945.
—RVGK (FHO and SME).
Units: June 1943, 17 Breakthrough Artillery Division.
June 1944: 1 Guards, 13, 17 Artillery Divisions.

7 Cavalry Corps
—Stalingrad Offensive, Nov. 1942.
—Ostrogosh Rossosh Op., Jan. 1943.
—Steppe Front, Apr. 1943.
—Reformed as 6 Guards Cavalry Corps.

7 Mechanized Corps
—Headquarters at Tula, Moscow Military District, June 1941.
—Bobruysk, Western Special Military District w/20 Army in the High Command Reserve, June 1941.
—Lepel area w/20 Army, July 1941.
—Reformed, Sep. 1942.
—Kirovograd w/5 Guards Army, Jan. 1944.
—Iasi Kishinev Op., w/37 Army, Aug. 1944.
—Debrecen, Hungary w/6 Guards Tank Army, Oct. 1944.
—Budapest Op., Dec. 1944.
—Hungary, Jan. 1945.
—Prague Op., May 1945.
—Regrouped to Far East w/6 Guards Tank Army, June 1945.
—Manchurian Op. w/6 Guards Tank Army, Aug. 1945.
Key Commanders: Gen-Maj V.I. Vinogradov, June 1941.
Units: June 1941: 14, 18 Tank, 1 "Moscow Minsk" Motorized Rifle Divisions.
Jan. 1944: 16, 34, 64 Mechanized, 41 Guards Tank Brigades, 237, 240 Tank Regiments.

7 Rifle Corps
—Dnepropetrovsk, July 1941.
—Stalingrad w/64 Army, Oct. 1942.
—Stalingrad offensive, Nov. 1942.
—Reformed into 35 Guards Rifle Corps, Apr. 1943.
—Novgorod w/59 and 8 Armies, Jan. 1944.
—East Pomeranian Op. w/3 Shock Army, Mar. 1945.
Units: Nov. 1942: 93, 96, 97 Rifle Brigades.

7 Independent Tank Corps
—Formed near Kalinin from Rotmistrov's 3 Guards Tank Brigade, Apr–May 1942.

—RVGK at Kalinin, June 1942.
—Voronezh Op. w/5 Tank Army, July 1942.
—Volya Corridor on Stalingrad axis w/1 Guards Army, Sep. 1942.
—RVGK w/5 Shock Army, Dec. 1942.
—Kotelnikovo w/5 Shock Army, Dec. 1942.
—Donbas Op., Dec. 1942.
—Reformed as 3 Guards Tank Corps, Jan. 1943.
—Second Formation at Kiev, Nov. 1943.
—Targul Frumos w/2 Tank Army, May 1944.
Key Commanders: P.A. Rotmistrov, May–Dec 1942.

8 Airborne Corps
—Formed 35 Guards Rifle Division, 1942.
—Second formation probably became Guards Airborne Division, Dec. 1942.

8 Breakthrough Artillery Corps
—RVGK (SME).
—Kursk w/11 Guards Army, July 1943.
—Berlin Op., Apr. 1945.
Units: June 1944: 3, 6 Breakthrough Artillery Divisions.

8 Cavalry Corps
—Activated at Orel and Tula, Jan–June 1942.
—Bryansk front, July 1942.
—Voronezh axis, Aug. 1942.
—Middle Don, Sep. 1942.
—Southwest Front, Oct. 1942.
—RVGK, Nov. 1942.
—Stalingrad offensive as mobile group w/5 Tank Army; heavy losses from air, Nov. 1942.
—Northern Donets, Dec. 1942.
—Raid in Debaltsev Region, Feb. 1943.
—Reformed as 7 Guards Cavalry Corps, 14 Feb., 1943.
Units: Jan. 1942: 21 Mountain, 55, 112 Cavalry Divisions.

8 Mechanized Corps
—Kiev Special Military District w/26 Army, July 1940.
—Dubno Lutsk w/26 Army; one of only four corps w/some T-34 and KV tanks, 26 June 1941.
—Striy, June 1941.
—Brody, July 1941.
—Basis for activating 38 Army on Southwest Front, July 1941.

—Smolensk, Aug. 1941.
—Moscow, Dec. 1941.
—Reformed, Sep. 1942.
—Kirovograd w/5 Guards Tank Army, Jan. 1944.
—East Prussian Op. w/2 Shock Army, Mar. 1945.
—Berlin Op., Apr. 1945.
—"Alexandrija."
Units: June 1941: 12, 34 Tank, 7 Motorized Rifle Divisions.
  Jan. 1944: 66, 67, 68 Mechanized, 116 Tank Brigades, 41, 69 Tank Regiments.

8 Rifle Corps
—Kiev Special Military Districts w/26 Army, July 1940.
—Przemysl, June 1941.
—Commander captured by Germans, Aug. 1941.
—Kharkov Offensive w/6 Army, May 1942.
—Tallinn, Aug. 1944.
—RVGK w/2 Shock Army, Sep. 1942.
—Kalinin Front, Aug. 1943.
—Muttu Island, Baltic Sea w/2 Shock Army, Sep. 1944.
—Tartu w/2 Shock Army, Sep. 1942.
—Leningrad Military District, Apr. 1946 (Feb. 1947 OB).
—"Estonian."
Units: June 1941: 72, 173 Rifle Divisions.
  Nov. 1944: 7, 249 Rifle Divisions.

8 Tank Corps
—Formed, Apr–May 1942.
—Pogorelo Gorodische Op. in front mobile group; had 165 tanks, Aug. 1942.
—Western Front, Aug. 1943.

9 Airborne Corps
—Formed 36 Guards Rifle Division, July 1942.
—Second formation probably formed a Guards Airborne Division, Dec. 1942.

9 Cavalry Corps
Units: June 1941: 4, 17, 44 Cavalry Divisions.

9 Mechanized Corps
—General reserve in Kiev-Zhitomir area, Kiev Special Military District, June 1941.

—In the tank battles at Dubno, June 1941.
—Lutsk, July 1941.
—Formed Tula, Moscow Military District, Sep. 1943.
—Dnieper, Oct. 1943.
—Fastov w/3 Guards Tank Army, Nov. 1943.
—Kiev w/3 Guards Tank Army, Nov. 1943.
—Zhitomir Berdichev Op., Jan. 1944.
—Proskurov Chernovtsy Op. w/3 Guards Tank Army (rest of war), Mar. 1944.
—RVGK, June 1944.
—Lvov Sandomir Op., July 1944.
—Vistula Oder Op., Jan. 1945.
—Silesian Op., Feb. 1945.
—Berlin Op. (Marienburg), Apr. 1945.
—Wunsdorf, Apr. 1945.
—Prague, May 1945.
—Cottbus, Germany w/3 Guards Mechanized Army, Aug. 1946 (Feb. 1947 OB).
—All mechanized brigades "Proskurov," Orders of Red Banner, Kutuzov.
—The 91 Tank Brigade "Proskurov" was commanded by I.I. Yakubovskiy.
—"Kiev, Zhitomir," Orders of Red Banner, Suvorov, Kutuzov.
Commanders: K.K. Rokossovski, June–July 1941.
Units: June 1941: 20, 35 Tank Divisions, 131 Motorized Divisions.
    Oct. 1943: 69, 70, 71 Mechanized Brigades, 47, 59 Guards, 166 Tank Regiments; 91 Independent Tank Brigade.

9 Independent Rifle Corps
—A 9 Rifle Corps was in the North Caucasus, May 1931.
—Formed at Simferopol, Odessa Military District, June 1941.
—Basis of 51 Army, Aug. 1941.
—Kerch, Oct. 1941.
—Krasnodar axis w/9 Army, Feb. 1943.
—North Caucasus, May 1943.
—Southwest Ukraine w/28 Army, 3 Ukrainian Front, Jan. 1944.
—Berlin w/5 Shock Army; Zhukov says had greatest success in city, Apr. 1945.
—Schwerin, Germany w/5 Mechanized Army, Jan. 1947 (Feb. 1947 OB).
Key Commanders: P.I. Batov, June 1941; Gen-Maj I.P. Rosly, Apr. 1945.
Units: June 1941: 106, 156, 234 Rifle, 32 Cavalry Divisions.
    Feb. 1943: 157 Rifle Brigade.
    Jan. 1944: 230, 301 Rifle Divisions.
    Jan. 1947: 30, 89, 94 Guards, 301 Rifle Divisions.

9 Independent Tank Corps
—Formed in the Tula, Kozelsk, Serpukov areas, Moscow Military District, Apr–May 1942.
—Moscow area, Aug. 1942.
—Kursk as Central Front reserve, July 1943.
—Belgorod Kharkov Op. w/60 Army, Aug. 1943.
—Ssevsk w/60 Army, Aug. 1943.
—To 1 Belorussian Front, June 1944.
—Belorussia Op. at Bobruysk w/3 Army, June 1944.
—Minsk, July 1944.
—Brest, July 1944.
—Radom Lodz Op. in Pulawy Bridgehead, Jan. 1945.
—Vistula Oder Op. w/33 Army, Jan. 1945.
—Breslau, Feb. 1945.
—East Pomeranian Op., Mar. 1945.
—Berlin Op., Apr. 1945.
—Germany as 9 Tank Division, Jan. 1946 (Feb. 1947 OB).
—Brandenburg, Germany, RVGK under Group of Occupation Forces HQ, June 1946 (Aug. 1946 OB)
—Independent tank corps.
—All tank brigades have Order of Red Banner.
—"Bobruysk, Berlin."
Commanders: G.S. Rudchenko, Aug. 1943.
Units: 23, 95, 108 Tank Brigades, 6 Motorized Rifle Brigade.

10 Airborne Corps
—Formed 41 Guards Rifle Division, June 1942.
—Second formation probably formed a Guards Airborne Division, Dec. 1942.

10 Breakthrough Artillery Corps
—Berlin Op., Apr. 1945.
—RVGK (FHO).
Key Commanders: Gen-Lt L.I. Kozhukov, 1945.
Units: Apr. 1945: 31 Artillery Division.

10 Cavalry Corps
—Reformed as 5 Guards Cavalry Corps, Nov. 1942.

10 Mechanized Corps
—Karelian Isthmus w/23 Army, June 1941.
—Transferred to Baltic Front, 27 June 1941.
—Lake Ilmen, July 1941.
—Niesse River, Apr. 1945.

—Manchuria w/6 Guards Tank Army as 10 Motorized Corps, Aug. 1945.
Units: June 1941: 21, 24 Tank, 198 Motorized Divisions.
   July 1941: 21 Tank, 70, 237 Rifle Divisions.
   Apr. 1945: 62 Tank, 29 Motorized Rifle Brigade.
   Aug. 1945: 72 Mechanized Brigade.

10 Rifle Corps
—Baltic Special Military District w/8 Army, June 1941.
—Tallinn w/8 Army, Aug. 1941.
—Newly reformed, Oct. 1942.
—Urukh River, Caucasus front, Oct. 1942.
—North Caucasus, May 1943.
—South Ukraine w/51 Army, Jan. 1944.
—Perekop w/51 Army, Apr. 1944.
—Sevastopol w/51 Army, May 1944.
—Riga w/51 Army, Oct. 1944.
—Memel, Oct. 1944.
Units: Oct. 1942: 43, 59, 106 Rifle Brigades.
   Jan. 1944: 216, 257, 263, 346 Rifle Divisions.
   Apr. 1944: 216, 257, 279 Rifle Divisions.
   Oct. 1944: 77, 204, 257 Rifle Divisions.
   Oct. 1944: 91, 279, 347 Rifle Divisions.

10 Tank Corps
—Formed in Leningrad Military District on basis of 11 Mechanized Corps, the original mechanized corps in the Soviet Army, 1938.
—Viipuri, Finland, Dec. 1939.
—Reformed, Apr–May 1942.
—With Popov's mobile group, Feb–Mar 1943.
—Badly defeated by Germans at Pavlograd, Mar. 1943.
—In reserve, Steppe Front, June 1943.
—Kursk w/5 Guards Tank Army, July 1943.
—Kursk counteroffensive w/Voronezh Front, Aug. 1943.
—Voronezh Front, Sep. 1943.
—Kiev, Nov. 1943.
—Korsun Shevchenkovskiy Op. w/2 Guards Tank Army, Jan. 1944.
—Lvov Sandomir Op, July 1944.
—SW of Lvov, July 1944.
—Mulhausen, Jan. 1945.
—East Prussian Op. w/5 Guards Tank Army, Feb. 1945.
—Furstenwalde, Germany as 10 Tank Division, June 1946 (Aug. 1946 OB).
—Independent corps.
Units: July 1944: 178, 186 Tank Brigades.

11 Cavalry Corps
—Rzhev, Jan. 1942.
—Vyazma, Feb. 1942.
—Destroyed Rzhev, July 1942.
Units: Jan. 1942: 18, 24, 82 Cavalry Divisions.

11 Mechanized Corps
—Formed on the basis of 11 Rifle Division in Leningrad Military District; first of mechanized corps with 45th, 1932.
—In the Red Army "general reserve," Nov. 1935.
—Expanded from division to corps size, Dec. 1935.
—Reformed in Leningrad Military District as 10 Tank Corps, 1938.
—Reactivated, Feb–Mar 1941.
—Grodno, Western Special Military District in mechanized group of I.V. Boldin, 3 Army, 22 June 1941.
—Probably destroyed by 24 June 1941.
Key Commanders: D.K. Mostovenk, 1941.
Units: June 1941: 29, 33 Tank, 204 Motorized Divisions.

11 Rifle Corps
—In Belorussia Military District, Dec. 1934.
—Western Dvina River w/8 Army, June 1941.
—Narva, Aug. 1941.
—Taman Peninsula, Mar. 1943.
—North Caucasus, May 1943.
—Taman area, Nov. 1943.
—Southwest Ukraine w/1 Guards Army, 1 Ukrainian Front, Jan. 1944.
—Proskurov Chernovsty Op. w/1 Guards Army, Mar. 1944.
Units: Jan. 1944: 271, 276, 316 Rifle Divisions.
     Nov. 1943: 304, 316, 414 Rifle Divisions.
     Nov. 1944: 271 Rifle Division.

11 Tank Corps
—Formed Apr–May 1942.
—Kharkov w/5 Tank Army, May 1942.
—Voronezh axis w/5 Tank Army, July 1942.
—RVGK w/2 Tank Army, Jan. 1943.
—Orel w/4 Tank Army, July 1943.
—With the Bryansk Front, Aug. 1943.
—To Southern Front, Sep. 1943.
—Melitopol Op., Oct. 1943.
—Belorussian Op. w/8 Guards and 47 Armies, June 1944.
—Lublin Brest Op. w/8 Guards Army; badly mauled, commander (P.U. Rudkin) relieved, July 1944.

—Mobile Group of 1 Belorussian Front w/2 and 7 Guards Cavalry Corps, July 1944.
—Magnusew Bridgehead w/69 Army, Aug. 1944.
—RVGK (MHJ), Jan. 1945.
—Vistula Oder Op. w/1 Belorussian Front, Jan. 1945.
—Radom Lodz Op. w/69 Army (Pulawy Bridgehead), Jan. 1945.
—East Pomeranian Op. w/1 Guards Tank Army, Mar. 1945.
—Berlin Op. w/1 Guards Tank Army, Apr. 1945.
—Germany as 11 Tank Division, Jan. 1946 (Feb. 1947 OB).
—Independent corps.
—"Berlin, Radom," Orders of Red Banner, Suvorov, Kutuzov.
Key Commanders: Gen Tolbukhin, Oct. 1943; P.N. Rudkin, July 1944; Gen-Maj Yuschuk, July 1944–May 1945.
Units: Oct. 1943: 20, 36, 65 Tank Brigades, 12 Motorized Rifle Brigade.

12 Cavalry Corps
—Known to have existed.

12 Mechanized Corps
—Formed in Baltic Special Military District, Feb–Mar 1941.
—Shauliai w/8 Army, Baltic Special Military District, June 1941.
—Counterattacks failed, July 1941.
Units: June 1941: 23, 28 Tank, 202 Motorized Divisions.

12 Rifle Corps
—Basis for formation of 36 Army, Transbaikal Military District, July 1941.

12 Tank Corps
—Raised Moscow Military District, May 1942.
—The 30th Tank Brigade replaced by 106 Tank Brigade from Urals, July 1942.
—Kozelsk, Aug. 1942.
—Ostrogosh Rossosh Op. w/3 Guards Tank Army, Jan. 1943.
—Kharkov, Feb. 1943.
—Pechengi and Chuguyev in Ukraine, Feb. 1943.
—Krasnograd; cut to pieces by Germans w/4 Tank Corps, Mar. 1943.
—Kursk, July 1943.
—Orel, 20 July 1943.
—Reformed as 6 Guards Tank Corps, 26 July 1943.
Units: June 1943: 86, 97, 106 Tank, 13 Motorized Rifle Brigades.

13 Cavalry Corps
—Lyuban, Jan. 1942.

—Volkhov River, Jan. 1942.
Key Commanders: Gen-Maj N. I. Gusev, Jan. 1942.
Units: Jan. 1942: 25, 80, 87 Cavalry Divisions.

13 Mechanized Corps
—Formed in Western Special Military District, Feb–Mar 1941.
—Bialystok, Western Special Military District w/10 Army, June 1941.
—Disbanded, July 1941.
—Second formation corps in Stalingrad offensive w/57 Army, Nov. 1942.
—Reserve of Stalingrad Front, Dec. 1942.
Key Commanders: P.N. Akhlyusgin, 1941.
Units: June 1941: 25, 31 Tank, 208 Motorized Divisions.

13 Mountain Rifle Corps
—Turkestan, 1919.
—Poland w/12 Army as Rifle Corps, Sep. 1939.
—Commander captured by Germans, Aug. 1941.
—Bukrin Bridgehead, Nov. 1943.
—Nis, Yugoslavia, Oct. 1944.
—Northwest of Baku, Nov. 1945, (Feb. 1947 OB).
Units: Nov. 1945: 400 Rifle Division.

13 Tank Corps
—Formed Stalingrad, Volga Military District, May 1942.
—Reformed Northeast of Surovikono, July 1942.
—Stalingrad axis w/1 Tank Army, July 1942.
—Stalingrad front w/64 Army, Sep. 1942.
—Stalingrad w/51 Army, Oct. 1942.
—RVGK, Oct. 1942.
—Stalingrad offensive, Nov. 1942.
—Converted to mechanized corps, kept tank corps designator (SME), Nov. 1942.
—Destroyed near Kalach, Dec. 1942.
—Deployment pattern implies independent corps.
—Reformed as 4 Guards Mechanized Corps, Jan. 1943.
—Second formation in RVGK (MHJ), Aug. 1943.
—Belgorod Kharkov Op., Aug. 1943.
Units: Nov. 1942: 17, 61, 62 Mechanized Brigades; all mechanized brigades until Jan. 1943.

14 Cavalry Corps
—Known to have existed, June 1944.

14 Mechanized Corps
—Kobrin area w/4 Army, Western Special Military District, June 1941.
—Pruzhany-Kobrin area, June 1941.
—Disbanded by 1942.
Units: June 1941: 22, 30 Tank , 205 Motorized Divisions.

14 Rifle Corps
—Odessa Military District, on Danube River w/9 Independent Army, June 1941.
—Destroyed near Kharkov w/6 Army, Feb. 1943.
—Novogorod Luga Op. w/59 Army, Jan. 1944.
—Dvinsk w/4 Shock Army, Aug. 1944.
—"Stalin."
Units: Jan. 1944: 191, 378 Rifle Divisions.
       Nov. 1944: 311 Rifle Divisions.

14 Tank Corps
—Formed, probably in North Caucasus Military District, Apr–May 1942.
—Stavropol axis/direction; fought on foot with no tanks, July 1942.
—Destroyed, Aug. 1942.
—Reformed as 6 Mechanized Corps, North Caucasus area, Nov. 1942.
Units: Jan. 1942: 136, 138, 139 Tank, 21 Motorized Rifle Brigades.

15 Cavalry Corps
—In the Transcaucasus Front, July 1942.
—Iran, Aug. 1943.
—Iran, July 1944.
Units: July 1944: 1, 23 Cavalry Divisions.

15 Mechanized Corps
—Formed Kiev Special Military District, Feb–Mar 1941.
—General reserve, Kiev-Zhitomir area, Kiev Special Military District, May 1941.
—Radekhov/Ostrog, Kiev Special Military District w/12 Army; one of only four corps w/some T-34 and KV tanks, June 1941.
—Attacked east of Radzekhuz on SW Front, 24 June 1941.
—Toporov region, July 1941.
—Kursk, at Prokhorovka, 12 July 1943.
—Lvov Sandomir Op., July 1944.
—Sofia, Bulgaria, w/10 Mechanized (former 37) Army, Dec. 1946 (Feb. 1947 OB).
Units: July 1944: 148 Rifle Division.

15 Rifle Corps
—Finland w/13 Army, Dec. 1939.
—Kovel, Kiev Special Military District w/5 Army, June 1941.
—Chernigov w/5 Army, Aug. 1941.
—Commander killed in action, Aug. 1941.
—Encircled at Kiev; broke out, Sep. 1941.
—Kantemirov, Dec. 1942.
—Lozovaya area, Feb. 1943.
—Torn apart by Germans at Pavlograd, Feb. 1943.
—Kursk w/13 Army, July 1943.
—Dnieper River w/13 Army, Sep. 1943.
—Chernigov/Pripyask w/13 Army, Sep. 1943.
—Ukraine w/60 Army, 1 Ukrainian Front, Jan. 1944.
—Ternopol w/60 Army, Mar. 1944.
—Main attack corps w/13 Army, Lvov-Sandomir Op., July 1944.
—Established Volkhov Corridor, July 1944.
—Sofia, Bulgaria, 1946 (Feb. 1947 OB).
Key Commanders: Col. I. I. Fedyuninski, June 1941; K.S. Moskalenko, Sep. 1941.
Units: July 1943: 8, 74, 148 Rifle Divisions.
Jan. 1944: 322, 336 Rifle Divisions.
Mar. 1944: 148, 322, 336 Rifle Divisions.

15 Tank Corps
—Formed in Belorussia Military District from a Mechanized Corps, 1938.
—Took part in "liberation" of western Ukraine (Poland), Sep. 1939.
—Broken up, Nov. 1939.
—Formed Moscow, May 1942.
—Ostrogosh Rossosh Op. w/3 Guards Tank Army, Jan. 1943.
—Pechengi and Chuguyev in Ukraine, Feb. 1943.
—Kharkov w/3 Guards Tank Army, Feb. 1943.
—Kursk w/3 Guards Tank Army, July 1943.
—Orel w/3 Guards Tank Army, Aug. 1943.
—Became 7 Guards Tank Corps, 26 July 1943.
Key Commanders: Gen-Maj M. S. Shumilov, June 1941.

16 Cavalry Corps
—Known to have existed, June 1944.

16 Mechanized Corps
—Poland w/12 Army, Sep. 1939.
—Kiev Special Military District w/18 Army, June 1941.
Units: June 1941: 15, 39 Tank, 240 Motorized Divisions.

16 Rifle Corps
—Belorussian Military District, Dec. 1934.
—Belorussian Maneuvers, Sep. 1936.
—Headquarters at Kaunus, Baltic Special Military District w/11 army, June 1941.
—Novorossiysk w/18 Army, Apr. 1943.
—Kerch Landing w/56 Army, Nov. 1943.
—Kerch Peninsula, Jan. 1944.
—Crimea (Sivash), Feb. 1944.
—Crimea w/Independent Coastal Army, Apr. 1944.
Units: Sep. 1936: 2, 5, 81 Rifle Divisions.
June 1941: 5, 23, 133, 188 Rifle Divisions.
Nov. 1943: 2, 32, 55, 128 Guards Rifle Divisions.
Jan. 1944: 227, 339, 383 Rifle Divisions.
Apr. 1944: 339, 383 Rifle Divisions.

16 Tank Corps
—Kharkov Op., May 1942.
—Stalingrad axis, July 1942.
—Volya Corridor, Stalingrad axis w/1 Guards Army, Aug. 1942.
—Stalingrad Counteroffensive, Nov. 1942.
—RVGK w/2 Tank Army, Jan. 1943.
—Kursk w/2 Tank Army, July 1943.
—Orel, Aug. 1943.
—Became 12 Guards Tank Corps, 1943.
—Uman Botosani Op. w/2 Guards Tank Army (second formation), Mar. 1944.
—Targul Frumos; made main attack on German 24 Panzer Division w/ 2 Guards Tank Army, May 1944.
—Lublin Brest Op. w/2 Guards Tank Army, July 1944.
—Magnusew Bridgehead w/8 Guards Army, Aug. 1944.
—Vistula Oder Op. as an independent corps of 1 Belorussian Front (captured German SIGINT document), Jan. 1945.
—"Uman," Order of Suvorov.
Units: May 1944: 107, 109, 164 Tank; 15 Motorized Rifle Brigades; 6 Guards Heavy Tank Breakthrough Regiment.

17 Cavalry Corps
—Formed Krasnodar, North Caucasus Military District, Jan—Apr 1942.
—Pavlovskaya, North Caucasus, Apr. 1942.
—Sea of Azov w/North Caucasus Front, July 1942.
—Became 4 Guards "Kuban Cossacks" Cavalry Corps, Aug. 1942.
Key Commanders: Gen-Lt N.Y. Kirichenko, Apr. 1942.
Units: Apr. 1942: 12, 13, 15, 116 Cavalry, 91 Rifle Divisions.

17 Mechanized Corps
—Western Special Military District as an independent corps, June 1941.
—Defended Lida, June 1941.
—Disbanded, Aug. 1941.
Units: June 1941: 27, 36 Tank, 209 Motorized Divisions.
    June 1941: 121, 143, 155 Rifle Divisions.

17 Rifle Corps
—Far East as 17 "Primorye" Corps in 1930's.
—Poland w/12 Army, Sep. 1939.
—Kiev Special Military District w/18 Army, June 1941.
—Uman Pocket w/12 Army, Aug. 1941.
—Formed basis for reactivation of 12 Army, Aug. 1941.
—North Caucasus, May 1943.
—Proskurov Chernovtsy Op. w/1 Guards Army, Mar. 1944.
Key Commanders: I.S. Koniev, 1930's.
Units: June 1941: 60, 96 Mountain Rifle, 164 Rifle Divisions.

17 Independent Tank Corps
—Formed Voronezh as a Kuban Cossack Corps, Apr–May 1942.
—Kharkov Op., May 1942.
—RVGK at Voronezh, July 1942.
—Stalingrad axis, July 1942.
—RVGK w/6 Army, Dec. 1942.
—Middle Don River, Dec. 1942.
—Kantemirovka, Dec. 1942.
—Became 4 Guards "Kantemirov" Tank Corps, 2 Jan. 1943.
—Second formation at Kursk, July 1943.
Key Commanders: Gen-Maj P.P. Poluboyarov, 1942–43.
Units: Dec. 1942: 66, 67, 174 Tank, 31 Motorized Rifle Brigades.

18 Cavalry Corps
—Far East, Aug. 1944.

18 Mechanized Corps
—Baltic Special Military District w/11 Army, June 1941.
—To Southern Front, June 1941.
—Never saw combat, disbanded by 1942.
Units: June 1941: 44, 47 Tank, 218 Motorized Divisions.

18 Independent Rifle Corps
—Far East, 1929.
—Basis for forming 35 Army, Far East Military District, July 1941.
—RVGK, Nov–Dec 1941.

—Moscow Counteroffensive, Dec. 1941.
—Second formation main attack corps for Ostrogosh Rossosh Op., Jan. 1943.
—Basis for activation of 69 Army, Feb. 1943.
—With Southwest Front, Aug. 1943.
—Third formation main attack corps for Belorussian Op. w/65 Army, June 1944.
—Second Ukrainian Front Reserve, Nov. 1944.
—Budapest, Dec. 1944.
—Vistula Oder Op.; breakthrough corps w/65 Army, Jan. 1945.
Units: June 1944: 4 Guards, 15, 37, 69 Rifle Divisions.
      Nov. 1944: 15, 69 Rifle Divisions.

18 Independent Tank Corps
—Formed as an independent corps, Apr–May 1942.
—RVGK at Voronezh, July 1942.
—To Don River front, July 1942.
—Stalingrad offensive w/57 Army, Nov. 1942.
—RVGK, Dec. 1942.
—Donbas, Southwest Front, Dec. 1942.
—With Popov mobile group, Feb–Mar 1943.
—Badly beaten by Germans near Pavlograd, Mar. 1943.
—Kursk, at Prokhorovka w/5 Guards Tank Army; highly touted; 30% losses, July 1943.
—Belgorod Kharkov Op. w/53 Army, Aug. 1943.
—Dnieper, Oct. 1943.
—Krivoi Rog w/5 Guards Tank Army, Oct. 1943.
—Melitopol Op., Oct. 1943.
—Znamenka, Dec. 1943.
—Kirovograd w/5 Guards Tank Army, Jan. 1944.
—Korsun Shevchenkovsky Op. w/53 Army, Jan. 1944.
—Proskurov Chernovtsy Op. w/5 Guards Tank Army, Mar. 1944.
—Targul Frumos w/5 Guards Tank Army, May 1944.
—Iasi Kishinev Op., Aug. 1944.
—RVGK w/26 Army, Nov. 1944.
—Szekesfehervar, Dec. 1944.
—Budapest, 46 Army zone, Dec. 1944.
—Lake Balaton, Mar. 1945.
—Bratislava, Apr. 1945.
—Austria w/9 Guards Army, Feb. 1946.
—Uman, Kiev MD, July 1946 (Sep. 1946 OB).
—"Znamenka," Order of Red Banner.
Key Commanders: I.D. Cheryakhovskiy, July 1942.
Units: Nov. 1942: 17, 61, 62 Mechanized Brigades.

July 1943: 110, 170, 181 Tank, 32 Motorized Brigades.
Aug. 1944: 110, 170, 181 Tank, 32 Motorized Brigades.

19 Mechanized Corps
—In general reserve at Zhitomir, Kiev Special Military District, 21 June 1941.
—Rovno, July 1941.
—Shepetovka, July 1942.
Key Commanders: K.K. Rokossovskiy, June 1941.
Units: June 1941: 40, 43 Tank, 213 Motorized Divisions.

19 Rifle Corps
—In Leningrad Military District, Jan. 1933.
—Viipuri axis w/7 Independent Army, Dec. 1939.
—Karelian Isthmus w/23 Army, May 1941.
—Belorussia w/50 Army, May 1944.
—Constanza, Rumania, possibly as a Motorized Rifle Division, Aug. 1946 (Feb. 1947 OB).
—"Perekop," Order of Red Banner.
Units: Aug. 1946: 213 Rifle Division.

19 Independent Tank Corps
—Formed, Apr–May 1942.
—Voronezh, Jan. 1943.
—Kursk as Central front reserve, June 1943.
—Kursk, July 1943.
—Trapped part of German 29 Corps near sea of Azov w/51 Army, Aug. 1943.
—Melitopol area w/51 Army, Oct. 1943.
—Southwest Ukraine w/3 Ukrainian Front, Jan. 1944.
—Sivash, Crimea, May 1944.
—Simferopol w/51 Army, Apr. 1944.
—RVGK, July 1944.
—Baltic coast, Shauliai area, Aug. 1944.
—Memel Op., Oct. 1944.
—Stara Zagora, Bulgaria as 19 Tank Division, Aug. 1946 (Aug. 1946).
—Withdrawn from Rumania by July 1947 (July 1947 OB).
—"Yevpatoriya."
Key Commanders: Gen. I.D. Vasileyev, 1943.
Units: Jan. 1944: 79, 101, 202 Tank, 26 Motorized Rifle Brigades.

20 Mechanized Corps
—Reformed as a tank corps in Transbaikal Military District, 1938.
—Borisov area, Western Special Military District, June 1941.

Key Commanders: A.G. Nikitin, June 1941.
Units: June 1941: 26, 38 Tank, 210 Motorized Division.

20 Rifle Corps
—Far East, Apr. 1937.
—Bogushev area, July 1941.
—Called 20 Assault Corps w/18 Assault Landing Army, Novorossiysk, Feb. 1943.
—Kuban Bridgehead, Novorossiysk w/18 Army, Apr. 1943.
—North Caucasus, Aug. 1943.
—Taman area, Oct. 1943.
—Kerch landing, Nov. 1943.
—Southwest Ukraine w/4 Ukrainian Front, Apr. 1944.
—Iasi, Apr. 1944.
—Targul Frumos, May 1944.
—Belorussian Op. w/28 Army, June 1944.
—Gumbinnen Op. w/28 Army, Jan. 1945.
—Koenigsberg area, Apr. 1945.
—Berlin Op. w/28 Army, Apr. 1945.
—Germany, 1946 w/5 Shock Army (Feb. 1947 OB).
Units: July 1941: 144, 160 Rifle Divisions.
Nov. 1943: 117, 128 Guards, 318 Rifle Divisions.
Apr. 1944: 55 Guards, 20 Rifle Divisions.

20 Tank Corps
—Formed in Transbaikal Military District from a mechanized corps, 1938.
—Reformed, Apr-May 1942.
—Don offensive w/61 Army, Nov. 1942.
—Kursk w/61 Army, July 1943.
—Orel Op., July 1943.
—To Southern Front, Sep. 1943.
—Melitopol Op., Oct. 1943.
—Kirovograd w/2 Ukrainian Front, Jan. 1944.
—Korsun Shevchenkovsky Op. w/5 Guards Tank Army, Jan. 1944.
—Uman Botosani Op. w/5 Guards Tank Army, Mar. 1944.
—Proskurov Chernovtsy Op. (Rybnitsa), Mar. 1944.
—Rzeszow, Poland as 20 Tank Division w/105 Rifle Corps, 7 Mechanized Army, Aug. 1946 (Feb. 1947 OB).
Units: Jan. 1944: 8 Guards, 80, 155 Tank, 7 Guards Motorized Rifle Brigades.

21 Mechanized Corps
—Moscow Military District, June 1941.
—Baltic Special Military District, June 1941.

Key Commanders: D.D. Lelyushenko.
Units: June 1941: 42, 46 Tank, 185 Motorized Divisions.

21 Rifle Corps
—Headquarters at Vitebsk, June 1941.
—Moldecheno area w/13 Army, June 1941.
—Commander captured by Germans, July 1941.
—Voronezh w/13 Army, Jan. 1943.
—RVGK w/37 Army, Sep. 1943.
—Kiev Op. w/38 Army, Nov. 1943.
—SW Ukraine w/38 Army, Jan. 1944.
—Rava Russkaya axis w/3 Guards Army, July 1944.
—Hungary w/4 Guards Army, Nov. 1944.
—Deployment pattern suggests Independent Corps.
Units: June 1941: 17, 24, 37, 50 Rifle Divisions.
      Nov. 1943: 74 Rifle Division.
      Jan. 1944: 100, 135, 155 Rifle Divisions.

21 Tank Corps
—Kharkov Op. w/6 Army, May 1942.
—Destroyed, May 1942 (FHO).
Units: May 1942: 64, 196, 198 Tank Brigades.

22 Mechanized Corps
—Lutsk area, Kiev Special Military District w/5 Army; one of only four corps w/some T-34 and KV tanks, June 1941.
—Disbanded by 1942.
Units: June 1941: 19, 41 Tank, 215 Motorized Divisions.

22 Rifle Corps
—Baltic Special Military District as an Estonian territorial corps w/27 Army, June 1941.
—Leningrad, Dno railroad station, July 1941.
—Kerch landing with 18 Army, Nov. 1943.
—Southwest Ukraine w/18 Army, Jan. 1944.
—Rava Russkaya axis w/3 Guards Army, July 1944.
—"Estonian."
Units: June 1941: 180, 182 Rifle Divisions.
      Nov. 1943: 117, 129 Guards, 317, 318 Rifle Divisions.
      Jan. 1944: 129 Guards, 71, 317 Rifle Divisions.

22 Tank Corps
—Formed, Apr-May 1942.
—Kalach, July 1942.

—Stalingrad w/4 Tank Army, July 1942.
—Destroyed in Kalach area, July 1942 (FHO).
—With the Southern Front, May 1943.
—Bialogard, Poland as 22 Tank Division, Apr. 1947 (Feb. 1948 OB).
Units: July 1942: 133, 175, 176, 182 Tank, 22 Motorized Rifle Brigades.

23 Mechanized Corps
—Orel Military District, May-June 1941.
—Western Special Military District in RVGK w/19 Army, June 1941.
—Converted to 23 Rifle Corps, July 1941.
Units: June 1941: 48, 51 Tank, 220 Motorized Divisions.

23 Independent Rifle Corps
—Belorussian Military District, Aug. 1939.
—Eastern Poland, Sep. 1939.
—Finland w/13 Army, Dec. 1939.
—Reactivated in Transcaucasus, possibly as 23 Mechanized Corps, 1940.
—Basis for forming 45 Army, July 1941.
—Reformed from 23 Mechanized Corps, July 1941.
—Voronezh w/13 Army, Jan. 1943.
—Kursk w/47 Army, July 1943.
—Belgorod Kharkov Op. w/6 Guards Army, Aug. 1943.
—RVGK w/37 Army, Sep. 1943.
—Bukrin Bridgehead, Oct-Nov 1943.
—Kiev w/38 Army, Nov. 1943.
—Southwest Ukraine w/60 Army, Jan. 1944.
—Rovno Lutsk Op. w/13 Army, Feb. 1944.
—Ternopol w/60 Army, Mar. 1944.
—Belorussian Op. June 1944.
—Lvov Sandomir Op. w/60 Army, July 1944.
—Iasi Kishinev Op. w/6 Guards Tank Army, Aug. 1944.
Units: Aug. 1943: 51, 52, 90 Guards Rifle Divisions.
   Jan. 1944: 8, 147, 226 Rifle Divisions.
   Aug. 1944: 78, 337 Rifle; 1, 3 Guards Rumanian Rifle Divisions.

23 Independent Tank Corps
—Formed, Apr–May 1942.
—Kharkov Offensive w/6 Army, May 1942.
—Kalach, July 1942.
—Stalingrad front w/4 Tank Army, Aug. 1942.
—Stalingrad; had only 17 tanks, Sep. 1942.
—Northern Donets, Dec. 1942.
—Reserve, Upyansk Suyatovo area, Apr. 1943.
—Kursk, July 1943.

—With Southwest Front, Aug. 1943.
—Dnieper River w/12 Army, Sep. 1943.
—Nearly destroyed in pocket near Pavlograd w/1 Guards Mechanized Corps, Sep. 1943.
—Melitopol Op., Oct. 1943.
—Zaporozhye Bridgehead w/8 Guards Army, Oct. 1943.
—Southwest Ukraine w/3 Ukraine Front, Jan. 1944.
—Novy Bug River, Nikolayev area, Apr. 1944.
—Iasi Kishinev Op. in cavalry-mechanized group w/5 Guards Cavalry Corps, Aug. 1944.
—Debrecen, Hungary (Ultra), Oct. 1944.
—Budapest area, Jan. 1945.
—Lake Balaton Op., Mar. 1945.
—Vienna w/9 Guards Army, Apr. 1945.
—Independent corps.
Units: May 1942: 3, 39, 135 Tank, 56 Motorized Rifle Brigades, 10 Guards Heavy Tank Breakthrough Regt.
Jan. 1944: 3, 39, 135 Tank, 56 Motorized Rifle Brigades.

24 Mechanized Corps
—Kiev Special Military District in general reserve, June 1941.
—Broken up, never committed to combat, summer 1941.
Units: June 1941: 45, 49 Tank, 216 Motorized Divisions.

24 Rifle Corps
—RVGK, June 1941.
—Baltic Special Military District w/27 Army, June 1941.
—Kursk w/60 Army, July 1943.
—Belgorod Kharkov Op., breakthrough corps w/60 Army, Aug. 1943.
—Kiev Op. w/60 Army, Nov. 1943.
—Rovno Lutsk Op. w/13 Army; main attack corps, Jan-Feb 1944.
—Lvov Sandomir Op. w/13 Army, July 1944.
—Berlin Op. w/3 Guards Army, Apr. 1945.
—Called Motorized Rifle Corps of 2 Ukrainian Front in Czechoslovakia, May 1945.
—Probably independent corps.
—"Latvian."
Units: June 1941: 181, 183 Rifle Divisions.
Jan. 1944: 121 Guards, 112, 140, 149, 287, 328 Rifle Divisions.
Nov. 1944: 8 Guards Airborne Division.

24 Tank Corps
—Formed in Voroshilovgrad area, Apr. 1942.
—Kharkov Op., May 1942.

—Novy Oskol, in Bryansk Front, June 1942.
—Stalingrad axis, July 1942.
—RVGK Oct. 1942.
—RVGK, Dec. 1942.
—Donets w/1 Guards and 3 Guards Army; at Tatsin, Dec. 1942.
—Wiped out at Tatsin, 28 Dec. 1942.
—Reformed as 2 Guards Tank Corps, Dec. 1942.
—Second formation corps at Prokhorovka, Kursk, July 1943.
—Sibiu, Rumania as 24 Tank Division, Jan. 1946 (July 1947 OB).
—Out of Rumania by July 1947 (July 1947 OB).
Key Commanders: Gen-Maj V.M. Badanov, Dec. 1942.
Units: Apr. 1942: 4 Guards, 2, 54 Tank, 24 Motorized Rifle Brigades.
　　　 Nov. 1942: 4 Guards, 54, 130 Tank, 24 Motorized Rifle Brigades.

25 Mechanized Corps
—Formed as Tank Corps, Kiev Military District, 1938.
—RVGK in Volga Military District w/21 Army, June 1941.
—Western Special Military District, June 1941.
—Southwest Front w/21 Army, Aug. 1941.
—Disbanded by 1942.
Units: June 1941: 50, 55 Tank, 219 Motorized Divisions.

25 Independent Rifle Corps
—North Caucasus, 1940.
—Independent Corps, Kharkov Military District, May 1941.
—RVGK w/19 Army, June 1941.
—Kharkov, 13 Aug. 1941.
—Formed basis of 52 Army, Southwest Front, Aug. 1941.
—Lvov Sandomir Op. w/69 Army, July 1944.
—Carpathian Duklinskiy Op. w/38 Army, Sep. 1944.
—Vistula Oder Op. and Radom w/69 Army, Jan. 1945.
—Berlin Op. w/69 Army, Apr. 1945.
Key Commanders: Gorbatov, May 1941.
Units: July 1944: 77 Guards, 4, 41 Rifle Divisions.
　　　 Jan. 1945: 77 Guards, 4, 214 Rifle Divisions.
　　　 Apr. 1945: 77 Guards, 4 Rifle Divisions.

25 Tank Corps
—Activated in Kiev Military District, reformed from 45 Mechanized Corps, 1938.
—Liberation of Western Ukraine (Eastern Poland), Sep. 1939.
—Eastern Poland w/12 Army, Sep. 1939.
—Reformed, Apr–May 1942.

—Stalingrad area, Oct. 1942.
—Don Front reserve, Nov. 1942.
—RVGK, Dec. 1942.
—Wiped out on Middle Don at Maryevka, 31 Dec. 1942.
—Reconstituted, Pavlograd-Sinelnikovo, 19 Feb. 1943.
—Destroyed near Pavlograd w/6 Army, Feb. 1943.
—Reactivated at Kursk (Western Front Reserve), July 1943.
—Orel, July 1943.
—Belgorod Kharkov Op. w/4 Tank Army, Aug. 1943.
—RVGK, Nov. 1943.
—Kiev Defensive Op., Dec. 1943.
—Zhitomir Berdichev Op. w/1 Ukrainian Front, Jan. 1944.
—Rovno Lutsk Op. w/13 Army, Jan. 1944.
—Novograd Volyinskiy, Jan. 1944.
—Lvov Sandomir Op., July 1944.
—In a cavalry-mechanized group of 1 Ukrainian Front w/1 Guards Cavalry Corps, July 1944.
—Carpathian Duklinskiy Op., Sep. 1944.
—Vistula Oder Op. w/3 Guards Army, Jan. 1945.
—Cottbus, Apr. 1945.
—Czechoslovakia, May 1945.
—Germany as 25 Tank Division w/4 Guards Mechanized Army, June 1946 (Aug. 1946 OB).
—Independent corps.
Units: July 1944: 111, 162, 175 Tank, 20 Motorized Rifle Brigades.

26 Mechanized Corps
—North Caucasus Military District w/19 Army, June 1941.
—Disbanded by 1942.

26 Rifle Corps
—Rovno, Aug. 1941.
—Kursk w/6 Army, July 1943.
—Magnuszew Bridgehead, Jan. 1945.
—Manchuria, Aug. 1945.
Units: Aug. 1941: 21, 135 Rifle Divisions.

26 Tank Corps
—Formed Moscow area, July 1942.
—Bryansk Front w/5 Tank Army, Sep. 1942.
—Stalingrad area, Oct. 1942.
—Southwest Front and Stalingrad offensive w/5 Tank Army, Nov. 1942.
—Closed Stalingrad Pocket at Kalach, Dec. 1942.
—Named 1 Guards Tank Corps, 8 Dec. 1942.

27 Mechanized Corps
—Probably in North Caucasus Military District, June 1941.
—Never committed to combat, broken up summer 1941.

27 Rifle Corps
—Formed in RVGK, Kiev area, June 1941.
—Southwest Front w/5 Army, June 1941.
—South of Kiev, Aug. 1941.
—RVGK, Apr. 1943.
—Headquarters used to form Headquarters, 18 Independent Rifle Corps in RVGK, Apr. 1943.
—Lvov Sandomir Op. w/13 Army, July 1944.
—Berlin Op., Apr. 1945.
Units: June 1941: 135 Rifle Division. Nov. 1944: 112 Rifle Division.

27 Tank Corps
—Stalingrad offensive w/5 Tank Army, Nov. 1942.
Key Commanders: Gen-Maj A.G. Rodin, Nov. 1942.
Units: Nov. 1942: 19, 157 Tank, 14 Motorized Rifle Brigades.

28 Mechanized Corps
—Transcaucasus Military District, June 1941.
—Basis for forming 47 Army, Transcaucasus Military District, July 1941.
—Second formation basis for reforming 48 Army, Apr. 1942.

28 Rifle Corps
—Finland w/7 Independent Army; formed from army reserve, Feb. 1940.
—Specially formed for assault on Viipuri, Feb. 1940.
—Responsible for defense of the Brest Fortress, June 1941.
—Slutsk, July 1941.
—Novgorod, July 1941.
—Kursk w/70 Army, July 1943.
—Dnieper River w/13 Army, Sep. 1943.
—Chernigov Bryansk Op. w/ 13 Army, Sep. 1943.
—Rovno Lutsk Op. w/13 Army, Feb. 1944.
—Lvov Sandomir Op. w/60 Army, July 1944.
—Petsamo Kirkenes Op., Sep. 1944.
Key Commanders: P.A. Kurochkin, June 1941.
Units: June 1941: 6, 42 Rifle Divisions.
July 1943: 140, 162, 181, 250, 280 Rifle Divisions.
Jan. 1944: 4 Guards Airborne, 70 Guards, 246, 415 Rifle Divisions.

28 Tank Corps
—Stalingrad w/1 Tank Army, July 1942.
—Basis for forming 4 Mechanized Corps, Oct. 1942.
—Kirovograd w/5 Guards Tank Army, Jan. 1944.

29 Rifle Corps
—Baltic Special Military District w/11 Army, June 1941.
—Kursk w/13 Army, July 1943.
—Dnieper, Oct. 1943.
—Belorussian Op., June 1944.
—Bobruysk w/48 Army, July 1944.
—"Lithuanian."
Units: June 1941: 179, 184 Rifle Divisions. July 1943: 15, 81, 307 Rifle Divisions.

29 Tank Corps
—Reserve, Ostrogosh area, Apr. 1943.
—Kursk w/5 Guards Tank Army at Prokhorovka; had 60% losses, July 1943.
—Belgorod Kharkov Op. w/5 Guards Tank Army (rest of war), Aug. 1943.
—Krivoi Rog, Oct. 1943.
—Znamenka, Dec. 1943.
—Kirovograd Op., Jan. 1944.
—Korsun Shevchenkovsky Op., Jan. 1944.
—Uman Botosani Op., Mar. 1944.
—Targul Frumos, May 1944.
—Vitebsk Orsha Op., June 1944.
—Vilnius, July 1944.
—Minsk, July 1944.
—East Prussia, Oct. 1944.
—East Prussian Op., Jan. 1945.
—East Prussian Op., Mar. 1945.
—Memel Op., Mar. 1945.
—The 25 Tank Brigade, Order of Lenin; 31 Tank Brigade, Order of Red Banner; 32 Tank Brigade, Orders of Lenin, Suvorov; 53 Motorized Rifle Brigade "Znamenka," Order of Suvorov.
—Order of Lenin.
Key Commanders: P.S. Beloborodov, Jan. 1945.
Units: May 1944: 25, 31, 32 Tank, 53 Motorized Rifle Brigades.

30 Mechanized Corps
—Far East Military District, June 1941.
Key Commanders: A.I. Getman, June 1941.

30 Rifle Corps
—RVGK in Archangelsk Military District w/28 Army, June 1941.
—Kursk w/60 Army, July 1943.
—Kiev Op. w/60 Army, Nov. 1943.
—Southwest Ukraine w/1 Ukraine Front, Jan. 1944.
—Proskurov Chernovtsy Op. w/1 Guards Army, Mar. 1944.
—Kamenets Podolsk w/4 Tank Army, Mar. 1944.
—Tried to stop breakout of 1 Panzer Army, Apr. 1944.
—Carpathian Uzhgorod Op. w/1 Guards Army, Sep. 1944.
—RVGK w/26 Army, Nov. 1944.
—Budapest, Jan. 1945.
—Lake Balaton w/26 Army, Mar. 1945.
—Craiova, Rumania as Motorized Corps, 1946 (Feb. 1947 OB).
Units: Jan. 1944: 121, 141 Rifle Divisions.
      Sep. 1944: 30, 141, 155 Rifle Divisions.

30 Tank Corps
—Activated in Ural Military District, Feb. 1943.
—With 4 Tank Army (later 4 Guards Tank Army), rest of war, 1943–45.
—Kursk, July 1943.
—Orel, July 1943.
—Bryansk, Aug. 1943.
—Became 10 Guards Tank Corps, 23 Oct. 1943.
—"Ural Volunteers."
Key Commanders: Gen-Lt A.G. Rodin, Aug. 1943.
Units: Feb. 1943: 197 "Sverdlovsk," 243 and 244 "Chelyabinsk," Tank Brigades, 30 "Unetchsk" Motorized Rifle Brigade.

31 Rifle Corps
—Far East MD, 1940.
—Transferred to west, 25 May 1941.
—General reserve as independent corps in Kiev-Zhitomir area, Kiev Special Military District, June 1941.
—Molodechno w/13 Army, June 1941.
—Lutsk, subordinate to Southwest Front, July 1941.
—Karelian Front, Aug. 1943.
—Petsamo Kirkenes Op. w/14 Army, Sep–Oct 1944.
—Probably an independent corps.
Units: June 1941: 17, 24, 31 Rifle Divisions.
      Oct. 1944: 83, 367 Rifle Divisions.

31 Independent Tank Corps
—Formed from at least 2 tank brigades and tank regiments of the 1 Tank Army, July 1943.
—Kursk, July 1943.
—Belgorod Kharkov Op. w/1 Tank Army, Aug. 1943.
—Lvov Sandomir Op. w/5 Guards Army, July 1944.
—With cavalry-mechanized group of 1 Ukrainian Front w/6 Guards Cavalry Corps, July 1944.
—Carpathian Duklinskiy Op. w/38 Army; had 72 tanks and 18 self-propelled guns, Sep. 1944.
—Dukla Pass, Oct. 1944.
—Sandomir Bridgehead w/187 tanks and 64 self-propelled guns, Jan. 1945.
—Vistula Oder Op. w/5 Guards Army (Czestochowa), Jan. 1945.
—Breslau w/5 Guards Army, Feb. 1945.
—Prague Op., May 1945.
Units: July 1944: 100, 237, 242 Tank, 65 Motorized Rifle Brigades.

32 Rifle Corps
—Smolensk w/16 Army, July 1941.
—With Southwest Front, Aug. 1943.
—Southwest Ukraine w/3 Guards Army, Jan. 1944.
—Berlin Op. w/5 Shock Army, Apr. 1945.
Units: July 1941: 46, 152 Rifle Divisions.
      Jan. 1944: 259, 266, 279 Rifle Divisions.
      Nov. 1944: 266 Rifle Division.

33 Rifle Corps
—RVGK in Archangelsk Military District w/28 Army, June 1941.
—Basis for forming 43 Army in RVGK, July 1941.
—Southwest Ukraine w/2 Ukraine Front, Jan. 1944.
—Targul Frumos w/27 Army, May 1944.
—Iasi Kishinev Op. w/27 Army, Aug. 1944.
—Debrecen, Hungary w/6 Guards Tank Army, Oct. 1944.
—Hungary w/27 Army, Mar. 1945.
Units: Jan. 1944: 50, 297 Rifle Divisions.
      May 1944: 93 Guards, 78, 202, 206 Rifle Divisions.
      Oct. 1944: 78, 337 Rifle, 1 Rumanian Volunteer Rifle Divisions.

34 Rifle Corps
—North Caucasus Military District, 1940.
—Transferred to Moscow area w/19 Army, May 1941.

—Southwest Ukraine w/46 Army, Jan. 1944.
Key Commanders: Gen-Lt M.A. Reiter, May 1941.
Units: Jan. 1944: 195, 236, 394 Rifle Divisions.
      Nov. 1944: 394 Rifle Division.

35 Rifle Corps
—Odessa Military District w/9 Independent Army, June 1941.
—Reserve corps of Voronezh Front, June 1943.
—Kursk, July 1943.
—With the Bryansk Front, Aug. 1943.
—Main attack corps in Belorussia Op. w/3 Army, June 1944.

36 Rifle Corps
—General reserve as independent corps, Kiev-Zhitomir area, Kiev Special Military District, June 1941.
—Dubno, subordinate to Southwest Front, July 1941.
—Kursk w/31 Army, July 1943.
—With the Western Front, Aug. 1943.
—Minsk, July 1944.
—Western Rumania as Motorized Rifle Corps, Jan. 1946 (July 1947 OB)..
—Gone from Rumania by July 1947 (1947-48 OBs).
—Probably an independent corps.
Key Commanders: Gen-Maj N.N. Oleshev, July 1943; Gen-Maj K.I. Provalov, July 1944.
Units: July 1943: 215, 274 Rifle Divisions.
      July 1944: 173, 220 Rifle Divisions.
      Nov. 1944: 174 Rifle Division.

37 Rifle Corps
—Kiev Special Military District, 1940.
—General Reserve in Kiev-Zhitomir area, Kiev Special Military District, June 1941.
—Near Brody w/6 Army, Southwest Front, June 1941.
—Commander captured by Germans, Aug. 1941.
—Taman area w/44 Army, May 1943.
—Southwest Ukraine w/3 Guards Army, Jan. 1944.
—Timosoara, Sep. 1944.
—Budapest w/46 Army, Dec. 1944.
—Probably an independent corps.
Units: Sep. 1940: 41, 97, 99 Rifle Divisions.
      Jan. 1944: 248, 416, 417 Rifle Divisions.
      Nov. 1944: 320 Rifle Division.

38 Rifle Corps
—Kursk w/50 Army, July 1943.
—With the Western Front, Aug. 1943.
—Belorussian Op. June 1944.

39 Mechanized Corps
—Leningrad, Nov. 1941.

39 Rifle Corps
—Lake Khasan, Aug. 1938.
—Far East, June 1941.
—Pyongyang, Korea, July 1946 (July 1947 OB).
Key Commanders: G.M. Shtern, Aug. 1938.
Units: Aug. 1938: 32, 39, 40 Rifle Divisions, 2 Mechanized Brigade.

40 Rifle Corps
—Smolensk area, June 1941.
—Basis for forming 44 Army in Transcaucasus Military District, July 1941.
—Kursk w/63 Army, July 1943.
—With the Bryansk Front, Aug. 1943.
—Belorussian Op. w/3 Army, June 1944.
—Lvov Sandomir Op. w/1 Ukrainian Front reserve, July 1944.
Units: June 1941: 68, 108 Rifle Divisions.
       May 1943: 41, 271, 348, 397 Rifle Divisions.

41 Rifle Corps
—RVGK, June 1941.
—To 27 Army, Baltic Special Military District, June 1941.
—Luga Line, July 1941.
—Mogilev w/13 Army, July 1941.
—Kursk w/3 Army, July 1943.
—Belorussian Op. w/3 Army, June 1944.
—Minsk, possibly w/28 Army, Feb. 1947 (Apr. 1947 OB).
Units: June 1941: 111, 118, 125 Rifle Divisions.
       May 1943: 110, 356, 415 Rifle Divisions.

42 Rifle Corps
—Kandalaksha, June 1941.
—Karelia, Kandalaksha axis, July 1941.
—Commander captured by Germans, July 1941.
—Belorussian Op., June 1944.

—Bobruysk w/48 Army, July 1944.
Key Commanders: Gen-Maj R.I. Panin, July 1944.
Units: July 1941: 122 Rifle Division.
       Nov. 1944: 170 Rifle Division.

43 Rifle Corps
—Luban Plain, Latvia, Aug. 1944.
—"Latvian."

44 Rifle Corps
—Minsk area w/13 Army, June 1941.
—Smolensk, July 1941.
—Basis for activating 54 Army, Moscow Military District, Aug. 1941.
—With the Kalinin Front, Aug. 1943.
—A main attack corps for Belorussian Op., July 1944.
—Dvina River w/4 Shock Army, Aug. 1944.

45 Mechanized Corps
—One of first two mechanized corps in Red Army, formed on the basis of the 45 Rifle Division in the Ukraine Military District; 11 Rifle Division the other, Oct. 1932.
—Kiev maneuvers, Sep. 1935.
—In the Red Army "general reserve," Nov. 1935.
—Mechanized division took name of corps, Dec. 1935.
—Kiev Special Military District, 1938.
Key Commanders: F.I. Golikov, 1938.
Units: Sep. 1935: 133, 134 Mechanized, 135 Machine Gun Brigades.

45 Rifle Corps
—Rogachev area, July 1941.
—Commander court-martialed, July 1941.
—Western Front w/31 Army, May 1943.
—Baltic area June 1943.
—With the Western Front, Aug. 1943.
—Belorussian Op., June 1944.
—Neman River w/5 Army, July 1944.
Key Commanders: Gen-Maj S.G. Poplavskiy, June 1943.
Units: July 1941: 138, 148, 187 Rifle Divisions.

46 Rifle Corps
—With the Bryansk Front, Aug. 1943.
—Bobruysk, June 1944.
—Oder Op.; main assault corps for 65 Army, Jan. 1945.

—South of Breslau, Poland, July 1946 (Feb. 1947 OB).
Units: July 1946: 17, 18 Rifle Divisions.

47 Independent Rifle Corps
—Bobruysk, 15 June 1941.
—Borisov, July 1941.
—Kursk w/40 Army, July 1943.
—Belgorod Kharkov Op. w/40 Army, Aug. 1943.
—Korsun Shevchenkovsky Op. w/6 Tank Army, Jan. 1944.
—Proskurov Chernovtsy Op. w/1 Guards Army, Mar. 1944.
—Targul Frumos w/27 Army, May 1944.
—Lvov Sandomir Op. as 1 Ukrainian Front reserve, July 1944.
—Oder Op., Apr. 1945.
—Berlin Op. w/70 Army, Apr. 1945.
Units: June 1941: 55, 121, 143 Rifle Divisions.
       Jan. 1944: 38, 136, 167, 180, 359 Rifle Divisions.

48 Independent Rifle Corps
—Activated, Mar. 1941.
—When Zakharov was the Odessa Special Military District's Chief of Staff, he obtained permission from Zhukov, Chief of the General Staff, to move this corps to the border region (MHJ); implies a High Command Reserve formation, June 1941.
—Odessa Military District border w/9 Independent Army, 22 June 1941.
—Beltsy, June 1941.
—Mogilev Podolsk in shock group w/2 Cavalry and 2 Mechanized Corps, July 1941.
—Nikolayev area w/9 Army, Aug. 1941.
—Basis for second formation of 6 Army, Aug. 1941.
—Kursk w/40 Army, July 1943.
—Belgorod Kharkov Op. w/69 Army, Aug. 1943.
—Vorskla River w/53 Army, Sep. 1943.
—Kirovograd w/53 Army, Jan. 1944.
—Spree River w/52 Army, Apr. 1945.
Key Commanders: R.Ya. Malinovskiy, Mar–Aug 1941; Gen-Maj Rogosniy, Apr. 1944.
Units: July 1943: 252 Rifle Division.
       Jan. 1944: 14 Guards, 252, 299 Rifle Divisions.
       Nov. 1944: 252 Rifle Division.

49 Rifle Corps
—Commander captured by Germans, Aug. 1941.
—Kursk w/53 Army, July 1943.

—Dnieper River w/7 Guards Army, Sep. 1943.
—Korsun Shevchenkovskiy Op. w/57 Army, Jan. 1944.
—Zvenigorod w/5 Guards Tank Army, Feb. 1944.
—Manchurian campaign, Aug. 1945.
—Deployment pattern suggests an independent corps.
Units: Sep. 1943: 15 Guards, 213 Rifle Division.
       Jan. 1944: 19, 223 Rifle Divisions.
       Feb. 1944: 6, 94 Guards, 84, 375 Rifle Divisions.

50 Mechanized Corps
—Tatsin, Dec. 1942.
—Identification doubtful; found only in Manstein's *Lost Victories*.

50 Rifle Corps
—Viipuri axis w/7 Independent Army, Dec. 1939.
—Karelian Isthmus w/23 Army, May 1941.
—Kursk w/38 Army, July 1943.
—RVGK w/37 Army, Sep. 1943.
—Kiev Offensive w/38 Army at Dnieper River; density of 416 guns, mortars per kilometer; highest of war to that time, Sep. 1943.
—Kiev w/38 Army, Nov. 1943.
—Fastov, Nov. 1943.
—Southwest Ukraine w/40 Army, 1 Ukrainian Front, Jan. 1944.
—Carpathian Mountains w/40 Army, Sep. 1944.
—Berlin Op. w/33 Army, Apr. 1945.
Units: May 1943: 167, 204, 240 Rifle Divisions.
       Nov. 1943: 136, 167 Rifle Divisions.
       Jan. 1944: 74, 163, 240 Rifle Divisions.
       Sep. 1944: 50, 74, 163 Rifle Divisions.
       Nov. 1944: 240 Rifle Divisions.

51 Rifle Corps
—RVGK in Ural Military District w/22 Army, June 1941.
—Nevel w/22 Army, July 1941.
—Kalach, July 1942.
—RVGK w/37 Army, Sep. 1943.
—Sumy w/38 Army, Sep. 1943.
—Kiev w/38 Army, Nov. 1943.
—Southwest Ukraine w/40 Army, 1 Ukrainian Front, Jan. 1944.
—Carpathians (Hungary) w/40 Army, Sep. 1944.
Units: July 1941: 98, 112, 170 Rifle Divisions.
       Sep. 1943: 167, 180, 232, 240, 340 Rifle Divisions.
       Nov. 1943: 167, 180 Rifle Divisions.

Jan. 1944: 167, 232, 340 Rifle Divisions.
Sep. 1944: 42 Guards Rifle Division.

52 Rifle Corps
—RVGK in Siberian Military District w/24 Army, June 1941.
—Kursk w/47 Army, July 1943.
—Southwest Ukraine w/18 Army, Jan. 1944.
—Lvov Sandomir Op. w/38 Army, July 1944.
—Carpathian Duklinsky Op. w/38 Army, Sep. 1944.
Units: Jan. 1944: 117 Guards, 24, 395 Rifle Divisions.
Sep. 1944: 304, 305, 340 Rifle Divisions.

53 Rifle Corps
—RVGK in Siberian Military District w/24 Army, June 1941.
—RVGK in Kursk area w/11 Army, May 1943.
—Kursk w/11 Army, July 1943.
—With the Bryansk Front, Aug. 1943.
—Bobruysk w/48 Army, June 1944.
Units: May 1943: 96, 369 Rifle Divisions.
Nov. 1944: 17 Rifle Division.

54 Rifle Corps
—With the Southern Front, May 1943.
—Southern Russia w/51 Army, Jan. 1944.
—Crimea w/2 Guards Army, Apr. 1944.
—Shauliai w/2 Guards Army, Aug. 1944.
Units: Jan. 1944: 91, 126, 315 Rifle Divisions.
Apr. 1944: 126, 315 Rifle Divisions.
Nov. 1944: 315 Rifle Division.

55 Rifle Corps
—Southern Russia w/51 Army, Jan. 1944.
—Crimea w/2 Guards Army, Apr. 1944.
Units: Jan. 1944: 87, 347, 387 Rifle Divisions.
Apr. 1944: 87, 347, 387 Rifle Divisions.

56 Rifle Corps
—Southern Sakhalin Island w/16 Army, Aug. 1945.
Units: Aug. 1945: 79 Rifle Division.

57 Independent Special Corps
—RVGK Corps when organized in Mongolia, 1938.
—Khalkin Gol, 1938.

—Became 1 Army Group, 15 July 1939.
—Second formation at Ulan Baator, 1938-39.
—Became 17 Army, July 1940.
Key Commanders: N.V. Feklenko, 1940.
Units: Aug. 1938: 36 Motorized Rifle Division, 6 Cavalry Brigade, 11 Tank, 7, 8, 9, Armored Car Brigades.

57 Rifle Corps
—May be third formation of 57 Independent Special Corps.
—Dnieper River w/37 Army, Sep. 1943.
—Southwest Ukraine w/37 Army, Jan. 1944.
—Iasi Kishinev Op. as 2 Ukrainian Front reserve, Aug. 1944.
Units: Jan. 1944: 15, 29 Guards, 228 Rifle Divisions.
 Sep. 1943: 62, 92, 110 Guards, 89 Rifle Divisions.

58 Rifle Corps
—Known to have existed.

59 Rifle Corps
—Known to have existed.

60 Rifle Corps
—Belorussian Op. w/43 Army, June 1944.
—Shauliai area w/43 Army, Aug. 1944.
Units: June 1944: 156, 235, 334 Rifle Divisions.

61 Rifle Corps
—RVGK in Orel Military District w/20 Army, June 1941.
—Mogilev w/13 Army, July 1941.
—Kursk w/21 Army, July 1943.
—Pulawy Bridgehead and Radom w/69 Army, Jan. 1945.
—Berlin Op. w/69 Army, Apr. 1945.
Key Commanders: F.A. Bakhunin, July 1941.
Units: July 1941: 53, 110, 172 Rifle Division.
 Jan. 1945: 134, 247, 274 Rifle Divisions.
 Apr. 1945: 134, 247, 274 Rifle Divisions.

62 Rifle Corps
—RVGK in Ural Military District w/22 Army, June 1941.
—Dvina River, July 1941.
—Nevel, July 1941.
—Commander killed in action, Aug. 1941.
—Mogilev Op. w/49 Army, June 1944.
—Berlin Op. w/33 Army, Apr. 1945.

Units: July 1941: 174, 186 Rifle Divisions.
　　　June 1944: 64, 330, 369 Rifle Divisions.
　　　Nov. 1944: 32, 63 Rifle Divisions.

63 Rifle Corps
—Formed, Dec. 1940.
—Volga Military District w/21 Army, June 1941.
—Mogilev w/21 Army, July 1941.
—Dnieper River at Rogachev, July 1941.
—Mount Kolokolnya, Leningrad Front, Dec. 1941.
—Southwest Ukraine w/5 Shock Army, Jan. 1944.
—Sivash, on Perekop Isthmus w/51 Army, Apr. 1944.
—Sevastopol, May 1944.
—Memel, Oct. 1944.
Key Commanders: Gen-Lt L.G. Petrovsky, July 1941; P.K. Koshevoi, May 1944.
Units: June 1941: 61, 117, 167 Rifle Divisions.
　　　Jan. 1944: 118, 267 Rifle Divisions.
　　　Apr. 1944: 263, 267, 417 Rifle Divisions.
　　　Oct. 1944: 77, 87, 417 Rifle Divisions.

64 Rifle Corps
—North Caucasus Military District, June 1941.
—Kiev Special Military District w/26 Army, July 1941.
—Kursk w/57 Army, July 1943.
—Southwest Ukraine w/57 Army, Jan. 1944.
—Belgrade w/57 Army, Oct. 1944.
—Hungary, Nov. 1944.
—Craiova, Rumania, 1946 (Feb. 1947 OB).
Units: Jan. 1944: 73, 78 Guards, 52 Rifle Divisions.
　　　Nov. 1944: 73 Guards, 19 Rifle Divisions.

65 Rifle Corps
—Mogilev w/13 Army, July 1941.
—Lenino, near Mogilev w/33 Army, Oct. 1943.
—Vilnius w/5 Army, July 1944.
—Gumbinnen Op. w/28 Army, Jan. 1945.
—Far East w/5 Army, Aug. 1945.
Units: Oct. 1943: 58, 149, 173 Rifle Divisions.
　　　July 1944: 93, 144, 371 Rifle Divisions.

66 Rifle Corps
—Volga Military District w/21 Army, June 1941.
—Berezina River w/21 Army, July 1941.

—Dnieper River w/12 Army, Sep. 1943.
—Southwest Ukraine w/6 Army, Jan. 1944.
—Iasi Kishinev Op., a main attack corps of 37 Army, Aug. 1944.
—Probably an independent corps.
Units: July 1941: 232 Rifle Division.
       Jan. 1944: 60 Guards, 203, 244, 333 Rifle Divisions.
       Nov. 1944: 244, 333 Rifle Divisions.

67 Rifle Corps
—In Moscow Military District, June 1941.
—To Western Front w/21 Army, June 1941.
—Melitopol Op., Oct. 1943.
—Korsun Shevchenkovskiy Op. w/40 Army, Jan. 1944.
—Carpathian Duklinskiy Op., Sep. 1944.
—Dukla Pass w/38 Army, Oct. 1944.
—Berlin Op. w/70 Army, Apr. 1945.
—Probably an independent corps.
Units: Jan. 1944: 167, 359 Rifle Divisions.
       Sep. 1944: 122, 140, 241 Rifle Divisions.

68 Rifle Corps
—Kursk w/40 Army, July 1943.
—Southwest Ukraine w/57 Army, Jan. 1944.
—Belgrade w/57 Army, Oct. 1944.
—Hungary w/4 Guards Army, Jan. 1945.
Units: Jan. 1944: 80 Guards, 93, 113 Rifle Divisions.
       Nov. 1944: 113 Rifle Division.
       Jan. 1945: 93, 252 (possibly) Rifle Divisions.

69 Rifle Corps
—Moscow, Moscow Military District, June 1941.
—Vitebsk area, July 1941.
—Kursk w/21 Army, July 1943.
—Belorussia w/33 Army, May 1944.
—Mogilev Op., Belorussia w/49 Army, June 1944.
—Grodno w/50 Army, July 1944.
—Probably an independent corps.
Units: June 1944: 42, 222 Rifle Divisions.

70 Rifle Corps
—Northern Front, Karelian Isthmus, 22 June 1941.
—To Baltic Front, 27 June 1941.
—Lenino, near Mogilev w/33 Army, Oct. 1943.

—Mogilev Op., on Western Dvina River w/49 Army, June 1944.
—Pomerania w/49 Army, Mar. 1945.
Units: Oct. 1943: 338, 371 Rifle Divisions.
   June 1944: 49, 199, 290 Rifle Divisions.

71 Rifle Corps
—Belorussian Op. w/31 Army, June 1944.
Units: June 1944: 88, 192, 351 Rifle Divisions.

72 Rifle Corps
—Belorussia w/33 Army, June 1944.
—Vilnius w/5 Army, July 1944.
—Manchurian Op. w/5 Army, Aug. 1945.
Units: May 1944: 70, 157, 344 Rifle Divisions.
   July 1944: 63, 215, 277 Rifle Divisions.

73 Rifle Corps
—Sieled Bridgehead, Dnieper River, Sep. 1943.
—Mirgorod, Oct. 1943.
—Cherkass, Nov. 1943.
—Southwest Ukraine w/52 Army, Jan. 1944.
—Korsun Shevchenkovsky Op., Jan. 1944.
—Rumania, Apr. 1944.
—Iasi Kishinev Op. w/37 Army, Aug. 1944.
—Vistula Oder Op.; a main attack corps, Jan. 1945.
—RVGK.
Key Commanders: Gen-Lt P.A. Batitskiy.
Units: Jan. 1944: 7 Guards Airborne, 62 Guards Rifle Divisions.
   July 1944: 337 Rifle Division.
   Nov. 1944: 294, 373 Rifle Divisions.

74 Rifle Corps
—Southwest Ukraine w/38 Army, Jan. 1944.
Units: Jan. 1944: 107, 183, 305 Rifle Divisions.

75 Rifle Corps
—Kursk w/53 Army, July 1943.
—Kirovograd w/53 Army, Jan. 1944.
—Yugoslavia, Sep. 1944.
—Belgrade w/57 Army, Oct. 1944.
—Danube River, Oct. 1944.
Units: Jan. 1944: 116, 213, 233 Rifle Divisions.

76 Rifle Corps
—Rovno Lutsk Op. w/13 Army, Jan–Feb 1944.
—Rava Russkaya w/3 Guards Army, July 1944.
Units: Jan. 1944: 6, 121 Guards, 112 Rifle Divisions.
   Feb. 1944: 6, 121 Guards, 181 Rifle Divisions.

77 Rifle Corps
—Gomel, June 1941.
—Kursk w/65 Army, July 1943.
—Kiev Op. w/60 Army, Nov. 1943.
—Rovno Lutsk Op. w/13 Army, Jan. 1944.
—To the newly formed 2 Belorussian Front from 13 Army, Feb. 1944.
—Belorussia w/47 Army, Mar. 1944.
—Belgrade area, Sep. 1944.
—Probably an independent corps.
Units: June 1941: 137, 151 Rifle Divisions.
   May 1943: 60, 69, 194, 246, 354 Rifle Divisions.
   Jan. 1944: 143, 397 Rifle Divisions.
   Mar. 1944: 60, 143, 260 Rifle Divisions.

78 Rifle Corps
—Southwest Ukraine, probably w/52 Army, Jan. 1944.
Units: Jan. 1944: 254, 373 Rifle Divisions.

79 Rifle Corps
—Schniedemuhl w/3 Shock Army, Feb. 1945.
—Kustrin Bridgehead, Mar. 1945.
—Berlin w/3 Shock Army, Apr. 1945.
—Stendal, Germany w/3 Mechanized Army, Aug. 1946 (Feb. 1947 OB).
Units: Nov. 1944: 207 Rifle Division.
   Apr. 1945: 150 Rifle Division.
   Oct. 1946: 150, 171, 207 Rifle Divisions.

80 Rifle Corps
—Belorussian Op. w/3 Army, June 1944.
—Brest w/65 Army, July 1944.
—Vistula Oder Op. w/61 Army, Jan. 1945.
—Probably an independent corps.

81 Rifle Corps
—Belorussia w/33 Army, May 1944.
—Mogilev Op. w/49 Army, June 1944.
—Probably an independent corps.
Units: June 1944: 32, 95, 153 Rifle Divisions.

82 Independent Rifle Corps
—Dnieper River w/37 Army, Oct. 1943.
—Southwest Ukraine w/37 Army, Jan. 1944.
—Iasi Kishinev Op. w/37 Army, Aug. 1944.
—Dnestrovskiy Op. w/37 Army, Aug. 1944.
—Plovdiv, Bulgaria w/37 Army, Sep. 1946 (Feb. 1947 OB).
Units: Oct. 1943: 1, 10 Guards Airborne, 5, 188 Rifle Divisions.
       Jan. 1944: 10 Guards Airborne, 28 Guards, 188 Rifle Divisions.
       Sep. 1946: 19 Mechanized Division.

83 Rifle Corps
—With 11 Guards Army, Dec. 1943.
—Dvinsk w/4 Shock Army, Aug. 1944.
—Riga w/51 Army, Oct. 1944.
—Possibly an independent corps.
—Sibiu, Rumania, July 1946 (Feb. 1947 OB).
Units: Dec. 1943: 234, 235, 360 Rifle Divisions.
       Oct. 1944: 264, 417 Rifle Divisions.
       July 1946: 24 Tank, 68 Guards, 68 Rifle Divisions.

84 Rifle Corps
—Vitebsk Op. w/39 Army, June 1944.
Units: June 1944: 158, 262 Rifle Divisions.

86 Rifle Corps
—Transbaikal w/36 Army, Aug. 1945.

87 Rifle Corps
—Ukrainian frontier district, Kiev Special Military District, June 1941.
—Rovno Lutsk Op. w/13 Army, Jan. 1944.

88 Rifle Corps
—Vistula River, Aug. 1944.

89 Rifle Corps
—Kursk w/61 Army, July 1943.
—Belorussia w/61 Army, Mar. 1944.
—Vistula Oder Op. w/61 Army; a main attack corps, Jan. 1945.
Units: Mar. 1944: 15, 356, 415 Rifle Divisions.
       Nov. 1944: 55 Rifle Division.

90 Rifle Corps
—Probably existed.

91 Rifle Corps
—Vistula Oder Op. w/69 Army, Jan. 1945.
—Radom Lodz w/69 Army, Jan. 1945.
—Berlin Op. w/69 Army, Apr. 1945.
Units: Jan. 1945: 117, 312, 370 Rifle Divisions.
       Apr. 1945: 117, 312, 370 Rifle Divisions.

92 Rifle Corps
—Vitebsk w/43 Army, June 1944.
Units: June 1944: 145, 204 Rifle Divisions, 55 Fortified Area.
       Nov. 1944: 235 Rifle Division.

93 Rifle Corps
—Latvia, Nov. 1944.
Units: Nov. 1944: 391 Rifle Division.

94 Rifle Corps
—Southwest Ukraine w/1 Guards Army, Jan. 1944.
—Proskurov Chernovtsy Op. w/1 Guards Army, Mar. 1944.
—Probably in Far East, Manchurian Op., Aug. 1945.
Units: Jan. 1944: 30, 99, 350 Rifle Divisions.

95 Rifle Corps
—Known to have existed.

96 Rifle Corps
—Belorussia w/70 Army, Mar. 1944.
—Vistula Oder Op. w/70 Army, Jan. 1945.
—East Prussian Op. w/70 Army, Mar. 1945.
Units: Mar. 1944: 185 Rifle Division.

97 Rifle Corps
—Probably in Baltic area, Nov. 1944.
Units: Nov. 1944: 372 Rifle Division.

98 Rifle Corps
—RVGK w/2 Shock Army, Sep. 1944.
—East Prussian Op. w/2 Shock Army, Mar. 1945.

99 Rifle Corps
—Svir River w/7 Independent Army, June 1944.
—Petsamo Kirkenes Op., w/14 Army, Oct. 1944.
Units: Oct. 1944: 10 Guards, 65, 114, 367 Rifle Divisions.

100 Rifle Corps
—Dvinsk w/4 Shock Army, Aug. 1944.
Units: Nov. 1944: 28 Rifle Division.

101 Rifle Corps
—Southwest Ukraine w/18 Army, Jan. 1944.
—Lvov Sandomir Op. w/38 Army, July 1944.
—Carpathian Duklinskiy Op. w/38 Army, Sep. 1944.
—Moravska Ostrava, Czechoslovakia w/38 Army, Mar–Apr 1945.
—Prague Op., May 1945.
Units: Jan. 1944: 161 Rifle Divisions.
　　　Sep. 1944: 70 Guards, 183, 211 Rifle Divisions.

102 Rifle Corps
—Lvov Sandomir Op. w/13 Army, July 1944.
—Vistula Oder Op. w/13 Army, Jan. 1945.
—Berlin Op. w/13 Army, Apr. 1945.
—Carpathian Military District (EUCOM Study), Jan. 1946.
Units: Apr. 1945: 147 Rifle Division.

103 Rifle Corps
—Latvia, Nov. 1944.
Units: Nov. 1944: 29 Guards, 154 Rifle Division.

104 Rifle Corps
—Korsun Shevchenkovskiy Op. w/40 Army, Jan. 1944.
—Targul Frumos w/40 Army, May 1944.
—Iasi Kishinev Op.; main attack corps of 37 Army, Aug. 1944.
—Nyirgyhaza, Hungary (Ultra), 23 Oct. 1944.
Units: Jan. 1944: 58, 133 Rifle Divisions.

105 Rifle Corps
—Belorussian Op. w/65 Army, June 1944.
—Danzig w/65 Army, Mar. 1945.
—Schreiberhau, Poland w/7 Mechanized Army, July 1946 (Feb. 1947 OB).
Units: June 1946: 2, 44, 108, 186, 325 Rifle Divisions.
　　　July 1946: 20 Tank Division.

106 Rifle Corps
—Known to have existed.

107 Rifle Corps
—Southwest Ukraine w/1 Guards Army, Jan. 1944.

—Proskurov Chernovtsy Op. w/1 Gds Army, Mar. 1944.
—Lvov Sandomir Op. w/38 Army, July 1944.
—Carpathian Uzhgorod Op. w/1 Guards Army, Sep. 1944.
Units: Jan. 1944: 127, 304, 328 Rifle Divisions.
  Sep. 1944: 129 Guards, 167, 276 Rifle Divisions.
  Nov. 1944: 127 Rifle Division.

108 Rifle Corps
—Leningrad w/2 Shock Army, Jan. 1944.
—East Prussian Op. w/2 Shock Army, Mar. 1945.
—Rugen Island w/70 Army, May 1945.

109 Rifle Corps
—Narva w/2 Shock Army, July 1944.
—Prob. Finnish Front, Nov. 1944.
—Leningrad Military District, 1946 (Feb. 1947 OB).
Units: Nov. 1944: 109 Rifle Division.
  Feb. 1947: 109, 131 Rifle Divisions.

110 Rifle Corps
—Known to have existed.

111 Rifle Corps
—Known to have existed.

112 Rifle Corps
—Novgorod Luga Op. w/59 Army, Jan. 1944.
Units: Jan. 1944: 2, 377 Rifle Divisions.

113 Rifle Corps
—Belorussian Op. w/31 Army, June 1944.
—Grodno w/31 Army, July 1944.
Units: June 1944: 62, 173, 174, 352 Rifle Divisions.
  Nov. 1944: 173 Rifle Division.

114 Rifle Corps
—Belorussia w/70 Army, Mar. 1944.
—Poland w/70 Army, Sep. 1944.
—East Prussian Op. w/70 Army, Mar. 1945.
Key Commanders: D.I. Rybishev, June 1944–May 1945.
Units: Mar. 1944: 38 Guards, 160 Rifle Divisions.
  Sep. 1944: 38 Guards, 36, 160 Rifle Divisions.

115 Rifle Corps
—Known to have existed.

116 Rifle Corps
—Leningrad Front w/2 Shock Army, Sep. 1944.
—East Prussian Op. w/2 Shock Army, Mar. 1945.
Units: Nov. 1944: 86, 291 Rifle Divisions.

117 Rifle Corps
—Known to have existed.

118 Rifle Corps
—Leningrad front w/2 Shock Army, Sep. 1944.
—RVGK w/2 Shock Army, Sep. 1944.

119 Rifle Corps
—Northern Finland, Sep. 1944.
—Petsamo Kirkenes Op. w/14 Army, Oct. 1944.
—To Latvia w/57 Army, Oct. 1944.

120 Rifle Corps
—Nevel w/20 Army, Oct. 1943.
—Rava Russkaya w/3 Guards Army, July 1944.
—Berlin Op. w/3 Guards Army, Apr. 1945.
—RVGK.
Units: Nov. 1944: 197, 273 Rifle Divisions.

121 Rifle Corps
—Oder River w/49 Army, Mar. 1945.

122 Rifle Corps
—Known to have existed.

123 Rifle Corps
—Known to have existed.

124 Rifle Corps
—Known to have existed.

125 Rifle Corps
—Belorussia w/47 Army, Mar. 1944.
—Warsaw Poznan Op. w/47 Army, Jan. 1945.

—Berlin Op., Apr. 1945.
Units: Mar. 1944: 76, 175, 328 Rifle Divisions.
       Jan. 1945: 60 Rifle Division.

126 Light Rifle Corps
—Petsamo Kirkenes Op. w/14 Army; made up of brigades, Oct. 1944.
—Berlin Op., Apr. 1945.
Units: Apr. 1945: 72 Naval Rifle Brigade.

127 Light Rifle Corps
—Petsamo Kirkenes Op. w/14 Army; made up of brigades, Oct. 1944.
—Moravka Ostrava, Czechoslovakia as mountain corps w/38 Army, Apr. 1945.

128 Rifle Corps
—Belorussian Op. w/1 Belorussian Front, June 1944.
—Bobruysk, July 1944.
—Lvov Sandomir Op., July 1944.
—Gumbinnen w/28 Army, Jan. 1945.
—Koenigsberg w/28 Army, Apr. 1945.
—Berlin w/28 Army, Apr. 1945.
—RVGK w/28 Army (SME), Apr. 1945.
—Brest Litovsk, Belorussian Military District, May 1947(Feb. 1948 OB).
—"Gumbinnen."
Key Commanders: Gen-Lt P.A. Batitskiy, June 1944.
Units: Apr. 1945: 152 Rifle Division.

129 Rifle Corps
—Warsaw Poznan Op. w/47 Army, Jan. 1945.
—Berlin Op. Apr. 1945.
Units: Jan. 1945: 132, 143, 260 Rifle Divisions.

130 Rifle Corps
—Latvia w/67 Army, Aug-Oct 1944.
—Latvia w/6 Guards Army, Sep. 1945 (Feb. 1947 OB).
—"Latvian."
Units: Nov. 1944: 43 Guards, 308 Rifle Divisions.
       Sep. 1945: 43 Guards, 43, 129 Rifle Divisions.

131 Rifle Corps
—Petsamo Kirkenes Op. w/14 Army, Sep. 1944.
—Pechenga area w/14 Army, Oct. 1944.

132 Rifle Corps
—Courland, East Prussia w/19 Army, Mar. 1945.
—Bornholm Island w/19 Army, May 1945.

133 Rifle Corps
—Szekesfehervar, Jan. 1945.
—Lake Balaton (Hron Bridgehead), Feb. 1945.

134 Rifle Corps
—Courland, East Prussia w/19 Army, Mar. 1945.

135 Rifle Corps
—Hungary, Nov. 1944.
—Szekesfehervar, Hungary Jan. 1945.

CHAPTER FOUR

Rifle Division Activations and Military District Summary

The following section details the *known* activation points of Rifle, Guards Airborne, Guards Rifle, some Guards Divisions, Mountain Divisions and Motorized Divisions. Divisions which were rifle divisions but later became guards are listed only once. This compendium will provide the reader with insight into the geographical distribution of the rifle division mobilization bases. It must be kept in mind that many activation bases in the western military districts were overrun by the Germans in the early days of the invasion and could not be used. The data is arranged alphabetically and lists the location of the division's activation, the military district and unit's identity. Units listed with an attached reference in parentheses, for example 309 (2F), reflect the unit number and the order of activation such as second formation (2F), third formation (3F) etc. All units are regular rifle divisions unless otherwise stated. This information has been extracted from declassified German FHO records available in NARS. The spelling of placenames, therefore, is originally German and has been modified accordingly.

LOCATION	MILITARY DISTRICT	DIVISIONS
Abakan	Siberian	309 (2F)
Agdam	Transcaucasus	402
Akmolinsk	Central Asia	29 (3F); 310; 387
Aktubinsk	Central Asia	312
Alexin	Moscow	119 (3F)
Alkalkalaki	Transcaucasus	407
Alma Ata	Central Asia	38 (2F); 316; 391
Archangelsk	Archangelsk	88; 362; 368
Artemovsk	Kharkov	162

Arzamas	Moscow	238 (2F)
Ashkabad	Central Asia	120
Astrakhan	North Caucasus	248 (2F); 248 (3F); 337; 349
Atkarsk	Volga	127 (2F); 350; 397
Achinsk	Siberian	91; 378
Baku	Transcaucasus	68; 71 Mtn; 317
Balachna	Moscow	145 (2F); 279 (2F)
Balachov	Volga	61; 99 (2F); 340
Barabash	Far East	92
Barnaul	Siberian	298 (2F); 315; 372
Belaya Tserkov	Kiev Special	159
Belev	Moscow	97 (3F)
Belgorod	Orel	145; 185; 299
Belokovorichi	Kiev Special	200
Berdichev	Kiev Special	100; 146
Berdyansk	Odessa	261
Besslan	North Caucasus	328 (2F)
Bikin	Far East	35; 422
Birobidzhan	Far East	34; 36
Biysk	Siberian	133; 233 (2F)
Blagoveshchensk	Far East	12; 204 (2F)
Bobruysk	Western Special	121
Bogolovo	Siberian	374
Borzya	Far East	321 (2F)
Bugulma	Volga	352
Buguruslan	Volga	206 (2F); 226 (2F); 358
Busuluk	Volga	200 (2F)
Chkalov (Orenburg)	Volga	360
Chaklovsk	Moscow	35 GRD
Chapayevsk	Volga	41 (2F); 153 (2F); 253 (2F)
Chaussy	Western Special	33
Chelyabinsk	Ural	85; 181 (2F)
Cherbarkul	Ural	166 (2F); 249 (2F); 373; 377
Cherepovets	Archangelsk	180 (2F); 286
Cherkassy	Kiev Special	190; 212
Chernigov	Kiev Special	187; 232
Chimkent	Central Asia	102 (2F)
Chita	Transbaikal	65; 93; 106 (4F); 116 (2F); 152 399

Rifle Division Activations and Military District Summary 175

Cholm	Leningrad	319 (2F)
Chuguyev	Kiev Special	295; 411
Citorol	Far East	87 (3F)
Dimitrov	Moscow	244; 305; 10 GARD; 98 GRD
Divisionnaya (Ulan Ude)	Far East	97 (2F)
Dmitriyev	Orel	277
Dnepropetrovsk	Odessa	196; 230; 273
Dorogobosh	Western Special	208 (3F)
Dorpat	Baltic Special	182
Dunaburg	Unidentified	23 (2F)
Dzerzhinsk	Moscow	93 (2F); 279
Engels	Volga	148
Fastov	Kiev Special	62
Frolov	North Caucasus	277 (2F)
Frunze	Central Asia	385
Gajassin	Kiev Special	173 Mtn; 218
Gajnovka	Western Special	208
Gomel	Western Special	143
Gori	Transcaucasus	392
Gorki	Moscow	17; 137; 160; 201; 322; 336; 418
Grozny	North Caucasus	242 Mtn (2F)
Gshatsk	Western Special	128; 56 GRD; 65 GRD
Gulbene	Baltic Special	181
Hiitola	Archangelsk	142
Iman	Far East	59
Irkutsk	Transbaikal	46
Ishevsk	Ural	98
Issakogorski	Archangelsk	2 (2F)
Ivanovo	Moscow	49 (2F); 117 (2F); 144; 207; 307; 36 GRD
Ivye	Western Special	209 Mtz
Kalinin	Moscow	48; 111 (2F); 138 (2F); 156 (2F); 157 (2F); 199 (2F); 260 25 GRD

Kaluga	Moscow	63 (2F); 95 (3F); 174 (3F); 266
Kalyasin	Moscow	290
Kamensk	North Caucasus	171
Kamychin	North Caucasus	333
Kamyshlov	Ural	375
Kanasch	Moscow	140 (3F)
Kandalaksha	Archangelsk	104
Kansk	Siberian	228 (2F); 382
Karelia	Leningrad	136 (2F)
Katta Kurgan	Central Asia	213 (2F)
Kazakh	Transcaucasus	236
Kazakhstan	Central Asia	238
Kazan	Volga	18; 141 (2F); 146 (2F); 147 (2F); 188; 334
Kemerovo	Siberian	71
Khabarovsk	Far East	78; 102 (3F); 205
Kharkov	Kharkov	219 Mtz
Kiev	Kiev Special	197; 218 (2F)
Kingisepp	Leningrad	11
Kirov	Ural	125; 131 (2F); 311; 355
Kirovobad	Transcaucasus	398
Kirovograd	Odessa	124
Kirovokan	Transcaucasus	406
Kirshatsch	Moscow	5 GARD
Kirssanov	Orel	219 (2F)
Kisner	Ural	88 (2F); 196 (2F)
Kologriv	Moscow	120 (2F)
Kolomna	Moscow	52 (2F0; 135 (2F); 251; 269
Korosten	Kiev Special	143 (2F); 193
Korotscha	Orel	92 GRD
Kostroma	Moscow	49; 118; 133 (2F); 234; 285; 328
Kotovki	Odessa	95
Kovrov	Moscow	299 (2F)
Kozelsk	Moscow	139
Kramatorsk	Kharkov	134
Krasnodar	North Caucasus	74, 106 (3F); 197 (2F); 302; 316 (3F); 347; 353; 359
Krasnogvardeysk	Leningrad	292
Krasnoufinsk	Ural	221
Krasnoyarsk	Siberian	94; 119
Kremenchug	Kiev Special	102; 116

Rifle Division Activations and Military District Summary 177

Krimskaya	North Caucasus	257 (2F); 110 GRD
Krivoi Rog	Kiev Special	41, 176
Kuba	North Caucasus	223
Kuibyshev	Volga	1 (2F); 55 (2F); 69 Mtz; 70; 117; 121 (3F); 197 (3F); 266 (3F); 348; 354; 356
Kungar	Ural	231
Kupyansk	Kharkov	240; 240 (2F)
Kurgan	Orel	165 (2F); 174
Kurgan	Ural	369
Kursk	Orel	55; 89; 309
Kussary	Transcaucasus	396
Kutaisi	Transcaucasus	38 (3F); 47 Mtn; 276 (2F); 388
Laurovo	North Caucasus	86
Leningrad	Leningrad	44 (2F); 67; 72; 72 (2F); 85 (2F); 90; 98 (3F); 109 (3F) 177 189; 191; 198 Mtz; 202 Mtz; 265 281
Leninikan	Transcaucasus	136; 136 (3F); 138 Mtn; 320 (2F); 446; 469
Lev Tolstoi	Moscow	49 GRD
Lgow	Orel	226 (3F)
Lipetsk	Orel	287 (2F); 294
Livny	Orel	278
Louti	Archangelsk	45 (3F); 83 (2F)
Lubertsy	Moscow	37 GRD
Lubny	Kharkov	75 Mtn; 81; 147; 287; 297
Luknya	Moscow	325 (2F)
Makhachkala	North Caucasus	91 (2F); 317 (2F); 319; 345; 414
Mariupol	Odessa	80
Maselskaya	Leningrad	176 (2F)
Matveyev	North Caucasus	130 (3F)
Melekess	Volga	58
Melitopol	Odessa	270
Minsk	Western Special	2; 13
Malechna	Moscow	16 (2F); 161
Mitschurinsk	Orel	161 (2F)
Mogilev	Western Special	343 (2F)
Molotov	Ural	170 (2F); 252 (2F)

Morschansk	Orel	325
Moscow	Moscow	1 Moscow Prol.; 14; 17 (2F); 29 (2F); 32 (2F); 51 (2F); 52; 60 (2F); 70 (2F); 76 (2F); 107; 110 (2F); 110 (3F); 113 (2F); 119 (2F); 126; 129; 129 (2F); 130 (2F); 139 (2F); 140 (2F); 155 (2F); 160 (2F); 172 (3F); 173 (2F); 242 Mtn; 282; 343; 344; 4 GARD; 8 GARD; 9 GARD; 34 GRD; 39 GRD; 40 GRD; 41 GRD; 100 GRD
Mozyr	Western Special	268
Murmansk	Archangelsk	205
Murom	Moscow	247
Nakichevan	Trancaucasus	47 Mtn (2F); 76
Nalchik	North Caucasus	115
Nanovo	Moscow	332
Naro Fominsk	Moscow	233 (2F)
Nelidovo	Moscow	201 (3F); 215 (2F)
Nevel	Moscow	1 (3F)
Nikolayev	Odessa	15
Nikopol	Odessa	235
Noginsk	Moscow	229; 6 GARD
Novgorod	Leningrad	16
Novocherkassk	North Caucasus	37; 118 (3F); 157
Novograd Volynskiy	Kiev Special	131
Novo Moskovsk	Odessa	275
Novorossiysk	North Caucasus	140 (4F)
Novosibirsk	Siberian	112 (2F); 199; 235 (2F); 258 (2F); 376
Novossil	Orel	211 (2F)
Novy Oskol	Orel	94 GRD
Odessa	Odessa	51
Omsk	Siberian	73; 178; 282 (2F); 308; 364; 384
Onenga	Archangelsk	234 (2F)
Opotschka	Moscow	155
Ordzhonikidze	North Caucasus	73 (2F); 165; 351 (2F)

Orechovo	Moscow	226
Orel	Orel	258; 271
Orsha	Western Special	164
Ostrogosh	Orel	149
Ovruch	Kiev Special	60, 195
Pavlograd	Odessa	206; 217 (2F); 255
Penza	Volga	57 Mtz; 184 (3F); 338
Perm	Ural	82 Mtz; 379
Petropavlovsk	Archangelsk	314
Petrozavodsk	Archangelsk	237
Pleskau	Leningrad	56
Podolsk	Moscow	273 (2F)
Polotsk	Western Special	5; 50
Poltava	Kharkov	25; 132; 264; 301
Priluki	Kiev Special	135
Prokladnyy	North Caucasus	175
Ramenskoye	Moscow	7 GARD
Romny	Kiev Special	130, 284
Rossosh	Orel	30 (2F)
Rostov	North Caucasus	38; 127; 192; 318 Mtn; 339
Rovno	Kiev Special	215
Ryazan	Moscow	8 (2F); 149 (2F)
Rybinsk	Moscow	198 (2F); 246; 291
Rylsk	Moscow	113; 122
Rzhev	Moscow	153 (3F); 154 (2F); 159 (3F)
Samarkand	Central Asia	78 (2F); 103 (2F); 109 (2F)
Sarapul	Ural	357
Saratov	Volga	53; 342
Shchekovo	Moscow	3 GARD
Schtschigry	Orel	283
Schlusselburg	Leningrad	120 (3F); 124 (3F); 201 (2F)
Semipalatinsk	Central Asia	8
Serpukov	Moscow	64 (2F); 252; 259; 267 (2F)
Shandansk	Volga	367
Simbirsk	Siberian	24
Simferopol	Odessa	172, 276, 421
Slavgorod	Siberian	312 (2F); 380
Slavyanka	Far East	40

Slavyansk	Moscow	141
Slavyansk	North Caucasus	227
Slonim	Western Special	29
Smolensk	Western Special	64
Solotonoscha	Kharkov	106; 304
Solnechnogorsk	Moscow	134 (2F)
Sortovala	Archangelsk	168
Sorotschninik	Volga	193 (2F)
Spassk	Far East	21; 98 (2F)
Ssaransk	Moscow	326
Ssucho Lug	Ural	167 (2F)
Ssuschinitsch	Western Special	212 (2F)
Ssyteschevka	Moscow	192 (2F)
Stalingrad	North Caucasus	181 (2F); 184 (2F); 266 (2F); 278 (2F); 335; 341; 351
Stalino	Kharkov	383
Stalinsk	Siberian	237 (2F)
Staniza	North Caucasus	156
Staritsa	Moscow	173 (3F)
Starobelsk	Kharkov	174 (2F)
Starodub	Orel	222
Staro Konstantinov	Kiev Special	216
Stary Oskol	Orel	267
Stepanavan	Transcaucasus	409
Sterlitamak	Ural	170
Suchum	Tanscaucasus	224
Sumgait	Transcaucasus	404; 416
Sumy	Kharkov	293
Svjatogorsk	Kharkov	264 (2F); 393
Sverdlovsk	Ural	87; 153; 175 (3F); 363; 365; 371
Svobodny	Far East	413
Taman	North Caucasus	117 GRD
Tambov	Moscow	19; 107 (2F); 239; 323; 331
Tashkent	Central Asia	69 (2F); 162 (3F); 194 Mtn; 389
Tejkovo	Moscow	1 GARD; 38 GRD
Terijok	Archangelsk	42
Tiflis (Tbilisi)	Transcaucasus	63 Mtn; 386; 394; 417
Tikhvin	Leningrad	92 (2F); 272
Tomsk	Siberian	166; 284 (2F); 366; 370; 443

Transbaikal	Transbaikal	109 Mtz; 114
Tscherbokssary	Moscow	139 (3F); 324
Tula	Moscow	84; 95 (2F); 96 (3F); 110; 167 254; 257; 280; 330; 2 Gds Mtz
Turga	Siberian	150 (2F)
Typki	Siberian	303 (2F)
Tyumen	Siberian	175 (2F)
Udshary	Transcaucasus	151; 151 (2F)
Ufa	Ural	46 (2F); 186; 214 (2F); 361
Ulyanovsk	Volga	15; 154
Uman	Kiev Special	99; 140
Ussuriysk	Far East	66; 105; 126
Valuki	Orel	93 GRD
Vaskelovo	Leningrad	46 (3F)
Vasniki	Moscow	316 (2F)
Velikiye Luki	Moscow	43
Verchnoye	Ural	41 (3F); 162 (2F)
Veissenstein	Baltic Special	180
Venden	Baltic Special	183
Vilnius	Western Special	179
Vinnitsa	Kiev Special	96; 169; 213
Vishny Volochek	Moscow	45 (2F); 123; 241; 245
Vishny Volochev	Leningrad	163
Vitebsk	Western Special	27
Vladimir	Moscow	10; 250; 262
Vladivostok	Far East	32; 39; 208 (2F); 415
Volkhovsk	Western Special	204 Mtz
Volochanks	Kharkov	253
Vologda	Archangelsk	24 (2F); 100 (2F); 111; 263
Volokolamsk	Moscow	229 (2F); 260 (2F)
Volsk	Volga	42 (2F); 346
Voronezh	Orel	124 (2F); 217; 270 (2F); 303; 305 (2F); 321; 327; 329
Voroshilov	Kharkov	23 (3F); 26
Voroshilovgrad	Kharkov	214; 395
Voroshilovsk	North Caucasus	103 Mtz; 203
Vyazma	Western Special	108; 112; 150; 220; 248
Yaroslavl	Moscow	243; 288
Yefremov	Moscow	5 (2F)

Yelez	Orel	287
Yelnaya	Western Special	207 (2F)
Yerevan	Transcaucasus	31; 89 (2F); 225; 261 (2F); 408
Yesk	North Caucasus	158
Yevlach	Transcaucasus	400
Yukhnov	Western Special	62 (2F)
Yuryev	Moscow	306
Zagorsk	Moscow	211
Zaporozhye	Kiev Special	274
Zhitomir	Kiev Special	44; 228
Zhmerinka	Kiev Special	97
Zlatoust	Siberian	381
Zvenigorod	Moscow	233; 2 GARD

This section details the activation of the total number of divisions by military district and year and gives the total number *known* to have been activated.

INTERNAL MILITARY DISTRICTS

DISTRICT	1941	1942	1943	1944	1945	TOTAL
Archangelsk	7	4	1	1		13
Central Asia	12	7				19
Kharkov	17	1				18
Moscow	65	47	22	3		137
North Caucasus	18	24	5			47
Orel	21	6	5			32
Siberian	16	16				32
Transcaucasus	18	7	2	2	1	30
Ural	18	14	1			33
Volga	14	19	1			34
TOTALS	206	145	37	6	1	395

FRONTIER MILITARY DISTRICTS

DISTRICT	1941	1942	1943	1944	1945	TOTAL
Baltic Special						
Far East	7	4		11	1	23
Kiev Special	8	2	2	1		13
Leningrad	7	3	5	1		16
Odessa	12					12

Transbaikal	4	4		1		9
Western Special	7		5	1	1	14
TOTALS	45	13	12	15	2	87

Rifle Divisions existing before 1941: 177
Formed in unidentified Military District: 65
Total number of Rifle Divisions known to have been activated: 724

CHAPTER FIVE

Artillery Divisions

Introduction
Divisions were formations of combined arms, combat support and combat service support designed to execute a single phase of a large operation such as a counterattack, delay, exploitation or penetration. Antiaircraft, artillery, cavalry, and rifle divisions existed in World War II. Antiaircraft divisions and cavalry divisions will not be detailed in the order of battle.

Artillery divisions served as the base of fire for major offensive or defensive operations. The division headquarters contained permanent planning, fire direction, reconnaissance, intelligence, and liaison staffs. It could control, without additional staff augmentation, up to 36 artillery battalions. The division was tailored according to the requirements of the intended operation and would be reinforced with RVGK assets as required. Certain divisions were designated "Breakthrough Artillery Divisions of the RVGK." They performed the task inherent in the name. Guards Rocket Barrage Divisions consisted of units with large numbers of rocket launchers which were capable of laying down a tremendous volume of area fire. They were particularly effective in supporting major attacks, in disrupting enemy assaults, and in combat in cities.

Rifle divisions constituted the most numerous force in the Red Army. Nearly 800 rifle divisions were formed at various times in the GPW although about 500 divisions appears to be the maximum force in existence at any one time. The mission of the rifle division was to engage the enemy in close combat. It contained three rifle regiments, an artillery regiment, and supporting arms and services.

As early as the Civil War, Red Army maneuver divisions were classified according to role, mobilization echelon, and commitment to the operational forces. Documents available in the National Archives show the 1920s classification system used the first three letters of the Cyrillic alphabet (A, B, V), and assigned different Table of Organization and Equipment (TO&E) strengths to each. Starting out World War II with a TO&E of 18,000 men, authorized rifle division strength was reduced several times. By 1943–44, NARS FHO documents show that the Civil War system had developed as follows:

Division A . . . a shock division *(udarnyie divisii)* . 12,000 men.
Division B . . . a "normal" division . . . . 9,000 men.
Division V . . . a "passive" (non-attack) division . . . 6,000 men.

The Germans noted that the strengths of the three types of divisions varied considerably from earlier equivalents and determined that manpower was directly related to the status and availability of human reserves.

The division existed in two forms, the guards rifle and the rifle division. The guards formations had a larger TO&E, better weapons, higher quality personnel, larger supporting services, and were always found in the key offensive and defensive sectors. It was not uncommon for rifle divisions to be augmented to 12,000 men (assault divisions) for breakthrough operations. Guards Airborne Divisions existed but for most of the war were used as rifle formations. These divisions were used as elite assault formations.

It should be noted that readers of this compilation should "cross reference" their research on divisions. For example, if a person wishes the complete history of the 45th Guards Rifle Division, that division should first be found. Upon locating the 45th, it will be seen that it was originally the 70th Rifle Division. A complete history of the 45th Guards Rifle Division, therefore, would include the history of the 70th Rifle Division up to the time it was designated "guards," plus the combat trail of the 45th Guards. The same approach would apply for any unit that became "guards," corps that became armies etc.

Artillery Divisions

1 Artillery Division
—Carried as existing in the Lithuanian Order of Battle, fall 1938.
—Finland w/13th Army as "Grendal's Special Detachment;" was a Top Secret unit at the time, 1939–40.
—Activated on Southwest Front as 1 Artillery Division of the RVGK, Oct. 1942.
—Kletskaya, near Stalingrad, w/21 Army, Nov. 1942.
—Stalingrad offensive w/21 and 65 Armies, Dec. 1942.
—Regiments upgraded to 3 brigades, 20 Feb. 1943.
—Reformed as 1 Guards Artillery Division of the RVGK, 1 Mar. 1943.
Units: Oct. 1942: 274, 275, 331 Howitzer Artillery; 1162, 1166 Gun Artillery; 468, 501, 1189 Antitank Regiments, 8, 16 Artillery Reconnaissance Battalions.

1 Guards Breakthrough Artillery Division
—Reformed as Guards from 1 Artillery Division, 1 Mar. 1943.

—Kursk in support of 13 and 70 Armies, July 1943.
—Glukhov w/60 Army, Aug. 1943.
—Dnieper, Sep. 1943.
—Kiev, Nov. 1943.
—Yampol, Mar. 1943.
—Lvov-Sandomir Op. w/13 Army, July 1944.
—Reformed as Guards Breakthrough Artillery Division of the RVGK, Nov. 1944.
—Sandomir-Silesia Op., Jan. 1945.
—Lower Silesia Op., Feb. 1945.
—Berlin w/3 Guards Army, Apr. 1945.
—With 7 Breakthrough Artillery Corps, 1943–1945.
—Austria, Jan. 1946, (Feb. 1947 OB).
—Lvov, Carpathian Military District w/5 Guards Artillery Division, Jan. 1947 (Feb. 1948 OB).
—The 1 Guards Artillery Brigade "Kiev," 2 Guards Artillery Brigade "Rechitsa," 3 Guards Artillery Brigade "Bachmach, Kiev."
—"Ssevsk, Glukhov," Orders of Lenin, Red Banner, Suvorov, Kutuzov, Bogdan Khmelnitskiy.
Units: Mar. 1943: 1 Guards Gun, 2 Guards Howitzer, 3 Guards Light Artillery Brigades.
June 1944: 1 Guards Gun, 2 Guards Howitzer, 3 Guards Light Artillery Brigades.

1 Guards Rocket Barrage* Division
—RVGK (SME).
*Sometimes rendered as Guards Mortar.

1 Tank Destroyer Division
—Voronezh Front, Jan. 1943.
Units: Jan. 1943: 6, 10 Tank Destroyer Brigades.

2 Breakthrough Artillery Division
—A 2 Artillery Division was carried in the Latvian Order of Battle (NARS), Fall 1938.
—RVGK.
—With 3 Baltic Front, June 1944.
Units: June 1943: 7 Howitzer Artillery Brigade.

2 Guards Breakthrough Artillery Division
—Formerly 4 Artillery Division, 1943.
—Taganrog, Aug. 1943.
—Supporting 51 Army, 4 Ukrainian Front, Feb. 1944.

—With 1 Baltic and 3 Belorussian Fronts, June 1944.
—"Taganrog."
Units: June 1944: 4 Guards Light, 5 Guards Howitzer Artillery, 6 Guards Gun Artillery, 20 Guards Howitzer Artillery, 114 Gun Artillery, 33 Rocket Barrage Brigades.

2 Guards Rocket Barrage Division
—RVGK (SME).
—Gorodok, Dec. 1943.
—"Gorodok."
Units: Dec. 1943: 3, 17, 26 Rocket Barrage Brigades, 24, 34, 526 Rocket Barrage Regiments.

3 Breakthrough Artillery Division.
—Zhitomir Berdichev Op., Jan. 1944.
—With 1 Ukrainian Front, 8 Breakthrough Artillery Corps, June 1944.
—Lvov-Sandomir Op. in support of 5 Guards Army, July 1944.
—Tiraspol, Aug. 1944.
—Poland, Jan. 1945.
—With 8 Breakthrough Artillery Corps.
—"Zhitomir," Orders of Lenin, Red Banner.
Units: June 1944–Jan. 1945: 1 Heavy Howitzer Artillery, 5 Gun Artillery, 15 Light Artillery, 25 Howitzer Artillery, 116 Heavy Howitzer Artillery, 168 Artillery Brigades, 7 Rocket Brigade.

3 Guards Breakthrough Artillery Division
—Formerly 8 Artillery Division, activated Moscow, Nov. 1942.
—With 5 Breakthrough Artillery Corps, 1943–45.
—Reformed as 3 Guards Artillery Division of the RVGK, 7 Mar. 1943.
—Reformed as a Guards Breakthrough Artillery Division of the RVGK, June 1943.
—On the Southwest Front w/5, 21, 31, 33 Armies, July 1943.
—Smolensk Op., Sep. 1943.
—Vitebsk Op., June 1944.
—Vilnius, July 1944.
—Neman River, Aug. 1944.
—East Prussian Op., Jan. 1945.
—Koenigsberg, Apr. 1945.
—Regrouped to Far East w/39 Army, May 1945.
—Khingan, Aug. 1945.
—"Vitebsk, Khingan," Orders of Red Banner, Suvorov, Kutuzov.
Units: May 1944: 7 Guards Light Artillery, 8 Guards Howitzer, 15 Guards

Gun Artillery Brigades; 208 Guards Artillery Regiment, 619 Observation Detachment.

3 Guards Rocket Barrage Division
—Activated in Moscow, Dec. 1942.
—RVGK (SME).
—Stalingrad, Jan. 1943.
—RVGK, Jan–Feb 1943.
—Orel, Apr. 1943.
—Dnieper, Sep. 1943.
—Kiev w/1 Ukrainian Front (to end of war), Nov. 1943.
—Zhitomir/Fastov, Dec. 1943.
—Korsun Shevchenkovskiy Op., Jan. 1944.
—Lvov-Sandomir Op., July 1944.
—Sandomir-Silesia Op., Jan. 1945.
—Breslau, Feb. 1945.
—Berlin, Apr. 1945.
—Prague, May. 1945.
—"Kiev," Orders of Red Banner, Kutuzov, Suvorov.
Units: July 1944: 4, 19 Guards, 32 Rocket Barrage Brigades; 312, 313 Guards Rocket Regiments.

4 Breakthrough Artillery Division
—Activated in the RVGK, Nov. 1942.
—Deployed from RVGK to Stalingrad, Nov. 1942.
—Renamed 2 Guards Artillery Division, 1943.
—Second formation raised, spring 1943.
—Kursk w/11 Guards Army, July 1943
—Koenigsbruck, Germany w/1 Guards Mechanzied Army, 24 Aug. 1946 (Feb. 1947 OB).

4 Guards Breakthrough Artillery Division
—Smolensk, Sep. 1943.
—Belorussian Op., June 1944.
—With 5 Breakthrough Artillery Corps, 1943–45.
—"Smolensk."
Units: June 1944: 10 Guards Howitzer Artillery, 11 Guards Light Artillery Brigades.

4 Guards Rocket Barrage Division
—RVGK (SME).
—Melitopol Op., Oct. 1943.
—South Russia with 4 Ukrainian Front, June 1944.

Units: June 1944: 20, 21 Rocket Barrage Brigades, 16, 36, 314 Rocket Barrage Regiments.

5 Breakthrough Artillery Division
—Kursk as part of 4 Breakthrough Artillery Corps, July 1943.
—Lenino (near Mogilev) w/33 Army, Oct. 1943.
—RVGK (FHO).
—Proskurov Chernovtsy Op., Mar. 1944.
—Belorussian Op. w/1 Belorussian Front, June 1944.
—Supporting 8 Guards Army in Magnuszew bridgehead, Aug. 1944.
—Weichsel, supporting 33 Army, Mar. 1945.
—With 4 Breakthrough Artillery Corps, 1943–45.
Units: Mar. 1944: 9 Howitzer Artillery, 15 Light Artillery, 24 Gun Artillery, 1 Rocket Barrage Brigades.
May 1944: 17, 18, 27, 68, 71, 95, 119 Artillery Brigades.

5 Guards Breakthrough Artillery Division
—Former 19 Artillery Division; at Stalingrad, Nov. 1942.
—Vyborg campaign, Svir River, June 1944.
—With 5 Breakthrough Artillery Corps, 1943–45.
—Lvov, Carpathian Military District w/1 Guards Artillery Divivision, June 1946 (Feb. 1947 OB).
—"Stalingrad."
Units: June 1944: 17 Heavy Howitzer Artillery, 18 Guards High Power Artillery, 23 Guards Light Artillery, 119 Heavy Howitzer Artillery Brigades.

5 Guards Rocket Barrage Division
—RVGK (SME).
—Baptism of fire, Kastornaya, "Katyusha equipped," Jan. 1943.
—RVGK, Jan. 1943.
—Kursk w/4 Breakthrough Artillery Corps, July 1943.
—Belorussian Op., June 1944.
—Iasi Kishinev Op., Aug. 1944.
—East Prussian Op., Jan. 1945.
—Berlin, Apr. 1945.
Units: June 1944: 16, 22, 23 Rocket Barrage Brigades.

6 Breakthrough Artillery Division
—With 8 Breakthrough Arty Corps, 1943–45.
—Belorussian Op., June 1944.

—Berlin Op., Apr. 1945.
—Rathenow, Germany with 4 Breakthrough Artillery Corps, 1946–49.
Units: Jan. 1946: 10 Artillery, 111 Howitzer Artillery Brigades.

6 Guards Breakthrough Artillery Division
—RVGK.
—Vistula Oder Op., Jan. 1945.
—Mongolia, June 1945.
—Manchuria, Aug. 1945.

6 Guards Rocket Barrage Division
—RVGK (SME).

7 Breakthrough Artillery Division
—Activated in the RVGK, Nov. 1942.
—RVGK to Stalingrad, Nov. 1942.
—Zaporozhye Bridgehead supporting 8 Guards Army, Oct. 1943.
—Vyborg Op., supporting 37 Guards Rifle Corps, June 1944.
—Regrouped to Rumania from Karelian Front via RVGK, July 1944.
—Tiraspol, Aug. 1944.
—Iasi Kishinev Op., Aug. 1944.
—Moldavia, Odessa Military District, May 1946 (EUCOM study and Apr. 1947 OB).
—"Zaporozhye."
Units: June 1944: 7 Gun Artillery, 25 Howitzer Artillery, 11 Light Artillery, 3 Rocket Barrage Brigades.

7 Guards Breakthrough Artillery Division
—RVGK

7 Guards Rocket Barrage Division
—Activated, Moscow, as Guards Rocket Barrage Division, Jan. 1943.
—RVGK (SME).
—Training until June, 1943.
—To 5 Breakthrough Artillery Corps for rest of war, July 1943.
—Spas-Demensk, supporting 33 Army in Smolensk Op., Aug. 1943.
—Lenino, Oct. 1943.
—Orsha Vitebsk area, Oct–Dec 1943.
—Belorussian Op., June 1944.
—Neman River, July 1944.
—Kaunos (Kovno), Aug. 1944.
—East Prussia, Oct. 1944.

—East Prussian Op., Jan. 1945.
—Koenigsberg, Apr. 1945.
—Zemland Peninsula, Apr. 1945.
—"Kaunos," Orders of Red Banner, Suvorov, Kutuzov.

8 Breakthrough Artillery Division
—Activated, Moscow, Nov. 1942.
—On Middle Don, Dec. 1942.
—Received a "unique" artillery regiment, Feb. 1943.
—Kharkov w/3 Tank Army, Feb. 1943.
—Reformed as 3 Guards Artillery Division of the RVGK, 7 Mar. 1943.
—Second formation raised at later date.
Units: Nov. 1942: 138, 206, 265 Howitzer, 38, 129 Gun Artillery, 288, 368, 374 Anti-Tank Regiments/Brigades; 619 Artillery Reconnaissance Battalion.
June 1944: 12 Gun Artillery, 28 Howitzer Artillery, 37 Light Artillery Brigades; 619 Artillery Reconnaissance Battalion.

9 Breakthrough Artillery Division
—RVGK.
—Zaporozhye Bridgehead supporting 8 Guards Army, Oct. 1943.
—With 3 Ukrainian Front, June 1944
—Szekesferhervar, Hungary supporting 4 Guards Army, Dec. 1944.
—Szentendre, Hungary, 1946 (Feb. 1947 OB).
—"Zaporozhye."
Units: June 1944: 30 Gun Artillery, 26 Light Artillery Brigades; 778 Artillery Reconnaissance Battalion.
Dec. 1944: 23 Howitzer Artillery, 115, 123 Gun Artillery, 10, 64 Mortar, 42 Antitank Brigades; 1440 Self-propelled Artillery Regiment.

10 Artillery Division
—Southwest Russia with 3 Ukrainian Front, June 1944.
—Gumbinnen, East Prussia in support of 28 Army, Jan. 1945.
Units: June 1944: 22 Light Artillery, 27 Gun Artillery Brigades, 621 Artillery Reconnaissance Battalion.

11 Artillery Division
—Activated in the RVGK, Nov. 1942.
—RVGK to Stalingrad,. Nov. 1942.
—Kirovograd, Jan. 1944.
—Probably Uman-Botosani Op. w/2 Ukrainian Front, Mar. 1944.

—Probably Targul Frumos w/2 Ukrainian Front, May 1944.
—Budapest, Dec. 1944.
—"Kirovograd."
Units: June 1944: 40 Howitzer Artillery, 45 Gun Artillery, 31 Light Artillery Brigades; 838 Artillery Reconnaissance Battalion.

12 Breakthrough Artillery Division
—Kursk with 4 Breakthrough Artillery Corps, July 1943.
—With 3 Belorussian Front, Belorussian Op., June 1944.
—Magnusew Bridgehead supporting 8 Guards Army, Aug. 1944.
—Pulawy Bridgehead (Radom-Lodz Op.), w/69 Army, Jan. 1945.
—With 4 Breakthrough Artillery Corps, 1943–45.
—Possibly at Plovdiv, Bulgaria, Jan. 1947 (Apr. 1947 OB).
Units: June 1944: 32 Howitzer Artillery, 41 Gun Artillery, 46 Light Artillery, 89 Heavy Howitzer, 104 Heavy Howitzer, 11 Rocket Barrage Brigades.
Feb. 1945: 32 Howitzer Artillery, 41 Gun Artillery, 46 Light Artillery, 89 Heavy Howitzer Artillery, 104 Heavy Howitzer Artillery, 125 Heavy Howizter Brigades, 11 Rocket Barrage Brigades.

13 Breakthrough Artillery Division
—RVGK.
—Kiev, Nov. 1943.
—Lvov-Sandomir Op., July–Aug. 1944.
—With 7 Breakthrough Artillery Corps, 1943–45.
—"Kiev," Order of Red Banner.
Units: June 1944: 42 Light Artillery, 47 Howitzer Artillery, 88 Heavy Howitzer Artillery, 91 Heavy Howitzer Artillery, 101 Heavy Howitzer Artillery, 17 Rocket Barrage Brigades.

14 Artillery Division
—Known to have existed.

15 Breakthrough Artillery Division
—Svir River, Vyborg Op., June 1944.
—East Prussian Op., Mar. 1945.
—RVGK.
—Order of Red Banner.
Units: June 1944: 35 Light Artillery, 18 Rocket Barrage Brigades.

16 Breakthrough Artillery Division
—RVGK.

—From Kursk, supporting 61 Army, to Voronezh Front, 15 July 1943.
—Kremenchug, supporting 5 Guards Army, Sep. 1943.
—Kirovograd, Jan. 1944.
—Uman-Botosani Op., Mar. 1944.
—"Kirovograd, Uman," Order of Red Banner.
Units: June 1944: 49 Light Artillery, 52 Howitzer Artillery, 61 Gun Artillery, 90 Heavy Howitzer, 109 High Power Artillery, 14 Mortar Brigades.

17 Breakthrough Artillery Division
—Activated Moscow area as 17 Artillery Division, Mar 1943.
—Mga w/8 Army, Mar. 1943.
—Received 97 Heavy Howitzer and 108 Super Heavy Howitzer Brigades; renamed 17 Breakthrough Artillery Division of the RVGK, Apr. 1943.
—Orel, Aug. 1943.
—Kiev, Nov. 1943.
—Kiev Defensive Op., Dec. 1943.
—Zhitomir-Berdichev Op., Jan. 1944.
—Korsun Shevchenkovskiy Op., Jan. 1944.
—Proskurov-Chernovtsy Op., Mar. 1944.
—Lvov-Sandomir Op. w/60 and 5 Guards Armies, July 1944.
—Sandomir-Silesia Op., Jan. 1945.
—Krakow, Jan. 1945.
—Ratibor, Berlin Op., Apr. 1945.
—With 7 Breakthrough Artillery Corps, 1943–45.
—"Kiev, Zhitomir," Orders of Lenin, Red Banner, Suvorov.
Units: June 1943: 22 Mortar, 32 Light Artillery, 50 Howitzer Artillery, 39 Gun Artillery, 97 Heavy Howitzer Artillery, 108 Super Heavy Howitzer Artillery Brigades. June 1944: 37 Light Arty, 39 Gun Artillery, 50 Howitzer Artillery, 92 Heavy Howitzer Artillery, 108 Heavy Howitzer Artillery, 22 Rocket Barrage Brigades.

18 Artillery Division
—Leningrad Front, June 1944.
—Klietz, Germany w/3 Mechanized Army, 19 Sep. 1946 (Feb. 1947 OB).
—"Gatchina" Order of Red Banner.
Units: June 1944: 6 Howitzer Artillery, 65 Light Artillery, 42 Rocket Barrage Brigades.

19 Artillery Division
—Activated in the RVGK, Nov. 1942.
—RVGK to Stalingrad, Nov. 1942.

—Became 5 Guards Artillery Division, 1943.
Units: Nov. 1942: 16 Light Artillery, 17 Heavy Howitzer Artillery, 18 Howitzer Artillery Brigades.

20 Breakthrough Artillery Division
—Kursk w/3 Army, June 1943.
—With 1 Baltic Front, June 1944.
—East Prussian Op., Feb. 1945.
Units: Sep. 1944: 52 Light Artillery, 60 Gun Artillery, 64 Howitzer Artillery, 93 Howitzer Artillery, 20 Rocket Barrage Brigades.

21 Artillery Division
—Dukhov, Sep. 1943.
—Baltic area, Sep. 1944.
—East Prussian Op., Feb. 1945.
—"Dukhovschina".
Units: Jan. 1945: 55 Howitzer Artillery, 65 Gun Artillery, 66 Gun Howitzer Artillery, 94 Heavy Howitzer, 103 Gun Artillery, 25 Rocket Barrage Brigades.

22 Breakthrough Artillery Division
—Gomel, Nov. 1943.
—"Gomel," Order of Red Banner.

23 Breakthrough Artillery Division
—RVGK.
—Leningrad Front, June 1944.
—East Prussian Op., Jan. 1945.
—"Gatchina."
Units: June 1944: 21 Heavy Howitzer Artillery, 38 Heavy Howitzer Artillery, 96 Heavy Howitzer Artillery, 120 Heavy Howitzer Artillery Brigades.

24 Artillery Division

25 Breakthrough Artillery Division
—With 3 Belorussian Front, June 1944.
—Ratibor, Mar. 1945.
Units: June 1944: 27 Guards Gun Artillery, 21 Rocket Barrage Brigades.

26 Artillery Division
—Crimea, supporting 51 Army, Apr. 1944.
—Southwest Russia w/4 Ukrainian Front, June 1944.

Units: June 1944: 56 Heavy Gun Artillery, 75 Light Artillery, 77 Howitzer Artillery Brigades.

27 Artillery Division
—With 2 Baltic Front, June 1944.
Units: June 1944: 74, 76, 78 Howitzer Artillery Brigades.

28 Artillery Division
—With Leningrad Front, June 1944.
Units: June 1944: 599 Howitzer Artillery Regiment.

29 Artillery Division
—Known to have existed.

30 Artillery Division
—Known to have existed.

31 Artillery Division
—Teltow Canal, Berlin Op. supporting 3 Guards Tank Army, Apr. 1945.
—Neuruppin, Germany, June 1946 (Feb. 1947 OB).

32 Artillery Division
—Known to have existed.

34 Breakthrough Artillery Division
—Southwest of Berlin, Germany, Jan. 1946 (Feb. 1947 OB).

38 Breakthrough Artillery Division
—Maritime Military District, Jan. 1947 (Feb. 1948 OB).

39 Artillery Division
—RVGK (FHO).
—With 3 Belorussian Front, June 1944.
Units: June 1944: 995 Howitzer Artillery, 1247, 1251 Light Artillery Regiments.

46 Artillery Division
—Known to have existed.

CHAPTER SIX

Guards Divisions

A total of 11 combined arms armies, 6 tank armies, a cavalry-mechanized group, 40 rifle, 12 tank, 9 mechanized and 14 aviation corps, and at least 117 rifle, 9 airborne, 17 cavalry, 6 artillery, 6 antiaircraft, 53 air and 7 mortar divisions became guards units. Some elite formations, such as guards mortar and guards airborne divisions, were designated guards upon their activation.

1 Guards Airborne Division
Units: 3, 6, 13 Guards Airborne Rifle, 4 Guards Airborne Artillery Regiments.
—Raised Tejkovo, Moscow Military District, from 4 Airborne Corps, probably in the RVGK, Dec. 1942.
—Vyazma, Dec. 1942.
—Demyansk, w/68 Army, Feb. 1943.
—Staraya Russa w/68 Army, Mar. 1943.
—Kremenchug, Sep. 1943.
—Dnieper River w/82 Independent Rifle Corps, 37 Army, Oct. 1943.
—Krivoi Rog-Kirovograd axis w/37 Army, Oct. 1943.
—Korsun Shevchenkovskiy op. w/53 Army (to end of war), Jan. 1944.
—Zvenigorod w/53 Army, Feb. 1944.
—Dniester River, Apr. 1944.
—Iasi Kishinev op., Aug. 1944.
—Hungary, Oct. 1944.
—Tisa river, Nov. 1944.
—Budapest, Dec. 1944.
—Czechoslovakian Mountains, Jan. 1945.
—Brno, May 1945.
—To Far East w/53 Army, June 1945.
—Khingan Mukden Op., Aug. 1945.
—North Korea, Jan. 1946 (Feb. 1947 OB).
—Probably an independent division.
—"Zvenigorod, Budapest," Orders of Red Banner, Suvorov, Bogdan Khmelnitskiy.

1 Guards Cavalry Division
—Activated near Balachov and Kherson, Oct. 1919.
—Designated 2 Cavalry Division; w/1 and 2 Cavalry Armies, Feb. 1920.
—Named in honor of M.F. Blinov, Mar. 1922.
—Redesignated 5 Cavalry Division, Aug. 1924.
—Designated Guards, w/1 Guards Cavalry Corps for rest of war, 26 Nov. 1941.
—Moscow axis, Nov. 1941.
—Zhizdra area, Aug. 1942.
—RVGK, Jan. 1943.
—Don Basin w/6 and 2 Tank Armies, Feb. 1943.
—Kharkov Op., Mar. 1943.
—Southwest Front reserve, Apr. 1943.
—Dnieper River, Sep. 1943.
—Kiev Op., Nov. 1943.
—Kiev Defensive Op. w/38 and 60 Armies, Dec. 1943.
—Kiev Zhitomir Op. w/1 Ukrainian Front, Jan. 1944.
—Rovno Lutsk Op. w/13 Army, Feb. 1944.
—Proskurov Chernovsty Op., Mar. 1944.
—Lvov Sandomir Op., w/Cavalry-Mechanized Group Baranov, July 1944.
—Carpathian Op., Sep. 1944.
—Sandomir Silesian Op. w/3 Guards Tank Army and 60 Army, Jan. 1945.
—Lower Silesian Op., Feb. 1945.
—Berlin Op., Apr. 1945.
—Prague Op., May 1945.
—"Stavropol, Zhitomir," Orders of Lenin, Red Banner, Suvorov, Bogdan Khmelnitskiy.

1 Guards Rifle Division
Units: 4, 7, 11 Guards Rifle, 20 Guards Artillery Regiment.
—Raised Berdichev, Kiev Military District, as 100 Rifle Division, before, 1941.
—Designated Guards, 18 Sep., 1941.
—Reformed as 1 Guards Mechanized Corps, Nov., 1942.
—Four Guards Rifle Regiment sent to 6 Guards Rifle Division, Nov. 1942.

1 Guards Rifle Division (second formation)
Units: 167, 169, 171 Guards Rifle, 35 Guards Artillery Regiment.
—Raised on order of the Revolutionary Committee as 1 "Moscow Proletarian" Rifle Division, Moscow, Dec. 1926.
—Two and 3 Rifle Regiments formed 126 and 115 Rifle Divisions; 1

Rifle Regiment formed the new 1 "Moscow Proletarian" Rifle Division, Sep. 1939.
—Reformed as 1 "Moscow Motorized Proletarian" Rifle Division, Jan. 1940.
—RVGK w/7 Mechanized Corps, June 1941.
—First unit to use the T-34 tank in combat, 30 June 1941.
—Temporarily designated 1 Tank Division; not equipped as tank division, Aug. 1941.
—Reformed as 1 Guards Motorized Rifle Division, Sep. 1941.
—Moscow w/33 Army, Oct. 1941.
—Right flank of Southwest Front, Dec. 1941.
—Vyazma axis, Jan–Apr 1942.
—Dorogobuzh, Mar. 1942.
—Bryansk Front w/48 Army, Aug. 1942.
—Rhzev Op., Nov. 1942.
—Reorganized as a Guards Rifle Division, Jan. 1943.
—To 11 Guards Army in the RVGK, May 1943.
—Orel Op. w/16 Guards Rifle Corps, 11 Guards Army, July 1943.
—Bryansk, Aug. 1943.
—Vitebsk axis, Nov. 1943–Apr. 1944.
—Gorodok, Dec. 1943.
—Belorussian Op., June 1944.
—Minsk, July 1944.
—Latvia, July 1944.
—Lithuania, Oct. 1944.
—East Prussian Op., Jan. 1945.
—Koenigsberg, Mar. 1945.
—Pillau (Baltiysk), Apr. 1945.
—Germany as the Group of Forces Germany Headquarters Reserve, May 1946 (Feb. 1947 OB).
—Reformed as a Motorized Rifle Division (SME), 1956–57.
—Dvina Maneuvers (SME), 1970.
—The 167 Guards Rifle Regiment Order of Red Star; 169 Guards Rifle Regiment Order of Red Banner; 171 Guards Rifle Regiment Order of Suvorov; 35 Guards Artillery Order of Kutuzov.
—"Proletarian, Moscow, Minsk," Orders of Lenin, Twice Red Banner, Orders Suvorov, Kutuzov.
Key Commanders: Col. A.I. Lizyukov, Nov. 1941; Gen-Maj N.A. Kropotin, 1943–44.

2 Guards Airborne Division
Units: 4, 5, 7 Guards Airborne Rifle and 3 Guards Airborne Artillery Regiments.

—Raised Zvenigorod, Moscow Military District, probably in the RVGK, Dec. 1942.
—RVGK w/18 Independent Guards Rifle Corps, Apr. 1943.
—Ponyri, w/18 Independent Guards Rifle Corps, 13 Army, May 1943.
—Kursk, (Ponyri) w/18 Independent Guards Rifle Corps, 13 Army, on the main defensive axis, July 1943.
—Dnieper River w/17 Guards Rifle Corps, 13 Army, Sep. 1943.
—Korsun Shevchenkovskiy Op., Jan. 1944.
—Proskurov Chernovtsy Op. w/47 Rifle Corps, 1 Guards Army, Mar. 1944.
—Leningrad Military District, Jan. 1946 (Feb. 1947 OB).
—Probably an independent division.
—"Carpathian, 2 u/i honorifics," Orders of Red Banner, Bogdan Khmelnitskiy.

2 Guards Cavalry Division
Units: 7 Guards Cavalry Regiment.
—Kashira w/43 Army, Dec. 1941.
—Sukinichi, Aug. 1942.
—Kiev Defensive Op., Dec. 1943.
—Kiev Zhitomir Op. w/1 Ukrainian Front, Jan. 1944.
—With 1 Guards Cavalry Corps during war, 1941–45.
—"Zhitomir, in the name of the Ukrainian SSR."

2 Guards Motorized Division
Units: 1, 2 Guards Motorized Rifle, 3 Guards Motorized Artillery Regiments.
—Formed Tula, Moscow Military District, as 107 Motorized Rifle Division, June 1941.
—Designated Guards, Feb. 1942.
—Rzhev Sychevka Op., Feb. 1942.
—Dissolved; absorbed into 2 Guards Mechanized Corps, Oct. 1942.
—The 1st Guards Motorized Rifle Regiment sent to 2 Guards Rifle Division, Oct. 1942.

2 Guards Rifle Division
Units: 1, 6 , 15 Guards Rifle, 21 Guards Artillery Regiment.
—Raised Kharkov, North Caucasus Military District, as 127 Rifle Division, July 1940.
—Designated Guards, 18 Sep. 1941.
—Glukhov, Sep. 1941.
—Kursk w/13 army, Dec. 1941.
—Rostov, Jan. 1942.

—Mius river, Feb–Mar 1942.
—Sevastopol, May 1942.
—Caucasus w/3 Guards Rifle Corps, July 1942.
—Terek River, Sep. 1942.
—Caucasus, w/37 Army, Aug–Nov 1942.
—Nalchik, North Caucasus w/37 Army, Jan. 1943.
—Krasnoarmeyskaya, Mar. 1943.
—Novorossiysk w/56 Army, Sep–Oct 1943.
—Kherson Gulf Bridgehead w/16 Rifle Corps, 56 Army, Nov. 1943.
—Crimea w/11 Guards Rifle Corps, Independent Coastal Army, Apr. 1944.
—Sevastopol, May 1944.
—Baltic area w/2 Guards Army (to end of war), July 1944.
—Memel, Oct. 1944.
—Latvia, Dec. 1944.
—East Prussian Op., Jan. 1945.
—Koenigsberg,, Apr. 1945.
—Awarded honorific "in the name of M.I. Kalinin," July 1946.
—Moscow, Jan. 1947 (EUCOM Study).
—Exercise Dvina as a Motorized Rifle Division (SME), 1970.
—"Show division" for Moscow parades, 1970's.
—The 1 Guards Rifle Regiment "Sevastopol," Orders of Red Banner, Suvorov, Alexander Nevsky; 6 Guards Rifle Regiment, "Sevastopol," Order of Red Banner; 15 Guards Rifle Regiment "Shauliai," Order of Red Banner; 21 Guards Artillery "Sevastopol," Order of Kutuzov.
—"Taman, in the name of M.I. Kalinin," Orders of Red Banner, Suvorov.
Key Commanders: Gen-Maj F.Z. Zakharov 1942–43; Gen-Maj A.P. Turchinskiy 1943–44.

3 Guards Airborne Division
Units: 2, 8, 10 Guards Airborne Rifle, 2 Guards Airborne Artillery Regiments.
—Raised Shchelkovo, Moscow Military District from 8 Airborne Corps; probably in the RVGK, Dec. 1942.
—Demyansk w/1 Shock Army, Jan. 1943.
—RVGK w/18 Independent Guards Rifle Corps, Apr. 1943.
—Kursk (Ponyri) w/18 Independent Guards Rifle Corps, 13 army, on main defensive axis, July 1943.
—Dnieper, Oct. 1943.
—Probably in the Kiev Op., Nov. 1943.
—Kiev Defensive Op. w/60 Army, Nov–Dec 1943.
—Zhitomir Berdichev Op., Jan. 1944.

—Prut River, Uman-Botosani Op. w/27 Army, Mar. 1944.
—Targul Frumos w/27 Army, May 1944.
—Iasi Kishinev Op. w/front shock group, Aug. 1944.
—Debrecen Op. w/4 Guards Army, Oct. 1944.
—Budapest, Nov. 1944.
—Lake Balaton, Mar. 1945.
—Vienna, Apr. 1945.
—Graz, May 1945.
—Probably an independent division.
—"Uman, Transylvania," Orders of Red Banner, Suvorov, Kutuzov.

3 Guards Cavalry Division
—With 2 Guards Cavalry Corps, 1942–45.

3 Guards Motorized Division
Units: 5, 6, 250 Guards Motorized Rifle, 66 Guards Artillery Regiments.
—Raised Bajan Tumen, Transbaikal Military District, July 1941 (FHO).
—Formed from 82 Motorized Rifle Division, Mar. 1942.
—Disbanded; incorporated into 6 Guards Mechanized Corps, June 1943.
—The 250 Guards Motorized Rifle Regiment to 83 Guards Rifle Division, Apr. 1943.
—Order of Red Banner.

3 Guards Rifle Division
Units: 5, 9, 13 Guards Rifle, 22 Guards Artillery Regiments.
—Raised Sverdlovsk, Ural Military District as 153 Rifle Division before 1941.
—Designated Guards, 18 Sep. 1941.
—Tikhvin area w/54 Army, Oct. 1941.
—Volkhov w/4 Army of the RVGK, Nov. 1941.
—Moscow w/16 Army, Dec. 1941.
—To Stalingrad, probably from the RVGK, Dec. 1942.
—Stalingrad axis, Dec. 1942.
—Kiev w/60 Army, Nov. 1943.
—South Ukraine w/13 Guards Rifle Corps, 2 Guards Army, Jan. 1944.
—Crimea w/13 Guards Rifle Corps, 2 Guards Army, Apr. 1944.
—Baltic region w/6 Guards Army, Oct. 1944.
—RVGK (FHO), Apr. 1945.
—Probably an independent division.
—"Yevpatoriya."

4 Guards Airborne Division
Units: 9, 12, 15 Guards Airborne Rifle, 1 Guards Airborne Artillery Regiments.

—Raised Moscow, Moscow Military District from Headquarters, 1 Airborne Corps, probably in the RVGK, Dec. 1942.
—RVGK to Demyansk w/1 Shock Army, Feb. 1943.
—Kursk axis w/53 Army in the RVGK, Mar. 1943.
—RVGK w/18 Guards Independent Rifle Corps, Apr. 1943.
—Kursk (Ponyri) w/18 Guards Independent Rifle Corps, 13 army, on the main defensive axis, July 1943.
—Orel, July 1943.
—Priluki w/60 Army, Sep. 1943.
—To 13 Army, Oct. 1943.
—Kiev Defensive Op., Nov–Dec 1943.
—Zhitomir Berdichev Op. w/28 Rifle Corps, 13 Army, Jan. 1944.
—Korsun Shevchenkovskiy Op. w/40 Army, Feb. 1944.
—Uman Botosani Op. w/40 Army, Mar. 1944.
—Khotin, Mar. 1944.
—Crossed Dniester River into Rumania, Mar. 1944.
—Targul Frumos w/52 Army, May, 1944.
—Iasi Kishinev Op. w/27 Army, Aug. 1944.
—Debrecen, Oct. 1944.
—Budapest, Dec. 1944.
—Hungary w/7 Guards Army (to end of war), Feb. 1945.
—Bratislava, Apr. 1945.
—Prague area, May 1945.
—Probably an independent division.
—"Ovruch, Pressburg" Orders of Red Banner, Suvorov, Bogdan Khmelnitskiy.

4 Guards Cavalry Division
—With 2 Guards Cavalry Corps, 1941–45.
—Moscow w/20 Army, Dec. 1941.
—Poland w/1 Guards Cavalry Corps, Mar. 1946 (Feb. 1947 OB).
—"Kuban Cossacks."

4 Guards Rifle Division
Units: 3, 8, 11 Guards Rifle, 23 Guards Artillery Regiments.
—Raised Minsk, Belorussia Military District as 161 Rifle Division before 1941.
—Located in Ural Military District, 22 June 1941.
—Designated Guards, 18 Sep. 1941.
—Tikhvin w/54 Army, Oct. 1941.
—With 4 Army of the RVGK, Volkhov, Leningrad Front, Nov. 1941.
—Basis for forming 6 Guards Rifle Corps, Feb. 1942.
—Stalingrad axis, Aug. 1942.

—Stalingrad offensive w/65 Army, Nov. 1942.
—Stalingrad Front w/5 Shock Army, Dec. 1942.
—Mius River w/31 Guards Rifle Corps, 5 Shock Army, Aug. 1943.
—Hungary w/31 Guards Rifle Corps, 4 Guards Army, Dec. 1944.
—RVGK, Apr. 1945 (FHO).
—Austria w/32 Guards Rifle Corps, 5 Guards Army, Nov. 1946 (Feb. 1947 OB).
—Uzhgorod Mukachevo, Carpathian Military District w/5 Guards Army, 1947 (Nov. 1947 OB).
—Probably an independent division of the RVGK.
—"Budapest," Orders of Red Banner, Bogdan Khmelnitskiy.

5 Guards Airborne Division
Units: 1, 11, 16 Guards Airborne Rifle, 6 Guards Airborne Artillery Regiments.
—Raised Kirshatsch, Moscow Military District, probably in the RVGK, Dec. 1942.
—Demyansk w/68 Army, Feb. 1943.
—Voronezh w/24 Army, Mar. 1943.
—Korsun Shevchenkovskiy Op. w/20 Guards Rifle Corps, 4 Guards Army, Jan. 1944.
—Zvenigorod, Feb. 1944.
—Dniester River, Apr. 1944.
—Iasi Kishinev Op., Aug. 1944.
—Hungary, w/4 Guards Army, Nov–Dec 1944.
—Budapest, Jan. 1945.
—Lake Balaton Op. Mar. 1945.
—"Zvenigorod," Order of Suvorov.

5 Guards Cavalry Division
—Stalingrad Axis, July 1942.
—With 3 Guards Cavalry Corps, 1942–45.
—North Caucasus Military District from the shrunken 5 Guards Cavalry Corps "Don Cossacks," 1946 (Feb. 1947 OB).

5 Guards Rifle Division
Units: 12, 17, 21 Guards Rifle, 24 Guards Artillery Regiment.
—Raised Moscow, Moscow Military District as 107 Rifle Division, Aug. 1939.
—Designated Guards, 26 Sep. 1941.
—Kaluga, Oct. 1941.
—Airlifted to Orel from the RVGK w/1 Guards Rifle Corps, Oct. 1941.
—Orel w/1 Guards Rifle Corps, 26 Army, Oct. 1941.

—Moscow Op. w/49 Army, Dec. 1941.
—In the Western Front reserve, May 1942–June 1943.
—Orel Op. w/36 Guards Rifle Corps, 11 Guards Army (rest of war), July 1943.
—Bryansk, Sep. 1943.
—Gorodok, Sep. 1943.
—Gorodok, Dec. 1943.
—Belorussian Op., June 1944
—Borisov, July 1944.
—Polotsk, July 1944.
—Gumbinnen axis, Oct. 1944.
—East Prussian Op., Jan. 1945.
—Koenigsberg, Apr. 1945.
—Pillau, May 1945.
—"Gorodok, Polotsk," Orders of Lenin, Red Banner, Suvorov.

6 Guards Airborne Division
Units: 14, 17 20 Guards Airborne Rifle, 8 Guards Airborne Artillery Regiments.
—RVGK when raised at Noginsk, Moscow Military District, from 6 Airborne Corps, Dec. 1942.
—Staraya Russa w/1 Shock Army, Mar. 1943.
—RVGK, Apr. 1943.
—Kursk (Prokhorovka), w/5 Guards Army, July 1943.
—Dnieper River, Sep. 1943.
—Kremenchug, Sep. 1943.
—Znamenka, Dec. 1943.
—Kirovograd w/33 Guards Rifle Corps, 5 Guards Army, Jan. 1944.
—Korsun pocket w/49 Rifle Corps, attached 5 Guards Tank Army, Jan. 1944.
—Uman Botosani Op. w/4 Guards Army, Mar. 1944.
—Dniester River, Apr. 1944.
—Targul Frumos, probably with 5 Guards Mechanized Corps, 5 Guards Tank Army, May 1944.
—Iasi Kishinev Op. w/7 Guards Army; took Targul Frumos, Aug. 1944.
—Debrecen Op., Oct. 1944.
—Hungary w/20 Guards Rifle Corps, 4 Guards Army, Nov. 1944.
—Budapest w/7 Guards Army (rest of war), Dec. 1944.
—Bratislava, Mar. 1945.
—Prague, May 1945.
—Probably an independent division.
—"Kremenchug, Znamenka, Iasi, Roman, Pressburg," Orders of Red Banner, Suvorov.

6 Guards Cavalry Division
—Activated as 14 Cavalry Division, 1 Cavalry Army, Feb. 1920.
—Honorific "in the name of General Parkhemenko," 1928.
—Designated Guards, Dec. 1941.
—With 3 Guards Cavalry Corps, 1941–45.
—Yeletsk axis, spring 1942.
—Stalingrad axis, July 1942.
—Stalingrad axis, Sep. 1942.
—Don Basin, Dec. 1942.
—RVGK, May 1943.
—Smolensk, Sep. 1943.
—Belorussian Op. in cavalry-mechanized group, June 1944.
—Grodno, July 1944.
—East Prussian Op., Jan. 1945.
—Elbe River, Apr. 1945.
—Southeast of Wittenberg, May 1945.
—"Grodno, Lida," Orders of Lenin, Red Banner, Suvorov, Kutuzov, Red Star.

6 Guards Rifle Division
Units: 4, 10, 25 Guards Rifle, 34 Guards Artillery Regiments.
—Raised Orel, Orel Military District as 120 Rifle Division, July 1941 (SME).
—Designated Guards, 26 Sep. 1941.
—RVGK, Sep. 1941.
—Airlifted to Orel w/1 Guards Rifle Corps from the RVGK, Oct. 1941.
—Orel Bryansk Defensive Op. w/1 Guards Rifle Corps 26 Army, Oct. 1941.
—Tula w/50 Army, Dec. 1941.
—Orel axis, May 1942.
—Bryansk Front w/48 Army, Aug. 1942.
—Kursk w/17 Guards Rifle Corps, 13 Army; later 60, 70 Armies, July 1943.
—Orel, Aug. 1943.
—Dnieper River w/17 Guards Rifle Corps, 13 Army, Sep. 1943.
—Crossed Pripet River, Sep. 1943.
—Kiev, Nov. 1943.
—Kiev Defensive Op., Dec. 1943.
—Zhitomir Berdichev Op., Jan. 1944.
—Rovno Lutsk Op. w/76 Rifle Corps, 13 Army; took Rovno, Feb. 1944.
—Zvenigorod w/53 Army, Feb. 1944.
—Lvov Sandomir Op., July 1944.
—Neisse River w/13 Army, Apr. 1945.

—Berlin Op., Apr. 1945.
—Prague Op., May 1945.
—The 4 Guards Rifle Regiment from original 1 Guards Rifle Division.
—"Rovno," Orders of Lenin, Red Banner, Suvorov.

7 Guards Airborne Division
Units: 18, 21, 29 Guards Airborne Rifle, 10 Guards Airborne Artillery
　　　Regiments.
—Raised Ramenskoye, Moscow Military District, probably in the RVGK, Dec. 1942.
—Demyansk w/68 Army, Feb. 1943.
—Voronezh w/24 Army, Mar. 1943.
—Korsun Shevchenkovskiy Op. w/73 Rifle Corps, 52 Army, Jan. 1944.
—Dniester River, Apr. 1944.
—Iasi w/53 Army, Apr. 1944.
—Targul Frumos w/53 Army, May 1944.
—Iasi Kishinev Op., Aug. 1944.
—Hungary w/20 Guards Rifle Corps, 4 Guards Army, Nov. 1944.
—Budapest, Jan. 1945.
—Probably an independent division.
—"Cherkassy, in the name of the Comintern," Order of Red Banner.

7 Guards Cavalry Division
Units: Jan. 1943: 111, 114, 116 Guards Cavalry Regiments.
—Activated at Voronezh as 31 Cavalry Division, July 1941.
—Kaluga w/1 Guards Cavalry Corps (most of war), Dec. 1941.
—Designated Guards, 5 Jan. 1942.
—Zhizder River, Aug–Sep 1942.
—Don Basin w/1 Guards Cavalry Corps, 6 army, Feb. 1943.
—Kharkov Op., Mar. 1943.
—Left Bank Ukraine, Sep. 1943.
—Dnieper River, Oct. 1943.
—Kiev Offensive Op., Nov. 1943.
—Kiev Defensive Op. w/60 Army at Korosten, Dec. 1943.
—Kiev Zhitomir Op. w/1 Ukrainian Front, Jan. 1944.
—Rono Lutsk Op. w/13 Army, Feb. 1944.
—San River, July 1944.
—Sanok, Poland, Aug. 1944.
—Czechoslovakian Mountains, Sep. 1944.
—Sandomir Silesian Op., Feb. 1945.
—Berlin Op., Apr. 1945.
—Elbe River, Apr. 1945.
—"Zhitomir," Orders of Red Banner, Suvorov, Bogdan Khmelnitskiy.

7 Guards Rifle Division
Units: 14, 20, 26 Guards Rifle, 25 Guards Artillery Regiments.
—Raised Smolensk, Moscow Military District as 64 Rifle Division, before June 1941.
—Designated Guards, Oct. 1941.
—Moscow w/49 Army, Nov. 1941.
—RVGK from 16 Army, Dec. 1941.
—Belgorod Kharkov Op. (Akhtyrka), Aug. 1943.
—Leningrad Military District, Aug. 1946 (EUCOM Study).
—Leningrad Military District w/7 Guards Rifle Corps, 10 Guards Army, Jan. 1946 (Feb. 1947 OB).
—Inactivated by Feb. 1948 (Feb 1948 OB).

8 Guards Airborne Division
Units: 22, 25, 27 Guards Airborne Rifle, 9 Guards Airborne Artillery Regiments.
—Raised Moscow Military District, probably from an airborne corps in the RVGK, Dec. 1942.
—Demyansk w/68 Army, Feb. 1943.
—Voronezh w/24 Army, Mar. 1943.
—Kirovograd w/24 Guards Rifle Corps, 7 Guards Army, Jan. 1944.
—Grigoriopol, Apr. 1944.
—Targul Frumos w/7 Guards Army, May 1944.
—RVGK w/39 Guards Rifle Corps, Independent Airborne Army, later 9 Guards army, Nov–Dec 1944.
—Redesignated 107 Guards Rifle Division, Dec. 1944.
—Southeast of Budapest, Feb. 1945.
—Vienna, Apr. 1945.
—Prague Op., May 1945.
—"Pervomaysk."

8 Guards Cavalry Division
—Probably in Southwest Poland, w/6 Guards Cavalry Corps, July 1944.
—Stalingrad, North Caucasus Military District w/4 Guards Cavalry Corps, Apr. 1946 (Feb. 1947 OB).

8 Guards Rifle Division
Units: 19, 23, 30 Guards Rifle, 27 Guards Artillery Regiments.
—Raised Alma Ata, Central Asia Military District as 316 Rifle Division, July 1941.
—Designated Guards, 18 Nov. 1941.
—Volokolamsk, Nov. 1941.

—Moscow, assault division of 16 Army in Moscow Counteroffensive, Dec. 1941.
—To the RVGK from 16 Army, 17 Dec. 1941.
—Orel w/11 Guards Army, July 1943.
—Belgorod Kharkov Op. (Akhtyrka) w/4 Guards Army, Aug. 1943.
—Served w/3 Shock Army off and on, 1942–44.
—Belorussia Op., June 1944.
—With 10 Guards Army 1944–45.
—Latvia, Jan. 1945.
—Leningrad Military District w/7 Guards Rifle Corps, 10 Guards Army, Apr. 1946 (Feb. 1947 OB).
—Alma Ata, Turkestan Military District, Sep. 1947 (1948 OBs).
—The 19 Guards Rifle Regiment has the honorific "Talgar."
—"Rzhev, Rechitsa, in the name of Panfilov" Orders of Lenin, Red Banner, Suvorov.
Key Commanders: Gen-Maj I.V. Panfilov, July–Nov. 1941; Gen-Maj I.M. Chistyakov, Jan–Apr 1942.

9 Guards Airborne Division
Units: 23, 26, 28 Guards Airborne Rifle, 7 Guards Airborne Artillery Regiments.
—SME says activated Moscow Military District, probably from 1 Airborne Corps in the RVGK, Dec. 1942.
—Demyansk w/1 Shock Army, Feb. 1943.
—RVGK, May 1943.
—Staraya Russa (w/5 Guards Army to end of war), May 1943.
—Kursk w/29 Tank Corps, 5 Guards Tank Army (Prokhorovka), July 1943.
—Poltava, Sep. 1943.
—Vorskla River, Sep. 1943.
—Kremenchug, Sep. 1943.
—Aleksandriya, Oct. 1943.
—Kirovograd w/33 Guards Rifle Corps, 5 Guards Army, Jan. 1944.
—Ivanovka, Mar. 1944.
—Pervomaysk, Apr. 1944.
—Lvov Sandomir Op., w/33 Guards Rifle Corps; main assault division, July 1944.
—Oder River, Jan. 1945.
—Sandomir Bridgehead, breakthrough division, Jan. 1945.
—Sandomir Silesia Op., Feb. 1945.
—Berlin Op., Apr. 1945.
—Spremberg, Apr. 1945.

—Prague Op., May 1945.
—"Poltava," Orders of Red Banner, Suvorov, Kutuzov.

9 Guards Cavalry Division
—Activated as 12 "Kuban Cossacks" cavalry division at Krasnodar, Jan. 1942.
—Units based on "volunteer 100's of the Kuban Cossack People's Militia," Jan. 1942.
—Designated Guards, 27 Aug. 1942.
—With 4 Guards Cavalry Corps, 1942–45.
—Mozdok region, Sep. 1942–Feb. 1943.
—Stavropol axis, Mar. 1943.
—Defended Bay of Taganrog Coast, Mar–July 1943.
—Don Basin, Aug–Sep 1943.
—Melitopol Op., Oct. 1943.
—Defended Sea of Azov Coast, Nov. 1943–Feb. 1944.
—Odessa, Apr. 1944.
—Belorussian Op., w/4 Guards Cavalry Corps in Cavalry-Mechanized Group Pliyev, June 1944.
—Slutsk, Slonim, Baranovichi, July 1944.
—Debrecen, Oct. 1944.
—Budapest, Dec. 1944.
—Bratislava Brno Op. w/1 Guards Cavalry-Mechanized Group, Mar. 1945.
—Prague Op., May 1945.
—Stalingrad, North Caucasus Military District w/4 Guards Cavalry Corps, May 1946 (Feb. 1947 OB).
—"Kuban Cossacks, Slonim, Luminets, Baranovichi," Twice order of Red Banner, Orders of Suvorov, Kutuzov, Bogdan Khmelnitskiy.

9 Guards Rifle Division
Units: 18, 22, 28 Guards Rifle, 31 Guards Artillery Regiments.
—Raised Khabarovsk, Far East Military District, as 78 "Siberian" Rifle Division, May 1940.
—Far East to European front, Oct. 1941.
—Istra, Moscow front, Nov. 1941.
—Designated Guards, 18 Nov. 1941.
—Vyazma, Jan. 1942.
—Oskol River, Stalingrad axis w/38 Army, July 1942.
—Krasnodar, Feb. 1943.
—Belgorod Kharkov Op., Aug. 1943.
—Vistula River w/8 Guards Army, Aug. 1944.
—Vistula Oder Op. w/5 Guards Army, Jan. 1945.

—Probably an independent division.
—Orders of Lenin, Red Banner.
Key Commanders: Col. A.P. Beloborodov, 1941–42.

10 Guards Airborne Division
Units: 19, 24, 30 Guards Airborne Rifle, 5 Guards Airborne Artillery Regiments.
—Formed, Dimitrov, Moscow Military District, probably from an airborne corps in the RVGK, Dec. 1942.
—Demyansk w/68 Army, Feb. 1943.
—Assault division for crossing Dnieper River w/82 Independent Rifle Corps, 37 Army, Oct. 1943.
—Southwest Ukraine w/82 Independent Rifle Corps, 37 army, Jan. 1944.
—Dniester River, Apr. 1944.
—Iasi Kishinev Op., Aug. 1944.
—RVGK, Aug. 1944 (FHO).
—Pecs, Hungary, Nov. 1944.
—Tulcea, Rumania, Jan. 1946 (Sep. 1947 OB).

10 Guards Cavalry Division
Units: 36, 40, 42 Guards Cavalry Regiments.
—Activated at Krasnodar as 13 "Kuban Cossack," Cavalry; Civil War veterans made up more than 75% of the division when it was formed, Jan. 1942.
—Basis of division units was the "volunteer hundreds of the Kuban Cossacks Peoples Militia," Jan. 1942.
—With 4 Guards Cavalry Corps, 1942–45.
—Designated Guards, 27 Aug. 1942.
—Mozdok region, Sep. 1942–Feb. 1943.
—Stavropol axis, Feb. 1943.
—Southern Front reserve, Mar. 1943.
—Rostov, Aug–Sep 1943.
—Melitopol Op., Oct. 1943.
—Defended Sea of Azov coast, Nov. 1943–Feb. 1944.
—Odessa, Apr. 1944.
—Belorussian Op. w/4 Guards Cavalry Corps, Cavalry-Mechanized Group Pliyev, June 1944.
—Slutsk, Slonim, Baranovichi w/Cavalry-Mechanzied Group Pliyev, July 1944.
—Debrecen Op., Oct. 1944.
—Budapest, Dec. 1944.
—Bratislava Brno Op. w/1 Guards Cavalry-Mechanzied Group, Mar. 1945.

—Prague Op., May 1945.
—Stalingrad, North Caucasus Military District w/4 Guards Cavalry Corps, Apr. 1946 (Feb. 1947 OB).
—All cavalry regiments Order of Red Banner; 36 Guards Cavalry Regiment also Orders of Suvorov, Alexander Nevskiy; 40 Guards Cavalry Regiment also Orders of Kutuzov, Alexander Nevskiy; 42 Guards Cavalry Regiment also Orders of Suvorov, Bogdan Khmelnitskiy.
—"Kuban Cossacks, Slutsk, Baranovichi," Orders of Red Banner, Suvorov, Kutuzov, Bogdan Khmelnitskiy.

10 Guards Rifle Division
Units: 24, 28, 35 Guards Rifle, 29 Guards Artillery Regiments.
—Activated at Moscow as 52 Rifle Division, 1935.
—Designated Guards, 25 Dec. 1941.
—Probably on the Murmansk front w/14 Army, 1942–44.
—Petsamo Kirkenes Op., w/99 Rifle Corps, 14 Army, Oct. 1944.
—Reequipped, Nov. 1944–Jan. 1945.
—East Prussia w/19 army (rest of war), Jan. 1945.
—Danzig area, Mar. 1945.
—Baltic coast near Colberg, Apr. 1945.
—Berlin Op., Apr. 1945.
—RVGK (FHO), Apr. 1945.
—The 35 Guards Rifle Regiment is also associated w/55 Guards Rifle Division.
—"Petsamo (Pechenga), Kirkenes," Twice Order of Red Banner, Orders of Alexander Nevskiy, Red Star.

11 Guards Airborne Division
—With 37 Guards Rifle Corps, Independent Airborne Army, Oct. 1944.
—RVGK, Nov–Dec 1944.
—Redesignated 104 Guards Rifle Division, Dec. 1944.

11 Guards Cavalry Division
—Tuapse Defensive Op. w/18 Army, 25 Sep–20 Dec, 1942.
—Korsun Shevchenkovskiy Op. w/5 Guards Cavalry Corps, 2 Ukrainian Front, Jan. 1944.
—Targul Frumos w/5 Guards Cavalry Corps, 7 Guards Army, May 1944.
—"Don Cossacks, Verchnedneprovsk."

11 Guards Rifle Division
Units: 27, 33, 40 Guards Rifle, 30 Guards Artillery Regiments.
—Raised Kazan, Volga Military District, Nov. 1939.

—Moscow as 18 Moscow People's Volunteer Division, Nov. 1941.
—Designated Guards, Jan. 1942.
—Orel w/8 Guards Rifle Corps, 11 Guards Army, July 1943.
—Bolkhov Op.; a breakthrough division, July 1943.
—Gorodok, Sep. 1943.
—Belorussian Op., June 1944.
—Orsha, June 1944.
—Vistula Oder Op.; a breakthrough division, Jan. 1945.
—East Prussia, Mar. 1945.
—"Gorodok, Kaunas (Kovno)."

12 Guards Airborne Division
—With 38 Guards Rifle Corps, Independent Airborne Army, Oct. 1944.
—RVGK, Nov-Dec 1944.
—Redesignated 105 Guards Rifle Division, Dec. 1944.

12 Guards Cavalry Division
—Tuapse Defensive Op. w/18 Army, 25 Sep-20 Dec 1942.
—Korsun Shevchenkovskiy Op. w/5 Guards Cavalry Corps, 2 Ukrainian Front, Jan. 1944.
—Targul Frumos, w/5 Guards Cavalry Corps, 7 Guards Army, May 1944.
—"Cherkassy."

12 Guards Rifle Division
Units: 29, 32, 37 Guards Rifle, 31 Guards Artillery Regiments.
—Raised Orel, Moscow Military District as 258 Rifle Division, July 1941.
—Designated Guards, Jan. 1942.
—Western Front reserve, Jan. 1942.
—Basis for forming 9 Guards Rifle Corps, Apr. 1942.
—Second formation division activated, 1942.
—Apparently w/9 Guards Rifle Corps, 61 Army entire war, 1942-45 (SME).
—Bolkhov axis, Nov. 1942.
—Mtsenk River, June 1943.
—Bolkhov Op. as breakthrough division, July 1943.
—Desna River, Sep. 1943.
—Dnieper River, Sep. 1943.
—Belorussia, Jan. 1944.
—Belorussia, Mar. 1944.
—Belorussia Op., June 1944.
—Sandomir Bridgehead, July 1944.
—Riga, Oct. 1944.

—Vistula Oder Op., jan. 1945.
—Berlin Op., Apr. 1945.
—Order of Red Banner, has an u/i honorific.

13 Guards Airborne Division
—RVGK, Jan. 1944.
—Redesignated 98 Guards Rifle Division, Jan. 1944.
—Second formation w/37 Guards Rifle Corps, Independent Airborne Army, Oct. 1944.
—RVGK, Nov–Dec 1944.
—Redesignated 103 Guards Rifle Division, Dec. 1944.

13 Guards Cavalry Division
—Dubno w/6 Guards Cavalry Corps, Feb. 1944.
—Probably in Southeast Poland w/6 Guards Cavalry Corps, Aug. 1944.

13 Guards Rifle Division
Units: 34, 39, 42 Guards Rifle, 32 Guards Artillery Regiments.
—SME says raised at Kursk from 3 Airborne Corps as 87 Rifle Division, Nov. 1941.
—Designated Guards, 19 Jan. 1942.
—Kharkov axis w/38 and 28 Armies, Mar–July 1942.
—Don River, July 1942.
—Refitted in Stalingrad Military District, Aug. 1942.
—RVGK, Sep. 1942.
—Stalingrad; took Mamaev Hill w/62 Army, Sep. 1942.
—RVGK, Feb–July 1943.
—Kursk w/5 Guards Army (to end of war), July 1943.
—Belogorod Kharkov Op.; broken through by SS Panzer Division "Das Reich," Aug. 1943.
—Vorskla River, Sep. 1943.
—Poltava, Sep. 1943.
—Kremenchug, Sep. 1943.
—Krivoi Rog, Oct. 1943.
—Kirovograd w/33 Guards Rifle Corps, Jan. 1944.
—Uman Botosani Op., Mar. 1944.
—Pervomaysk, Mar. 1944.
—Lvov Sandomir Op. w/32 Guards Rifle Corps, July 1944.
—Vistula Oder Op. (Czestochowa) w/32 Guards Rifle Corps; 42 Guards Rifle Regiment the assault regiment, Jan. 1945.
—Lower Silesia, Feb–Apr 1945.
—Berlin Op.; in shock grouping, Apr. 1945.
—Prague, May 1945.

—Austria, (Feb. 1947 ob) as 13 Guards Motorized, later mechanized division w/32 Guards Rifle Corps, 1946 (Feb. 1948 OB).
—"Poltava, Silesia, Transylvania," Orders of Lenin, twice Red Banner, Suvorov, Kutuzov.
Key Commanders: Gen-Maj Rodimtsev, 1941–43.

14 Guards Airborne Division
—RVGK, Jan. 1944.
—Reformed as 99 Guards Rifle Division, Jan. 1944.
—Second formation with 39 Guards Rifle Corps, Independent Airborne Army, Oct. 1944.
—RVGK, Nov–Dec 1944.
—Redesignated 114 Guards Rifle Division, Dec. 1944.
—Southeast of Budapest w/9 Guards Army, Feb. 1945.
—Prague Op., May 1945.

14 Guards Cavalry Division
—Former 21 Mountain Cavalry Division, 1941.
—Designated Guards, 14 Feb. 1943.
—With 7 Guards Cavalry Corps (rest of war), 1943–45.
—Chernigov, Sep. 1943.
—Mozyr, Jan. 1944.
—Lublin Brest op., July 1944.
—East Pomeranian Op., Feb. 1945.
—Berlin Op., Apr. 1945.
—Brandenburg, Apr. 1945.
—"Lublin."

14 Guards Rifle Division
Units: 36, 38, 41 Guards Rifle, 33 Guards Artillery Regiments.
—Activated at Vinnitsa, Dec. 1923.
—Designated "in the name of Jana Fabritsiusa," Sep. 1929.
—Reformed as 96 Mountain Rifle Division, Apr. 1940.
—Designated Guards, 24 Jan. 1942.
—With 37 Army, Jan. 1942.
—Izyum axis w/57 Army, Feb. 1942.
—RVGK w/5 Reserve Army, June 1942.
—Stalingrad axis w/21 and 63 Armies, June 1942.
—Stalingrad offensive w/5 Tank Army, Nov. 1942.
—Don Basin, Jan–Feb 1943.
—Kharkov Defensive Op., Mar. 1943.
—Belgorod Kharkov Op., Aug. 1943.
—Dnieper River, Sep. 1943.

—Krivoi Rog, Oct–Dec 1943.
—Kirovograd w/48 Rifle Corps, 53 Army, Jan. 1944.
—Zvenigorod w/53 Army, Feb. 1944.
—Uman Botosani Op. w/5 Guards Army, Mar. 1944.
—Crossed Dniester River, Apr. 1944.
—Lvov Sandomir Op. w/33 Guards Rifle Corps, 5 Guards Army, July 1944.
—Sandomir Bridgehead as breakthrough division, Jan. 1945.
—Vistula Oder w/5 Guards Army, Jan. 1945.
—Breslau, Feb. 1945.
—Dresden, May 1945.
—Prague Op. w/5 Guards Army, May 1945.
—Papa, Hungary w/31 Guards Rifle Corps, 5 Guards Army, Sep. 1946 (Feb. 1947 OB).
—"Vinnitsa, in the name of Jana Fabritsiusa," Orders of Lenin, Red Banner, Kutuzov.

15 Guards Airborne Division
—RVGK, Jan. 1944.
—Redesignated 100 Guards Rifle Division, Jan. 1944.

15 Guards Cavalry Division
—Former 55 Cavalry Division, 1941.
—Designated Guards, 14 Feb. 1943.
—With 7 Guards Cavalry Corps (rest of war), 1943–45.
—Chernigov, Sep. 1943.
—Mozyr, Jan. 1944.
—Lublin Brest Op., July 1944.
—East Pomeranian Op., Feb. 1945.
—Berlin Op., Apr. 1945.
—Brandenburg, Apr. 1945.
—"Lublin."

15 Guards Rifle Division
Units: 44, 47, 50 Guards Rifle, 43 Guards Artillery Regiments.
—Raised as 17 "Gorki" Rifle Division, 1918.
—In civil war, received Order of Red Banner, honorific "in the name of K.Ye. Voroshilov," 1922.
—Reactivated at Gorki as 136 Rifle Division, Sept. 1939.
—Finnish War 1939–40.
—To Leninakan, Transcaucasus after Finnish War, 1940.
—Designated Guards, 16 Feb. 1942.
—Don Basin, Feb–Apr 1942.

—RVGK, June 1942.
—Kharkov Offensive w/28 Army, June 1942.
—To Stalingrad from 57 Army, July 1942.
—Stalingrad area w/64 Army, July 1942.
—Stalingrad area w/51 Army, Oct. 1942.
—Kharkov w/3 Tank Army, Jan. 1943.
—Volchansk w/7 Guards Army, Apr. 1943.
—Kursk w/7 Guards Army, July 1943.
—Kharkov w/7 Guards Army, Aug. 1943.
—Dnieper River w/49 Rifle Corps, 7 Guards Army, Sep. 1943.
—Southwest Ukraine w/57 Rifle Corps, 37 Army, Jan. 1944.
—Liberated Krivoi Rog, Feb. 1944.
—Odessa area, Mar–Apr 1944.
—Dniester River, took Tiraspol, Apr. 1944.
—RVGK, June 1944.
—Lvov Sandomir Op. w/34 Guards Rifle Corps, 5 Guards Army (to end of war), July 1944.
—Poland, summer–fall 1944.
—Vistula Oder Op., Jan. 1945.
—RVGK, Apr. 1945 (FHO).
—Berlin Op., Apr. 1945.
—Prague, May 1945.
—Rumania, 1946 (Feb. 1947 OB).
—The 44 Guards Rifle Regiment "Silesia," Orders of Red Banner, Alexander Nevsky; 47 Guards Rifle Regiment "Prague," Orders of Red Banner, Bogdan Khmelnitskiy; 50 Guards Rifle Regiment "Czestochowa," Red Banner; 43 Guards Artillery "Oder," Orders of Red Banner, Suvorov.
—"Kharkov, Prague," Orders of Lenin, twice Red Banner, Suvorov, Kutuzov.
Key Commanders: Gen-Maj Ye.I. Vasilenko 1941–44.

16 Guards Airborne Division
—With 38 Guards Rifle Corps, Independent Airborne Army, later 9 Guards Army, Oct. 1944.
—RVGK, Nov–Dec 1944.
—Redesignated 106 Guards Rifle Division, Dec. 1944.

16 Guards Cavalry Division
—Former 112 Cavalry Division, June 1941.
—Designated Guards, 14 Feb. 1943.
—With 7 Guards Cavalry Corps (rest of war), 1943–45.
—Chernigov, Sep. 1943.

—Mozyr, Jan. 1944.
—Lublin Brest Op., July 1944.
—East Pomeranian Op., Feb. 1945.
—Berlin Op., Apr. 1945.
—Brandenburg, Apr. 1945.
—Thuringia, Germany, Mar. 1946; (Aug. 1946 OB).
—"Bashkirich, Lublin."

16 Guards Rifle Division
Units: 43, 46, 49 Guards Rifle, 44 Guards Artillery Regiments.
—Raised Ural Military District as 249 Rifle Division from "picked frontier guards," before July 1941.
—Designated Guards, Feb. 1942.
—Orel Op. w/16 Guards Rifle Corps, 11 Guards Army, July 1943.
—Karachev, Aug. 1943.
—Orsha, June 1944.
—Neman River, July 1944.
—Koenigsberg, Mar–Apr 1945.
—RVGK (FHO), Apr. 1945.
—Baltic Military District, 1947 (Feb. 1948 OB).
—"Karachev, Orsha, Neman," Orders of Lenin, Red Banner.

17 Guards Cavalry Division
—Brest area w/2 Guards Cavalry Corps, Aug. 1944.

17 Guards Rifle Division
Units: 45, 48, 52 Guards Rifle, 26 Guards Artillery Regiments.
—Raised at Krasnoyarsk, Siberia Military District as 119 Rifle Division, before 1941.
—Designated Guards, Mar. 1942.
—Kalinin Front w/41 Army, May 1942.
—Dukhov, Sep. 1943.
—Gomel w/3 Army, Nov. 1943.
—Vitebsk w/5 Guards Rifle Corps, 39 Army; assault division, June 1944.
—Borodino area, July 1944.
—Kovno, Aug. 1944.
—Vistula Oder Op. w/5 Guards Army, Jan. 1945.
—RVGK, Apr. 1945 (FHO).
—Chinhsien, China w/5 Guards Rifle Corps, 39 Army, Feb. 1947 (Feb. 1948 OB).
—"Dukhov, Vitebsk, Kaunas (Kovno)," Order of Red Banner.

18 Guards Rifle Division
Units: 51, 53, 58 Guards Rifle and 52 Guards Artillery Regiments.

—Raised Biysk, Siberia Military District as 133 Rifle Division before 1941.
—Guards, Mar. 1942.
—Orel Op. w/36 Guards Rifle Corps, 11 Guards Army, July 1943.
—RVGK, Apr. 1945 (FHO).
—Danzig, Poland w/70 Army, Apr. 1946 (Feb. 1947 OB).
—Siberia Military District, 1948 (EUCOM Study).

19 Guards Rifle Division
Units: 54, 56, 61 Guards Rifle, 45 Guards Artillery Regiments.
—Raised Novosibirsk, Siberia Military District as 336 Rifle Division (FHO), Nov. 1941.
—Activated at Tomsk, Siberia Military District as 366 Rifle Division (SME), Aug–Nov 1941.
—To 2 Shock Army in Leningrad area, Nov. 1941.
—Guards, 17 Mar. 1942.
—Leningrad area w/2 Shock Army, May 1942.
—Veliki Luki w/3 Shock Army, Dec 1942–Feb 1943.
—Central Front w/39 Army (to end of war), Aug. 1943.
—Rudna, Aug. 1943.
—Smolensk Op., Sep. 1943.
—Vitebsk axis, Oct. 1943-Mar 1944.
—Took Borisov, July 1944.
—Vitebsk, w/5 Guards Rifle Corps; assault division, July 1944.
—Took Kaunos, Aug. 1944.
—East Prussia, Oct. 1944.
—East Prussian Op., Jan. 1945.
—Koenigsberg, Apr. 1945.
—Zemland Peninsula, Apr. 1945.
—RVGK, Apr. 1945 (FHO).
—Regrouped to Far East w/39 Army, May 1945.
—Mukden Khingan Op., Aug. 1945.
—"Rudnya, Borisov, Khingan," Orders of Lenin, Red Banner, Suvorov.

20 Guards Rifle Division
Units: 55, 57, 60 Guards Rifle, 46 Guards Arty Regiments.
—Raised in Kurgan, Ural Military District as 174 Rifle Division, Aug. 1940.
—Designated Guards, 17 Mar. 1942.
—Rzhev Op. w/31 Army, Aug–Sep 1942.
—Stalingrad axis, Dec. 1942.
—To Southwest Front, Feb. 1943.
—North of Donestk w/6 Army, Mar. 1943.
—Dnieper River w/46 Army, Oct. 1943.

—Krivoi Rog, Dec. 1943.
—Nikopol Krivoi Rog Op. w/6 Guards Rifle Corps, 46 Army; took Krivoi Rog, Feb. 1944.
—Odessa w/46 Army, Apr. 1944.
—Iasi Kishinev Op. w/6 Guards Rifle Corps, 37 Army, Aug. 1944.
—Bulgaria w/37 Army, Sep. 1944.
—Reequipped, Oct. 1944.
—Budapest w/57 Army (to end of war), Nov. 1944.
—Lake Balaton Op., Mar. 1945.
—Vienna, Mar. 1945.
—RVGK, Apr. 1945 (FHO).
—Graz, May 1945.
—Focsani, Rumania as 25 Mechanized Division, Jan. 1946 (July 1947 OB).
—"Krivoi Rog, Lower Dniester, Danube," Orders of Red Banner, Suvorov.

21 Guards Rifle Division
Units: 59, 64, 69 Guards Rifle, 47 Guards Artillery Regiments.
—Raised at Ufa, Ural Military District as 361 Rifle Division, Oct. 1941.
—Guards, Mar. 1942.
—Velkiye Luki w/3 Shock Army, Nov. 1942.
—Nevel Op. w/3 Shock Army Mobile Group, Oct. 1943.
—Belorussian Op., June 1944.
—Polotsk, July 1944.
—"Nevel, Polotsk."

22 Guards Rifle Division
Units: 62, 65, 67 Guards Rifle, 48 Guards Artillery Regiments.
—Raised Sverdlovsk, Ural Military District as 363 Rifle Division, Sep. 1941.
—Guards, Mar. 1942.
—Northwest Front w/53 Army, Apr. 1942.
—Germany 1946, (Feb. 1947 OB).
—"Latvian," Order of Lenin.

23 Guards Rifle Division
Units: 49, 63, 66 Guards Rifle, 68 Guards Artillery Regiment.
—Raised Archangelsk, Archangelsk Military District as 88 Rifle Division before 1941.
—Designated Guards, Mar. 1942.
—Karelian Front w/23 Army, Mar. 1942.
—Northwest Front w/1 Shock Army, July 1943.

—Kiev Defensive Op., Dec. 1943.
—Kiev Zhitomir Op., Jan. 1944.
—Ostrov w/1 Shock Army, July 1944.
—Schniedemuhl, Jan. 1945.
—Kustrin Bridgehead w/3 Shock Army, Apr. 1945.
—Biederitz, Germany w/12 Guards Rifle Corps, 3 Mechanized Army, Sep. 1946 (Feb. 1948 OB).
—"Walcz, Dno."

24 Guards Rifle Division
Units: 70, 71, 72 Guards Rifle, 50 Guards Artillery Regiments.
—Raised Vologda, Archangelsk Military District as 111 Rifle Division, June 1940.
—Designated Guards, Mar. 1942.
—Leningrad (Volkhov area), 1941–42.
—Sinyavino (Leningrad), July 1942.
—To Stalingrad axis w/2 Guards Army, Dec. 1942.
—North Caucasus, Jan. 1943.
—Rostov, Feb. 1943.
—Ukraine, fall 1943.
—Southwest Ukraine w/10 Guards Rifle Corps, 28 Army, Jan. 1944.
—Crimea w/13 Guards Rifle Corps, 2 Guards Army, Apr. 1944.
—Sevastopol, Crimea, May 1944.
—Lithuania, Oct. 1944.
—East Prussian Op., Jan. 1945.
—Koenigsberg, Mar. 1945.
—The 71 Guards Rifle Regiment Orders of Red Banner, Bogdan Khmelnitskiy; 72 Guards Rifle Regiment "Koenigsberg."
—"Yevpatoriya," Order of Red Banner.
Key Commanders: Gen-Maj P.K. Koshevoy 1942–43; Gen-Maj P.I. Sakeyev (KIA) 1943; Col. G.Ya. Kolesnikov 1944; Col. P.N. Domrachev, 1944–45.

25 Guards Rifle Division
Units: 73, 78, 81 Guards rifle, 53 Guards Artillery Regiments.
—Formed at Kalinin, Moscow Military District as 25 Guards Rifle Division on basis of 2 Guards Red Banner Rifle Brigade (former 71 Naval Rifle Brigade), Apr–May 1942.
—RVGK w/2 Reserve Army, May 1942.
—Kharkov Offensive w/6 Army, May–June 1942.
—Storozhevoye Bridgehead, Aug–Nov 1942.
—Ostrogosh Rossosh Bridgehead w/40 Army, Jan. 1943.
—Kharkov w/3 Tank Army, Feb. 1943.

—Taranovka, Mar. 1943.
—Sinelnikov, Sep. 1943.
—Dnieper River w/6 Army, Oct. 1943.
—Krivoi Rog w/8 Guards Army, Oct. 1943.
—Kirovograd w/53 Army, Dec. 1943.
—With 26 Guards Rifle Corps, 2 Ukrainian Front, Jan. 1944.
—Korsun Shevchenkovskiy Op. w/53 Army, Jan. 1944.
—Uman Botosani Op., Mar. 1944.
—Iasi, Apr. 1944.
—Targul Frumos, May 1944.
—Iasi Kishinev Op. (Focsani), Aug. 1944.
—Carpathian Mountain passes (Husi), Aug. 1944.
—RVGK (FHO), Aug. 1944.
—Hungary w/7 Guards Army, Oct. 1944.
—Budapest, Jan. 1945.
—Bratislava Brno Op., Apr. 1945.
—Prague, May 1945.
—Motorized Rifle Division by 1964 (SME).
—Honorific "in the name of V.I. Chapayev" to carry on traditions of 25 Rifle Division (SME).
—Awarded Lenin Jubilee Prize, 1970.
—Garrisoned in Kiev Military District, 1982 (MHJ).
—The 73 Guards Rifle Regiment "Pugachev;" 78 Guards Rifle Regiment "Stepan Razin;" 81 Guards Rifle Regiment "Domaska."
—"Sinelnikov, Budapest," Orders of Red banner, Suvorov, Bogdan Khmelnitskiy, in the name of V.I. Chapayev.
Key Commanders: Gen-Maj T.K. Kolomiyets 1942; Col. K.V. Bilyutin 1943; Gen-Maj Shafarenko, 1942–43.

26 Guards Rifle Division
Units: 75, 77, 79 Guards Rifle, 57 Guards Artillery Regiments.
—Raised at Chita, Transbaikal Military District as 93 Rifle Division "East Siberian," 1936.
—Designated Guards, 20 Apr. 1942.
—Bryansk axis w/20, 33, 16 and 11 Guards Armies, 1942–43.
—Orel Op. w/8 Guards Rifle Corps, 11 Guards Army, July 1943.
—East Belorussia w/11 Guards Army, Oct. 1943.
—Gorodok w/11 Guards Army (apparently to end of war), Dec. 1943.
—Orsha, June 1944.
—Berezina River, June 1944.
—Borisov, July 1944.
—East Prussia, Aug. 1944.
—East Prussia, Jan. 1945.
—Koenigsberg, Mar. 1945.

—Pillau, Apr. 1945.
—Rugenwalde, Poland w/70 Army, Nov. 1946 (Feb. 1947 OB).
—"East Siberian, Gorodok," Orders of Red Banner, Suvorov.

27 Guards Rifle Division
Units: 74, 76, 83 Guards Rifle and 54 Guards Artillery Regiments.
—Takes history from 75 Naval Rifle later 3 Guards Rifle Brigade; activated in 2 Shock Army (SME), Dec. 1941.
—Honorific "Omsk" to preserve combat traditions of 27 Rifle Division (SME).
—Raised Sselisharovo, Moscow Military District as 3 Guards Rifle Brigade, May 1942 (FHO).
—Reformed as 27 Guards Rifle Division, 21 May 1942.
—Kalinin Front w/39 and 52 Armies, Aug. 1942.
—Stalingrad front w/1 Guards, 24, 65 and 66 Armies, Aug. 1942.
—Stalingrad Counteroffensive w/65 Army, Nov. 1942.
—Stalingrad, breakthrough division of 62 army, Jan. 1943.
—With 29 Guards Rifle Corps, 8 Guards Army (to end of war), Mar. 1943.
—Don Basin, Aug. 1943.
—Barvenkovo, Sep. 1943.
—Zaporozhye Bridgehead, 10–14 Oct. 1943.
—Korsun Shevchenkovskiy Op., Jan. 1944.
—Ingulets River, Mar. 1944.
—Odessa, Apr. 1944.
—Sandomir Bridgehead, July 1944–Jan. 1945.
—Vistula Oder Op.; breakthrough division, Jan. 1945.
—Poznan, Feb. 1945.
—Kustrin Bridgehead, Feb. 1945.
—Berlin Op., Apr. 1945.
—Koslin, Poland w/70 Army, Apr. 1947 (Feb. 1948 OB).
—"Omsk, Novobug, Korsun, Posen," Orders of Red Banner, Bogdan Khmelnitskiy.

28 Guards Rifle Division
Units: 86, 89, 92 Guards Rifle, 61 Guards Artillery Regiments.
—Raised at Weissenstein, Ostsee as 180 Rifle Division before 1941.
—Designated Guards, May 1942.
—Kharkov w/53 Army, Aug. 1943.
—Southwest Ukraine w/82 Independent Rifle Corps, 37 Army, Jan. 1944.
—Iasi Kishinev Op. w/37 Army, Aug. 1944.
—Bulgaria w/10 Mechanized Army, Sep. 1946 (Feb. 1947 OB).
—"Kharkov."

29 Guards Rifle Division
Units: 87, 90, 93 Guards Rifle, 62 Guards Artillery Regiments.
—Formed Vladivostok, Far East Military District as 32 Rifle Division, 1934.
—Guards, May 1942.
—Southwest Ukraine w/57 Rifle Corps, 37 Army, Jan. 1944.
—Riga, Oct. 1944.
—"Yelnaya, Riga."

30 Guards Rifle Division
Units: 94, 96, 98 Guards Rifle, 63 Guards Artillery Regiments.
—Raised Kazakstan, Central Asia Military District as 238 Rifle Division, 1941.
—Guards, May 1942.
—Kiev Defensive Op., Dec. 1943.
—Kiev Zhitomir Op., Jan. 1944.
—Riga, Oct. 1944.
—Weimar, Germany w/9 Rifle Corps, 5 Mechanized Army, Aug. 1946 (Feb. 1947 OB).
—"Latvian, Riga, Zhitomir," Order of Red Banner.

31 Guards Rifle Division
Units: 95, 97, 99 Guards Rifle, 64 Guards Artillery Regiments.
—Raised Yaroslavl, Moscow Military District as 328 Rifle Division (SME), Sep. 1941.
—Guards, 24 May 1942.
—Bryansk, July 1942.
—Orel axis, Feb. 1943.
—Orel w/16 Guards Rifle Corps, 11 Guards Army (rest of war), July 1943.
—Vitebsk, Belorussian Op., June 1944.
—Neman River, July 1944.
—East Prussia, Oct. 1944.
—East Prussian Op., Jan. 1945.
—Gvardeysk, Feb. 1945.
—Koenigsberg, Apr. 1945.
—"Vitebsk" Orders of Lenin, Red Banner, Suvorov.

32 Guards Rifle Division
Units: 80, 82, 85 Guards Rifle, 58 Guards Artillery Regiments.
—Formed in the North Caucasus Military District from 2 Airborne Corps, May 1942.
—Maikop Tuapse Line, July 1942.

—From Taman to Krasnodar, Caucasus w/18 Army, Aug. 1942.
—Tuapse Defensive Op. w/18 Army, Sep–Dec 1942.
—Krasnodar, Jan. 1943.
—Kuban River, Feb. 1943.
—Kerch landing w/16 Rifle Corps, 56 Army, Nov. 1943.
—Crimea w/11 Guards Rifle Corps, 4 Ukrainian Front, Apr. 1944.
—Sevastopol, May 1944.
—South of Shauliai, Aug. 1944.
—Budapest, Dec. 1944.
—Hungary, Jan. 1945.
—"Taman, Sevastopol, Budapest, Feodosiya," Orders of Red Banner, Suvorov.

33 Guards Rifle Division
Units: 84, 88, 91 Guards Rifle, 59 Guards Artillery Regiments.
—Formed in the North Caucasus Military District from 3 Airborne Corps, June 1942.
—RVGK w/7 Reserve Army, June 1942.
—To Stalingrad axis (Kalach area), w/62 Army, July 1942.
—South Ukraine w/1 Guards Rifle Corps, 2 Guards Army, Jan. 1944.
—Crimea w/1 Guards Rifle Corps, 51 Army, Apr. 1944.
—Sevastopol, May 1944.
—Siauliai, Aug. 1944.
—Riga, Oct. 1944.
—Silesia, Jan. 1945.
—Koenigsberg; assault division (84 Guards Rifle Regiment was assault regiment), Apr. 1945.
—Baltic Military District, Apr. 1946, (EUCOM study).
—Developed "Laws of the Soviet Guards."
—"Sevastopol, Silesia, Ponowiec, Siauliai, Riga."

34 Guards Rifle Division
Units: 103, 105, 107 Guards Rifle, 84 Guards Artillery Regiments.
—Formed in Moscow, Moscow Military District from 7 Airborne Corps, Aug. 1942.
—To Stalingrad axis w/28 Army, Aug. 1942.
—Stalingrad Counteroffensive w/28 Army, Nov. 1942.
—Mius River w/31 Guards Rifle Corps, 5 Shock Army, Aug. 1943.
—Iasi Kishinev Op., Aug. 1944.
—RVGK, Aug. 1944 (FHO).
—Hungary w/31 Guards Rifle Corps, 4 Guards Army, Sep–Dec 1944.
—Lake Balaton Op. w/31 Guards Rifle Corps, 4 Guards Army, Mar. 1945.

—Gdansk, Mar. 1945.
—"Jenakiyevo."

35 Guards Rifle Division
Units: 100, 101, 102 Guards Rifle, 112 Guards Artillery Regiments.
—Raised Chaklovsk, Moscow Military District from 8 Airborne Corps, Aug. 1942.
—Stalingrad w/57 and 62 Armies, Aug–Oct 1942.
—Counterattacked near Stalingrad, 23 Aug. 1942.
—RVGK, Oct. 1942.
—Stalingrad Counteroffensive w/1 Guards Army, Nov. 1942.
—RVGK, Dec. 1942.
—Don Basin w/Southwest Front, Dec. 1942.
—Starobelsk, Jan. 1943.
—Took Pavlograd, Feb. 1943.
—Kharkov Defensive Op., Mar. 1943.
—Lozovaya, Sep. 1943.
—Dnieper River w/8 Guards Army (to end of war), Oct. 1943.
—Krivoi Rog, Oct. 1943.
—Nikopol/Krivoi Rog w/4 Guards Rifle Corps, Jan. 1944.
—Ingulets River, Mar. 1944.
—Odessa, Apr. 1944.
—Lublin Brest Op., July 1944.
—Vistula River, Aug. 1944.
—Magnuszew Bridgehead, Aug. 1944–Jan. 1945.
—Warsaw Poznan Op., Jan. 1945.
—Kustrin Bridgehead, Feb. 1945.
—Berlin w/4 Guards Rifle Corps, Apr. 1945.
—"Lozovaya," Orders of Red Banner, Suvorov, Kutuzov.

36 Guards Rifle Division
Units: 104, 106, 108 Guards Rifle, 65 Guards Artillery Regiments.
—Formed Ivanov, Moscow Military District from 9 Airborne Corps, Aug. 1942.
—Stalingrad front w/57 and 64 Army, Aug. 1942–Feb. 1943.
—Donetsk River w/64 Army, Mar. 1943.
—Kursk w/7 Guards Army (Southeast of Belgorod), July 1943.
—Belgorod Kharkov area, Aug. 1943.
—Dnieper River, Sep. 1943.
—Kirovograd w/24 Guards Rifle Corps, 7 Guards Army, Jan. 1944.
—Uman Botosani Op. w/5 Guards Army, Mar. 1944.
—Prut River, Apr. 1944.
—Iasi, Apr. 1944.

—Targul Frumos, May 1944.
—Iasi Kishinev Op., w/7 Guards Army, Aug. 1944.
—Debrecen Op. w/7 Guards Army, Oct. 1944.
—Hungary w/7 Guards Army, Oct. 1944–Jan. 1945.
—Lake Balaton w/26 Army, Mar. 1945.
—Vienna, Mar. 1945.
—The 104 Guards Rifle Regiment is "Iasi."
—"Dneprovsk," Orders of Red Banner, Suvorov, Kutuzov.

37 Guards Rifle Division
Units: 109, 114, 118 Guards Rifle, 86 Guards Artillery Regiments.
—Raised at Lubertsy, Moscow Military District from 1 Airborne Corps, July 1942.
—SME says activated at Moscow from 1 Airborne Corps, Aug. 1942.
—Southwest Front w/4 Tank Army, Aug. 1942.
—Don River, Sep. 1942.
—Stalingrad w/62 Army (Barrikady, Tractor factories), Oct. 1942.
—Called elite division in Stalingrad, Oct. 1942.
—Destroyed in Tractor Factory, Stalingrad, Oct. 1942.
—RVGK, Dec. 1942.
—Central Front w/65 Army (rest of war), Feb. 1943.
—Army reserve on Sevsk axis, June 1943.
—Orel, Aug. 1943.
—Left Bank Ukraine, Aug–Oct 1943.
—Southeast Belorussia, Jan. 1944.
—Bobruysk Op, main assault division of 18 Independent Rifle Corps, 65 Army, June 1944.
—Slonim, July 1944.
—Narew River, Sep. 1944.
—Vistula Oder Op., Jan. 1945.
—East Prussia Op. w/2 Shock Army, Feb. 1945.
—Gdansk, Mar. 1945.
—Berlin Op., Apr. 1945.
—Rostock, May 1945.
—"Rechitsa," twice Order of Red Banner, Orders of Suvorov, Kutuzov, Bogdan Khmelnitskiy.

38 Guards Rifle Division
Units: 110, 113, 115 Guards Rifle, 88 Guards Artillery Regiments.
—Formed from 4 Airborne Corps at Tejkovo, Moscow Military District, July 1942.
—To Stalingrad axis, Aug. 1942.
—"Volga Corridor" w/1 Guards Army, Sep. 1942.

—Stalingrad Counteroffensive, Nov. 1942.
—RVGK, Dec. 1942.
—Donbas w/Southwest Front, Dec. 1942.
—Lozovaya, Sep. 1943.
—Belorussia w/114 Rifle Corps, 70 Army, Mar. 1944.
—Danzig area w/70 Army, Mar. 1945.
—RVGK, Apr. 1945 (FHO).
—"Lozovaya" Order of Red Banner.

39 Guards Rifle Division
Units: 112, 117, 120 Guards Rifle, 87 Guards Artillery Regiments.
—Formed in Moscow, Moscow Military District from 5 Airborne Corps, Aug. 1942.
—To Stalingrad axis w/1 Guards Army, Aug. 1942.
—"Volga Corridor" w/1 Guards Army, Sep. 1942.
—Stalingrad w/62 Army; 4 months in Red October Factory, Sep. 1942.
—Stalingrad Offensive, Nov. 1942.
—Izyum Barvenkovo axis w/8 Guards Army (to end of war), Aug. 1943.
—Zaporozhye Bridgehead, 10–14 Oct. 1943.
—Dnepropetrovsk, Oct. 1943.
—Southwest Ukraine w/28 Guards Rifle Corps, Jan. 1944.
—Novy Bug, Mar. 1944.
—Odessa, Apr. 1944.
—Lvov Sandomir Op., July 1944.
—Vistula River, Magnuszew Bridgehead, Aug. 1944–Jan. 1945.
—Warsaw Poznan Op., Jan. 1945.
—Posen w/28 Guards Rifle Corps, Feb. 1945.
—Kustrin Bridgehead, Feb. 1945.
—Berlin, took the Tiergarten, Apr. 1945.
—Rudolstadt, Germany w/4 Guards Rifle Corps, 8 Guards Army, Aug. 1946 (Feb. 1947 OB).
—The 117, 120 Guards Rifle Regiments, 87 Guards Artillery are "Posen."
—"Barvenkovo," Orders of Lenin, twice Red Banner, Suvorov, Bogdan Khmelnitskiy.

40 Guards Rifle Division
Units: 111, 116, 119 Guards Rifle, 90 Guards Artillery Regiments.
—Formed Moscow, Moscow Military District from 6 Airborne Corps, Aug. 1942.
—Stalingrad w/1 Guards Army, Aug. 1942.
—Stalingrad Counteroffensive w/65 Army, Nov. 1942.
—Stalingrad Counteroffensive w/5 Tank Army, Dec. 1942.

—Don Basin w/5 Shock Army, Jan–Feb 1943.
—Mius River w/31 Guards Rifle Corps, 5 Shock Army, Aug. 1943.
—Yenakiev, Sep. 1943.
—Krivoi Rog Nikopol w/46 Army, Jan. 1944.
—Odessa, Apr. 1944.
—Iasi Kishinev Op., Aug. 1944.
—Hungary w/31 Guards Rifle Corps, 46 Army, Nov. 1944.
—Budapest w/21 Guards Rifle Corps, 4 Guards Army, Dec. 1944–Feb. 1945.
—Vienna, Mar. 1945.
—"Jenakiyevo (Yenakiev), Danube," Orders of Red Banner, Suvorov.

41 Guards Rifle Division
Units: 122, 124, 126 Guards Rifle, 89 Guards Artillery Regiments.
—Formed at Moscow, Moscow Military District from 10 Airborne Corps, June 1942.
—Stalingrad axis, Aug. 1942.
—"Volga Corridor" w/1 Guards Army, Sep. 1942.
—Stalingrad Counteroffensive, Nov. 1942.
—RVGK, Dec. 1942.
—Donbas, Dec. 1942.
—Kirovograd w/24 Guards Rifle Corps, 7 Guards Army, Jan. 1944.
—Korsun Shevchenkovskiy Op. w/24 Guards Rifle Corps, 7 Guards Army; Zhukov says distinguished itself, Jan. 1944.
—Uman Botosani Op. w/4 Guards Army, Mar. 1944.
—Dniester River, Apr. 1944.
—Iasi Kishinev Op., Aug. 1944.
—Hungary w/21 Guards Rifle Corps, 4 Guards Army, Nov. 1944.
—Budapest w/4 Guards Army, Jan. 1945.
—"Korsun, Kishinev, Budapest" Order of Red Banner.

42 Guards Rifle Division
Units: 127, 132, 136 Guards Rifle, 75 Guards Artillery Regiments.
—Formed on basis of the 1 Guards Red Banner Rifle Brigade; called "The Guards Red Banner Rifle Division," July 1942.
—Rzhev Defensive Op., Aug. 1942.
—Renamed 42 Guards Rifle Division, Sep. 1942.
—Stalingrad, Nov. 1942.
—Rzhev Bridgehead w/31 Army, Mar. 1943.
—RVGK w/5 Guards Army, Steppe Front, May 1943.
—Kursk, July 1943.
—Belgorod Kharkov Op., Aug. 1943.
—Priluki, Sep. 1943.

—Dnieper River w/40 Army, Oct. 1943.
—Kiev, Nov. 1943.
—Kiev Zhitomir Defensive Op., Dec. 1943.
—Zhitomir Berdichev Op., Jan. 1944.
—Uman Botosani Op., Mar. 1944.
—Prut River, Mar. 1944.
—Targul Frumos w/7 Guards Army, May 1944.
—Iasi Kishinev Op., Aug. 1944.
—Hungarian border (Carpathian Mountains), w/51 Rifle Corps, 40 Army, Sep. 1944.
—Debrecen Op., Oct. 1944.
—Budapest, Nov 1944–Feb 1945.
—Western Carpathian Mountains, Mar. 1945.
—Prague Op. w/53 Army, May 1945.
—Probably an independent division.
—"Priluki, Prut," Orders of Lenin, Red Banner, Bogdan Khmelnitskiy.
Key Commanders: Gen-Maj F.A. Bobrov, Sep. 1944.

43 Guards Rifle Division
Units: 121, 123, 125 Guards Rifle, 94 Guards Artillery Regiments.
—Raised Gorki, Moscow Military District as 201 Rifle Division, Aug. 1941.
—Guards, Oct. 1942.
—Probably on Northwest Front, 1942–43.
—Into Northwest Front Reserve, May 1943.
—Northwest Front Reserve w/14 Guards Rifle Corps, July 1943.
—Baltic area, Sep. 1944.
—Baltic Military District w/129 Rifle Corps, 6 Guards Army, Oct. 1945 (Feb. 1947 OB).
—"Latvian."

44 Guards Rifle Division
Units: 128, 130, 133 Guards Rifle, 95 Guards Artillery Regiments.
—Raised at Kurgan, Ural Military District as 5 Rifle Division "Saratov" (SME), 1918.
—Renamed "Vitebsk" Rifle Division, 1921.
—Raised Polotsk, Western Special Military District as 5 Rifle Division before 1941 (FHO).
—Designated Guards, 5 Oct. 1942.
—Stalingrad offensive w/1 Guards Army, Nov. 1942.
—Don Rostov railroad, Jan. 1943.
—Gomel Op. w/65 Army (to end of war), Nov. 1943.
—Bobruysk Op. w/Indpendent 18 Rifle Corps; breakthrough division, June 1944.

—Baranovichi, July 1944.
—Bug River, Aug. 1944.
—Narev River, Sep. 1944.
—Vistula Oder Op., 65 Army reserve, Jan. 1945.
—Warsaw Poznan Op., Jan. 1945.
—East Prussia Op.; breakthrough division, Jan. 1945.
—Danzig area, Mar. 1945.
—Oder Op. as 65 Army reserve, Apr. 1945.
—The 128 and 130 Guards Rifle Regiments, 95 Guards Artillery, "Stettin," 133 Guards Rifle Regiment "Gdansk."
—"Baranovichi, Vitebsk," Orders of Lenin, Red Banner, Suvorov.

45 Guards Rifle Division
Units: 129, 131, 134 Guards Rifle, 96 Guards Artillery Regiments.
—SME says raised at Kuibyshev, Volga Military District as 70 Rifle Division, 1934.
—FHO says raised at Kingisepp, Leningrad Military District as 70 Rifle Division, before 1941.
—The 70 Rifle Division was designated one of the four best divisions in the Red Army, Oct., 1940.
—Designated Guards; one regiment made up of naval infantry, 16 Oct. 1942.
—Leningrad area w/67, 55, 42 and 2 Shock Armies, Jan. 1943–Feb. 1944.
—Leningrad Offensive w/67 Army as breakthrough division, Jan. 1943.
—Krasnoselysk, Jan. 1944.
—Out of combat and reequipped, probably in RVGK, Mar–June 1944.
—Karelia, June 1944.
—Breakthrough division for Vyborg Op. w/21 Army, June 1944.
—Ema-Igi River w/30 Guards Rifle Division, 2 Shock Army, Sep. 1944.
—Tallinn w/2 Shock Army, Sep. 1944.
—Estonia w/30 Guards Rifle Corps, 2 Shock Army, Oct. 1944.
—Defended Tallinn coast w/8 Army, Nov. 1944.
—Courland Peninsula, Feb–May 1945.
—Ventspils, May 1945.
—All regiments have the honorific "Leningrad."
—Awarded honorific "in the name of A.A. Zhdanov," Oct. 1948.
—Probably an independent division.
—"Krasnoselysk, in the name of A.A. Zhdanov," Orders of Lenin, Red Banner.

46 Guards Rifle Division
Units: 135, 139, 141 Guards Rifle, 97 Guards Artillery Regiments.

—Raised Starobelsk, Kharkov Military District, as 170 Rifle Division, Apr. 1942.
—Designated Guards, Oct. 1942.
—From Don Front to Veliki Luki, Oct. 1942.
—Velikiye Luki w/3 Shock Army, Dec. 1942.

47 Guards Rifle Division
Units: 137, 140, 142 Guards Rifle, 99 Guards Artillery Regiments.
—Raised Ulyanovsk, Volga Military District as 154 Rifle Division before 1941.
—Designated Guards, Oct. 1942.
—To Stalingrad area, Oct. 1942.
—Stalingrad Counteroffensive w/5 Tank Army, Nov. 1942.
—Smolensk, Sep. 1943.
—Southwest Ukraine w/4 Guards Rifle Division, 8 Guards Army, Jan. 1944.
—Vistula River w/8 Guards Army, Aug. 1944.
—Magnuszew Bridgehead, Aug. 1944.
—The 140 Guards Rifle Regiment is also associated w/49 Guards Rifle Division.

48 Guards Rifle Division
Units: 138, 143, 146 Guards Rifle, 98 Guards Artillery Regiments.
—Raised Svyatogorsk, Kharkov Military District as 264 Rifle Division (second formation), May 1942.
—Designated Guards, Oct. 1942.
—Ostrogosh Rossosh Op. w/3 Tank Army, Jan. 1943.
—Kharkov Op. w/3 Tank Army, Feb. 1943.
—Dnieper River, Oct. 1943.
—Krivoi Rog w/27 Guards Rifle Corps, 37 Army, Jan. 1944.
—Gumbinnen, Oct. 1944.
—RVGK, Apr. 1945 (FHO).
—Teltow Canal, Berlin Op, Apr. 1945.
—"Krivoi Rog, Gumbinnen," Order of Red Banner.

49 Guards Rifle Division
Units: 144, 147, 149 Guards Rifle, 100 Guards Artillery Regiments.
—Raised Lev Tolstoi, Moscow Military District, Nov. 1942.
—Designated Guards, Nov. 1942.
—To Stalingrad axis, Dec. 1942.
—Probably in Southern Russia, 1943.
—South Ukraine w/13 Guards Rifle Corps, 2 Guards Army, Jan. 1944.
—Budapest, Jan. 1945.
—"Budapest."

50 Guards Rifle Division
Units: 148, 150, 152 Guards Rifle, 119 Guards Artillery Regiments.
—Raised Voronezh, Oral Military District as 124 Rifle Division (second formation), Dec. 1941.
—Designated Guards, Nov. 1942.
—Stalingrad Counteroffensive w/5 Tank Army, Nov. 1942.
—With 3 Guards Army, Dec. 1942.
—North Caucasus area w/5 Shock Army, Apr. 1943.
—Stalina, Sep. 1943.
—Zaporozhye Bridgehead w/8 Guards Army, 10–14 Oct. 1943.
—South Ukraine w/3 Guards Rifle Corps, 5 Shock Army, Jan. 1944.
—Nikopol, Feb. 1944.
—RVGK, Mar. 1944 (SME).
—Nikolayev, Apr. 1944.
—Belorussia w/28 Army, May 1944.
—Belorussian Op. w/3 Guards Rifle Corps, 28 Army, June 1944.
—Baranovichi w/28 Army, July 1944.
—Gumbinnen w/28 Army, Oct. 1944.
—East Prussia Op, Jan. 1945.
—Koenigsberg, Apr. 1945.
—Berlin, Apr. 1945.
—Prague, May 1945.
—Baranovichi, Belorussia Military District w/3 Guards Rifle Corps, 28 Army, May 1947 (Feb. 1948 OB).
—"Stalina (Donetsk), Nikopol, Baranovichi, Gumbinnen, Insterburg" Twice order of the Red Banner, Orders of Suvorov, Kutuzov.

51 Guards Rifle Division
Units: 154, 156, 158 Guards Rifle, 122 Guards Artillery Regiments.
—Raised Nakichevan, Transcaucasus Military District as 76 Rifle Division, before June 1941.
—Designated Guards, Nov. 1942.
—Kursk w/6 Guards Army, July 1943.
—Kharkov w/23 Rifle Corps, 6 Guards Army, Aug. 1943.
—Vitebsk, June 1944.
—Prague, May 1945.
—"Vitebsk, Polotsk, Armansk," Order of Red Banner.
Key Commanders: Col. (later Army General) V.A. Penkovskiy May–Aug 1942.

52 Guards Rifle Division
Units: 151, 153, 155 Guards Rifle, 124 Guards Artillery Regiments.
—Activated at Voronezh, Orel Military District as an NKVD Motorized Rifle Division, Dec. 1941.

—Redesignated 8 NKVD Motorized Rifle Division, Jan. 1942.
—Reformed as 63 Rifle Division, July 1942.
—Served w/21 and later 6 Guards Armies, summer 1942.
—Designated Guards while at Stalingrad, Nov. 1942.
—Belgorod w/21 Army, Mar. 1943.
—Voronezh Front w/23 Guards Rifle Corps, Apr. 1943.
—Kursk w/6 Guards Army, badly beat up by German attacks; called crack unit, July 1943.
—Belgorod Kharkov w/23 Rifle Corps, 6 Guards Army, Aug. 1943.
—RVGK, Sep. 1943.
—Nevel Op. w/2 Baltic Front, Oct. 1943.
—Leningrad Novgorod Op. w/6 Guards and 3 Shock Armies, Nov–Dec 1943.
—Baltic area w/1 Shock Army, Apr–Oct 1944.
—Riga, Oct. 1944.
—RVGK w/3 Shock Army, Nov. 1944.
—Warsaw Poznan Op., w/3 Shock Army, Jan. 1945.
—Berlin w/12 Guards Rifle Corps, 3 Shock Army, Apr. 1945.
—"Grunische," may mean the color green in German, from the NKVD border guards color rather than a location honorific.
—Probably an independent division.
—"Grunische, Riga, Walcz, Berlin, Latvian" Orders of Lenin, Suvorov, Kutuzov.

53 Guards Rifle Division
Units: 157, 159, 161 Guards Rifle, 123 Guards Artillery Regiments.
—Raised Moscow, Moscow Military District as 130 Rifle Division; former 3 Moscow Communists and Workers Rifle Division, Oct. 1941.
—Designated Guards, Dec. 1942.
—Into Northwest Front Reserve, May 1943.
—Northwest Front Reserve w/14 Guards Rifle Corps, July 1943.
—Dnieper River, Sep. 1943.
—Targul Frumos, May 1944.
—Riga, Oct. 1944.
—Moscow Military District, Apr. 1946 (EUCOM Study).
—"Riga," Order of Red Banner.

54 Guards Rifle Division
Units: 160, 162, 163 Guards Rifle, 125 Guards Artillery Regiments.
—Raised Kalinin, Moscow Military District on basis of 51 Rifle Brigade as 119 Rifle Division (second formation), Apr–July 1942.
—Designated Guards, 16 Dec. 1942.
—RVGK, Dec. 1942.

—Stalingrad, Dec. 1942.
—Donbas w/Southwest Front, Dec. 1942.
—Voroshilovgrad area w/3 Guards and 51 Armies, Mar–July 1943.
—Don Basin w/5 Shock Army, Aug–Sep 1943.
—With 5 Shock Army to Feb. 1944.
—Makeyevka, Sep. 1943.
—Donetsk, Sep. 1943.
—Melitopol Op., Oct. 1943.
—Nikopol-Krivoi Rog w/3 Guards Rifle Corps, 5 Shock Army, Jan–Feb 1944.
—RVGK w/28 Army (to end of war), Feb. 1944.
—Odessa, Apr. 1944.
—Vitebsk Orsha Op., June 1944.
—Brest, July 1944.
—Gumbinnen axis, Oct. 1944.
—East Prussia Op. (Gumbinnen); breakthrough division, Jan. 1945.
—Koenigsberg, Apr. 1945.
—RVGK, Apr. 1945 (FHO).
—Berlin Op., Apr. 1945.
—Brest, Belorussia w/128 Rifle Corps, 28 Army, May 1947 (Feb. 1948 OB).
—"Makeyevka, Baranovichi, Slonim, Luminets, Gumbinnen," Orders of Lenin, Red Banner, Suvorov, Kutuzov.

55 Guards Rifle Division
Units: 164, 166, 168 Guards Rifle, 92 Guards Artillery Regiments.
—Takes its history from 3 and 4 "Ural" Rifle Divisions, Aug. 1918.
—These divisions combined into 4 Rifle, later 30 Rifle Division.
—Raised Dnepropetrovsk, Kiev Military District as 30 Rifle division (FHO).
—Designated Guards, 18 Dec. 1942.
—Krasnodar w/56 Army, Feb. 1943.
—Novorossiysk, spring 1943.
—Novorossiysk w/shock group of 18 Army; received first award of the Order of Suvorov, Sep. 1943.
—Primorsky, Taman Peninsula, Oct. 1943.
—Kerch Landing w/56 Army, Nov. 1943.
—With 20 Rifle Corps, 4 Ukrainian Front, Apr. 1944.
—Kerch Peninsula w/11 Guards Rifle Corps, Independent Coastal Army, Apr. 1944.
—Probably at Sevastopol, May 1944.
—Vitebsk Orsha Op. w/28 Army, June 1944.
—Pinsk, July 1944.

—East Prussia, Oct. 1944.
—Berlin Op., Apr. 1945.
—RVGK, Apr. 1945 (FHO).
—Prague Op., May 1945.
—Irkutsk, Pinsk," Orders of Lenin, three times Red Banner, Order of Suvorov, in the name of the Supreme Soviet of the RSFSR.
Key Commanders: B.N. Arshintsev, Sep. 1943.

56 Guards Rifle Division
Units: 254, 256, 258 Guards Rifle, 187 Guards Artillery Regiments.
—Formed Gshatsk, Moscow Military District from 74 and 91 "Stalin" Brigades, Jan. 1943.
—Velikiye Luki w/3 Shock Army, Jan. 1943.
—Smolensk, Sep. 1943.
—Shepetovka, July 1944.
—Tentatively identified, Moscow Military District, 1947 (Feb. 1948 OB).
—The 254 Guards Rifle Regiment honorific "in the name of Alexander Matrosov."
—"Smolensk, Shepetovka."

57 Guards Rifle Division
Units: 170, 172, 174 Guards Rifle, 128 Guards Artillery Regiments.
—Raised Chapayevsk, Kiev Military District as 153 Rifle Division, Mar. 1942.
—Designated Guards, Jan. 1943.
—Don River, Jan. 1943.
—Southwest Ukraine w/4 Guards Rifle Corps, 8 Guards Army, Jan. 1944.
—Vistula River w/8 Guards Army, Aug. 1944.
—Berlin Op. w/8 Guards Army, Apr. 1945.
—Naurnburg, Germany w/28 Guards Rifle Corps, 8 Guards Mechanized Army, 1946 (Feb. 1947 OB).
—Naurnburg, Germany as a motorized rifle division, 1947 (Feb. 1948 OB).

58 Guards Rifle Division
Units: 173, 175, 178 Guards Rifle, 130 Guards Artillery Regiments.
—Raised Kuybushev, Volga Military District as 1 Rifle Division (first formation), 5 Reserve Army (SME), June 1942.
—Raised Melekess, Volga Military District as 344 Rifle Division (FHO), Mar. 1942.
—Designated Guards, 31 Dec. 1942.
—Voroshilovgrad, Feb. 1943.
—Kharkov Defensive Op. w/1 Guards Army, Feb. 1943.

—Belgorod Op. w/57 Army, Aug. 1943.
—Krasnograd, Sep. 1943.
—Krivoi Rog axis w/57 Army, Oct–Dec 1943.
—Krivoi Rog Nikopol area w/27 Guards Rifle Corps, 37 Army, Jan. 1944.
—Odessa, Apr. 1944.
—Lvov Sandomir Op. w/34 Guards Rifle Corps, 5 Guards Army (rest of war), July 1944.
—Sandomir Silesia Op., Jan. 1945.
—Silesian Operations, Feb–Mar 1945.
—Berlin Op., Apr. 1945.
—Torgau, Elbe River; first Soviet unit to meet Americans, Apr. 1945.
—RVGK, Apr. 1945 (FHO).
—Dresden, May 1945.
—"Krasnograd, Prague" Orders of Lenin, Red Banner, Suvorov.
Key Commanders: Gen-Maj V.V. Rusakov, 1945.

59 Guards Rifle Division
Units: 176, 179, 183 Guards Rifle, 127 Guards Artillery Regiments.
—Raised Krasnodar, North Caucasus Military District as 197 Rifle Division (2nd formation), Mar. 1942.
—Raised Armavir, North Caucasus Military District as 197 Rifle Division (FHO), Mar. 1942.
—Designated Guards, Jan. 1943.
—Don Basin, Aug–Sep 1943.
—Kramatorsk, Sep. 1943.
—Zaporozhye Bridgehead w/3 Guards Army, Oct. 1943.
—Krivoi Rog/Nikopol w/34 Guards Rifle Corps, 3 Guards Army, Jan. 1944.
—Odessa, Apr. 1944.
—Dniester River, Apr. 1944.
—Iasi Kishinev Op. w/46 Army (to end of war), Aug. 1944.
—Bulgaria, Sep. 1944.
—Debrecen Op., Oct. 1944.
—Budapest, Jan. 1945.
—Vienna, Mar–Apr 1945.
—RVGK, Apr. 1945.
—Linz, May 1945.
—"Kramatorsk, Nikopol, Budapest, Lower Dniester," Orders of Red Banner, Suvorov, Bogdan Khmelnitskiy.

60 Guards Rifle Division
Units: 177, 180, 185 Guards Rifle, 132 Guards Artillery Regiments.

—Raised near Stalingrad, North Caucasus Military District as 278 Rifle Division (second formation), Jan. 1942.
—Designated Guards, Jan. 1943.
—Pavlograd w/4 Guards Rifle Corps, Feb. 1943.
—Zaporozhye Bridgehead w/12 Army, Pct. 1943.
—Southwest Ukraine w/66 Rifle Corps, 6 Army, Jan. 1944.
—RVGK (FHO), Apr. 1945.
—Berlin Op. w/5 Shock Army, Apr. 1945.
—Probably an independent division.
—"Pavlograd, Dnepropetrovsk," Order of Red Banner.

61 Guards Rifle Division
Units: 181, 187, 189 Guards Rifle, 129 Guards Artillery Regiments.
—Raised in Belaya Tserkov, Kiev Special Military District as 159 Rifle Division, June 1940.
—Designated Guards, Jan. 1943.
—Zaporozhye Bridgehead w/3 Guards Army, Oct. 1943.
—Kovel Lutsk Op. w/34 Guards Rifle Corps, 3 Guards Army, Jan. 1944.
—Berlin Op. w/28 Army, Apr. 1945.
—RVGK w/28 Army (SME), Apr. 1945.
—"Slavyarsk, Lutsk, Lower Dniester."

62 Guards Rifle Division
Units: 182, 184, 186 Guards Rifle, 131 Guards Artillery Regiments.
—Raised Karsk, Volga Military District as 127 Rifle Division (second formation), Jan. 1942.
—Designated Guards, Jan. 1943.
—Ostrogosh Rossosh Op., Jan. 1943.
—Kharkov w/3 Tank Army, Feb. 1943.
—Possibly in the RVGK w/6 Guards Army, Apr. 1943.
—Southwest Front w/1 Guards Army, July 1943.
—RVGK w/37 Army, Aug. 1943.
—Kremenchug area w/57 Rifle Corps, 37 Army, Sep. 1943.
—Krivoi Rog, Oct. 1943.
—Cherkask w/52 Army, Dec. 1943.
—Korsun Shevchenkovskiy Op. w/4 Guards Army, Jan. 1944.
—Zvenigorod w/73 Rifle Corps, 52 Army, Jan. 1944.
—Uman Botosani Op. w/4 Guards Army, Mar. 1944.
—Iasi, Apr. 1944.
—Targul Frumos, May 1944.
—Iasi Kishinev Op. w/52 Army, Aug. 1944.
—Hungary w/20 Guards Airborne Rifle Corps, 4 Guards Army, Nov. 1944.

—Budapest w/20 Guards Airborne Rifle Corps, 4 Guards Army, Jan. 1945.
—Vienna, Mar–Apr 1945.
—Sopron, Hungary w/31 Guards Rifle Corps, 5 Guards Army, Sep. 1946 (Feb. 1947 OB).
—Probably an independent division.
—"Jassy, Roman, Budapest, Zvenigorod," Orders of Red Banner, Suvorov, Bogdan Khmelnitskiy.

63 Guards Rifle Division
Units: 188, 190, 192 Guards Rifle, 133 Guards Artillery Regiments.
—Raised Karelia, Leningrad Military District as 136 Rifle Division, Mar. 1942.
—Designated Guards, Jan. 1943.
—Leningrad Offensive w/42 Army, Jan. 1943.
—Leningrad Offensive w/42 Army, Jan. 1944.
—Assault division of Leningrad Front at Narva, Feb. 1944.
—Estonia w/30 Guards Rifle Corps, 2 Shock Army, mentioned in the Supreme Commanders Order of the Day, Sep. 1944.
—Baltic coast w/30 Guards Rifle corps, 2 Shock Army, Nov. 1944.
—One regiment "Lenin Komsomol," Orders of Red Banner, Kutuzov.
—"Krasnosel'skaya, Leningrad," Order of Red Banner (MHJ).
Key Commanders: Gen-Maj A.F. Shchlegov, Apr. 1943.

64 Guards Rifle Division
Units: 191, 194, 197 Guards Rifle, 134 Guards Artillery Regiments.
—Raised Voronezh, Orel Military District as 327 Rifle Division, Nov. 1941.
—Designated Guards, Jan. 1943.
—Leningrad Offensive w/42 Army, Jan. 1944.
—Vyborg, June 1944.
—Tallinn area w/30 Guards Rifle Corps, 2 Shock Army, Sep. 1944.
—"Vyborg."

65 Guards Rifle Division
Units: 255, 257, 259 Guards Rifle, 190 Guards Artillery Regiments.
—Raised near Gshatsk, Moscow Military District from 75 and 78 Rifle Brigades, Apr. 1943.
—Designated Guards, Apr. 1943.
—Riga, Oct. 1944.
—"Riga, Latvian."

66 Guards Rifle Division
Units: 145, 193, 195 Guards Rifle, 135 Guards Artillery Regiments.

—Raised at Sumy, Kharkov Military District as 293 Rifle Division, Aug. 1941.
—Designated Guards, Jan. 1943.
—Belgorod Kharkov Op. Aug. 1943.
—Poltava, Sep. 1943.
—Korsun Shevchenkovskiy Op. w/20 Guards Rifle Corps, 4 Guards Army, Jan. 1944.
—Lvov Sandomir Op., July 1944.
—Carpathian Mountains, Sep. 1944.
—Mukachevo Uzhgorod Op. w/1 Guards Army, Sep. 1944.
—Dunovar, Hungary, Sep–Oct 1944.
—Budapest, Jan. 1945.
—Possibly an independent division.
—"Poltava, Carpathian, Budapest, Ungvar," one other u/i honorific.

67 Guards Rifle Divsion
Units: 196, 199, 201 Guards Rifle, 138 Guards Artillery Regts.
—Raised Solotonoscha, Kharkov Military District as 304 Rifle Division, Aug. 1941.
—Designated Guards, Jan. 1943.
—Belgorod, Mar. 1943.
—Kursk w/22 Guards Rifle Corps, 6 Guards Army, July 1943.
—Vitebsk Orsha Op., June 1944.
—"Vitebsk."

68 Guards Rifle Division
Units: 198, 200, 202 Guards Rifle, 136 Guards Artillery Regiments.
—Raised Kiev Military District as 96 Rifle Division, July 1942.
—Designated Guards, Feb. 1943.
—Voronezh, w/24 Army, Mar. 1943.
—Ryzhev Kanev Bridgehead, Dnieper River w/40 Army, Sep. 1943.
—Southwest Ukraine w/17 Guards Rifle Corps, 38 Army, Jan. 1944.
—Proskurov Chernovsty Op., Mar. 1944.
—Lvov Sandomir Op., July 1944.
—Lvov, July 1944.
—Alba Julia, Rumania w/83 Rifle Corps, Oct. 1946; gone by July 1947 (1947–48 OBs).
—"Lvov, Proskurov," Order of Red Banner.

69 Guards Rifle Division
Units: 204, 206, 208 Guards Rifle, 79 Guards Artillery Regiments.
—Raised Kologriv, Moscow Military District as 120 Rifle Division, Aug. 1941.

—Designated Guards, Feb. 1943.
—Voronezh, Mar. 1943.
—Korsun Shevchenkovskiy Op. w/21 Guards Rifle Corps, 4 Guards Army, Jan. 1944.
—Iasi, Apr. 1944.
—Targul Frumos, May 1944.
—Iasi Kishinev Op., Aug. 1944.
—Hungary w/21 Guards Rifle Corps, 4 Guards Army, Dec. 1944.
—Belorussian Military District, Jan. 1947 (Feb. 1948 OB).
—"Jassy, Roman."

70 Guards Rifle Division
Units: 203, 205, 207 Guards Rifle, 137 Guards Artillery Regiments.
—Raised Kalinin, Moscow Military District as 138 Mountain Rifle Division, Sep. 1939.
—Designated Guards, 6 Feb. 1943.
—Orel area, Apr. 1943.
—Kursk, w/17 Guards Rifle Corps, 13 Army, July 1943.
—Glukhov, Aug. 1943.
—Dnieper River w/17 Guards Rifle Corps, 13 Army, Sep. 1943.
—Desna River, Sep. 1943.
—Bachmach, Sep. 1943.
—Southwest Ukraine w/28 Rifle Corps, 13 Army, Jan. 1944.
—Vinnitsa, Mar. 1944.
—Proskurov Chernovsty Op., Mar. 1944.
—Lvov Sandomir Op. w/38 Army (to end of war), July 1944.
—Lvov, July 1944.
—Carpathian Duklinskiy Op. w/101 Rifle Corps, Sep. 1944.
—Krakow, Jan–Feb 1945.
—Prague Op., May 1945.
—Carpathian Military District, May 1947 (EUCOM Study).
—"Glukhov, Lvov," Orders of Lenin, twice Red Banner, Orders of Suvorov, Kutuzov, Bogdan Khmelnitskiy.

71 Guards Rifle Division
Units: 210, 213, 219 Guards Rifle, 151 Guards Artillery Regiments.
—Takes history from 1 "Ust-Medvedits" Rifle Division (SME), Oct. 1918.
—Redesignated 23 Rifle Division in 1920's.
—Raised Dunaburg, Ostsee as 23 Rifle Division (FHO), before Dec. 1941.
—Designated Guards, 1 Mar. 1943.
—Kharkov Defensive Op., Mar. 1943.
—With 6 Guards Army (to end of war), Apr. 1943.
—Kursk w/22 Guards Rifle Corps, July 1943.

—RVGK, Sep. 1943.
—To 2 Baltic Front, Oct. 1943.
—Polotsk axis, Nov–Dec 1943.
—Belorussian Op., June 1944.
—Vitebsk, July 1944.
—Riga and Memel, Oct. 1944.
—Courland Peninsula, Nov 1944–Apr. 1945.
—Baltic Military District, Oct. 1945 (EUCOM study).
—Leningrad Military District, Apr. 1946 (Feb. 1947 OB).
—"Kharkov, Vitebsk," Orders of Lenin, Red Banner.

72 Guards Rifle Division
Units: 222, 224, 229 Guards Rifle, 155 Guards Artillery Regiments.
—Raised Akmolinsk, Central Asia Military District as 29 Rifle Division, Dec. 1941.
—Designated Guards, 1 Mar. 1943.
—Kursk w/70 Army, July 1943.
—Dnieper River w/25 Guards Rifle Corps, 7 Guards Army, Sep. 1943.
—Krasnograd, Sep. 1943.
—Kirovograd w/25 Guards Rifle Corps, 7 Guards Army, Jan. 1944.
—Targul Frumos w/7 Guards Army, 2 May 1944.
—Iasi Kishinev Op., Aug. 1944.
—"Krasnograd, Borislav, Bolgrad, Roman, Pressburg" Order of Red Banner.

73 Guards Rifle Division
Units: 209, 211, 214 Guards Rifle, 153 Guards Artillery Regiments.
—Formed Alma Ata, Central Asia Military District as 38 Rifle Division (second formation), Jan. 1942.
—Designated Guards, 1 Mar. 1943.
—Kursk w/25 Guards Rifle Corps, 7 Guards Army, July 1943.
—Dnieper River w/24 Guards Rifle Corps, 7 Guards Army, Sep. 1943.
—Vorskla River, w/5 Guards Army, Sep. 1943.
—Southwest Ukraine w/64 Rifle Corps, 57 Army, Jan. 1944.
—Belgrade w/57 Army, Oct. 1944.
—Hungary, Dec. 1944.
—The 209 Guards Rifle Regiment "Abganerovskiy," 27 Jan. 1943; 211 Guards Rifle Regiment "Basarginskiy," 27 Jan. 1943; 214 Guards Rifle Regiment "Voropanovskiy," 27 Jan. 1943; 153 Guards Artillery Regiment "Urazovskiy," 27 Jan. 1943.
—"Stalingrad, Danube."

74 Guards Rifle Division
Units: 226, 236, 240 Guards Rifle Regiments.

—Raised at Vishny Volochek, Moscow Military District as 45 Rifle Division, July 1941.
—Designated Guards, 1 Mar. 1943.
—Zaporozhye Bridgehead w/8 Guards Army, Oct. 1943.
—Nikopol w/29 Guards Rifle Corps, 8 Guards Army, Jan. 1944.
—Vistula River w/8 Guards Army, Aug. 1944.
—"Nikopol."

75 Guards Rifle Division
Units: 212, 231, 241 Guards Rifle, 159 Guards Artillery Regiments.
—Raised Tula, Moscow Military District on basis of 13 NKVD Motorized Rifle Division; later 95 Rifle Division (second formation), Sep. 1942.
—Reformed as a Guards Division, 1 Mar. 1943.
—Kursk (Ponyri), w/17 Guards Rifle Corps, 13 Army, July 1943.
—Left Bank Ukraine w/70 and 60 Armies, Sep. 1943.
—Kiev op. w/60 Army, Oct–Nov 1943.
—Belorussia w/65 Army, Jan–June 1944.
—Belorussian Op.; assault division of 65 Army, June 1944.
—To 61 Army (rest of war), Aug. 1944.
—Riga, Oct. 1944.
—Vistula Oder Op., Jan. 1945.
—East Pomeranian Op., Feb. 1945.
—Berlin Op., Apr. 1945.
—Tula, Moscow Military District, May 1946 (Feb. 1947 OB).
—"Bachmach, Bobruysk, Baranovichi, Riga," twice Order of Red Banner, Order of Suvorov.

76 Guards Rifle Division
Units: 234, 237, 239 Guards Rifle and 154 Guards Artillery Regiments.
—Lineage of 22 "Krasnodar" Rifle Division, formed 1918 and 74 "Taman" Rifle Division (SME), formed in 1924.
—Raised Novocherkassk, North Caucasus Military District from 157 Rifle Division (FHO), 1939.
—Designated Guards, 1 Mar. 1943.
—Chernigov, Sep. 1943.
—Belorussia w/9 Guards Rifle Corps, 61 Army, Mar. 1944.
—Odessa, Apr. 1944.
—Crimea, May 1944.
—Belorussian Op, June 1944.
—Brest, July 1944.
—Vistula Oder Op., Jan. 1945.
—Danzig w/70 Army, Mar. 1945.
—Wismar, Germany linked up w/British 6 Airborne Division, May 1945.
—Returned to USSR, winter 1945.

—Irkutsk, East Siberian Military District, 1947 (Feb. 1948 OB).
—Reformed as Guards Airborne Division after the war (SME).
—The 234 Guards Rifle Regiment "Black Sea," Order of Kutuzov; 237 Guards Rifle Regiment "Torun," Order of Red Banner; 239 Guards Rifle Regiment "Danzig," Order of Red Banner; 154 Guards Artillery Regiment, Order of Red Banner.
—"Chernigov, Brest-Litovsk, Torun, Radom," Order of Red Banner.

77 Guards Rifle Division
Units: 215, 218, 221 Guards Rifle, 156 Guards Artillery Regiments.
—Raised Moscow, Moscow Military District as 21 Moscow People's Militia Rifle Division, July 1941.
—Named 173 Rifle Division (second formation), Aug. 1941.
—Designated Guards, 1 Mar. 1943.
—Orel Op. w/61 Army, July–Aug. 1943.
—RVGK, Aug. 1943.
—Chernigov, Sep. 1943.
—Kalinkovichi, Jan. 1944.
—Belorussia w/9 Guards Rifle Corps, 61 Army, Mar. 1944.
—Kovel w/69 Army (rest of war), Apr. 1944.
—Belorussian Op., June 1944.
—Lublin Brest Op., July 1944.
—Pulawy Bridgehead w/25 Rifle Corps, 69 Army, Aug. 1944–Jan. 1945.
—Vistula Oder Op., breakthrough division, Jan. 1945.
—Oder River, Feb. 1945.
—Kustrin Bridgehead, Feb. 1945.
—Berlin Op. w/25 Rifle Corps, Apr. 1945.
—Magdeburg, May 1945.
—The 1st Battalion, 215 Guards Rifle Regiment called the "Battalion of Glory" for Pulawy Bridgehead Battle, Jan. 1945.
—"Chernigov, Kalinkovichi, Radom, Brandenburg," Orders of Lenin, Red Banner, Suvorov.

78 Guards Rifle Division
Units: 223, 225, 228 Guards Rifle, 158 Guards Artillery Regiments.
—Raised Blagoveshchensk, Far East as 204 Rifle Division, Sep. 1941.
—Designated Guards, Mar. 1943.
—Kursk w/25 Guards Rifle Corps, w/7 Guards Army, July 1943.
—Dnieper River w/24 Guards Rifle Corps, 7 Guards Army, Sep. 1943.
—Zaporozhye Bridgehead w/8 Guards Army, Oct. 1943.
—Southwest Ukraine w/64 Rifle Corps, 57 Army, Jan. 1944.
—Iasi w/53 Army, Apr. 1944.

—Targul Frumos w/53 Army, May 1944.
—Lvov Sandomir Op. w/34 Guards Rifle Corps, 5 Guards Army, July 1944.
—Vistula Oder Op. w/5 Guards Army, Jan. 1945.
—Prague Op., May 1945.
—Leningrad Military District, 1947, (Feb. 1948 OB).
—"Oder."

79 Guards Rifle Division
Units: 216, 220, 227 Guards Rifle, 172 Guards Artillery Regiments.
—Raised Tomsk, Siberia Military District, as 443 Rifle Division, Dec. 1941.
—Redesignated 284 Rifle Division (second formation), Mar. 1942.
—Defended Mamaev, Red October and Barrikady at Stalingrad, Sep. 1942.
—Designated Guards, 1 Feb. 1943.
—Zaporozhye Bridgehead w/8 Guards Army, 10–14 Oct. 1943.
—Nikopol w/28 Guards Rifle Corps, 8 Guards Army, Jan. 1944.
—Odessa, Apr. 1944.
—Lublin Brest Op., July 1944.
—Lvov Sandomir Op. w/8 Guards Army (rest of war), July 1944.
—Magnuszew Bridgehead, July 1944–Jan. 1945.
—Warsaw Poznan Op., Jan. 1945.
—South of Kustrin, Feb. 1945.
—Berlin, Apr. 1945.
—"Zaporozhye, Nikopol, Lublin," Orders of Lenin, Red Banner, Suvorov, Bogdan Khmelnitskiy.

80 Guards Rifle Division
Units: 217, 230, 232 Guards Rifle, 171 Guards Artillery Regiments.
—Raised Barnaul, Siberia Militray District as 298 Rifle Division (second formation), Jan. 1942.
—Designated Guards, Mar. 1943.
—Southwest Ukraine w/68 Rifle Corps, 57 Army, Jan. 1944.
—Uman, Mar. 1944.
—Iasi, Apr. 1944.
—Targul Frumos w/53 Army, May 1944.
—Hungary w/20 Guards Airborne Rifle Corps, 4 Guards Army, Nov. 1944.
—"Uman."
Key Commanders: Gen-Maj A.Ye. Yakovlev, Nov. 1944; Col. V.I. Chizov, Dec. 1944.

81 Guards Rifle Division
Units: 233, 235, 238 Guards Rifle, 173 Guards Artillery Regiments.
—Raised at Bikin, Far East Military District as 422 Rifle Division, Apr. 1942.
—Designated Guards, Mar. 1943.
—Kursk W/25 Guards Rifle Corps, 7 Guards Army, July 1943.
—Dnieper River w/25 Guards Rifle corps, 7 Guards Army, Sep. 1943.
—Krasnograd, Sep. 1943.
—Kirovograd w/25 Guards Rifle Corps, 7 Guards Army, Jan. 1944.
—Targul Frumos w/18 Independent Tank Corps, 5 Guards Tank Army, May 1944.
—Iasi Kishinev Op., Aug. 1944.
—Prague, May 1945.
—"Krasnograd, Iasi, Roman, Pressburg," Order of Red Banner.

82 Guards Rifle Division
Units: 242, 244, 246 Guards Rifle, 195 Guards Artillery Regiments.
—Raised Borzya, Transbaikal Military District as 321 Rifle Division (second formation), Apr. 1942.
—Designated Guards, Mar. 1943.
—Zaporozhye Bridgehead w/8 Guards Army, Oct. 1943.
—Southwest Ukraine w/29 Guards Rifle Corps, 8 Guards Army, Jan. 1944.
—Lvov Sandomir Op., July 1944.
—Vistula Oder Op.; breakthrough division, Jan. 1945.
—Posen w/8 Guards Army, Feb. 1945.
—Muncheberg, Apr. 1945.
—Gotha, Germany w/29 Guards Rifle Corps, 8 Guards Mechanized Army, Oct. 1946 (Feb. 1947 OB).
—Left Germany for Soviet Union in 1947 (Sep. 1947 OB).
—"Zaporozhye, Yarzevo," Order of Red Banner.

83 Guards Rifle Division
Units: 248, 250, 252 Guards Rifle Regts.
—Raised at Divisionnaya, Transbaikal Military District as 97 Rifle Division (second formation), Jan. 1942.
—Designated Guards, Apr. 1943.
—The 250 Guards Rifle Regiment associated w/3 Guards Motorized Rifle Division, 1942.
—Tuapse Defensive Op. w/18 Army, Sep–Dec 1942.
—Bolkhov Op. w/11 Guards Army; breakthrough division, July 1943.
—Orel Op. w/8 Guards Rifle Corps, 11 Guards Army, July 1943.
—Gorodok, Sep. 1943.

—Vitebsk Orsha Op., June 1944.
—East Prussia, Nov. 1944.
—Danzig area w/11 Guards Army, Apr. 1945.
—Had a naval infantry regiment in its composition, Apr. 1945.
—"Gorodok, Vitebsk, Molodetschino," Order of Red Banner.

84 Guards Rifle Division
Units: 243, 245, 247 Guards Rifle, 186 Guards Artillery Regiments.
—Raised Moscow, Moscow Military District as 4 "Kuibyshev" (Moscow) People's Militia Division, Aug. 1941.
—Reformed as 110 Rifle Division (second formation), Sep. 1941.
—Designated Guards, 10 Apr. 1943.
—Orel w/36 Guards Rifle Corps, 11 Guards Army (to end of war), July 1943.
—Karachev, Aug. 1943.
—Breakthrough division on Nevel-Vitebsk axis, Oct–Dec 1943.
—Vitebsk Orsha Op.; breakthrough division, June 1944.
—Neman River, July 1944.
—East Prussia, Aug. 1944.
—East Prussian Op., Jan. 1945.
—Memel, Mar. 1945.
—Koenigsberg, Apr. 1945.
—Pillau, Apr. 1945.
—"Karachev, Orel, Orsha, Memel, Neman," Orders of Red Banner, Suvorov.

85 Guards Rifle Division
Units: 249, 251, 253 Guards Rifle, 188 Guards Artillery Regiments.
—Raised Kostroma, Moscow Military District as 118 Rifle Division (second formation), June 1941.
—Designated Guards, Apr. 1943.

86 Guards Rifle Division
Units: 260, 263, 265 Guards Rifle, 191 Guards Artillery Regiments.
—Raised at Spassk, Far East Military District as 98 Rifle Division (second formation), Oct. 1941.
—Designated Guards, Apr. 1943.
—South Ukraine w/1 Guards Rifle Corps, 2 Guards Army, Jan. 1944.
—Kherson, Mar. 1944.
—Nikolayev, May 1944.
—Odessa, May 1944.
—Budapest, Jan. 1945.
—Had naval infantry in its composition.

—"Budapest, Odessa, Berislav, Kherson, Nikolayev," Orders of Lenin, Red Banner, Suvorov.

87 Guards Rifle Division
Units: 261, 262, 264 Guards Rifle, 192 Guards Artillery Regiments.
—Raised Krasnograd, Kharkov Military District as 300 Rifle Division, July 1941.
—Designated Guards, Apr. 1943.
—South Ukraine w/13 Guards Rifle Corps, 2 Guards Army, Jan. 1944.
—Crimea w/13 Guards Rifle Corps, 2 Guards Army, Apr. 1944.

88 Guards Rifle Division
Units: 266, 269, 271 Guards Rifle, 194 Guards Artillery Regiments.
—Existed before the war as a covering division (99 Rifle Division), Kiev Special Military District, Aug. 1940.
—First formation of that division commanded by A.A. Vlasov, 1940–41.
—The 99 Rifle Division was designated as the best division in the Soviet Army by MSU Timoshenko, Oct. 1940.
—Raised Balaschov, Volga Military District (second formation, FHO), Aug. 1942.
—Designated Guards, Apr. 1943.
—Zaporozhye Bridgehead w/8 Guards Army, Oct. 1943.
—Southwest Ukraine w/28 Guards Rifle Corps, 8 Guards Army, Jan. 1944.
—Kustrin Bridgehead (Seelow Heights), w/8 Guards Army, Apr. 1945.
—Reichenbach, Germany w/29 Guards Rifle Corps, 8 Guards Mechanized Army, Apr. 1946, (Aug. 1946 OB).
—"Zaporozhye," Orders of Red Banner, Suvorov, Bogdan Khmelnitskiy.

89 Guards rifle division
Units: 267, 270, 273 Guards Rifle, 196 Guards Artillery Regiments.
—Raised Gorki, Moscow Military District as 160 Rifle Division (second formation), Nov. 1941.
—Designated Guards, Apr. 1943.
—Kursk w/6 Guards Army, July 1943.
—Belgorod; first unit in city, 5 Aug. 1943.
—Kharkov w/69 Army, Aug. 1943.
—Iasi, Apr. 1944.
—Targul Frumos, May 1944.
—Oder Vistula Op. as breakthrough division, Jan. 1945.
—Seized Kustrin Bridgehead w/5 Shock Army, Feb. 1945.

—Berlin Op. w/5 Shock Army, Apr. 1945.
—Rostock, Germany w/9 Rifle Corps, as a Guards Motorized Division, 1946 (Feb. 1947 OB).
—Koenigsberg w/5 Mechanized Army, by Feb. 1947 (EUCOM Study).
—"Belgorod, Kharkov," Order of Red Banner.

90 Guards Rifle Division
Units: 268, 272, 274 Guards Rifle, 193 Guards Artillery Regiments.
—Raised Morschansk, Orel Military District as 325 Rifle Division, Oct. 1941.
—Designated Guards, Apr. 1943.
—Kursk w/6 Guards Army, July 1943.
—Belgorod Kharkov Op. w/23 Rifle Corps, 6 Guards Army, Aug. 1943.
—Vitebsk Op., June 1944.
—RVGK, Apr. 1945 (FHO).
—"Vitebsk."

91 Guards Rifle Division
Units: 275, 277, 279 Guards Rifle, 195 Guards Artillery Regiments.
—Raised Tula, Moscow Military District as 257 Rifle Division, July 1941.
—SME says raised Kalinin, Moscow Military District from 257 Rifle Division (second formation), 1941.
—Designated Guards, 18 Apr. 1943.
—Assigned to 39 Army (rest of war), July 1943.
—Smolensk, Sep. 1943.
—Dukhov (Duchovschtschina), Sep. 1943.
—Vitebsk, Jan. 1944.
—Vitebsk Op. w/5 Guards Rifle Corps; assault division, July 1944.
—Memel Op., Oct. 1944.
—East Prussia, South of Taurage, Nov. 1944.
—Gvardeysk, Jan. 1945.
—Koenigsberg, Apr. 1945.
—To Far East w/39 Army, May 1945.
—Khingan Mukden Op., Aug. 1945.
—Port Arthur, China w/5 Guards Rifle Corps, 39 Army, Aug. 1946 (Feb. 1947 OB).
—"Dukhov, Khingan," Orders of Lenin, Red Banner, Suvorov.

92 Guards Rifle Division
Units: 276, 280, 282 Guards Rifle, 197 Guards Artillery Regiments.
—Raised at Korotscha, Orel Military District from 12 Guards and 149 Rifle Brigade, Apr. 1943.
—Stalingrad, fall 1942.

—Kursk w/57 Rifle Corps, 37 Army, July 1943.
—Dnieper River w/57 Rifle Corps, 37 Army, 24–28 Sep. 1943.
—Iasi Kishinev Op. w/37 Army, Aug. 1944.
—Bulgaria w/37 Army, Jan. 1946 (Aug. 1946 OB).
—"Stalingrad, Danube."

93 Guards Rifle Division
Units: 278, 281, 285 Guards Rifle, 198 Guards Artillery Regiments.
—Raised Valuki, Orel Military District from 12, 13 Guards, 92, 96 Rifle Brigades, Apr. 1943 (FHO).
—Activated on basis of 13 Guards Independent and 92 Red Banner Rifle Brigades (SME).
—Kursk w/69 Army, July 1943.
—Belgorod Kharkov Op.; liberated both cities w/69 Army, Aug. 1943.
—RVGK, Sep. 1943.
—Krivoi Rog area w/35 Guards Rifle Corps, 5 Guards Army, Dec. 1943.
—Krivoi Rog w/7 Guards Army, Jan. 1944.
—Kirovograd w/35 Guards Rifle Corps, 5 Guards Army, Jan. 1944.
—Uman Botosani Op., Mar. 1944.
—Crossed Dniester and Prut Rivers, Apr. 1944.
—Iasi, Apr. 1944.
—Targul Frumos w/33 Rifle Corps, 27 Army and 2 Tank Army, May 1944.
—Iasi Kishinev Op.; took Ploesti, Aug. 1944.
—Crossed Transylvanian Alps, Sep. 1944.
—Debrecen Op., Oct. 1944.
—Budapest w/27 Army, Nov. 1944.
—Budapest w/7 Guards Army, Jan. 1945.
—Lake Balaton (Hron Bridgehead), Feb. 1945.
—Brno Bratislava Op., Apr. 1945.
—Prague w/53 Army, May 1945.
—Probably an independent division.
—"Kharkov, Prague, Pressburg," Twice Order of Red Banner, Orders of Kutuzov, Suvorov.

94 Guards Rifle Division
Units: 283, 286, 288 Guards Rifle, 199 Guards Artillery Regiments.
—Raised Novy Oskol, Orel Military District from 14 Guards and 96 Rifle Brigades, Apr. 1943.
—Kursk, July 1943.
—Belgorod, Aug. 1943.
—Kirovograd w/35 Guards Rifle Corps, 5 Guards Army, Jan. 1944.
—Zvenigorod w/49 Rifle Corps, 5 Guards Tank Army, Feb. 1944.
—Vistula Oder Op. as a breakthrough division, Jan. 1945.

—Kustrin Bridgehead w/5 Shock Army, Feb. 1945.
—Berlin w/5 Shock Army, Apr. 1945.
—Schwerin, Germany w/9 Rifle Corps, 5 Mechanized Army, 1946 (Feb. 1947 OB).
—"Pomeranian," Order of Red Banner.
Key Commanders: Lt-Col B.I. Baranov, Feb. 1945; Gen-Maj I.G. Gasporyan, Apr. 1945.

95 Guards Rifle Division
Units: 284, 287, 290 Guards Rifle, 233 Guards Artillery Regiments.
—FHO says raised Bugurusslan, Volga Military District from 226 Rifle Division (second formation), Sep. 1942.
—SME says raised Zaporozhye, Kiev Special Military District as 226 Rifle Division, July–Aug 1942.
—RVGK, Aug–Oct 1942.
—RVGK, Feb. 1943.
—Designated Guards, 4 May 1943.
—Kursk (west of Prokhorovka) w/5 Guards Army, July 1943.
—Belgorod Kharkov Op., Aug–Sep 1943.
—Poltava, Sep. 1943.
—Vorskla River w/5 Guards Army, Sep. 1943.
—Kremenchug, Sep. 1943.
—Dnieper River w/5 Guards Army, Oct. 1943.
—Znamenka, Dec. 1943.
—Southwest Ukraine w/32 Guards Rifle Corps, 5 Guards Army, Jan. 1944.
—Dniester River, Apr. 1944.
—Lvov Sandomir Op. w/32 Guards Rifle Corps, 5 Guards Army, July 1944.
—Vistula Oder Op. w/5 Guards Army, Jan. 1945.
—Sandomir Silesia Op., Feb. 1945.
—Breslau, Mar. 1945.
—Berlin Op., Apr. 1945.
—Prague Op., May 1945.
—Austria w/32 Guards Rifle Corps, 5 Guards Army as a Motorized Rifle Division, 1946–47 (Feb. 1948 OB).
—"Poltava, Znamenka, Oder," Orders of Lenin, Red Banner, Suvorov, Bogdan Khmelnitskiy.

96 Guards Rifle Division
Units: 291, 293, 295 Guards Rifle, 234 Guards Arty Regiments.
—History from 43 Independent Rifle Brigade, activated at Novosibirsk, Siberia Military District, Oct. 1941.

—Reformed as 258 Rifle Division (second formation) at Mozhaisk; w/ 1 Shock Army, Jan. 1942.
—To 5 Shock Army, Dec. 1942–Mar. 1944.
—Designated Guards, 4 May 1943.
—Ilovaisk, Don Basin, Sep. 1943.
—Melitopol Op., Oct. 1943.
—Nikopol area w/3 Guards Rifle Corps, 5 Shock Army, Jan. 1944.
—Nikolayev, Mar. 1944.
—Belorussian Op. w/3 Guards Rifle Corps, 28 Army (rest of war), June 1944.
—Minsk, July 1944.
—Lublin Brest Op. (Brest), July 1944.
—East Prussia, Oct. 1944.
—East Prussian Op. w/128 Rifle Corps, 28 Army, Jan. 1945.
—Berlin Op., Apr. 1945.
—RVGK, Apr. 1945 (FHO).
—Czechoslovakia, May 1945.
—Slanovichi, Belorussia Military District w/3 Guards Rifle Corps, 28 Army, May 1947 (Feb. 1948 OB).
—"Ilovaysk, Gumbinnen, Insterberg," Orders of Lenin, Red Banner, Suvorov.

97 Guards Rifle Division
Units: 289, 292, 294 Guards Rifle, 232 Guards Artillery Regiments.
—Raised Voroshilovsk, North Caucasus Military District as 343 Rifle Division, Sep. 1941.
—Designated Guards, May 1943.
—Belgorod Kharkov Op. w/5 Guards Army, Aug. 1943.
—Vorskla River w/5 Guards Army, Sep. 1943.
—Kirovograd w/32 Guards Rifle Corps, 5 Guards Army, Jan. 1944.
—Poltava, Apr. 1944.
—Lvov Sandomir Op. w/32 Guards Rifle Corps, 5 Guards Army, July 1944.
—Vistula Oder Op. w/5 Guards Army, Jan. 1945.
—Germany, Mar. 1945.
—Torgau w/5 Guards Army, Apr. 1945.
—Prague, May 1945.
—The 289 Guards Rifle Regiment "Vistula," Order of Kutuzov; 292 Guards Rifle Regiment, Order of Red Star; 294 Guards Rifle Regiment, Order of Alexander Nevskiy.
—"Poltava," Orders of Red Banner, Suvorov, Bogdan Khmelnitskiy.
Key Commanders: Gen-Maj M.A. Vsenko 1942–43; Gen-Maj I.I. Antsiferov 1943–44; Col. A.P. Garan, 1945.

98 Guards Rifle Division
Units: 296, 299, 302 Guards Rifle Regiments.
—Raised Dmitrov, Moscow Military District from 18, 19, 20 Guards Independent Airborne Brigades (FHO), Dec. 1943.
—RVGK when formed from 13 Guards Airborne Rifle Division, Jan. 1944.
—Karelian Front w/37 Guards Rifle Corps, May 1944.
—Svir River w/37 Guards Rifle Corps, 7 Army, June 1944.
—With the Independent Airborne Army, Oct. 1944.
—RVGK w/9 Guards Army, Nov–Dec 1944.
—Southeast of Budapest, Feb. 1945.
—Vienna, Apr. 1945.
—Prague Op., May 1945.
—Reformed as an airborne division after war.
—"Svir."

99 Guards Rifle Division
Units: 297, 300, 303 Guards Rifle, 241 Guards Artillery Regiments.
—Formed from 6, 13, 15 Airborne Brigades (FHO), Jan. 1944.
—RVGK when formed from 14 Guards Airborne Division, Jan. 1944.
—Kiev Zhitomir Op., Jan. 1944.
—Karelian Front w/37 Guards Rifle Corps, May 1944.
—Svir River, w/37 Guards Rifle Corps, 7 Army, June 1944.
—Petsamo Kirkenes Op., Oct. 1944.
—With the Independent Airborne Army, Oct. 1944.
—RVGK w/9 Guards Army, Nov–Dec 1944.
—Southeast of Budapest, Feb. 1945.
—Hungary w/9 Guards Army, Mar. 1945.
—Vienna, Apr. 1945.
—Prague, May 1945.
—Pisek, 11 May 1945.
—The 297 Guards Rifle Regiment, Orders of Kutuzov, Alexander Nevskiy; 300 Guards Rifle Regiment, Order of Kutuzov; 303 Guards Rifle Regiment, Orders of Kutuzov, Alexander Nevskiy.
—"Svir, Petsamo, Kirkenes, Zhitomir," Orders of Red Banner, Kutuzov.

100 Guards Rifle Division
Units: 298, 301, 304 Guards Rifle, 243 Guards Artillery Regiments.
—Raised Moscow, Moscow Military District from 9, 10, and 12 Guards Independent Airborne Brigades (FHO), Jan. 1944.
—RVGK when formed from 15 Guards Airborne Rifle Division, Jan. 1944.
—Karelian Front w/37 Guards Rifle Corps, May 1944.

—Svir River w/37 Guards Rifle Corps, 7 Army, June 1944.
—With the Independent Airborne Army, Oct. 1944.
—RVGK w/9 Guards Army, Nov-Dec 1944.
—Southeast of Budapest, Feb. 1945.
—Vienna, Apr. 1945.
—Prague Op., May 1945.
—"Svir."

101 Guards Rifle Division
—Activated Moscow, Moscow Military District as 14 Rifle Division, 1932.
—Petsamo Kirkenes Op., Oct. 1944.
—Designated Guards, 29 Oct. 1944.
—East Prussian Op. w/19 Army, Jan. 1945.
—Danzig area w/19 Army, Mar. 1945.
—Berlin Op. w/2 Shock Army, Apr. 1945.
—Rugen Island, Baltic Sea, Apr. 1945.
—RVGK (FHO), Apr. 1945.
—"Petsamo," Orders of Red Banner, Suvorov, Red Star.

102 Guards Rifle Division
—Raised in Chita, Transbaikal Military District on the basis of 193 Rifle Regiment as 65 Rifle Division, July 1939.
—Designated Guards, 29 Dec. 1944.
—Grodno w/19 Army, Jan. 1945.
—East Pomeranian Op., Feb. 1945.
—Danzig area w/19 Army, Mar. 1945.
—Gdynia, Apr. 1945.
—RVGK (FHO), Apr. 1945.
—Eisenach, Germany, w/29 Guards Rifle Corps, 8 Guards Mechanized Army, Jan. 1946 (Feb. 1947 OB).
—"Novgorod, Pomeranian," Orders of Red Banner, Suvorov, Red Star.

103 Guards Rifle Division
—RVGK when formed from 13 Guards Airborne Division, Dec. 1944.
—Southeast of Budapest w/37 Guards Rifle Corps, 9 Guards Army, Feb. 1945.
—Vienna, Apr. 1945.
—Prague Op., May 1945.

104 Guards Rifle Division
Units: 332, 346 Guards Rifle Regiments.
—RVGK when formed from 11 Guards Airborne Division, Dec. 1944.

—Southeast of Budapest w/38 Guards Rifle Corps, 9 Guards Army, Feb 1945.
—Vienna, Apr. 1945.
—Prague Op., May 1945.

105 Guards Rifle Division
—RVGK when formed from 12 Guards Airborne Division, Dec. 1944.
—Southeast of Budapest w/38 Guards Rifle Corps, 9 Guards Army, Feb. 1945.
—Vienna, Apr. 1945.
—Prague Op., May 1945.

106 Guards Rifle Division
—Belgrade, Oct. 1944.
—Budapest w/46 Army, Dec. 1944.
—RVGK when formed from 16 Guards Airborne Division, Dec. 1944.
—Southeast of Budapest w/38 Guards Rifle Corps, 9 Guards Army, Feb. 1945.
—Vienna, Apr. 1945.
—Prague Op., May 1945.

107 Guards Rifle Division
—RVGK when formed from 8 Guards Airborne Division, Dec. 1944.
—Southeast of Budapest w/39 Guards Rifle Corps, 9 Guards Army, Feb. 1945.
—Vienna, Apr. 1945.
—Prague Op., May 1945.

108 Guards Rifle Division
Units: 305, 308, 311 Guards Rifle Regiments.
—Formed from 10 Guards Rifle Brigade, July 1943.
—Budapest, Jan. 1945.
—"Budapest" Orders of Red Banner, Suvorov.

109 Guards Rifle Division
Units: 306, 307, 312 Guards Rifle Regiments.
—Formed from 6 and 9 Guards Rifle Brigades, probably by July 1943.
—Southwest Ukraine w/10 Guards Rifle Corps, 28 Army, Jan. 1944.
—"Borislav," Orders of Red Banner, Suvorov.

110 Guards Rifle Division
Units: 307, 310, 313 Guards Rifle, 247 Guards Artillery Regiment.

—Raised near Krimskaya, North Caucasus Military District from 5 and 7 Guards Rifle Brigades (FHO), July 1943.
—Activated Voronezh, Orel Military District on basis of 5 and 7 Order of Red Banner Guards Rifle Brigades as 110 Guards Order of Red Banner Rifle Division (SME), July 1943.
—Dnieper River w/57 Rifle Corps, 37 Army, Sep. 1943.
—Attacked by German 39 Infantry Division, 6 Panzer, 2 SS Panzer Divisions in Dnieper Bridgehead, Sep. 1943.
—Kremenchug, Sep. 1943.
—Dnieper River w/57 Rifle Corps, 37 Army, Oct. 1943.
—Aleksandriya, Dec. 1943.
—Znamenka, Dec. 1943.
—Kirovograd w/32 Guards Rifle Corps, 5 Guards Army, Jan. 1944.
—Korsun Shevchenkovskiy Op. w/32 Guards Rifle Corps, 5 Guards Army, Jan. 1944.
—Uman Botosani Op. w/53 Army, Mar 1944.
—Iasi, Apr. 1944.
—Targul Frumos, May 1944.
—Iasi Kishinev Op., Aug. 1944.
—Timiaosara, Hungary, Sep. 1944.
—Eger, Hungary, Nov. 1944.
—To Czechoslovakia, Mar. 1945.
—Redeployed to Far East, July 1945.
—Mukden Khingan Op., Aug. 1945.
—"Alexandriya, Znamenka, Khingan," Twice Order of Red Banner, Order of Suvorov.

112 Guards Rifle Division
—Known to have existed.

114 Guards Rifle Division
—RVGK when formed from 14 Guards Airborne Division, Dec. 1944.
—Southeast of Budapest w/39 Guards Rifle Corps, 9 Guards Army, Apr. 1945.
—Prague Op., May 1945.

116 Guards Rifle Division
—Known to have existed.

117 Guards Rifle Division
Units: 333, 335, 338 Guards Rifle, 308 Guards Artillery Regiments.
—Raised in Taman, North Caucasus from 8 Guards, 81, 107 Naval Rifle Brigades, Oct. 1943.

—Kerch landing w/22 Rifle Corps, 18 Army, Nov. 1943.
—Berdichev w/52 Rifle Corps, 18 Army, Jan. 1944.
—Lvov Sandomir Op., July 1944.
—Vistula River w/8 Guards Army, Aug. 1944.
—Vistula Oder Op., Jan. 1945.
—Berlin Op., Apr. 1945.
—Potsdam, May 1945.
—Carpathian Military District, Mar. 1946, (Feb. 1947 OB).
—The 335 Guards Rifle Regiment was made up of seamen from the 81 Naval Rifle Brigade; The regiment has the Orders of Suvorov and Bogdan Khmelnitskiy.
—"Berdichev, Petrikov, Kielce."

118 Guards Rifle Division
—Formed from 7 Rifle Division "Estonian," reported in Pravda, 28 June 1945.
—Leningrad Military District w/8 Guards Rifle Corps, 10 Guards Army, Apr. 1946 (Feb. 1947 OB).

119 Guards Rifle Division
Units: 341, 343, 344 Guards Rifle, 325 Guards Artillery Regiments.
—Raised Cholm, Leningrad Military District from 11 and 15 Guards Naval Rifle Brigades, Oct. 1943.

120 Guards Rifle Division
Units: 334, 336, 339 Guards Rifle Regiments.
—Raised in Omsk, Siberia Military District as 308 Rifle Division, Apr. 1942.
—Stalingrad, defended Barrikady Factory w/62 Army, fall 1942.
—RVGK as 308 Rifle Division, Dec. 1942–Mar. 1943 (SME).
—Orel w/3 Army (rest of war), July 1943.
—Designated Guards, Sep. 1943.
—Gomel, Nov. 1943.
—Dnieper River, Dec. 1943.
—Rogachev, Feb. 1944.
—Belorussian Op., June 1944.
—Bialystok, July 1944.
—Ostrolenka, Sep. 1944.
—East Prussian Op., Jan. 1945.
—Berlin area, Apr. 1945.
—RVGK (FHO), Apr. 1945.
—Named in honor of the Belorussian SSR, as a Guards Motorized Rifle Division, 1967.

—"Rogachev, Bialystok, in the name of the Belorussian SSR," Orders of Red Banner, Suvorov, Kutuzov.

121 Guards Rifle Division
Units: 337, 340, 342 Guards Rifle, 313 Guards Artillery Regiments.
—Raised in Saratov, Volga Military District as 342 Rifle Division, Sep–Nov 1941.
—Designated Guards, Sep. 1943.
—Bryansk, Sep. 1943.
—Gomel w/3 Army, Nov. 1943.
—Rovno Lutsk Op. w/76 Rifle Corps, 13 Army (to end of war), Feb. 1944.
—Rogachev, Feb. 1944.
—Lvov Sandomir Op., on Lvov axis, July 1944.
—San River, July 1944.
—Sandomir Bridgehead, Aug–Dec 1944.
—Kielce, Vistula Oder Op., Jan. 1945.
—Silesian Op., Feb. 1945.
—Berlin Op., Apr. 1945.
—Wittenberg, Apr. 1945.
—Prague Op., May 1945.
—Carpathian Military District, Mar. 1946 (EUCOM Study).
—"Gomel, Rogachev, Kielce," Orders of Lenin, Red Banner, Suvorov.

122 Guards Rifle Division
—Formed from 249 Rifle Division "Estonian," reported in Pravda, 28 June 1945.
—Leningrad Military District w/8 Guards Rifle Corps, 10 Guards Army, Apr. 1946 (Feb. 1947 OB).

128 Guards Mountain Rifle Division
Units: 315, 323, 327 Guards Mountain Rifle Regiments.
—Raised Ashkabad, Central Asia Military District as 83 Mountain Rifle Division, before 1941.
—Designated Guards, Oct. 1943.
—Caucasus, Oct. 1943.
—Kerch, as reserve of the Independent Coastal Army, Jan. 1944.
—Crimea w/3 Mountain Rifle Corps, 4 Ukrainian Front, Apr. 1944.
—Sevastopol, May 1944.
—Carpathian Mountains, Sep. 1944.
—Lower Silesian Op., jan. 1945.
—Carpathian Military District, Mar. 1946 (EUCOM Study).
—Probably an independent division.

—"Turkestan, Carpathian Mountains, Katowice, Feodosiya, Sevastopol."

129 Guards Rifle Division
Units: 320, 325, 330 Guards Rifle Regiments.
—Kerch Landing w/22 Rifle Corps, 18 Army, Nov. 1943.
—Zhitomir Berdichev area w/22 Rifle Corps, 18 Army, Dec. 1943–Jan. 1944.
—Lvov Sandomir Op., July 1944.
—Carpathian Uzhgorod Op. w/107 Rifle Corps, 1 Guards Army, Sep. 1944.
—Kazatin area, Carpathian Military District, Feb. 1946 (Feb. 1947 OB).
—"Zhitomir, Lvov."

CHAPTER SEVEN

Rifle Divisions

1 Moscow Proletarian Motorized Rifle Division
Units: 6, 175, 356 Rifle, 13 Artillery Regiments.
—Formed as Independent Moscow Rifle Regiment, 1924.
—Reformed as Moscow Proletarian Rifle Division; Moscow Rifle Regiment became 1 Rifle Regiment, Feb. 1927.
—Used to form 3 new divisions; 1 Rifle Regiment formed new Moscow Proletarian Rifle Division, 2 Rifle Regiment formed 126 Rifle Division, 3 Rifle Regiment became 115 Rifle Division, Aug. 1939.
—New Moscow Proletarian Rifle Division had 6, 175, 356 Rifle, 13 Artillery Regiments, Aug. 1939.
—Reformed as motorized rifle division, Jan. 1940.
—RVGK w/7 Mechanized Corps at Tula, June 1941.
—Borisov, first use of T-34 tanks, 30 June 1941.
—Berezina River, July 1941.
—Orsha w/20 Army, July 1941.
—On Minsk-Moscow Highway w/22 Army, July 1941.
—Reformed as 1 Tank Division but not equipped, Aug. 1941.
—Yartsevo area w/16 Army, Sep. 1941.
—Reformed as 1 Guards Motorized Rifle Division, 21 Sep. 1941.
—Later reformed as 1 Guards Rifle Division (1st formation), then 1 Guards Mechanized Corps, Nov. 1942.
—Independent division.
Key Commanders: Col. Ya.G. Kyeyser, June 1941.

1 Rifle Division
Units: 408, 412, 415 Rifle, 1076 Artillery Regiments.
—Formed from 1 Moscow Detachment of Red Guards of Special Designation, Belorussia, 1918.
—First Army reformed into 1 Rifle Division, Jan. 1921.
—Archangelsk, June 1941.
—Western Special Military District w/1 Rifle Corps, 10 Army, June 1941.
—SME says activated Kuibyshev, Volga Military District w/5 Reserve Army in RVGK, June 1942.

—Stalingrad w/63 Army, July 1942.
—Stalingrad offensive w/1 Guards Army, Nov. 1942.
—Reformed as 58 Guards Rifle Division, 31 Dec. 1942.
—Third formation activated at Nevel, Moscow Military District, Jan. 1944.
—Gdynia area w/70 Army, Mar. 1945.

2 Rifle Division
Units: 13, 200, 261 Rifle, 164 Artillery Regiments.
—Was 2 Border Division, Western Front, 1921.
—Raised in Minsk, prior to 1935.
—Minsk, Belorussian Military District, 1935.
—Belorussian Maneuvers w/16 Rifle Corps, Sep. 1936.
—North of Grodno w/3 Army, June 1941.
—First formation destroyed in Novgorod Pocket, fall 1941.
—Second formation raised at Issakogorskiy, Arkhangelsk Military District, Jan. 1942.
—Sevastopol w/Independent Coastal Army, May 1942.
—Novgorod-Luga Op. w/112 Rifle Corps, 59 Army, Jan. 1944.
—"Verkne-Udinsk, Transbaikal."
Key Commanders: I.V. Koniev, 1935.

3 Rifle Division
Units: 18, 70, 64 Rifle, 65 Artillery Regiments.
—Raised in Far East Military District before 1940.
—Finland, 1940.
—Petrozavodsk, Oct. 1941.
—The 264 Rifle Regiment also associated with 241 Rifle Division, Oct. 1941.
—In Far East w/2 Independent Red Banner Army, Apr. 1943.
—In 2 Independent Red Banner Army, Aug. 1945.
—Birobidzhan, Transbaikal Military District, Jan. 1947 (Apr. 1947 OB).

4 Rifle Division
Units: 39, 101, 220 Rifle, 40 Artillery Regiments.
—On western front, 1921.
—Received honorific "in the name of the German Proletariat," 1923.
—Headquarters in Minsk until 1923.
—Belorussian Maneuvers w/5 Rifle Corps, Sep. 1936.
—Transcaucasus Military District w/3 Rifle Corps, 46 Army, July 1941.
—Caucasus Mountains, Aug. 1942.
—Baltic Special Military District w/11 Army, Apr. 1943.
—RVGK w/11 Army, May 1944.
—Pulawy Bridgehead w/25 Rifle Corps, 69 Army; had only six rifle battalions, Jan. 1945.

—Berlin Op. w/25 Rifle Corps, 69 Army, Apr. 1945.
—"Beshitsa."

5 Rifle Division
Units: 142, 190, 336 Rifle, 27 Artillery Regiment.
—Activated Kurgan, as 5 Rifle Division "Saratov," 1918 (SME).
—Regrouped to western front by Lenin's order, 1920
—Received honorific "in the name of the Czechoslovakian Proletariat," 1923.
—In Moscow Military District, 1933.
—Belorussian Maneuvers w/16 Rifle Corps, Sep. 1936.
—First formation raised Polotsk, Western Special Military District (FHO), 1936.
—Baltic Special Military District W/16 Rifle Corps, 11 Army as covering division, June 1941.
—With Reserve Army Group as an independent division, Oct. 1941.
—Moscow axis w/30 Army, Dec. 1941.
—Demyansk, Jan. 1942.
—First formation became 44 Guards Rifle Division, 5 Oct. 1942.
—Second formation Yefremov, Moscow Military District, Sep–Oct 1942.
—Distinguished itself at Orel, Aug. 1943.
—Dnieper River w/82 Independent Rifle Corps, 37 Army, Oct. 1943.
—East Prussian Op., Jan. 1945.
—RVGK (FHO), Apr. 1945.
—Probably an independent division.
—"Orel, Volkovsk, Bialystok, Tannenberg," Orders of Lenin, Red Banner, Kutuzov, Suvorov.

6 Rifle Division
Units: 84, 125, 333 Rifle Regiments.
—Brest Fortress w/28 Rifle Corps, 4 Army, June 1941.
—Ochkino w/13 Army, Sep. 1941.
—Stalingrad axis, June 1942.
—Orel, Aug. 1943.
—Southwest Ukraine w/26 Guards Rifle Corps, 2 Ukrainian Front, Jan. 1944.
—Targul Frumos, May 1944.
—Iasi Kishinev Op., Aug. 1944.
—Stralsund, Germany w/5 Mechanized Army, Sep. 1946 (Feb. 1947 OB).
—Possibly an independent division.
—"Orel, Roman, in the name of MSU Tolbukin," Twice Order of Red Banner, Order of Suvorov.

7 Rifle Division
Units: 27, 300, 354 Rifle Regiments.
—Kiev Special Military District w/8 Mechanized Corps, 26 Army, June 1941.
—Solnechnogorsk, Nov. 1941.
—Into Northwest Front reserve, May 1943.
—Northwest Front reserve w/14 Guards Rifle Corps, July 1943.
—Baltic area, July 1944.
—RVGK (FHO), Aug. 1944.
—Reformed as 118 Guards Rifle Division, reported in Pravda, 28 June 1945.
—Southwest Leningrad Military District w/8 Guards Rifle Corps, 10 Guards Army, Apr. 1946 (Feb. 1947 OB).
—"Estonian."

8 Rifle Division
Units: 151, 229, 310 Rifle, 62 Artillery Regiments.
—In Belorussia, 1918.
—Received honorific "Minsk" while on western front, 1921.
—Raised at Semipalitinsk, Kazakstan, Central Asia Military District, before 1936.
—Belorussian Maneuvers w/5 Rifle Corps, Sep. 1936.
—Western Special Military District w/1 Rifle Corps, 10 Army, June 1941.
—Destroyed in Minsk pocket, fall 1941.
—Second formation raised; in Bryansk Front w/48 Army, Apr. 1942.
—Voronezh, Jan. 1943.
—Kursk w/15 Rifle Corps 13 Army, July 1943.
—Pripet River, Fall 1943.
—Southwest Ukraine w/23 Rifle Corps, 60 Army, Jan. 1944.
—Rovno Lutsk Op. w/23 Rifle Corps, 13 Army, Jan–Feb 1944.
—Yampol, Mar. 1944.
—Carpathian Mountains w/27 Guards Independent Rifle Corps, 13 Army; Grigorenko stated it had only 50% of its normal complement of 12,000 men; i.e. it was an "A" division, Sep. 1944.
—Poprad, Czechoslovakia (Cz.), Jan. 1945.
—Kydne, Cz., Mar. 1945.
—Pardubice, Cz., May 1945.
—Zwickau, Germany, 15 May 1945.
—Dissolved and absorbed by a rifle division of 52 Army, May 1945.
—Grigorenko was Chief of Staff of this division, 1944–45.
—Probably an independent division.
—"Yampol, Carpathian, Dzerzhinski, Minsk."

9 Mountain Rifle Division
Units: 36, 121, 193, 1329 Rifle, 256 Artillery Regiments.
—Formed Kursk as 1 "Kursk" Rifle Division, July–Sep 1918.
—Redesignated 1 Caucasus Rifle Division, 1922.
—Named in honor of Georgian SSR, 1928.
—Reformed as Mountain Division, 1930.
—Designated 9 Mountain Rifle Division, 1936.
—Batumi w/40 Rifle Corps, 46 Army, June 1941.
—Turkish border, 1941–42.
—Elements made amphibious landing at Feodosiya w/44 Army, Dec. 1941.
—Tuapse w/46 Army, Dec. 1942.
—Maikop w/56 Army, Jan. 1943.
—Krasnodar w/37 Army, Feb. 1943.
—Kuban w/56 Army, Apr–Aug 1943.
—Into RVGK; reformed as 9 "Plastun, Krasnodar," Orders of Red Banner, Red Star Rifle Division. Had Rifle Regiments of "100's" and Plastun Reconnaissance/Guard Battalions, Sep. 1943.
—Taman Peninsula w/Independent Coastal Army, Jan–Feb 1944.
—Lvov Sandomir Op. w/5 Guards Army, July 1944.
—Sandomir Silesia Op. w/60 Army, Jan–Feb 1945.
—Krakow, Jan. 1945.
—Silesian Op., Mar. 1945.
—Morava Ostrova Op., Apr. 1945.
—Prague Op., May 1945.
—Independent division.
—"Plastun, Krasnodar, Batum, Krakow," Orders of Red Banner, Kutuzov, Red Star in the name of the Georgian SSR.

10 Rifle Division
Units: 62, 98, 204 Rifle, 30 Artillery Regiments.
—Regrouped from eastern to western front by Lenin Order, 1920.
—Raised at Vladimir, Moscow Military District (FHO), Sep. 1939.
—Tallin w/8 Army, June 1941.
—Riga, June 1941.
—Estonia, Aug. 1941.
—Krasnoye Selo, Sep. 1941.
—Leningrad w/8 and 42 Armies, Sep. 1941.
—RVGK (FHO), Apr. 1945.
—Order of Red Banner.

11 Rifle Division
Units: 163, 219, 320 Rifle, 72 Artillery Regiments.

—In the Civil War as 11 "Petrograd" Rifle Division, 1919.
—When part of 19 Rifle Corps, served as basis for 11 Mechanized Corps; one of the first two such formations in the Red Army, 1932.
—Reactivated at Kingisepp, Leningrad Military District, 1936.
—Baltic Special Military District w/8 Army, June 1941.
—Latvia, June 1941.
—Kingisepp, Aug. 1941.
—Estonia, Aug. 1941.
—Krasnoye Selo, Sep. 1941.
—Leningrad w/8 Army, Sep. 1941.
—Probably on Leningrad Front, 1941–44.
—Oranienbaum w/2 Shock Army, Jan. 1944.
—"Leningrad."

12 Rifle Division
Units: 57, 192, 214 Rifle, 7 Artillery Regiments.
—Raised at Blagoveshchensk, Far East by 1934.
—Brest w/4 Army, June 1941.
—Reformed in East, after June 1941.
—Redeployed to western front w/26 Army, Dec. 1941.
—Tambovka, Far East w/2 Independent Red Banner Army; 43 Tank Brigade colocated, Apr. 1943.
—Far East w/2 Independent Red Banner Army, Aug. 1945.
—Sakhalin Island, Far East Military District, 1946 (July 1947 OB).
—"Panfilov."

13 Rifle Division
Units: 119, 172, 296 Rifle, 48 Artillery Regiments.
—In Minsk Fortified Area, Sep. 1936.
—Raised at Minsk (FHO) by 1937.
—Western Special Military District w/5 Rifle Corps, 10 Army, June 1941.
—Leningrad w/42 Army, Sep. 1941.
—Probably on Leningrad Front, 1942–43.
—Leningrad Op. w/67 Army, Jan. 1943.
—Far East Military District, Nov. 1947 (Feb. 1948 OB).

14 Rifle Division
Units: 135, 155, 325 Rifle, 95 Artillery Regiments.
—Raised Moscow, Moscow Military District, 1922.
—Finland, 1939–40.
—Murmansk w/14 Army, June 1941.

—Kandalaksha axis, July 1941.
—Commander captured by Germans, Aug. 1941.
—Karelian Front 1941-44.
—Petsamo Kirkenes Op. w/14 Army, Sep.1944.
—Reformed as 101 Guards Rifle Division, 29 Oct. 1944.
—Second formation in East Prussia, Feb. 1945.
—White Sea Military District, Sep. 1946, (EUCOM Study).
—Northwest of Petrozavodsk, 1946 (Feb. 1947 OB).
—"Petsamo Kirkenes."

15 Rifle Division
Units: June 1941: 47, 321 Motorized, 14 Tank, 203 Motorized Artillery Regiments.
July 1941: 47, 321, 676 Rifle, 203 Artillery Regiments.
—Formed at Ulyanovsk, 1918.
—Motorized, Sep. 1939.
—Bessarabia, Bucovina campaign, June 1940.
—Odessa Military District w/2 Mechanized Corps, 9 Army, June 1941.
—Beltsy; badly mauled, July 1941.
—Reorganized as Rifle Division, Aug. 1941.
—Sevastopol, Nov. 1941.
—Voronezh, Jan. 1943.
—Kursk w/29 Rifle Corps, 13 Army, July 1943.
—Belorussia w/89 Rifle Corps, 61 Army, Mar. 1944.
—Ternopol, Apr. 1944.
—Sivash, Crimea, Apr. 1944.
—Crimea, May 1944.
—Belorussia Op. w/18 Rifle Corps, 65 Army, June 1944.
—Iasi Kishinev Op., Aug. 1944.
—East Pomeranian Op. (Stargard), w/65 Army, Mar. 1945.
—Stettin and Gdansk w/65 Army, Mar. 1945.
—Rostock, May 1945.
—Bulgaria, 1946 w/37 Army (EUCOM Study).
—Transcaucasus Military District, postwar period (SME).
—"Sivash, Stettin," Order of Lenin, twice Order of Red Banner, Order of Suvorov.

16 Rifle Division
Units: 156, 167, 249 Rifle, 224 Artillery Regiments.
—Received honorific "in the name of Kikvidze," Belorussia, 1921.
—Raised at Novgorod, Leningrad Military District, Oct. 1939.
—Baltic Special Military District w/27 Army, June 1941.

—Destroyed near Mga, Leningrad front, summer 1941.
—Second formation raised at Malechna, Moscow Military District, Dec. 1941.
—Stalingrad axis, July 1942.
—Kursk w/48 Army, July 1943.
—Shauliai w/5 Guards Tank Army, Aug. 1944.
—Lithuania w/2 Guards Army, Sep–Oct 1944.
—Lithuania w/11 Guards Army, Oct. 1946 (Feb. 1947 OB).
—Probably an independent division.
—"Latvian," Order of Red Banner.

17 Rifle Division
Units: First Formation: 55, 271, 278 Rifle, 20 Artillery Regiments; Second Formation: 1312, 1314, 1316 Rifle, 320 Artillery Regiments.
—First formation raised at Gorki, Moscow Military District, by 1920.
—Berezina River, 1920.
—Koniev commanded as 17 "Nizhni-Novgorod Rifle Division," in 1930's.
—Finnish War, 1939–40.
—Western Special Military District w/21 Rifle Corps, 10 Army, June 1941.
—Molodecheno w/31 Rifle Corps, 13 Army, July 1941.
—Destroyed at Vyazma, Oct. 1941.
—The 55 Rifle Regiment to 176 Rifle Division, 271 Rifle Regiment to 181 Rifle Division, 278 Rifle Regiment to 175 Rifle Division, after Oct. 1941.
—Second formation from 17 Moscow People's Militia Rifle Division, Moscow, Moscow Military District, after Oct. 1941.
—Moscow axis w/43 Army, Nov. 1941.
—Belorussian Op., June 1944.
—East Prussian Op. w/48 Army, Jan. 1945.
—Southwest Poland w/46 Rifle Corps, July 1946 (Feb. 1948 OB).
—"Moscow, Rezkaja, Bobruysk," Order of Red Banner.

18 Rifle Division
Units: First Formation: 97, 208, 316 Rifle, 3 Artillery Regiments; Second Formation: 414, 419, 424 Rifle, 1027 Artillery Regiments.
—Raised Kazan, Volga Military District, Nov. 1939.
—North of Lake Ladoga, Finland w/8 Army, Dec. 1939.
—Orel Military District w/20 Army, June 1941.
—RVGK w/22 Army, July 1941.
—Volokolamsk, Nov. 1941.
—Moscow w/16 Army, Dec. 1941.

—First formation associated with 18 People's Militia Rifle Division, Dec. 1941.
—Designated 11 Guards Rifle Division, Jan. 1942.
—Second formation raised at Ryazan, Moscow Military District as an independent division in the RVGK, Apr. 1942.
—The 3 Artillery Regiment to 67 Rifle Division, Apr. 1942.
—RVGK as an independent rifle division, July 1942.
—Kletskaya w/4 Tank Army, Stalingrad axis, July 1942.
—Danzig area w/19 Army, Mar. 1945.
—Southern Leningrad or southwest Poland w/105 Rifle Corps, 7 Mechanized Army, July 1946 (Feb. 1947 OB).
—Independent division.

19 Rifle Division
Units: June 1941: 32, 282, 315 Rifle Regiments; 1943: 32, 315, 1310 Rifle, 90 Artillery Regiments.
—Raised Tambov, July 1922.
—Honorific "Tambov," 1923.
—Honorifics "Voronezh, Worker's" Red Banner Rifle Division, 1925.
—Raised at Voronezh, Orel Military District (FHO), by 1936.
—Orel Military District, June 1941.
—Yelnaya area w/24 Army; Zhukov says fought well, Aug. 1941.
—In Reserve Front w/24 Army, Sep. 1941.
—Moscow w/10 Army, Dec. 1941.
—Mozhaisk w/5 Army, Jan. 1942.
—June 1942 w/5 Army at Sichevka, June 1942.
—RVGK, Jan–Feb 1943.
—Kharkov, Feb. 1943.
—To Southwest front w/3 Tank and 57 Armies, Mar. 1943.
—Kharkov, July 1943.
—Belgorod 1943.
—Dnieper River w/24 Guards Rifle Corps, 7 Guards Army, Sep. 1943.
—Krivoi Rog, Oct–Dec 1943.
—Southwest Ukraine w/49 Rifle Corps, 57 Army, Jan. 1944.
—Right Bank Ukraine w/64 Rifle Corps, 57 Army, Feb. 1944.
—Rumania, Aug. 1944.
—Bulgaria, Sep. 1944.
—Belgrade Op., Oct. 1944.
—Hungary, Nov. 1944.
—Bratislava, Apr. 1945.
—Czechoslovakia, May 1945.
—Southern Germany as Motorized Rifle Division, 1946 (Feb. 1947 OB).
—"Voronezh, Shumilov, Proletariat," Order of Red Banner.

20 Mountain Rifle Division
Units: 67, 174, 265 Rifle, 61 Artillery Regiments.
—Designated one of four best divisions in Red Army by Timoshenko, Transcaucasus Military District, Aug. 1940.
—Transcaucasus Military District, w/40 Rifle Corps, 45 Army, July 1941.
—Caucasus Mountains, June 1942.
—Pseashkita/Belorechenskaya Passes, North Caucasus, Aug. 1942.
—Krasnodar w/56 Army, Jan. 1943.
—Novorossiysk, Jan. 1943.
—Krimskaya, Mar. 1943.
—Southern Ukraine w/20 Rifle Corps, 4 Ukrainian Front, Jan. 1944.
—Reformed as rifle division, May 1944.
—Berlin Op w/28 Army, Apr. 1945.
—RVGK (FHO), Apr. 1945.
—Germany, 1946 (Feb. 1947 OB).

21 Rifle Division
Units: 94, 116, 326 Rifle, 78 Artillery Regiments.
—From eastern to western front by Lenin order, 1920.
—Raised at Spassk, Far East Military District by 1935.
—To western front, Oct. 1941.
—Finnish Front, Nov. 1941.
—Hungary w/26 Army, Mar. 1945.
—"Perm," Order of Red Banner.

22 Rifle Division
Units: 191, 201, 211, 246 Rifle, 157 Artillery Regiments.
—Far East, 1938.
—In Far East Military District, June 1941.
—Grodekovo, Far East w/1 Independent Red Banner Army, Apr. 1943.
—Far East w/1 Independent Red Banner Army, Aug. 1945.
—The 191 Rifle Regiment is associated with 201 Rifle Division.

23 Rifle Division
Units: 89, 117, 225 Rifle Regiment, 211 Artillery Regiments.
—Raised in North Caucasus Military District before Aug. 1932.
—Received Order of Lenin at Kharkov, Aug. 1932.
—Baltic Special Military District w/16 Rifle Corps, 11 Army, June 1941.
—Jonava, June 1941.
—Destroyed, July 1941.
—Second formation raised at Dunaburg, Ostsee, before Dec. 1941.
—RVGK w/3 Shock Army, Dec. 1941.
—Stalingrad axis, Aug. 1942.

—Reformed as 71 Guards Rifle Division, 1 Mar. 1943.
—Third formation raised at Voroshilov, Kharkov Military District, May 1943.
—Stalingrad offensive w/65 Army, Nov. 1942.
—Kursk, July 1943.
—Kiev, Nov. 1943.
—Zhitomir, Dec. 1943.
—Zhitomir Berdichev Op., Jan. 1944.
—Belorussian Op., June 1944.
—Riga, Oct. 1944.
—"Kharkov, Vitebsk, Kiev, Riga, Zhitomir," Orders of Lenin, Red Banner.

24 Rifle Division
Units: 7, 168, 274 Rifle, 160 Artillery Regiments.
—Activated Simbirsk (Ulyanovsk) as 1 "Simbirsk" Rifle Division, June–July 1918.
—Liberated Lenin's home town of Simbirsk (Ulyanovsk) and Samara in Civil War, 1919.
—In Mozyr Group on western front, May 1920.
—Called "Iron" Division, 25 Oct. 1921.
—Redesignated 24 Rifle Division, Apr. 1922.
—Finland w/7 Army, 1939–40.
—Redeployed to Western Special Military District w/21 Rifle Corps, 13 Army, 22 June 1941.
—Molodechno w/31 Rifle Corps, 13 Army, July 1941.
—Minsk Pocket w/10 Army; lost banner, Aug. 1941.
—Deactivated in disgrace for losing banner and dropped from rolls of Red Army (SME), 27 Dec. 1941.
—Second formation raised Vologda, Archangelsk Military District; lost all orders, history of original division, Feb. 1942.
—Kalinin Front w/3 Shock Army, Mar. 1942.
—Velikiye Luki, May 1942.
—RVGK, Aug. 1942.
—To Stalingrad axis, Aug. 1942.
—Volga Corridor w/1 Guards Army, Sep. 1942.
—Stalingrad area w/4 Tank, 1 Guards, 24, 1 Tank and 65 Armies, Sep–Nov. 1942.
—Stalingrad offensive w/65 Army, Nov. 1942.
—Stalingrad, Jan. 1943.
—Pskol River w/62 Army, Feb–Apr 1943.
—Don Basin w/1 Guards Army, Aug. 1943.
—Krivoi Rog w/37 Army, Oct. 1943.

—Banner found by D.N. Tyapin (later made honorary member of 1 Company, 7 Rifle Regiment); had not been captured by Germans, Oct. 1943.
—Kiev, W/18 Army, Nov. 1943.
—Zhitomir Berdichev area; took Berdichev, Dec 1943–Jan 1944.
—Southwest Ukraine w/52 Rifle Corps, 18 Army, Jan. 1944.
—By NKO order, the unit received all history, orders of original division, 20 Feb. 1944.
—Proskurov Chernovtsy Op. w/18 and 1 Guards Armies, Mar. 1944.
—Carpathian Mountains w/18 Army, Apr. 1944.
—Lvov Sandomir Op. w/11 Guards Independent Rifle Corps, July 1944.
—Uzhgorod Mukachevo Op. w/2 Guards Army, Oct. 1944.
—Carpathian Mountains, Sep. 1944.
—East Carpathian Op., Czechoslovakia, w/18 Army, Jan. 1945.
—Morava Ostrava Op., Apr. 1945.
—Northwest of Petrozavodsk, Leningrad Military District, 1946 (Feb. 1947 OB).
—Reformed into Motorized Rifle Division after war (SME).
—Awarded Order of October Revolution (SME), Oct. 1978.
—Independent division.
—"Samara, Ulyanovsk, Berdichev, Carpathian, Iron," Three times Order of Red Banner, Orders of Suvorov, Bogdan Khmelnitskiy.
Key Commanders: K.N. Galitskiy, June–July 1941; F.A. Prokhorov, Feb. 1942–May 1945.

25 Rifle Division
Units: 31, 54, 287 Rifle, 69 Artillery Regiments.
—Raised in Civil War; commanded by Chapayev, 1918.
—Reactivated at Poltava, Kharkov Military District, 1925.
—Received Order of Lenin, Feb. 1933.
—Finland, 1939–40.
—Odessa Military District w/9 Army, June 1941.
—In the Coastal Group, Odessa, July 1941.
—Sevastopol; two battalions of 287 Rifle Regiment made up of naval infantry, Nov. 1941.
—Sevastopol w/Independent Coastal Army, May 1942.
—Destroyed Sevastopol, July 1942.
—Zvenigorod w/53 Army, Feb. 1944.
—Riga area w/51 Army, Aug. 1944.
—The 31 Rifle Regiment associated w/40 Rifle Division, 287 Rifle Regiment w/51 Rifle Division.
—Combat traditions and history now preserved in 25 Guards Motorized Rifle Division (SME).
—"In the name of Chapayev," Order of Lenin.

26 Rifle Division
Units: 87, 312, 349 Rifle, 187 Artillery Regiments.
—Raised at Voroshilov, Far East Military District by 1935.
—Ussuriysk, 1935.
—Far East Military District, June 1941.
—Transferred to West (northern sector), Oct. 1941.
—Demyansk w/27 Army, Feb. 1943.
—Staraya Russa area w/34 Army, Mar. 1943.
—Tilsit, Oct. 1944.
—"Stalin, Tilsit, Zlatoust" Twice Order of Red Banner.

27 Rifle Division
Units: 132, 239, 345 Rifle, 53 Artillery Regiments.
—Civil War Rifle Division, 1920.
—First formation raised at Vitebsk, Wesyern Special Military District (FHO), before June 1941.
—Grodno area w/4 Rifle Corps, 3 Army, June 1941.
—Grodno w/3 Army, June 1941.
—Destroyed in Minsk pocket, July 1941.
—Second formation raised in Arkhangelsk Military District, Aug. 1941.
—Sredniy and Rybachiy Peninsula, Sep. 1941.
—Karelian Front w/26 Army, Mar. 1942.
—History to new 27 Guards Rifle Division (SME), Apr–May 1942.
—Danzig area w/19 Army, Mar. 1945.
—Germany w/5 Mechanized Army, 1946; gone by Feb. 1947 OB.

28 Mountain Rifle Division
Units: 88, 144, 235 Rifle, 112 Artillery Regiments.
—In North Caucasus Military District, Oct. 1935.
—Sochi, North Caucasus Military District as a mountain rifle division before 1941.
—The 235 Rifle Regiment is associated w/20 Mountain Rifle Division.
—RVGK w/20 Army, June 1941.
—Destroyed in Kiev Pocket, Sep. 1941.
—Second formation raised in Archangelsk Military District, before May 1942.
—Velikiye Luki, May 1942.
—Velikiye Luki w/3 Shock Army, Dec. 1942.
—Nevel Op., Oct. 1943.
—Targul Frumos, May 1944.
—Tblisi, March 1946 (Aug. 1946 OB).
—"Nevel," Order of Red Banner.

29 Rifle Division

Units: First Formation: 34, 106, 128 Rifle, 151 Artillery Regiments; Second Formation: 1294, 1296, 1298 Rifle, 974 Artillery Regiments; Third Formation 106, 128, 299 Rifle, 77 Artillery Regiments; Fourth Formation: 106, 128, 302 Rifle, 77 Artillery Regiments.
—Regrouped from eastern to western front by Lenin order, 1920.
—Raised Slonim, Western Special Military District before 1941.
—Western Special Military District w/6 Mechanized Corps, 10 Army, June 1941.
—Destroyed in Minsk pocket, July 1941.
—Second formation raised Moscow from 7 Reserve (People's Militia) Rifle Division, July 1941.
—Destroyed in Vyazma pocket, Oct. 1941.
—Third formation raised at Akmolinsk, Archangelsk Military District, Dec. 1941.
—RVGK w/1 Reserve Army, June 1942.
—Stalingrad front w/64 Army, July 1942.
—Reformed as 72 Guards Rifle Division, Mar. 1943.
—Fourth formation raised from 10 Rifle, 68 Naval Rifle, 40 Motorized Regiment, Feb. 1943.
—Kirovograd, Jan. 1944.

30 Rifle Division

Units: 35, 71, 256 RR, 59 Arty.
—Activated as 3/4 Ural Rifle Division; redesignated 30 Rifle Division, Aug. 1918.
—Received Order of Lenin, 1934.
—Bessarabian Op., 1940.
—Reformed as Mountain Rifle Division, 1941.
—Prut River, Odessa Military District w/48 Rifle Corps, 9 Independent Army, June 1941.
—Division commander court-martialed, July 1941.
—Basis for forming 29 Army, July 1941.
—Dnepropetrovsk, Aug. 1941.
—Southern Front w/9 Army, Oct–Nov 1941.
—Rostov, Mar. 1942.
—North Caucasus w/56 Army, distinguished itself at Pavlovskaya, Aug. 1942.
—Reformed as 55 Guards Rifle Division, 18 Dec. 1942.
—Second formation raised Rossosh, Orel Military District from 119, 161 Rifle Brigades, Apr. 1943.
—Kiev, Nov. 1943.
—Zhitomir, Dec. 1943.

—Zhitomir Berdichev Op. w/94 Rifle Corps, 1 Guards Army, Jan. 1944.
—Carpathian Uzhgorod Op. w/30 Rifle Corps, 1 Guards Army, Sep. 1944.
—Probably an independent division.
—"Kiev, Irkutsk, Carpathian, Stryy, Zhitomir," Orders of Lenin, twice Red Banner, in the name of the RSFSR.

31 Rifle Division
Units: 75, 248, 818 Rifle, 32 Artillery.
—Raised at Yerevan, Transcaucasus Military District before 1941.
—Transcaucasus Military District w/23 Rifle Corps, 45 Army, July 1941.
—Taganrog, Oct. 1941.
—RVGK w/56 Independent Army, Oct. 1941.
—Rostov w/56 Independent Army, Nov. 1941.
—Southern Front w/56 Independent Army, June 1942.
—Tuapse w/18 Army, Sep. 1942.
—Stalingrad, Nov. 1942.
—Maikop w/46 Army, Jan. 1943.
—Northeast of Krasnodar, Feb. 1943.
—Kursk, July 1943.
—Southwest Ukraine w/26 Guards Independent Rifle Corps, 2 Ukrainian Front, Jan. 1944.
—Iasi Kishinev Op., Aug. 1944.
—Vistula Oder Op., Jan. 1945.
—Probably an independent division.
—"Stalingrad, Kishinev, Oder," Order of Bogdan Khmelnitskiy.

32 Rifle Division
Units: 17, 113, 322 Rifle, 133 Artillery Division.
—Raised Vladivostok, Far East Military District as a Siberian Rifle Division, 1934.
—Lake Khasan w/39 Rifle Corps, Manchurian Border, Aug. 1938.
—Razdolnoye, Far East Military District, June 1941.
—Transferred to West (central sector), Sep. 1941.
—Yelnaya, Oct. 1941.
—Borodino w/5 Army, Oct. 1941.
—Mozhaisk defense line w/5 Army, Nov. 1941.
—Mozhaisk w/5 Army, Jan. 1942.
—Reformed as 29 Guards Rifle Division, May 1942.
—Second formation raised Moscow, Moscow Military District, May 1942.
—Belorussia w/33 Army, May 1944.
—Mogilev w/81 Rifle Corps, 49 Army, July 1944.
—Baltic area, Sep. 1944.

—The 17th Rifle Regiment has the Order of the Red Banner.
—Order of Red Banner.

33 Rifle Division
Units: 73, 82, 164 Rifle, 44 Artillery Regiments.
—Received honorific "Kuban," on western front, 1920.
—Territorial rifle division brought up to full TO&E and deployed from Belorussian to Moscow Military District for an exercise, 1928.
—Raised at Chaussy, Western Special Military District, Sep. 1939.
—Baltic Special Military District w/6 Rifle Corps, 11 Army as a covering division, June 1941.
—RVGK w/3 Shock Army, Dec. 1941.
—Stalingrad offensive w/21 Army, Nov. 1942.
—Cholm (Kholm), Leningrad Front, Oct. 1943.
—Ostrov w/1 Shock Army, July 1944.
—Berlin Op., Apr. 1945.
—Halberstadt, Germany w/12 Guards Rifle Corps, 3 Mechanized Army, Sep. 1946 (Feb. 1947 OB).
—Probably an independent division.
—"Cholm, Samarsk."

34 Rifle Division
Units: 83, 134, 327 Rifle, 145 Howitzer Artillery, 360 Artillery Regiments.
—Raised at Birobidzhan, Far East Military District, 1934.
—The 134 Rifle Regiment associated w/75 Rifle Division.
—Babatevo, Far East w/15 Army, "Front Command Khabarovsk," Apr. 1943.
—Manchurian Campaign w/15 Army, Aug. 1945.
—Birobidzhan, Transbaikal Military District, 1947 (Nov. 1947 OB).

35 Rifle Division
Units: 183, 196, 352 Rifle, 119 Artillery Regiments.
—Raised at Bikin, Far East Military District, by 1937.
—Far East Military District, June 1941.
—Far East w/18 Rifle Corps, July 1941.
—Bikin, Far East w/35 Army in "Front Command Khabarovsk," Apr. 1943.
—Far East, Aug. 1945.

36 Motorized Rifle Division
Units: 24, 76, 149 Motorized Rifle, 175 Artillery, 184 Howitzer Artillery Regiments.

—Raised Birobidzhan, Far East Military District as a Motorized Rifle Division, 1934.
—Chita, 1937.
—To Ulan Ude, 1938.
—Khalkin Gol, Aug. 1938.
—Sayn Shanda, w/17 Army, "Front Command Chita," Apr. 1943.
—Kursk, July 1943.
Key Commanders: Gen-Major Petrov, Apr. 1943.

37 Rifle Division
Units: 20, 91, 247 Rifle, 170 Artillery Regiments.
—Raised at Novocherkassk, North Caucasus Military District, 1919.
—Western Military District, 1924.
—Belorussian Maneuvers as an independent division, Sep. 1936.
—Western Special Military District w/10 Army, June 1941.
—Molodechno w/21 Rifle Corps, 13 Army, July 1941.
—Petrozavodsk axis, Shiya River, Sep. 1941.
—Riga, Oct. 1944.
—Graudents w/2 Shock Army, Feb. 1945.
—Pomeranian Op. w/2 Shock Army, Mar. 1945.
—Order of Red Banner.

38 Rifle Division
Units: 29, 48, 343 Rifle, 214 Artillery Regiments.
—Raised at Rostov, North Caucasus Military District, 1920.
—RVGK w/19 Army, June–July 1941.
—RVGK w/43 Army, July 1941.
—Smolensk w/43 Army, July 1941.
—Nearly destroyed at Yartsevo, July 1941.
—Yartsevo w/16 Army, Sep. 1941.
—Destroyed in Vyazma pocket, Oct. 1941.
—Second formation raised Alma Ata, Central Asia, Jan. 1942.
—To Stalingrad from 57 Army, July 1942.
—Stalingrad w/64 Army, Aug–Nov 1942.
—Stalingrad front w/51 Army, Dec. 1942.
—Reformed as 73 Guards Rifle Division, Mar. 1943.
—Third formation raised at Kutaisi, Transcaucasus Military District, Apr. 1943.
—Dnieper River w/40 Army, Sep. 1943.
—Southwest Ukraine w/47 Rifle Corps, 27 Army, Jan. 1944.
—Targul Frumos w/104 Rifle Corps, 40 Army, May 1944.
—The 343 Rifle Regiment is associated w/129 Rifle Division.
—Probably an independent division.
—Order of Red Banner.

39 Rifle Division
Units: 50, 199, 254 Rifle, 15 Artillery, 87 Howitzer Artillery Regiments.
—Former 1 Transbaikal Rifle Division, 1920s–30s.
—Rokossovskiy was a regimental commander in the division, circa 1930.
—Raised Vladivostok, Far East Military District (FHO), by 1937.
—Lake Khasan w/39 Rifle Corps, Aug. 1938.
—Far East, June 1941.
—Tschekunda, Far East w/15 Army, "Front Command Khabarovsk," Apr. 1943.
—Kursk, July 1943.
—Far East w/1 Independent Red Banner Army, Aug. 1943.
—Far East w/1 Independent Red Banner Army, Aug. 1945.
—Baku, Transcaucasus Military District, 22 Mar. 1946 (Feb. 1947 OB).
—"Pacific," Orders of Red Banner, Kutuzov.
Key Commanders: Petrov, 1957–60.

40 Rifle Division
Units: 31, 178, 231 Rifle, 82 Artillery, 107 Howitzer Artillery Regiments.
—Raised Slavyanka, Far East Military District, by 1934.
—The 31 Rifle Regiment associated w/25 Rifle District.
—Razdolnoye, Far East Military District, 1937.
—Lake Khasan w/39 Rifle Corps, Manchuria; won Order of Lenin, Aug. 1938.
—Only regular division left in Far East after units left for West in fall 1941 (Grigorenko).
—Kraskino, Far East w/25 Army, "Front Command Khabarovsk," Apr. 1943.
—Manchurian campaign, Aug. 1945.
—Pyongyang, North Korea w/25 Army, Jan. 1947 (Feb. 1947 OB).
—"Bogashev," Order of Lenin.

41 Rifle Division
Units: 102, 139, 244 Rifle, 132 Artillery Regiment.
—First formation raised at Krivoi Rog, Kiev Special Military District, 1940.
—Headquarters in Rava Russkaya, w/37 Rifle Corps, Kiev Special Military District, 1940.
—Lvov w/6 Army as a covering division, June 1941.
—Destroyed, Kiev pocket, Sep. 1941.
—Second formation raised Chapayevsk, Volga Military District, Mar. 1942.
—Destroyed Izyum pocket, May 1942.

—Third formation raised Verchovye, Ural Military District, from 118 Rifle Brigade, Oct. 1942.
—Kursk w/40 Rifle Corps, 63 Army, July 1943.
—Vistula Oder Op. w/69 Army, Jan. 1945.
—Grabow, Germany w/5 Mechanized Army, June 1946 (Feb. 1947 OB).

42 Rifle Division
Units: 44, 455, 459 Rifle, 472 Artillery Regiments.
—Existed in 1931.
—Raised Terijok, Archangelsk Military District, Feb. 1940.
—Finnish War, Mar. 1940.
—Western Special Military District w/28 Rifle Corps, 4 Army, June 1941.
—Defended Brest fortress w/4 Army, July 1941.
—Second formation raised Volsk, Volga Military District, Jan. 1942.
—RVGK w/66 Army, Aug. 1942.
—Smolensk, Sep. 1943.
—Lenino (near Mogilev) w/33 Army, Oct. 1943.
—Belorussia w/33 Army, May 1944.
—Mogilev w/69 Rifle Corps, 49 Army, June 1944.
—Grodno, July 1944.
—Danzig area w/49 Army, Mar. 1945.
—Crivitz, Germany w/5 Mechanized Army, July 1946 (Aug. 1946 OB).
—"Smolensk, Grodno, Kalinin," Order of Red Banner.

43 Rifle Division
Units: 65, 147, 708 Rifle, 162 Artillery Regiments.
—Raised Velikiye Luki, Moscow Military District before 1941.
—Northeast of Murmansk w/23 Army, June 1941.
—Moscow axis w/30 Army, Dec. 1941.
—Oranienbaum w/2 Shock Army, Jan. 1944.
—Latvia w/130 Rifle Corps, 6 Guards Army, Oct. 1945 (Feb. 1947 OB).

44 Rifle Division
Units: 25, 146, 305 Rifle, 122 Artillery Regiments.
—Civil War division, 1918–22.
—Raised Zhitomir, Kiev Military District before 1939.
—Finland as Motorized Rifle Division w/9 Army, destroyed by Finns at Suomussalmi, Dec. 1939.
—Kiev Special Military District w/12 Army, June 1941.
—Destroyed Belaya Tserkov, Sep. 1941.
—Second formation raised Leningrad, Leningrad Military District, Oct. 1941.

—Tikhvin, Oct. 1941.
—Attacked w/4 Army near Leningrad, Nov. 1941.
—Airlifted to Tikhvin, Nov. 1941.
—Tschudowo (Chudovo), Leningrad Front, Jan. 1944.
—Riga, Oct. 1944.
—Hungary, Dec. 1944.
—"Tschudowo, Riga."

45 Rifle Division
Units: 10, 61, 253 Rifle, 178 Artillery Regiments.
—Formed as 45 Red Banner Rifle Division, Berdichev, Kiev Military District, 1923.
—Made into a Mechanized Corps in the Ukraine; one of first two in Red Army w/11 Mechanized Corps (Leningrad), 1932.
—Vladimir Volynskiy w/5 Army, June 1941.
—Reactivated Vishniy Voloschok, Moscow Military District (FHO), July 1941.
—Destroyed Vyazma pocket, Oct. 1941.
—Kharkov w/6 Army, June 1942.
—To Stalingrad, Oct. 1942.
—Stalingrad w/62 Army, Nov. 1942.
—Second formation became 74 Guards Rifle Division, Mar. 1943.
—Third formation raised at Louti, Archangelsk Military District from 67 Naval Rifle Brigade, May 1943.
—Zaporozhye, Sep. 1943.
—Petsamo Kirkenes Op. w/14 Army, Sep. 1944.
—RVGK, Apr. 1945.
—White Sea Military District, 1946 (Feb. 1947 OB).
—"Zaporozhye," Order of Red Banner.

46 Rifle Division
Units: 176, 314, 340 Rifle, 393 Artillery Regiments.
—Raised Irkutsk, Transbaikal Military District, before 1941.
—RVGK w/32 Rifle Corps, 16 Army, July 1941.
—Ostrov area, July 1941.
—Destroyed at Yelnaya, July 1941.
—Second formation raised in Ufa, Ural Military District, after July 1941.
—Destroyed Volkhov pocket w/2 Shock Army, June 1942.
—Third formation from 1 NKVD Division, raised in Vaskelevo, Leningrad Military District, Sep. 1942.
—Leningrad area w/67 Army, Oct. 1942.
—Lutsk, Feb. 1944.
—Greifswald, Jan. 1945.

—Danzig area w/2 Shock Army, Mar. 1945.
—Germany w/5 Shock Army, 1946 (Feb. 1947 OB).
—"Lutsk," Order of Suvorov.

47 Mountain Rifle Division
Units: 145, 148, 334, 353 Rifle, 559 Artillery Regiments.
—With the Mozyr Group on the Western Front, May 1920.
—Raised Kutaisi, Transcaucasus Military District, by 1932.
—Transcaucasus Military District w/3 Rifle Corps, 46 Army, June 1941.
—RVGK to 38 Army, Sep. 1941.
—Main attack division in Poltava Offensive w/38 Army, Sep. 1941.
—Kharkov sector w/38 Army, Oct. 1941.
—Kharkov offensive w/6 Army, May 1942.
—Destroyed Izyum pocket, May 1942.
—Second formation from 21 Rifle Brigade, Nakichevan, Transcaucasus Military District, after May 1942.
—Reformed as a rifle division; 145 Rifle Regiment detached, Jan. 1945.
—Nevel, Oct. 1943.
—"Nevel," Order of Suvorov.
Key Commanders: Col. V.G. Chernov, Sep. 1941.

48 Rifle Division
Units: 268, 301, 328 Rifle, 10 Artillery Regiments.
—Raised Kalinin, Moscow Military District, 1939.
—Riga w/8 Army, June 1941.
—Oranienbaum area, Oct. 1941.
—With the Maritime Operational Group, Nov. 1941.
—On Mount Kolokolnya, Leningrad Front, Dec. 1941.
—"Kalinin, Ropsha," Order of Red Banner.

49 Rifle Division
Units: First Formation: 15, 212, 222 Rifle, 31 Artillery Regiments; Second Formation: 212, 222, 551 Rifle, 31 Artillery Regiments.
—Raised Kostroma, Moscow Military District, 1918.
—Finnish War, 1939–40; mutinied, 8 Jan. 1940.
—Brest area w/4 Army, June 1941.
—Destroyed Minsk, July 1941.
—Second formation raised in Ivanovo, Moscow Military District, Nov. 1941.
—RVGK w/66 Army, Aug. 1942.
—Stalingrad axis w/66 Army, Aug. 1942.
—Stalingrad offensive w/24 Army, Nov. 1942.
—Kursk w/50 Army, July 1943.

—Krasnaya Slobodka, July 1943.
—Roslavl, Aug. 1943.
—The 15 Rifle Regiment to 147 Rifle Division; 551 Rifle Regiment from 103 Motorized Division.
—Mogilev Op., w/70 Rifle Corps, 49 Army, June 1944.
—Berlin Op., Apr. 1945.
—"Roslavl," Order of Red Banner.

50 Rifle Division
Units: 2, 49, 359 Rifle, 202 Artillery Regiments.
—Raised Polotsk, Moscow Military District, before 1939.
—Klin, Moscow Military District, 1939.
—Western Special Military District w/13 Army, June 1941.
—Yelnaya w/16 Army, Sep. 1941.
—Roslavl w/19 Army, Oct. 1941.
—Mozhaisk defense line w/5 Army, Nov. 1941.
—Mozhaisk w/5 Army, Jan. 1942.
—Kursk, w/21 Army, July 1943.
—Zaporozhye, Sep. 1943.
—Southwest Ukraine w/33 Rifle Corps, 2 Ukrainian Front, Jan. 1944.
—Kirovograd versus Panzergrenadier Division "Grossdeutschland," Jan. 1944.
—Targul Frumos w/27 Army, May 1944.
—Probably in the Iasi Kishinev Op., Aug. 1944.
—Berlin Op., Apr. 1945.
—Probably an independent division.
—"Zaporozhye, Kirovograd," Order of Red Banner.

51 Rifle Division
Units: First formation: 1299, 1301, 1303 Rifle, 975 Artillery Regiments;
Second formation: 23, 287, 348 Rifle, 300 Artillery Regiments.
—Raised Odessa Military District, before 1941.
—Odessa Military District w/9 Army, June 1941.
—Coastal Army, Odessa Area, July 1941.
—Kiev Pocket w/37 Army, Aug. 1941.
—Destroyed Vyazma pocket, Oct. 1941.
—Second formation raised from 8 Moscow People's Militia Division, at Moscow, Moscow Military District after Oct. 1941.
—Caucasus, Oct. 1942.
—Caucasus w/44 Army, Jan. 1943.
—Perekop, Mar. 1944.
—Belorussian Op., June 1944.

—The 287 Rifle Regiment is associated w/25 Rifle Division; 300 Artillery Regiment w/176 Rifle Division.
—"Perekop, Vitebsk, Polotsk," Orders of Red Banner, Suvorov.

52 Rifle Division
Units: Firtst formation 58, 112, 205 Rifle, 158 Artillery Regiments; Second formation 429, 431, 439 Rifle, 1028 Artillery Regiments.
—The reserve of the Belorussian Revvoensoviet, 1919.
—Raised Moscow, Moscow Military District, 1935.
—Poland, Sep. 1939.
—Murmansk w/14 Army, Dec. 1939.
—Finland, 1939–40.
—Murmansk area w/14 Army, June 1941.
—Kandalaksha w/14 Army, July 1941.
—Karelia w/14 Army, Aug. 1941.
—Reformed as 10 Guards Rifle Division, 25 Dec. 1941.
—Second formation raised Kolomna, Moscow Military District, Jan. 1942.
—Southwest Ukraine w/64 Rifle Corps, 57 Army, Jan. 1944.
—Had some naval infantry in its composition.

53 Rifle Division
Units: 12, 223, 475 Rifle, 36 Artillery Regiments.
—Raised Saratov, Volga Military District, Oct. 1939.
—RVGK w/21 Army, July 1941.
—RVGK in Reserve Front w/43 Army, July 1941.
—Mogilev w/61 Rifle Corps, 21 Army, July 1941.
—Yelnaya area w/43 Army, Sep. 1941.
—Moscow axis w/43 Army, Nov. 1941.
—Dnieper River w/25 Guards Corps, 7 Guards Army, Sep. 1943.
—Dnieper River w/37 Army, Sep. 1943.
—Uman, Jan. 1944.
—Targul Frumos, May 1944.
—"Uman, Pugachev, " Order of Lenin.

54 Rifle Division
Units: 81, 118, 337 Rifle, 86 Artillery Regiment.
—Russo-Finnish War w/9 Army, 1939–40.
—Leningrad Front w/7 Independent Army, June 1941.
—Karelian Front w/26 Army, May 1942.
—Karelian Front w/26 Army, Jan. 1944.
—RVGK (FHO), Apr. 1945.

55 Rifle Division
Units: 107, 111, 228 Rifle, 84 Artillery Regiments.
—Kursk, Orel Military District, Sep. 1938.
—Slutsk, Western Special Military District, w/47 Rifle Corps in Western Front reserve, June 1941.
—Velikiye Luki, June 1941.
—Destroyed in Kiev pocket, Sep. 1941.
—Second formation raised at Kuybyshev, Volga Military District, Dec. 1941.
—Mozyr, Jan. 1944.
—Berlin Op. w/28 Army, Apr. 1945.
—"Ssevsk, Mozyr," Order of Red Banner.

56 Rifle Division
Units: 37, 184, 213 Rifle, 113 Artillery Regiments.
—Raised Pleskau, Leningrad Military District as a territorial division, before 1930.
—Leningrad, 1930.
—Lake Ladoga w/8 Army, Jan. 1940.
—North of Grodno w/4 Rifle Corps, 3 Army as a covering division, June 1941.
—Leningrad w/42 Army, Sep. 1941.
—Riga, Oct. 1944.
—Probably in Silesia, Feb. 1945.
—"Riga, Walcz, Pushkin, Temruk," Orders of Red Banner, Kutuzov, Bogdan Khmelnitsky.

57 Motorized Division
Units: 80, 127, 293 Motorized Rifle, 105 Motorized Artillery Regiments.
—In Mozyr Group, Western Front, May 1920.
—Raised Penza, Volga Military District, 1932.
—Olovnaya, Far East Military District, 1937.
—Khalkhin Gol, Aug. 1938.
—Mongolia, July 1941.
—Schamor, w/17 Army, "Chita Front Command," Apr. 1943.
—Manchuria w/6 Guards Tank Army, Aug. 1945.
—Order of Red Banner.

58 Mountain Rifle Division
Units: 170, 279, 335 Rifle, 244 Artillery Regiment.
—Raised at Cherkassy, Kiev Military District, 1932.
—Kiev Special Military District w/12 Army, June 1941.

—In Uman Pocket; commander captured by Germans, Aug. 1941.
—Lenino (near Mogilev) w/33 Army, Oct. 1943.
—Korsun Shevchenkovskiy Op. w/104 Rifle Corps, 40 Army, Jan. 1944.
—Vistula Oder Op., Jan. 1945.
—Plovdiv, Bulgaria as Motorized Rifle Division, Jan. 1947 (July 1947 OB).
—"Oder."

59 Rifle Division
Units: 5, 124, 194 Rifle, 37 Artillery Regiments.
—Raised Iman, Far East Military District before 1941.
—The 194 Rifle Regiment is associated with 60 and 162 Rifle Divisions.
—Duchovskoye, Far East w/1 Independent Red Banner Army, Apr. 1943.
—Far East w/1 Independent Red Banner Army, Aug. 1945.

60 Rifle Division
Units: First formation 194, 224, 358 Rifle, 83 Artillery Regiments; Second formation 1281, 1283, 1285 Rifle, 969 Artillery Regiments.
—Raised Ovruch, Kiev Military District, before 1941.
—Kiev Special Military District w/12 Army, June 1941.
—Kiev Special Military District w/18 Army, June 1941.
—Khotin, July 1941.
—Dissolved; 194 Rifle Regiment to 52 Rifle Division; 224 Rifle Regiment to 162 Rifle Division; 358 Rifle Regiment to 136 Rifle Division, Aug. 1941.
—Second formation raised in Moscow, Moscow Military District from 1 Moscow Militia Rifle Division, Aug. 1941.
—Moscow w/49 Army, Dec. 1941.
—Kursk area w/77 Rifle Corps, 65 Army, May 1943.
—Southwest axis w/65 Army, Aug. 1943.
—Belorussia w/77 Rifle Corps, 47 Army, Mar. 1944.
—Lublin axis; relieved by Guards Rifle Divisions shortly before Lvov-Sandomir offensive; indicates this unit was not an assault division, July 1944.
—Warsaw, Jan. 1945.
—Warsaw Poznan Op., w/125 Rifle Corps, 47 Army, Jan. 1945.
—"Ssevsk, Praga, Warsaw," Orders of Lenin, Red Banner, Suvorov, Red Star.

61 Rifle Division
Units: 66, 221, 307 Rifle, 55 Artillery Regiments.
—Raised at Balaschov, Volga Military District before 1933.
—Kiev Military District, 1933.

—RVGK w/63 Rifle Corps, 21 Army, June 1941.
—Sancharo, North Caucasus Military District, Aug. 1942.
—Leninakan, North Caucasus to 9 Army, Aug. 1942.
—Krasnodar w/56 Army, Jan. 1943.
—Abinskaya w/56 Army, Mar. 1943.
—Southwest Ukraine w/10 Guards Rifle Corps, 28 Army, Jan. 1944.
—Belorussia Op., June 1944.
—RVGK (FHO), Apr. 1945.
—Berlin Op. w/128 Rifle Corps, 28 Army, Apr. 1945.
—Belorussia, Sep. 1947 (EUCOM study).
—"Baranovichi, Slonim, Luminets," Order of Red Banner.

62 Rifle Division
Units: 104, 123, 306 Rifle, 89 Artillery Regiments.
—Raised Fastov, Kiev Military District, Sep. 1939.
—Kovel w/5 Army, June 1941.
—Stalingrad w/62 Army, Aug. 1942.
—Dissolved; absorbed by 343 Rifle Division, Nov. 1942.
—Second formation raised from 44 Rifle Brigade, in the Western Special Military District, Apr. 1943.
—Kursk w/21 Army, July 1943.
—Assault crossing of Dnieper River w/52 Army, Nov. 1943.
—Belorussian Op. w/113 Rifle Corps, 31 Army, June 1944.
—Grodno, July 1944.
—RVGK (FHO), Apr. 1945.
—Order of Red Banner.

63 Mountain Rifle Division
Units: 226, 291, 346 Rifle, 26 Artillery Regiments.
—Raised at Tiflis, Transcaucasus Military District, before 1941.
—Transcaucasus Military District w/47 Army, July 1941.
—Amphibious assault on Feodosiya w/44 Army, Dec. 1941.
—Stalingrad axis w/28 Army, June 1942.
—To Stalingrad from 28 Army, July 1942.
—Reformed as a rifle division, Aug. 1942.
—Stalingrad offensive w/21 Army, Nov. 1942.
—Reformed as 52 Guards Rifle Division, Nov. 1942.
—Second formation raised at Kaluga, Moscow Military District from 45, 86 Rifle Brigades, May 1943.
—Kursk w/21 Army, July 1943.
—Belorussian Op., June 1944.
—Vilnius w/72 Rifle Corps, 5 Army, July 1944.
—Kovno, Aug. 1944.

—Kuibyshev, Transbaikal Military District, Jan. 1947 (Feb. 1948 OB).
—"Vitebsk, Vilnius, Kaunas."

64 Rifle Division
Units: First formation: 30, 159, 288 Rifle, 163 Artillery Regiments; Second formation: 433, 440, 451 Rifle, 1029 Artillery Regiments.
—In Belorussia Military District, 1935.
—Raised at Smolensk, Western Special Military District, w/40 Rifle Corps, before Feb. 1939.
—Minsk w/13 Army, June 1941.
—Yelnaya area w/16 Army, Sep. 1941.
—Reformed as 7 Guards Rifle Division, 26 Sep. 1941.
—The 30 Rifle Regiment to 102 Rifle Division; 288 Rifle Regiment to 181 Rifle Division, Sep. 1941.
—Second formation raised at Serpukhov, Moscow Military District, Mar. 1942.
—Volga Corridor w/1 Guards Army, July 1942.
—Near Stalingrad; mutinied, had to be disciplined, Aug. 1942.
—Stalingrad offensive w/66 Army, Nov. 1942.
—Mogilev Op. w/62 Rifle Corps, 49 Army, June 1944

65 Rifle Division
Units: 38, 60, 311 Rifle, 6 Guards Artillery Regiments.
—Raised at Chita, Transbaikal Military District, Feb. 1941.
—Probably at Borzya, Transbaikal Military District, w/12 Rifle Corps, 36 Army, July 1941.
—To western front, Oct. 1941.
—Probably on Leningrad Front, 1941–44.
—Novgorod Luga Op. w/6 Rifle Corps, 59 Army, Jan. 1944.
—Petsamo Kirkenes Op. w/99 Rifle Corps, 14 Army; had 6,641 personnel and was the breakthrough division of 14 Army, Oct. 1944.
—Reformed as 102 Guards Rifle Division, 29 Dec. 1944.
—"Novgorod," Order of Red Banner.

66 Rifle Division
Units: 33, 108, 341 Rifle, 161 Artillery Regiment.
—Raised Ussuriysk, Far East Military District in 1930's.
—Far East w/18 Independent Rifle Corps, July 1941.
—At Spassk, Far East w/1 Independent Red Banner Army, "Front Command Khabarovsk," Apr. 1943.
—In the Second Baltic Front w/10 Guards Army, Jan. 1944.
—Zvenigorod w/53 Army, Feb. 1944.
—Far East w/35 Army, Aug. 1945.

—Probably an independent division.
Key Commanders: Gen-Major Goncharov, Apr. 1943.

67 Rifle Division
Units: 9, 452, 719 Rifle, 3 Artillery Regiment.
—Raised Leningrad, Leningrad Military District before 1941.
—Baltic Special Military District w/27 Army, May 1941.
—Libau (Liepaja), W/8 Army, 22 June 1941.
—Probably on Finnish Front, 1942–45.
—RVGK, Apr. 1945 (FHO).
—White Sea Military District, 1947 (Feb. 1948 OB).
—Three Artillery Regiment is associated w/18 Rifle Division.

68 Rifle Division
Units: 313, 430 Rifle, 130 Artillery Regiments.
—Raised Baku, Transcaucasus Military District, before 1941.
—Sibiu, Rumania w/83 Rifle Corps, Dec. 1946 (Feb. 1947 OB).

69 Rifle Division
Units: 120, 237, 303 Rifle, 118 Artillery Regiments.
—Raised Kuibyshev, Volga Military District as a Motorized Division in the 1930's.
—Destroyed as 69 Motorized Division, Nov. 1941.
—Second formation raised at Tashkent, Central Asia Military District, Dec. 1941.
—Kursk, July 1943.
—Belorussia Op. w/18 Independent Rifle Corps, 65 Army, June 1944.
—Stettin area w/65 Army, Mar. 1945.
—Rumania, 1946, (Feb. 1947 OB).
—"Ssevsk, Slonim, Luminets," Orders of Red Banner, Suvorov.

70 Rifle Division
Units: 68, 252, 329 Rifle, 221 Artillery Regiments.
—Activated Kuibushev, Volga Military District (SME), 1934.
—Mannerheim Line w/7 Army, Mar, 1940.
—Vyborg; distinguished itself in the Finnish War, Mar. 1940.
—Designated one of four best divisions in Red Army by Timoshenko, Leningrad Military District, Aug. 1940.
—In reserve at Leningrad, June 1941.
—Solsty w/11 Army, June 1941.
—From 23 Army to Luga defense line, July 1941.
—Lake Ilmen, July 1941.
—Novgorod Sector, July 1941.

—Sols'tsa, w/11 Army, July 1941.
—Novgorod, w/48 Army, Aug. 1941.
—Leningrad front w/55 Army, Sep. 1941–Apr. 1942.
—Neva River, Leningrad Front, Sep. 1942.
—Reformed as 45 Guards Rifle Division, 16 Oct. 1942.
—Second formation raised at Moscow, Moscow Military District from 70 Rifle Brigade, Mar. 1943.
—Kursk w/21 Army, July 1943.
—Belorussia w/72 Rifle Corps, 33 Army, May 1944.
—Baltic area, Sep. 1944.
—The 329 Rifle Regiment was primarily composed of naval infantry, Sep. 1942.
—An independent division.
—Order of Lenin.
Key Commanders: M.P. Kirponos, Mar. 1940.

71 Rifle Division
Units: 126, 131, 367 Rifle, 237 Artillery Regiments.
—Raised Kemerovo, Siberian Military Division by June 1941.
—To western front, July 1941.
—Petrozavodsk, Leningrad Military District w/7 Independent Army, July 1941.
—Leningrad area w/32 Army, Mar. 1942.
—Kursk w/26 Guards Rifle Corps, 27 Army, July 1943.
—Akhtyrka w/27 Army, Aug. 1943.
—Southwest Ukraine w/22 Rifle Corps, 18 Army, Jan. 1944.
—Baranow bridgehead, July 1944.
—Vistula Oder Op., Jan. 1945.
—Gdynia area w/70 Army, Mar. 1945.
—The 131 Rifle Regiment associated w/78 Rifle Division; 237 Rifle Regiment w/229 Rifle Division.
—"Siberian, Torun, Kuzbas, Proletarian."

72 Rifle Division
Units: 14, 133, 187 Rifle, 9 Artillery Regiments.
—Raised Leningrad, Leningrad Military District before June 1941.
—Przemysl as a covering division, 8 Rifle Corps, 26 Army, June 1941.
—Destroyed near Tiraspol, July 1941.
—Second formation raised Leningrad, Leningrad Military District from 7 Naval Infantry Brigade, Dec. 1941.
—Nevel Op., Oct. 1943.
—Leningrad Military District, Oct. 1945 (EUCOM study).
—"Nevel, Pavlovsk," Orders of Red Banner, Suvorov.

73 Rifle Division
Units: 392, 413, 471 Rifle, 11 Artillery Regiments.
—First formation raised Omsk, Siberian Military District, July 1940.
—Finland, 1940.
—Far East Military District, June 1941.
—Smolensk w/20 Army, July 1941.
—With the Reserve Front, Sep. 1941.
—Destroyed Vyazma pocket, Oct. 1941.
—Second formation raised at Ordzhonikidze, North Caucasus Military District, Feb. 1942.
—Southern Front w/24 Army, May 1942.
—Stalingrad axis, July 1942.
—Kursk w/48 Army, July 1943.
—Probably in the Gomel Rechitsa Op., Oct. 1943.
—Belorussian Op., June 1944.
—Probably in the Vistula Oder Op., Jan. 1945.
—Berlin Op. w/48 Army, Apr. 1945.
—"Novosybkov, Shlobin, Slonim, Luminets, Siberian" Orders of Red Banner, Suvorov, Kutuzov.

74 Rifle Division
Units: 78, 109, 360 Rifle, 6 Artillery Regiments.
—Raised at Krasnodar, North Caucasus Military District, before June 1941.
—Odessa Military District w/9 Army, June 1941.
—Stalingrad offensive w/21 Army, Nov. 1942.
—Voronezh, Jan. 1943.
—Kursk w/15 Rifle Corps, 13 Army, July 1943.
—Kiev w/21 Rifle Corps, 38 Army, Nov. 1943.
—Probably in the Kiev Defensive Op., Dec. 1943.
—Zhitomir Berdichev Op. w/50 Rifle Corps, 40 Army, Jan. 1944.
—Targul Frumos, w/104 Rifle Corps, 40 Army, May 1944.
—Iasi Kishinev Op., Aug. 1944.
—Carpathian Mountains w/50 Rifle Corps, 40 Army, Sep. 1944.
—Poznan, Feb. 1945.
—The 109 Rifle Regiment associated w/176 Rifle Division, 6 Artillery w/102 Rifle Division.
—"Kiev, Bucharest," Order of Red Banner.

75 Mountain Rifle Division
Units: 28, 115, 134 Rifle, 68 Artillery Regiments.
—Raised Lubny, Kharkov Military District, May 1939.
—Tolvajarvi, Finland; composed of Belorussians, Dec. 1939.

—North of Lake Ladoga as 8 Army reserve, Jan. 1940.
—Brest w/4 Army, June 1941.
—Destroyed in the Kiev Pocket, Aug. 1941.
—New regiments came from 75 Mountain and 8 Motorized Divisions after Aug. 1941.
—Vyazma, Jan. 1942.
—Iran, 1944.
—Far East Military District, Jan. 1946 (Feb. 1948 OB).

76 Mountain Rifle Division
Units: 93, 207, 216 Rifle, 817 (later 80 Guards) Artillery Regiments.
—Raised Nakichevan, Transcaucasus Military District, before June 1941.
—Transcaucasus Military District w/47 Army, July 1941.
—From RVGK to 38 Army, Sep. 1941.
—Poltava Offensive w/38 Army, Sep. 1941.
—Kharkov sector w/38 Army, Oct. 1941.
—Reinhard Gehlen, Chief FHO, supposedly had agents in this division, 1942.
—Captured German plans for the summer offensive when northeast of Kharkov w/21 Army, June 1942.
—To Stalingrad axis from 21 Army, July 1942.
—Reformed as a rifle division, Aug. 1942.
—Stalingrad offensive w/21 Army, Nov. 1942.
—Reformed as 51 Guards Rifle Division, Nov. 1942.
—Second formation raised at Moscow, Moscow Military District, May 1943.
—Kursk, w/21 Army, July 1943.
—Yelnaya, Sep. 1943.
—Kovel Lutsk Op., Jan. 1944.
—Belorussia w/125 Rifle Corps, 47 Army, Mar. 1944.
—Warsaw, Jan. 1945.
—The 817 Artillery Regiment to 273 Rifle Division.
—Possibly an independent division.
—"Yelnaya, Kovel, Praga-Warsaw."
Key Commanders: Gen-Maj V.A. Penkovskiy, May–Aug 1942.

77 Mountain Rifle Division
Units: 105, 276, 324 Rifle, 239 Artillery Regiments.
—Raised Baku, Transcaucasus Military District, 1930.
—Transcaucasus Military District w/40 Rifle Corps, 44 army, July 1941.
—To western front, Dec. 1941.
—Converted to Rifle Division, June 1942.
—Tuapse to Novorossiysk, Aug. 1942.

—Taman, Aug. 1942.
—Novorossiysk w/47 Army, Sep. 1942.
—Caucasus, 1943.
—Southwest Ukraine w/10 Guards Rifle Corps, 28 Army, Jan. 1944.
—Crimea, Apr. 1944 w/51 Army.
—Sapun Heights, Sevastopol, May 1944.
—Riga area w/51 Army, Aug. 1944.
—Dobele area, Sep. 1944.
—Memel w/63 Rifle Corps, Oct. 1944.
—Probably an independent division.
—"Simferopol, Azerbaijan, in the name of Ordhonikidze," Orders of Red Banner, Suvorov.

78 Rifle Division
Units: First formation: 40, 131, 258 Rifle, 159 Artillery regiments; 453, 458, 464 Rifle, 1030 Artillery Regiments.
—Raised Khabarovsk, Far East Military District as a Siberian Rifle Division, 1940.
—Far East Military District w/18 Indepedent Rifle Corps, July 1941.
—To western front (central sector), Nov. 1941.
—Istra reservoir w/16 Army, Nov. 1941.
—Reformed as 9 Guards Rifle Division, Nov. 1941.
—Second formation raised at Samarkand, Central Asia Military District, Mar. 1942.
—Zaporozhye, Sep. 1943.
—Kirovograd w/35 Guards Rifle Corps, 5 Guards Army, Jan. 1944.
—Zvenigorod w/53 Army, Feb. 1944.
—Gorny Tikich River w/27 Army, Mar. 1944.
—Targul Frumos w/33 Rifle Corps, 27 Army, May 1944.
—Iasi Kishinev Op. w/23 Rifle Corps, 6 Guards Tank Army, Aug. 1944.
—Debrecen, Hungary w/33 Rifle Corps, 6 Guards Tank Army, Oct. 1944.
—Probably an independent division.
—"Zaporozhye, Debrecen, Tomsk," Order of Suvorov.

79 Mountain Rifle Division
Units: 157, 165, 179 Mountain Rifle, 204 Artillery, 487 Howitzer Artillery Regiments.
—Far East, June 1941.
—Nikoleyevsk, Far East in Northern Army Group of "Front Command Khabarovsk," Apr. 1943.
—Sakhalin Island w/56 Rifle Corps, 16 Army, Aug. 1945.
—Far East Military District, Nov. 1947 (Feb. 1948 OB).

80 Rifle Division
Units: 77, 153, 218 Rifle, 88 Artillery Regiments.
—Raised Mariupol, Odessa Military District, Feb. 1939.
—In reserve, Kiev Special Militray District, June 1941.
—To Southwest Front, June 1941.
—Ukraine, spring 1943.
—Zvenigorod w/53 Army, Feb. 1944.
—Poland, Feb. 1945.
—"Lyuban, Kattowice, Donbas."

81 Rifle Division
Units: 410, 467, 519 Rifle, 346 Artillery Regiments.
—Raised at Lubny, Kharkov Military District, by 1936.
—All regiments associated w/102 Rifle Division.
—Belorussian Maneuvers w/16 Rifle Corps, Sep. 1936.
—Kiev Special Military District w/4 Mechanized Corps, as a motorized division 6 Army, June 1941.
—Caucasus Front, Dec. 1942.
—Voronezh, Jan. 1943.
—Kursk w/29 Rifle Corps, 13 Army; in path of main attack, July 1943.
—Kalinkovichi, Jan. 1944.
—Cholm, Jan. 1944.
—Poland, Feb. 1945.
—"Kalinkovichi, Cholm, Kaluga."

82 Rifle Division
Units: 210, 250, 601 Rifle, 795 Artillery Regiments.
—Formed at Perm, Ural Military District as a Motorized Rifle Division, 1932.
—In Belorussia Military District; included 242 Rifle Regiment, 1935.
—To Far East Military District from Ural Military District, 1938.
—Khalkin Gol, 1939.
—Far East, June 1941.
—Moscow w/5 Army, Dec. 1941.
—Mozhaisk, Jan. 1942.
—Motorized Division until, Mar. 1942.
—The 82 Motorized Division became 3 Guards Motorized Rifle Division, Mar. 1942; that unit later became 6 Guards Mechanized Corps, June 1943.
—Second formation formed from 64 Naval Rifle Brigade, by July 1942.
—Pogorelo Gorodische Op. w/20 Army, Aug. 1942.
—Voronezh, Jan. 1943.
—Poland, Jan. 1945.

—"Jarzewo," Orders of Lenin, Red Banner, Suvorov.
Key Commanders: I.I. Fedyuninskiy, 1940.

83 Mountain Rifle Division
Units: First formation: 45, 100, 150, 428 Rifle, 67 Artillery Regiments;
Second formation: 11, 26, 46 Rifle, 588 Artillery Regiments.
—Raised Ashkabad, Central Asia Military District, before 1942.
—Staraya Russa, Mar. 1942.
—Tuapse, North Caucasus MD, Sep. 1942.
—Krasnodar, w/56 Army, Jan. 1943.
—Kuban, Feb. 1943.
—Abinskaya w/56 Army, Mar. 1943.
—Reformed as 128 Guards Mountain Rifle Division, Oct. 1943.
—Second formation raised at Loutti, Archangelsk Military District, from 61 and 85 Naval Rifle Brigades, Jan. 1944.
—Karelia, May 1944.
—Petsamo Kirkenes Op. w/31 Rifle Corps, 14 Army; had 5761 personnel, Oct. 1944.
—"Turkmen."

84 Rifle Division
Units: 41, 201, 382 Rifle, 74 Artillery Regiments.
—Raised at Tula, Moscow Military District, before 1928.
—In Moscow Military District maneuvers as a territorial division, 1928.
—In Moscow Military District maneuvers, a total of 5272 men of this division moved a "great distance" and were airlanded, Sep. 1936.
—Mannerheim Line (Vyborg), Feb. 1940.
—Vilno w/3 Mechanized Corps, July 1940.
—Baltic Special Military District w/3 Mechanized Corps, 8 Army, June 1941.
—To Stalingrad, Aug. 1942.
—Volga Corridor w/1 Guards Army, Sep. 1942.
—Stalingrad offensive w/24 Army, Nov. 1942.
—Voronezh w/24 Army, Mar. 1943.
—Kursk, w/53 Army, July 1943.
—Kharkov w/53 Army, Aug. 1943.
—Kirovograd w/35 Guards Rifle Corps, 5 Guards Army, Jan. 1944.
—Zvenigorod w/5 Guards Tank Army, Feb. 1944.
—Iasi, Apr. 1944.
—Targul Frumos, May 1944.
—Iasi Kishinev Op., Aug. 1944.
—Hungary, w/4 Guards Army, Nov. 1944.

—Probably an independent division.
—"Kharkov, Kishinev, Budapest," Order of Red Banner.

85 Rifle Division
Units: 59, 103, 141 Rifle, 167 Artillery Regiments.
—Raised at Chelyabinsk, Ural Military District, by June 1941.
—Grodno area w/4 Rifle Corps, 3 Army, June 1941.
—Destroyed at Minsk, July 1941.
—Second formation raised at Leningrad, Leningrad Military District, after July 1941.
—Belorussian Op., June 1944.
—"Chelyabinsk, Leningrad, Pavlovsk, Slutsk."

86 Rifle Division
Units: 169, 284, 330 Rifle, 248 Artillery Regiments.
—Raised at Laurovo, North Caucasus Military District, Feb. 1941.
—North Caucasus Military District, June 1941.
—Neva River, Leningrad Front, Sep. 1941–Apr. 1942.
—Leningrad, w/67 Army, Oct. 1942.
—Leningrad offensive (Schlusselberg), w/67 Army, Jan. 1943.
—Leningrad Front w/42 Army, Jan. 1944.
—Tartu, Sep. 1944.
—East Prussia, Jan. 1945.
—Krasnogvardeysk, Jan. 1945.
—Danzig area w/2 Shock Army, Mar. 1945.
—"Gatschina, Tartu, Dorpat, Krasnogvardeysk."

87 Rifle Division
Units: First formation: 16, 96, 283 Rifle, 97 Artillery Regiments; Second and third formations: 1378, 1379, 1382 Rifle, 1381 Artillery Regiments.
—Raised at Sverdlovsk, Ural Military District, 1937.
—Vladimir Volyinskiy, 24 June 1941.
—Probably destroyed, summer 1941.
—Second formation formed from 3 Airborne Corps, Nov. 1941.
—Reformed as 13 Guards Rifle Division, Jan. 1942.
—Third formation raised at Citorol, Far East Military District, May 1942.
—Probably in Central Russia w/27 Army, May 1942.
—To the Stalingrad axis, July 1942.
—Stalingrad w/62 Army; had less than 800 men, Sep. 1942.
—RVGK, Stalingrad area, Nov. 1942.
—RVGK w/5 Shock Army, Dec. 1942.

—Stalingrad area w/2 Guards Army, Dec. 1942.
—South Ukraine w/55 Rifle Corps, 51 Army, Jan. 1944.
—Crimea w/55 Rifle Corps, 2 Guards Army, Apr. 1944.
—Memel w/63 Rifle Corps, Oct. 1944.
—Probably an independent division.
—RVGK (FHO), Apr. 1945.

88 Rifle Division
Units: 426, 611, 758 Rifle, 401 Artillery Regiments.
—Raised at Archangelsk, Archangelsk Military District, before Sep. 1939.
—Finnish War w/9 Army, 1939–40.
—Archangelsk, June 1941.
—Kandalaksha axis, July 1941.
—RVGK, Archangelsk area, Aug. 1941.
—Reformed as 23 Guards Rifle Division, Mar. 1942.
—Second formation raised Kisner, Ural Military Division, Apr. 1942.
—Belorussia w/71 Rifle Corps, 31 Army, June 1944.
—East Prussia, Feb. 1945.
—RVGK (FHO), Apr. 1945.
—"Vitebsk, Masurian," Order of Red Banner.

89 Rifle Division
Units: 390, 400, 526 Rifle, 262 Artillery Regiments.
—Raised at Kursk, Orel Military District, before June 1941.
—Western Special Military District w/5 Rifle Corps, 10 Army, June 1941.
—Smolensk as attack division, July 1941.
—Destroyed Vyazma pocket w/19 Army, Oct. 1941.
—Second formation raised at Yerevan, Transcaucasus Military District, Jan. 1942.
—Turkish frontier to Terek River, Aug. 1942.
—North Caucasus w/58 Army, Jan. 1943.
—Kharkov w/53 Army, Aug. 1943.
—Novorossiysk and Blagovesnchensk, Sep. 1943.
—Novorossiysk, Sep. 1943.
—Dnieper River w/57 Rifle Corps, 37 Army, Oct. 1943.
—Taman area, Nov. 1943.
—Kerch as reserve of the Independent Coastal Army, Jan. 1944.
—Zvenigorod w/53 Army, Feb. 1944.
—Crimea w/Independent Coastal Army, Apr. 1944.
—Pomeranian Op., Jan. 1945.
—Pomerania, Feb. 1945.
—Yerevan, Transcaucasus Military District, Apr. 1946 (Feb. 1947 OB).

—Possibly an independent division.
—"Armenian, Taman, Pomeranian, Siberian," Orders of Lenin, Kutuzov, Red Star.

90 Rifle Division
Units: 19, 173, 286 Rifle, 96 Artillery Regiments.
—Raised in Leningrad, Leningrad Military District, 1936.
—South of Luga w/8 Army, July 1941.
—Mount Kolokolnya, Leningrad Front, Dec. 1941.
—Probably with the Leningrad Front, 1942–44.
—Oranienbaum area w/108 Rifle Corps, 2 Shock Army, Jan. 1944.
—Narva Op, Feb. 1944.
—Probably in Estonia, Sep. 1944.
—Probably in East Prussia, Jan. 1945.
—Danzig area w/2 Shock Army, Mar. 1945.
—Germany w/5 Mechanized Army, July 1946, (Aug. 1946 OB).
—"Perm," Order of Red Banner.

91 Rifle Division
Units: 503, 561, 613 Rifle, 321 Artillery Regiments.
—Raised Achinsk, Siberia Military District, Sep. 1939.
—Moscow Military District, June 1941.
—RVGK w/19 Army, July 1941.
—Assault division in Smolensk offensive, July 1941.
—Destroyed Vyazma, w/19 Army, Oct. 1941.
—Second formation raised at Mahachkala, North Caucasus Military District, Apr. 1942.
—Pavlovskaya w/17 Cavalry Corps, Apr. 1942.
—North Caucasus w/51 Army, July 1942.
—To Stalingrad axis, Aug. 1942.
—Stalingrad area w/51 Army, Oct. 1942.
—Stalingrad Front w/51 Army, Dec. 1942.
—Kursk w/21 Army, July 1943.
—Melitopol, Sep. 1943.
—South Ukraine w/54 Rifle Corps, 51 Army, Jan. 1944.
—Crimea, 1 Guards Rifle Corps, 51 Army, Apr. 1944.
—Riga area w/51 Army, Aug. 1944.
—Memel w/10 Rifle Corps, Oct. 1944.
—"Melitopol."

92 Rifle Division
Units: 22, 203, 317 Rifle, 60 Artillery Regiments.
—Raised at Barabash, Far East Military District, by Apr. 1937.

—To western front, Nov. 1941.
—Leningrad w/4 Army, Nov. 1941.
—Destroyed at Volkhov, June 1942.
—Second formation raised from 20 NKVD division at Tikhvin, Leningrad Military District, after June 1942.
—Assault crossing of Dnieper w/52 Army, Nov. 1943.
—Order of Red Banner.

93 Rifle Division
Units: 51, 129, 266 Rifle, 100 Artillery Regiments.
—Raised Chita, Transbaikal Military District, 1936.
—Called "East Siberian," by NKO order, Oct. 1936.
—Transbaikal Military District w/12 Rifle Corps, 36 Army, July 1941.
—To west w/43 Army, Oct. 1941.
—Moscow, Nov. 1941.
—Moscow offensive w/43 Army, Dec. 1941.
—Mozhaisk w/33 Army, Jan. 1942.
—Reformed as 26 Guards Rifle Division, 20 Apr. 1942.
—Second formation raised at Dzerzhinsk, Moscow Military District, July 1942.
—Southwest Ukraine w/68 Rifle Corps, 57 Army, Jan. 1944.
—Dniester River, Apr. 1944.
—Vilnius w/65 Rifle Corps, 5 Army, July 1944.
—Krajevo, Yugoslavia, 26 Oct. 1944 (Ultra).
—Danube River w/68 Rifle Corps, 4 Guards Army, Jan. 1945.
—Bulgaria, as new type Rifle Division w/37 Army, 1946 (EUCOM Study, Apr. 1947 OB).
—Probably an independent division.
—"Mirgorod, Lower-Dniester, East Siberian."

94 Rifle Division
Units: 9, 64, 152 Rifle, 97 Artillery, 259 Howitzer Artillery Regiments.
—Raised at Krasnoyarsk, Siberia Military District by 1941.
—Transbaikal Military District w/12 Rifle Corps, 36 Army, July 1941.
—Matzeyewski, w/36 Army in "Front Command Chita," Apr. 1943.
—Ternopol, Apr. 1944.
—The 152 Rifle Regiment is associated w/20 Rifle Division.
—"Krasnoyarsk."
Key Commanders: Col. Ivanov, Apr. 1943.

95 Rifle Division
Units: 90, 161, 241 Rifle, 57 Artillery Regiments.
—Raised at Kotovki, Odessa Military District as a Motorized Division, about 1940.

—Odessa Military District w/9 Independent Army; on the Rumanian border, June 1941.
—From 9 Independent Army to the Independent Coastal Army in the Odessa area, July 1941.
—Odessa, Aug. 1941.
—Sevastopol; had naval rifle and naval infantry in 90 and 161 Rifle Regiments, Dec. 1941.
—Destroyed at Sevastopol with the Independent Coastal Army as, May 1942.
—Second formation raised at Tula, Moscow Military District as a rifle division on the basis of 13 NKVD Motorized Rifle Division, Sep. 1942.
—Badly mauled by Germans in the Stalingrad area, Sep. 1942.
—To Stalingrad w/62 Army, Sep. 1942–Jan. 1943.
—Reformed as 75 Guards Rifle Division, 1 Mar. 1943.
—Third formation raised at Kaluga, Moscow Military District, Apr. 1943.
—Kursk w/21 Army, July 1943.
—Belorussia w/ 33 Army, May 1944.
—Mogilev Op. w/81 Rifle Corps, 49 Army, June 1944.
—Prob. Iasi Kishinev Op., Aug. 1944.
—Probably an independent division.
—"Moldavia."

96 Mountain Rifle Division
Units: First formation 43, 155, 209, 651 Rifle, 573 Artillery Regiments; Second formation: 1381, 1384, 1389 Rifle, 1059 Artillery Regiments; Third formation: 331, 338, 350 Rifle, 1059 Artillery Regiments.
—Raised at Vinnitsa, Kiev Military District, Dec. 1923.
—Named in honor of Jana Fabritsiusa (SME), Sep. 1929.
—Kiev Special Military District w/12 Army, June 1941.
—Kiev w/18 Army, June 1941.
—Reformed as a rifle division, Oct. 1941.
—Southern Front w/37 Army, Nov. 1941.
—Reformed as 14 Guards Rifle Division, Jan. 1942.
—Second formation raised at unknown location, July 1942.
—Stalingrad offensive w/21 Army, Nov. 1942.
—Stalingrad Front w/51 Army, Dec. 1942.
—Reformed as 68 Guards Rifle Division, Feb. 1943.
—Belorussia w/11 Army, Feb. 1943.
—Third formation raised from 116, 117 Rifle Brigades at Tula, Moscow Military District, Mar. 1943.
—RVGK w/11 Army, May 1943.
—Gomel Op., Oct. 1943.
—Belorussian Op., June 1944.

—Allenstein w/48 Army, Jan. 1945.
—Berlin Op., Apr. 1945.
—Possibly an independent division.
—"Gomel, Slonim, Luminets," Order of Suvorov.

97 Rifle Division
Units: 69, 136, 233 Rifle, 47 Artillery Regiments.
—Raised Zhmerinka, Kiev Special Military District, before 1940.
—Kiev maneuvers w/6 Rifle Corps, won General Staff Challenge Cup, Oct. 1940.
—Rava Russkaya w/6 Army as a covering division, June 1941.
—Destroyed Kiev, Sep. 1941.
—Second formation raised at Divisionnaya, Transbaikal Military District, Jan. 1942.
—Reformed as 83 Guards Rifle Division, Apr. 1943.
—Third formation raised at Belev, Moscow Military District from 108, 110 Rifle Brigades, May 1943.
—Vitebsk Orsha Op., June 1944.
—Vilnius, w/5 Army, July 1944.
—Hungary, Oct. 1944.
—Jaroslav, Poland, July 1946 (Feb. 1947 OB).
—"Vitebsk," Order of Red Banner.

98 Rifle Division
Units: 4, 166, 308 Rifle, 153 Artillery Regiments.
—Raised at Ishevsk, Ural Military District, Feb. 1941.
—RVGK w/51 Rifle Corps, 22 Army, July 1941.
—Destroyed at Vyazma, Oct. 1941.
—Second formation raised at Spassk, Far East Military District, Oct. 1941.
—Stalingrad w/62 Army, less than 800 men, Sep. 1942.
—Manych River w/Popov's mobile group, Jan. 1943.
—Reformed as 86 Guards Rifle Division, Apr. 1943.
—Third formation raised at Leningrad, Leningrad Military District from 250 Rifle Brigade, Apr. 1943.
—Leningrad Offensive w/2 Shock Army, Jan. 1944.
—RVGK w/2 Shock Army, Sep. 1944.
—"Ropsha."

99 Rifle Division
Units: 1, 197, 206 Rifle, 22 Artillery Regiments.
—Raised Uman, Kiev Special Military District before 1939.
—Considered a crack division under A.A. Vlasov, Aug. 1940.

—Won "Challenge Red Banner," w/33 Corps (Zhukov); designated best division in Red Army by Timoshenko, Aug. 1940.
—Kiev maneuvers, Oct. 1940.
—Przemsyl w/26 Army as a covering division, June 1941.
—Retook Przemsyl; Red Banner for bravery, July 1941.
—Berdichev, July 1941.
—Kiev, Aug. 1941.
—Tatsinkaya w/37 Army, Oct. 1941.
—Destroyed at Izyum w/6 Army, May 1942.
—Second formation raised at Balachov, Volga Military District, Aug. 1942.
—RVGK w/66 Army, Aug. 1942.
—To Stalingrad, Sep. 1942.
—Stalingrad offensive w/66 Army, Nov. 1942.
—Reformed as 88 Guards Rifle Division, Apr. 1943.
—Third formation raised from 99 Rifle Brigade, May 1943.
—Zhitomir Berdichev Op. w/94 Rifle Corps, 1 Guards Army, Jan. 1944.
—Carpathian Mountains, Sep. 1944.
—Vienna w/46 Army, Apr. 1945.
—Probably an independent division.
—"Zhitomir, Carpathian," Order of Red Banner.
Key Commanders: Gen. A.A. Vlasov, Aug. 1940.

100 Mountain Rifle Division
—Reported by Germans at Petropavlosk, Far East as part of "Front Command Khabarovsk," Apr. 1943.

100 Rifle Division
Units: First formation: 85, 331, 355 Rifle, 34 Artillery Regiments; Second formation: 454, 460, 472 Rifle, 1031 Artillery Regiments.
—Raised at Berdichev, Kiev Military District as 45 Red Banner Rifle Division, 1 Nov. 1923.
—Reformed from 1 Rifle Regiment, Moscow Proletarian Rifle Division, Jan. 1940.
—Karelian Isthmus, Mannerheim Line, Feb. 1940.
—Minsk w/2 Rifle Corps, 13 Army; had to mobilize to achieve combat readiness, June 1941.
—Minsk, July 1941.
—Yelnaya salient; fought well (Zhukov), Aug. 1941.
—The 355 Rifle Regiment was awarded the Order of Lenin, Aug. 1941.
—Reserve Front w/24 Army, Sep. 1941.
—Reformed as 1 Guards Rifle Division, 18 Sep. 1941.
—Second formation raised at Vologda, Archangelsk Military District, Mar. 1942.

—Stalingrad axis, Aug. 1942.
—Southwest Ukraine w/21 Rifle Corps, 38 Army, Jan. 1944.
—Belorussian Op. w/60 Army, June 1944.
—Possibly an independent division.
—Orders of Lenin, Red Banner.

101 Motorized Rifle Division
Units: 138, 373 Rifle Regiments.
—Roslavl w/30 Army, Oct. 1941.
—Moscow axis w/30 Army, Nov. 1941.
—In the Operational Group of Western Front, Moscow, Dec. 1941.
—Sakhalin Island as a rifle division, Aug. 1945.

102 Rifle Division
Units: First and second formation: 410, 467, 519 Rifle, 346 Artillery; Regiments; Third formation 16, 30, 40 Rifle, 6 Artillery Regiments.
—Raised Kremenchug, Kiev Special Military District, June 1941.
—RVGK w/21 Army, July 1941.
—Yelnaya area w/24 Army, Sep. 1941.
—Dissolved, Oct. 1941.
—Second formation raised at Chimkent, Kazakstan, Central Asia Military District, Jan. 1942.
—Stalingrad axis, June 1942.
—Probably destroyed, summer 1942.
—Third formation from Far East NKVD Division, raised at Khabarovsk, Far East Military District, after June 1942.
—To Europe, Dec. 1942.
—RVGK w/70 Army, Feb. 1943.
—Demyansk w/70 Army, Feb. 1943.
—Kursk area w/28 Rifle Corps, 70 Army, May 1943.
—Kursk, July 1943.
—Novgorod Luga Op., Jan. 1944.
—Belorussian Op., June 1944.
—"Far East, Novgorod, Ssevsk, Bobruysk," Order of Red Banner.

103 Rifle Division
Units: First formation: 551, 583 Rifle, 271 Artillery Regiments; Second formation: 393, 583, 688 Rifle, 271 Artillery Regiments.
—Finnish War, Feb. 1940.
—Raised Voroshilovsk, Transcaucasus Military District as a Motorized Division, Mar. 1941.
—North Caucasus Military District, June 1941.

—Yelnya sector w/24 Army, Aug. 1941.
—Destroyed Vyazma Pocket, Oct. 1941.
—Second formation raised as a rifle division at Samarkand, Central Asia Military District, Jan. 1942.
—Kharkov w/6 Army, May 1942.
—Destroyed Izyum, May 1942.

104 Rifle Division
Units: 217, 242, 273 Rifle, 290 Artillery Regiments.
—Raised Kandalaksha, Archangelsk Military District, before Dec. 1939.
—Petsamo axis w/14 Army, Dec. 1939.
—Kandalaksha axis w/14 Army, July 1941.
—Kandalaksha w/19 Army, Apr. 1942.
—RVGK w/27 Army, May 1942.
—Rumania as a Motorized Rifle Division w/9 Mechanized Army, Jan. 1946 (Feb. 1947 OB).

105 Rifle Division
Units: 53, 130, 267 Rifle, 102 Artillery Regiments.
—Raised Ussuriysk, Far East Military District, by June 1941.
—Far East w/25 Army, June 1941.
—At Pokrovka, Far East w/1 Independent Red Banner Army, "Front Command Khabarovsk," Apr. 1943.
—Kharkov w/53 Army, Aug. 1943.
—Far East, Aug. 1945.
—North Korea w/25 Army, Apr. 1946 (Feb. 1947 OB).

106 Rifle Division
Units: First formation: 1, 2, 3 Motorized Rifle Regiment; Second and third formation: 397, 442, 534 Rifle, 553 Artillery Regiments; Fourth formation: 43, 188, 236 Rifle, 352 Artillery Regiments.
—One of four divisions in Red Army with "double" numbering.
—First formation raised Solotonoscha, Kharkov Military District, before June 1941.
—Moscow Military District, June 1941.
—To Crimea and 9 Independent Rifle Corps, June 1941.
—Was 106 Motorized Division to 28 Aug. 1941.
—Reserve Front w/24 Army, Aug. 1941.
—Destroyed Vyazma pocket, Oct. 1941.
—Second formation raised, Oct. 1941.
—Destroyed at Kerch, Nov. 1941.
—Third formation raised at Krasnodar, North Caucasus Military District, Dec. 1941.

—Rostov w/56 Army, Jan. 1942.
—Stalingrad axis, June 1942.
—Destroyed in Caucasus; remnants to 242/318 Rifle Divisions, Aug. 1942.
—Fourth formation raised from the Transbaikal NKVD Rifle Division at Chita, Nov. 1942.
—RVGK w/70 Army, Feb. 1943.
—Demyansk w/28 Rifle Corps, 70 Army, Feb. 1943.
—Kursk, July 1943.
—Dnieper River, Sep. 1943.
—Berlin w/3 Guards Army, Apr. 1945.
—Probably an independent division.
—"Dnieper, Transbaikal."

107 Rifle Division
Units: First formation: 586, 630, 765 Rifle, 347 Artillery Regiments; Second formation: 504, 516, 522 Rifle, 1032 Artillery Regiments.
—Raised in Moscow, Moscow Military District, before June 1941.
—In Moscow Military District, June 1941.
—RVGK w/24 Army, Aug. 1941.
—Distinguished itself at Voloskovo w/24 Army, Aug. 1941.
—Yelnaya, Aug. 1941.
—Reserve Front w/24 Army, Sep. 1941.
—Reformed as 5 Guards Rifle Division, Oct. 1941.
—Second formation raised at Tambov, Orel Military District, Mar. 1942.
—RVGK w/3 Reserve, later 60 Army, July 1942.
—Ostrogosh Rossosh Op. w/40 Army, Jan. 1943.
—Southwest Ukraine w/74 RC, 38 Army, Jan. 1944.
—Krakow, Jan. 1945.
—In Far East, Aug. 1945.
—Probably an independent division.
—"Kremjanez, Krakow, Kattowice."

108 Rifle Division
Units: 407, 444, 539 Rifle, 575 Artillery Regiments.
—Raised Vyazma, Western Special Military District, Mar. 1941.
—Minsk w/44 Rifle Corps, 13 Army, June 1941.
—Smolensk, July 1941.
—Yartsevo area w/16 Army, Sep. 1941.
—Zvenigorod w/33 Army, Nov. 1941.
—Mozhaisk w/5 Army, Jan. 1942.
—Far East 108 Rifle Division formed from elements of 22 and 59 Rifle Divisions w/99, 208, 316 Rifle Regiments. Reported in 1 Independent Red Banner Army, "Front Command Khabarovsk," Apr. 1943.

—Kursk w/11 Guards Army, May 1943.
—Vistula Oder Op., Jan. 1945.
—Hungary w/26 Army, Mar. 1945.
—Probably an independent division.
—Breslau, Poland, June 1946 (Aug. 1946 OB).

109 Rifle Division
Units: 381, 602, 702 Rifle, 404 Artillery Regiments.
—Raised in Transbaikal Military District as a Motorized Division w/16 Army, July 1940.
—Transbaikal Military District w/5 Mechanized Corps, 16 Army, May 1941.
—To western Russia (central sector), May 1941.
—RVGK w/5 Mechanized Corps, 16 Army, June 1941.
—Shepetovka, July 1941.
—Smolensk w/16 Army; destroyed there, Aug. 1941.
—Second formation raised at Samarkand, Central Asia Military District, Aug. 1941.
—Leningrad (Pulkovo) w/42 Army, Sep. 1941.
—Destroyed at Sevastopol, May 1942.
—Third formation raised at Leningrad, Leningrad Military District from 21 Security Division, Aug. 1942.
—Leningrad w/42 Army, Jan. 1944.
—Bratislava, Apr. 1945.
—RVGK (FHO), Apr. 1945.
—Leningrad Military District, Oct. 1946 (Feb. 1947 OB).

110 Rifle Division
Units: First formation: 397, 411, 425 Rifle, 355 Artillery Regiments; Second formation: 1287, 1289, 1291 Rifle, 971 Artillery Regiments.
—Raised Tula, Moscow Military District, before July 1941.
—RVGK w/61 Rifle Corps, 21 Army, July 1941.
—Destroyed Mogilev, Aug. 1941.
—Second formation raised at Moscow, Moscow Military District from 4 Moscow Militia Division "Dno," Aug. 1941.
—Distinguished itself at Borovsk (Zhukov), Nov. 1941.
—Mozhaisk w/33 Army, Jan. 1942.
—Reformed as 84 Guards Rifle Division, Apr. 1943.
—Third formation formed from 105 Rifle and 116 Naval Rifle Brigades at Moscow, Moscow Military District, May 1943.
—Kursk w/41 Rifle Corps, 3 Army, July 1943.
—Poland, Feb. 1945.
—"Verchnij, Dneprovsk, Osowiec."

111 Rifle Division
Units: 399, 468, 532 Rifle, 286 Artillery Regiments.
—Raised Vologda, Archangelsk Military District, June 1940.
—RVGK w/41 Rifle Corps, June 1941.
—Baltic Special Military District w/41 Rifle Corps, June 1941.
—Luga Line, June 1941.
—Ostrov, July 1941.
—Reformed as 24 Guards Rifle Division, Mar. 1942.
—Second formation raised at Kalinin, Moscow Military District, June 1942.
—Ostrogosh Rossosh Op. w/3 Tank Army, Jan. 1943.
—Kursk w/68 Army, July 1943.
—Belgorod Kharkov Op., Aug. 1943.
—Kirovograd w/33 Guards Rifle Corps, 5 Guards Army, Jan. 1944.
—Iasi, Apr. 1944.
—Targul Frumos, May 1944.
—Possibly an independent division.
—"Alexandrija."

112 Rifle Division
Units: 385, 436, 524 Rifle, 436 Artillery Regiments.
—Raised Vyazma, Western Special Military District, by July 1941.
—RVGK w/51 Rifle Corps, 22 Army, July 1941.
—Destroyed Vyazma, Oct. 1941.
—Second formation raised at Novosibirsk, Siberia Military District, Apr. 1942.
—RVGK w/1 Reserve Army; may have had a large number of men from penal units, June 1942.
—To Stalingrad w/64 Army, July 1942.
—Stalingrad w/62 Army, had 150 men, Sep. 1942.
—Stalingrad, Red October Factory w/62 Army, Nov. 1942.
—Kiev w/60 Army, Nov. 1943.
—Korosten, Dec. 1943.
—Kiev Defensive Op., Dec. 1943.
—Zhitomir Berdichev Op., Jan. 1944.
—Southwest Ukraine w/112 Rifle Corps, 13 Army, Jan. 1944.
—Rovno Lutsk w/24 Rifle Corps, 13 Army, Feb. 1944.
—"Rylsk, Korosten."

113 Rifle Division
Units: First formation: 513, 679, 725 Rifle, 451 Artillery Regiments; Second formation: 1288, 1290, 1292 Rifle, 972 Artillery Regiments.

—Raised Rylsk, Moscow Military District, Aug. 1939.
—Western Special Military District w/10 Army, June 1941.
—Destroyed in Minsk Pocket, July 1941.
—Second formation raised from 5 Moscow People's Militia Division "Frunze," Moscow, Moscow Military District, July 1941.
—Moscow axis w/53 Army, Dec. 1941.
—Vyazma, Jan. 1942.
—Mozhaisk w/33 Army, Jan. 1942.
—Rogan (Kharkov area) w/6 Army, Mar. 1943.
—Southwest Ukraine w/68 Rifle Corps, 57 Army, Jan. 1944.
—Dniester River, Apr. 1944.
—"Lower Dniester, Frunze," Order of Red Banner.

114 Rifle Division
Units: 363, 536, 763 Rifle, 405 Artillery Regiments.
—Raised, Transbaikal Military District, June 1941.
—Transbaikal Military District w/12 Rifle Corps, 36 Army, July 1941.
—To western front, Oct. 1941.
—Svir River, Oct. 1941.
—Petsamo Kirkenes Op., w/99 Rifle Corps, 14 Army; had 6,418 personnel, Oct. 1944.
—RVGK (FHO), Apr. 1945.

115 Rifle Division
Units: 292, 576, 638 Rifle, 313 Artillery Regiments.
—Raised Nalchik, North Caucasus Military District from 3 Rifle Regiment, Moscow Proletarian Rifle Division, 1940.
—Northeast of Murmansk w/23 Army, June 1941.
—Vyborg area, June–Aug 1941.
—Arbuzovo, Leningrad Front, Sep. 1941.
—Neva River, Aug. 1942.
—Leningrad Front, 1942–44.
—Novgorod Luga Op. w/54 Army, Jan. 1944.
—Cholm, Jan. 1944.
—Poland, Jan. 1945.
—"Cholm."

116 Rifle Division
Units: 441, 548, 656 Rifle, 406 Artillery Regiments.
—Raised Kremenchug, Kharkov Military District, before June 1941.
—Odessa Military District w/9 Independent Army, June 1941.
—RVGK to Zhitomir, July 1941.
—Zhitomir area w/26 Army, July 1941.

—Destroyed Kiev, Sep. 1941.
—Second formation raised at Chita, Transbaikal Military District, Dec. 1941.
—Sulak, North Caucasus Military District as an independent rifle division, Aug. 1942.
—To Stalingrad, Aug. 1942.
—Stalingrad offensive w/66 Army, Nov. 1942.
—Belgorod Kharkov Op. w/53 Army, Aug. 1943.
—Vorskla River w/53 Army, Sep. 1943.
—Kirovograd w/75 Rifle Corps, 53 Army, Jan. 1944.
—Targul Frumos w/52 Army, May 1944.
—RVGK (FHO), Apr. 1945.
—Baltic Military District, Jan. 1946 (Feb. 1947 OB).
—Independent division.
—"Kharkov."

117 Rifle Division
Units: First formation: 240, 269, 275 Rifle, 322 Artillery Regiments; Second formation had 820 Rifle vice 269 Rifle Regiment.
—Raised Kuibyshev, Volga Military District, Aug. 1939.
—RVGK w/63 Rifle Corps, 22 Army, July 1941.
—Destroyed at Kiev; 269 Rifle Regiment to 136 Rifle Division, Sep. 1941.
—Second formation raised at Ivanovo, Moscow Military District, Jan. 1942.
—Kerch landing, Nov. 1943.
—Pulawy Bridgehead w/91 Rifle Corps, 69 Army; had six rifle battalions, Jan. 1945.
—Posen, Feb. 1945.
—Berlin Op. w/91 Rifle Corps, 69 Army, Apr. 1945.
—"Posnan."

118 Rifle Division
Units: 398, 463, 527 Rifle, 604 Artillery Regiments.
—Raised at Kostroma, Moscow Military District, June 1941.
—RVGK w/41 Rifle Corps, June 1941.
—Baltic Special Military District w/41 Rifle Corps, June 1941.
—Kingisepp, June 1941.
—Pskov, July 1941.
—Destroyed at Vyazma, Oct. 1941.
—Second formation raised; became 85 Guards Rifle Division, Apr. 1943.
—Third formation raised at Novocherkassk, North Caucasus Military District from 52, 152 Rifle Brigades, May 1943.

—Melitopol Op., Oct. 1943.
—South Ukraine w/63 Rifle Corps, 5 Shock Army, Jan. 1944.
—Lvov Sandomir Op. w/5 Guards Army, July 1944.
—RVGK, Apr. 1945 (FHO).
—"Melitopol."

119 Rifle Division
Units: 365, 421, 634 Rifle, 349 Artillery Regiments.
—Raised Krasnoyarsk, Siberia Military District, before July 1941.
—RVGK w/30 Army, July 1941.
—Reserve Front w/24 Army, Sep. 1941.
—Reformed as 17 Guards Rifle Division, Mar. 1942.
—Second formation raised at Moscow, Moscow Military District, Mar. 1942.
—To Stalingrad area, Oct. 1942.
—Stalingrad offensive, w/5 Tank Army, Nov. 1942.
—Reformed as 54 Guards Rifle Division, Dec. 1942.
—Third formation raised from 161 Rifle Brigade at Alexin, Moscow Military District, Apr. 1943.
—Germans reported a 119 Rifle Division at Barabash as part of 25 Army, "Front Command Khabarovsk," Apr.1943.
—Kursk w/21 Army, July 1943.
—Baltic area, Sep. 1944.

120 Rifle Division
Units: First formation: 401, 474, 540 Rifle, 120 Artillery Regiments;
Second and third formations: 289, 538, 534 Rifle, 1033 Artillery Regiments.
—Raised Ashkabad, Central Asia Military District, before Aug.1941.
—Yelnya, Aug. 1941.
—Reserve Front w/24 Army, Sep. 1941.
—Reformed as 6 Guards Rifle Division, 26 Sep. 1941.
—Second formation raised at Kologriv, Moscow Military District, Aug. 1942.
—RVGK w/66 Army, Aug. 1942.
—To Stalingrad axis w/66 Army, Aug. 1942.
—Stalingrad offensive w/24 Army, Nov. 1942.
—Reformed as 69 Guards Rifle Division, Feb. 1943.
—Third formation raised Schlusselburg, Leningrad Military District from 11 Rifle Brigade, Apr. 1943.
—Narva, Feb. 1944.
—Krasnogvardeysk, Jan. 1945.
—Vistula Oder Op. w/117 Rifle Corps, 21 Army, Jan–Feb 1945.

—Leningrad Military District, Jan. 1946 (EUCOM Study).
—"Gatchina, Narva, Krasnogvardeysk," Order of Red Banner.

121 Rifle Division
Units: 383, 574, 705 Rifle, 297 Artillery Regiments.
—Raised at Bobruysk, Western Special Military District, before June 1941.
—Bobruysk w/17 Mechanized Corps, June 1941.
—Baranovichi w/Western Front Reserve (47 Independent Rifle Corps), June 1941.
—Sevastopol; 383 Rifle Regiment primarily composed of border guards and naval infantry, Dec. 1941.
—RVGK w/3 Reserve later 60 Army, July 1942.
—Rylsk, Aug. 1943.
—Seim River (Rylsk), Aug. 1943.
—Dnieper River w/60 Army, Sep. 1943.
—Kiev w/60 Army, Nov. 1943.
—Shepetovka area w/30 Rifle Corps, 60 Army, Jan. 1944.
—"Rylsk, Kiev," Order of Red Banner.

122 Rifle Division
Units: 420, 596, 715 Rifle, 285 Artillery Regiments.
—Raised at Rylsk, Orel Military District, Apr. 1939.
—Kandalaksha axis w/9 Army, Finnish War, Feb. 1940.
—Kandalaksha w/14 Army, July 1941.
—Kandalaksha area w/19 Army, Apr. 1942.
—Probably Leningrad Front, 1943–44.
—Carpathian Duklinskiy Op. w/67 Rifle Corps, 38 Army, Sep. 1944.

123 Rifle Division
Units: 245, 255, 272 Rifle, 495 Artillery Regiments.
—Raised at Vishny Volochek, Leningrad Military District, 1939.
—Mannerheim Line, Finland; first unit through line, Feb. 1940.
—Northeast of Murmansk w/23 Army, June 1941.
—Vyborg area, June 1941.
—Leningrad Front, 1942–43.
—Leningrad Offensive w/67 Army, Jan. 1943.
—Novgorod Luga Op., Jan. 1944.
—"Luga, Ordzhonikidze," Order of Lenin.

124 Rifle Division
Units: 622, 406, 781 Rifle, 469 Artillery Regiments.
—Raised Kirovograd, Odessa Military District, Sep. 1939.
—Kovel w/5 Army as a covering division, June 1941.

—Encircled near Milyatin; broke out, June 1941.
—Commander killed in action, July 1941.
—Rovno, Aug. 1941.
—Destroyed in Kiev pocket, Sep. 1941.
—Second formation raised at Voronezh, Orel Military District, Dec. 1941.
—Kharkov offensive, May 1942.
—To Stalingrad axis from 21 Army, June 1942.
—Stalingrad offensive w/5 Tank Army, Nov. 1942.
—Reformed as 50 Guards Rifle Division, Nov. 1942.
—Third formation raised at Schlusselburg, Leningrad from 56, 102, 138 Rifle Brigades, Apr. 1943.
—Mga, July 1943.
—Belorussian Op., June 1944.
—Neman, July 1944.
—To Far East w/39 Army, May–June 1945.
—Manchuria w/39 Army, Aug. 1945.
—"Mga, Neman."

125 Rifle Division
Units: 466, 657, 749 Rifle, 414 Artillery Regiments.
—Raised at Kirov, Ural Military District, before June 1940.
—Baltic Special Military District w/8 Army, June 1941.
—Taurage, June 1941.
—Overrun in Tilsit, 22 June 1941.
—Riga, 29 June 1941.
—Encircled near Lake Peipus, July 1941.
—Krasnoye Selo, Leningrad Front w/8 Army, Sep. 1941.
—Pulkovo w/42 Army, Sep. 1941.
—Probably Leningrad Front, 1942–44.
—Krasnoye Selo, Leningrad Offensive, Jan. 1944.
—Krasnogvardeysk, Jan. 1945.
—Vistula Oder Op., Jan. 1945.
—Maritime Military District, 1947 (Feb. 1948 OB).
—"Kingisepp, Krasnoye Selo, Gatschina, Oder, Krasnogvardeysk," Order of Red Banner.

126 Rifle Division
Units: 366, 539 (later 690), 550 Rifle, 358 Artillery Regiments.
—Raised at Moscow Military District from 2 Proletarian Rifle Regiment, 1 Moscow Proletarian Rifle Division, Dec. 1940.
—One of four units in Red Army with double division numbers.
—Alytus, Baltic Special Military District w/11 Army, June 1941.
—Neman River crossings, June 1941.

—Second formation raised at Voroshilov, Far East Military District while first still active, Sep. 1941.
—Vadino station, Vyazma area, Oct. 1941.
—Moscow, Dec. 1941.
—First formation of division broken up, Dec. 1941.
—Second formation in the RVGK w/5 Reserve Army as an independent division, Siberian Military District, June 1942.
—To Stalingrad front, July 1942.
—Stalingrad w/64 Army, Aug. 1942.
—Kuperosnoye w/62 Army, Sep. 1942.
—Stalingrad area w/51 Army, Oct–Dec 1942.
—Melitopol, Sep. 1943.
—South Ukraine w/54 Rifle Corps, 51 Army, Jan. 1944.
—Crimea w/54 Rifle Corps, 2 Guards Army, Apr. 1944.
—Probably an independent division.
—"Gorlovka, Melitopol," Orders of Red Banner, Suvorov.

127 Rifle Division
Units: First formation: 395, 535, 875 Rifle, 423 Artillery Regiments; Second and third formation: 547, 549, 555, 1034 Artillery Regiments.
—Raised at Rostov, North Caucasus Militry District (FHO), July 1939.
—Raised at Kharkov, Kharkov Military District (SME), July 1940.
—North Caucasus Military District, June 1941.
—RVGK w/16 Army, July 1941.
—Yelnaya, July 1941.
—Reserve Front w/24 Army, Sep. 1941.
—Reformed as 2 Guards Rifle Division, 18 Sep. 1941.
—Second formation raised at Atkarsk, Volga Military District, Feb. 1942.
—RVGK w/5 Reserve Army, May 1942.
—Stalingrad axis w/63 Army, July 1942.
—Reformed as 62 Guards Rifle Division, Jan. 1943.
—Third formation raised from 52, 98 Rifle Brigades at Kuibyshev, Volga Military District, May. 1943.
—Southwest Ukraine w/107 Rifle Corps, 1 Guards Army, Jan. 1944.
—Czestochowa, Jan. 1945.
—"Czestochowa, Kielce," Order of Red Banner.

128 Rifle Division
Units: 374, 533, 741 Rifle, 292 Artillery Regiments.
—Raised at Gshatsk, Western Special Military District, before June 1941.
—Alytus, Baltic Special Military District w/11 Army, June 1941.
—Mga w/48 Army, Aug. 1941.
—Tikhvin w/54 Army, Oct. 1941.

—Leningrad Offensive Op., Jan. 1942.
—Leningrad Op. w/2 Shock Army, Jan. 1943.
—Vistula Oder Op., Jan. 1945.
—Lower Silesian Op., Feb. 1945.
—"Plaskow, Kattowice, Oder."

129 Rifle Division
Units: First formation: 343, 438, 457 Rifle, 664 Artillery Regiments; Second formation: 438, 457, 518 Rifle, 664 Artillery Regiments.
—Raised at Moscow, Moscow Militry District from 2 Moscow Militia Division, June 1941.
—RVGK w/19 Army, June 1941.
—Smolensk w/16 Army, July 1941.
—Smolensk pocket w/16 Army, Aug. 1941.
—Yartsevo w/16 Army, Sep. 1941.
—Destroyed Vyazma, Oct. 1941.
—Second formation raised at Moscow, Moscow Military District, Oct. 1941.
—Moscow axis w/20 Army, Dec. 1941.
—Stalingrad area w/63 Army, Mar. 1943.
—RVGK w/65 Army, Mar. 1943.
—Distinguished itself at Orel, Aug. 1943.
—Poland, July 1944.
—Baltic area w/1 Shock Army, Oct. 1944.
—RVGK (FHO), Apr. 1945.
—Baltic Military District w/130 Rifle Corps, 6 Guards Army, Nov. 1946 (Feb. 1947 OB).
—The 343 Rifle Regiment to 38 Rifle Division.
—Probably an independent division.
—"Orel, Volkhov, Bialystok, Latvian."

130 Rifle Division
Units: 371, 528, 664 Rifle, 363 Artillery Regiments.
—Raised at Romny, Kharkov Military District, Aug. 1939.
—In the Kiev Special Military District reserve, June 1941.
—Destroyed Vyazma Pocket, Oct. 1941.
—Second formation from 3 Moscow Communist Rifle Division which had been formed from the Moscow Worker's Rifle Division, Moscow, Moscow Military District, 22 Jan. 1942.
—Northwest Front w/53 Army, Apr. 1942.
—Reformed as 53 Guards Rifle Division, Dec. 1942.
—Third formation raised from 152, 156, 159 Rifle Brigades, at Matveyev Kurgan, North Caucasus Military District, Jan. 1943.
—Kurgan, North Caucasus Military Division, Apr. 1943.

—Taganrog, Aug. 1943.
—Ukraine w/28 Army, Nov. 1943.
—Belorussian Op., June 1944.
—Brest, July 1944.
—East Prussia Op., Jan. 1945.
—East Prussia Op., Mar. 1945.
—RVGK (FHO), Apr. 1945.
—"Taganrog, Gumbinnen, Baranovichi, Brest
—Litovsk," Order of Red Banner.

131 Rifle Division
Units: First formation: 593, 695, 743 Rifle, 409 Artillery Regiments;
 Second formation: 482, 593, 743 Rifle, 409 Artillery Regiments.
—Raised at Novograd Volynsky, Kiev Special Military District, Nov. 1939.
—Lutsk, in Kiev Special Military District Reserve w/9 Mechanized Corps as a Motorized Division, June 1941.
—Destroyed at Kiev, Sep. 1941.
—Second formation raised at Kirov, Ural Military District as an independent division of the RVGK, Jan. 1942.
—The 695 Rifle Regiment was transferred to 221 Rifle Division.
—RVGK as an independent division, June 1942.
—Southwest Front w/1 Tank Army when it was organized, July 1942.
—Stalingrad w/64 Army, July 1942.
—Stalingrad w/62 Army, Aug. 1942.
—Oranienbaum w/2 Shock Army, Jan. 1944.
—Narva, Feb. 1944.
—Narva w/2 Shock Army, July 1944.
—RVGK (FHO), Apr. 1945.
—Leningrad Military District, 1946 (Feb. 1947 OB).
—Independent division.
—"Narva, Ropsha."

132 Rifle Division
Units: 498, 605, 712 Rifle, 425 Artillery Regiments.
—Raised Poltava, Kharkov Military District, before June 1939.
—Southern Front w/45 Rifle Corps, 13 Army, June 1941.
—RVGK w/16 Army, July 1941.
—Encircled in Bryansk area, Sep. 1941.
—Voronezh, Jan. 1943.
—Dnieper River w/60 Army, Sep. 1943.
—Warsaw Poznan Op. w/47 Army, Jan. 1945.
—Vistula Oder Op.; breakthrough rifle division w/47 Army, Jan. 1945.

—Berlin Op. w/47 Army, Apr. 1945.
—"Bachmach," Order of Red Banner.

133 Rifle Division
Units: 418, 521, 681 Rifle, 400 Artillery Regiments.
—Raised Biysk, Siberia Military District before June 1941.
—Baltic Special Military District w/16 Rifle Corps, 11 Army, June 1941.
—Reserve Front w/24 Army, Sep. 1941.
—Moscow axis w/26 Army, Dec. 1941.
—Reformed as 18 Guards Rifle Division, Mar. 1942.
—Second formation raised at Kostroma, Moscow Military District, June 1942.
—Smolensk, Sep. 1943.
—Korsun Shevchenkovskiy Op. w/104 Rifle Corps, 40 Army, Jan. 1944.
—Targul Frumos w/7 Guards Army, May 1944.
—Iasi Kishinev Op., Aug. 1944.
—"Smolensk, Transylvania" Order of Red Banner.

134 Rifle Division
Units: 515, 629, 738 Rifle, 410 Artillery Regiments.
—Raised Kramatorskaya, Kharkov Military District, June 1941.
—RVGK w/19 Army, July 1941.
—Destroyed, Vyazma, Oct. 1941.
—Second formation raised at Solnechnogorsk, Moscow Military District, Feb. 1942.
—Kalinin Front w/41 Army, May 1942.
—Pulawy Bridgehead w/61 Rifle Corps, 69 Army; breaktrough division, had six rifle battalions, Jan. 1945.
—Berlin Op. w/61 Rifle Corps, 69 Army, Apr. 1945.
—"Verdino, Brandenburg, u/i honorific" Order of Red Banner.

135 Rifle Division
Units: 396, 497, 791 Rifle, 276 Artillery Regiments.
—Raised Kiev Special Military District, Sep. 1939.
—Vladimir Volyinsky, Kiev Special Military District, 24 June 1941.
—Rovno w/27 Rifle Corps, 40 Army, Aug. 1941.
—Southwest Front w/40 Army, Sep. 1941.
—Destroyed Kiev, Sep. 1941.
—Second formation raised Kolomna, Moscow Military District, Feb. 1942.
—Kalinin Front w/41 Army, May 1942.
—RVGK w/70 Army, Oct. 1943.
—Kiev Op. w/60 Army, Nov. 1943.
—SW Ukraine w/21 Rifle Corps, 38 Army, Jan. 1944.

—Targul Frumos w/40 Army, May 1944.
—Vistula Oder Op., Jan. 1945.
—Possibly an independent division.
—"Kattowice."

136 Rifle Division
Units: First formation: 387, 541, 733 Rifle, 291 Artillery Regiments; Second and third formation: 269, 270, 342 Rifle, 343 Artillery Regiments.
—Raised Leninakan, Transcaucasus Military District from 50 Rifle Regiment of 17 "Gorki" Rifle Division (FHO), before 1939.
—SME says raised in Gorki, Moscow Military District, Sep. 1939.
—Finland, 1940.
—Transcaucasus Military District w/23 Rifle Corps, 45 Army, July 1941.
—Southern Front w/9 Army, Oct. 1941.
—Reformed as 15 Guards Rifle Division, Feb. 1942.
—Second formation raised in Karelia, Leningrad Military District, Mar. 1942.
—Leningrad offensive (Schlusselburg), w/67 Army, Jan. 1943.
—Reformed as 63 Guards Rifle Division, Jan. 1943.
—Third formation raised at Leninakan, Transcaucasus Military District, Feb. 1943.
—Kiev, Nov. 1943.
—Southwest Ukraine w/47 Rifle Corps, 38 Army, Jan. 1944.
—Korsun Shevchenkovskiy Op. w/40 Army, Jan. 1944
—Zvenigorod, Feb. 1944.
—Targul Frumos, May 1944.
—Gdynia area w/70 Army, Mar. 1945.
—Berlin Op. w/70 Army, Apr. 1945.
—"Kiev, Zvenigorod."

137 Rifle Division
Units: 409, 624, 771 Rifle, 17 Artillery Regiments.
—Raised Gorki, Moscow Military District, (Note: 17 "Gorki" Rifle Division had 17 Artillery), before Feb. 1939.
—Designated one of four best divisions in Red Army by Timoshenko, Moscow Military District, Aug. 1940.
—Moscow Military District w/67 Rifle Corps, June 1941.
—RVGK w/22 Army, July 1941.
—Central Front w/13 Army, Sep. 1941.
—Voronezh, Jan. 1943.
—Kursk w/48 Army, July 1943.

—Belorussia Op., June 1944.
—Carpathian Mountains w/18 Army, Sep. 1944.
—Northern Poland w/48 Army, Mar. 1945.
—Czechoslovakia, Apr. 1945.
—"Bobruysk."

138 Mountain Rifle Division
Units: 344, 650, 768 Rifle, 295 Artillery Regiments.
—Raised Leninakan, Transcaucasus Military District, 1939.
—Transcaucasus Military District w/23 Rifle Corps, 45 Army, June 1941.
—RVGK w/22 Army, July 1941.
—Caucasus and Crimea, Dec. 1941–Mar. 1942.
—Destroyed at Kerch, May 1942.
—Reformed as 138 Rifle Division, Second Formation, May 1942.
—Crimea w/51 Army, June 1942.
—North Caucasus w/51 Army, July 1942.
—Stalingrad axis w/51 Army, Aug. 1942.
—Aksai River, North Caucasus Military District, Aug. 1942.
—Stalingrad w/62 Army in Barrikady Factory; absorbed remnants of 37 Guards Rifle Division, Oct. 1942.
—Reformed as 70 Guards Rifle Division, 6 Feb. 1942.
—Second formation raised at Kalinin, Moscow Military District from 6 Naval Infantry and 109 Motorized Rifle Brigade, May 1943.
—Southwest Ukraine w/21 Guards Rifle Corps, 4 Guards Army, Jan. 1944.
—Zvenigorod w/53 Army, Feb. 1944.
—Carpathian Op., Sep. 1944.
—"Carpathian, u/i honorific," Order of Red Banner.

139 Rifle Division
Units: First and third formation: 364, 609, 718 Rifle, 354 Artillery Regiments; Second formation: 1300, 1302, 1304 Rifle, 976 Artillery Regiments.
—Raised Kozelsk, Moscow Military District, Sep. 1939.
—Tolvajarvi, Finnland; composed of Belorussians, Dec. 1939.
—Finnish War w/8 Army, Jan. 1940.
—Destroyed in Uman Pocket as a Motorized Division, Aug. 1941.
—Second formation raised at Moscow, Moscow Military District from 9 Moscow People's Militia Rifle Division, July 1941.
—Destroyed at Vyazma, Oct. 1941.
—Third formation raised at Tscherbokssary, Moscow Military District, Jan. 1942.

—Kursk w/10 Army, July 1943.
—Gdynia area w/49 Army, Mar. 1945.
—"Roslavl, Osowiec, Kirov, Lebedin," Orders of Red Banner, Suvorov.

140 Rifle Division
Units: First and third formation: 445, 637, 798 Rifle, 309 Artillery; Second formation: 1305, 1307, 1309 Rifle, 977 Artillery Regiments; Fourth formation 96, 258, 283 Rifle, 371 Artillery Regiments.
—Raised at Uman, Kiev Special Military District, Sep. 1939.
—In Kiev Special Military District Reserve, June 1941.
—Destroyed Nikolayev, Aug. 1941.
—Second formation raised at Moscow, Moscow Military District from 13 Moscow People's Rifle Division "Rastokin," July 1941.
—Destroyed Vyazma, Oct. 1941.
—Third formation raised at Kanasch, Moscow Military Division, Jan. 1942.
—Southern Front w/24 Army, May 1942.
—Dissolved; remnants to 242 Mountain Rifle Division, Aug. 1942.
—Fourth formation raised at Novorossiysk, Siberia Military District from Siberian NKVD Rifle Division, Nov. 1942.
—RVGK w/70 Army, Feb. 1943.
—Kursk w/28 Rifle Corps, 70 Army, July 1943.
—Zhitomir Berdichev Op. w/24 Rifle Corps, 13 Army, Jan. 1944.
—Novograd Volynskiy, Jan. 1944.
—Rovno Lutsk Op. w/60 Army, Jan. 1944.
—Proskurov Chernovtsy Op. w/60 Army, Mar. 1944.
—Lvov, July 1944.
—Carpathian Duklinskiy Op., w/67 Rifle Corps, 38 Army, Sep. 1944.
—Prague, May 1945.
—Probably an independent division.
—"Siberian, Novgorod, Seversk, Lvov," Order of Lenin, twice Order of Red Banner, Orders of Suvorov, Kutuzov.

141 Rifle Division.
Units: 687, 745, 796 Rifle, 186 Artillery Regiments.
—Raised Slavyansk, Moscow Military District, Sep. 1939.
—In Kiev Special Military District Reserve, June 1941.
—Destroyed at Nikolayev, Aug. 1941.
—Second formation raised at Kazan, Volga Military District, Jan. 1942.
—Kharkov Offensive w/6 Army, June 1942.
—Ostrogosh Rossosh Op. w/40 Army, Jan. 1943.
—Voronezh w/60 Army, Jan. 1943.
—RVGK w/70 Army, Oct. 1943.

—Kiev w/60 Army, Nov. 1943.
—Southwest Ukraine w/30 Rifle Corps, 1 Ukrainian Front, Jan. 1944.
—Stanislav, Aug. 1944.
—Carpathian Uzhgorod Op. w/30 Rifle Corps, 1 Guards Army, Sep. 1944.
—Probably an independent division.
—"Kiev, Stanislav, Drohobycz, Carpathian, Pressburg," Orders of Red Banner, Bogdan Khmelnitskiy.

142 Rifle Division
Units: 461, 588, 946 Rifle, 344 Artillery Regiments.
—Raised at Hiitola, Archangelsk Military District before June 1941.
—Northeast of Murmansk w/23 Army, June 1941.
—Trapped against Lake Ladoga by Germans; escaped, Aug. 1941.
—Finnish Front, Sep 1942–June 1943.
—Graudents w/2 Shock Army, Feb. 1945.
—Pomeranian Op. w/2 Shock Army, Mar. 1945.
—Order of Red Banner.

143 Rifle Division
Units: 487, 635, 800 Rifle, 287 Artillery Regiments.
—Raised at Gomel, Western Military District, before June 1941.
—Baranovichi w/Western Front Reserve (47 Independent Rifle Corps), June 1941.
—Central Front w/13 Army, Sep. 1941.
—Destroyed at Bryansk, Oct. 1941.
—Second formation raised at Korosten, Kiev Military District, Dec. 1943.
—Southwest Ukraine w/77 Rifle Corps, 47 Army, Jan. 1944.
—Rovno Lutsk Op. w/77 Rifle Corps, 13 Army, Jan–Feb 1944.
—Kovel, Feb. 1944.
—Warsaw Poznan Op., Jan. 1945.
—Vistula Oder Op. w/47 Army, Jan. 1945.
—Warsaw, Jan. 1945.
—"Konotop, Korosten, Kovel, Praga, Warsaw."

144 Rifle Division
Units: 449, 612, 785 Rifle, 308 Artillery Regiments.
—Raised Ivanov, probably in Moscow Military District, Sep–Oct 1939.
—Finnish War, Feb–Mar 1940.
—In Moscow Military District, 22 June 1941.
—To 20 Rifle Corps, 20 Army, 23 June, 1941.
—RVGK w/16 Army, July 1941.
—Right Bank Dnieper, July 1941.

—Mozhaisk, Nov. 1941.
—Moscow area w/20 and 5 Armies, Nov. 1941–Jan. 1942.
—Mozhaisk w/5 Army, Jan. 1942.
—Defensive operations on Smolensk axis, Aug. 1942–July 1943.
—Smolensk Op., Sep. 1943.
—Belorussian Op., w/5 Army, June 1944.
—Vilnius w/65 Rifle Corps, 5 Army, July 1944.
—Kaunus, Aug. 1944.
—East Prussia, Oct. 1944.
—East Prussian Op., Jan. 1945.
—Koenigsberg, Apr. 1945.
—To Far East w/5 Army, May 1945.
—Manchurian Op. w/5 Army, Aug. 1945.
—"Vilna, Vitebsk, Kovno, Insterberg," Orders of Red Banner, Suvorov, Kutuzov, Alexander Nevsky.

145 Rifle Division
Units: 403, 599, 729 Rifle, 277 Artillery Regiments.
—Raised at Belgorod, Orel Military District, by June 1941.
—Orel Military District, June 1941.
—RVGK w/43 Army, July 1941.
—Smolensk w/43 Army, July 1941.
—Destroyed, Roslavl Pocket, Aug. 1941.
—Yelnaya area w/43 Army. Sep. 1941.
—Second formation raised at Balachna, Moscow Military District, Jan. 1942.
—Cholm, Leningrad Front, Jan. 1944.
—Vitebsk w/92 Rifle Corps, 43 Army, June 1944.
—Baltic area, Sep. 1944.
—Poland, Jan. 1945.
—Maritime Military District, Jan. 1947 (Feb. 1948 OB).
—"Cholm."

146 Rifle Division
Units: 512, 608, 698 Rifle, 280 Artillery Regiments.
—Raised at Berdichev, Kiev Special Military District, July 1940.
—In the Kiev Special Military District Reserve, June 1941.
—Destroyed at Kiev, Sep. 1941.
—Second formation raised at Kazan, Volga Military District, Jan. 1942.

147 Rifle Division
Units: 45, 600, 640 Rifle, 379 Artillery Regiments.
—Raised at Lubny, Kharkov Military District, Sep. 1939.

—Odessa Military District w/9 Independent Army, June 1941.
—Kiev, July 1941.
—Kiev Pocket w/37 Army, Aug. 1941.
—Destroyed at Kiev, Sep. 1941.
—Second formation raised at Kazan, Volga Military District, Apr. 1942.
—RVGK w/7 Reserve Army, June 1942.
—Stalingrad w/62 Army, July 1942.
—Akhtyrka w/27 Army, Aug. 1943.
—Southwest Ukraine w/23 Rifle Corps, 60 Army, Jan. 1944.
—Berlin Op. w/102 Rifle Corps, 47 Army, Apr. 1945.

148 Rifle Division
Units: 496, 507, 654 Rifle, 326 Artillery Regiments.
—Raised at Engels, Volga Military District, before July 1941.
—RVGK w/45 Rifle Corps, 21 Army, July 1941.
—Central Front w/13 Army, Sep. 1941.
—Voronezh, Jan. 1943.
—Kursk, w/18 Guards Independent Rifle Corps, 13 Army, July 1943.
—Dnieper River w/13 Army, Sep. 1943.
—Chernigov, Sep. 1943.
—Southwest Ukraine w/18 Guards Independent Rifle Corps, 60 Army, Jan. 1944.
—Shepetovka, Mar. 1944.
—Ternopol, Mar. 1944.
—Lvov Sandomir Op. w/15 Rifle Corps, 60 Army, July 1944.
—Lvov, July 1944.
—Poland, Feb. 1945.
—Possibly an independent division.
—"Chernigov, Shepetovka, Lvov, Debica, Shumsk," Orders of Red Banner, Suvorov.

149 Rifle Division
Units: 479, 568, 744 Rifle, 314 Artillery Regiments.
—Raised at Ostrogosh, Orel Military District, before June 1941.
—In Orel Military District, June 1941.
—RVGK w/43 Army, July 1941.
—Smolensk, July 1941.
—Yelnaya area w/43 Army, Sep. 1941.
—Destroyed Vyazma, Oct. 1941.
—Second formation raised at Ryazan, Moscow Military District, Jan. 1942.
—Lenino (near Mogilev) w/65 Rifle Corps, 33 Army, Oct. 1943.
—Southwest Urkraine w/24 Rifle Corps, 13 Army, Jan. 1944.

—Novograd Volyinskiy, Jan. 1944.
—Rovno Lutsk Op. w/24 Rifle Corps, 13 Army, Jan–Feb 1944.
—"Novograd Volyinskiy," Orders of Red Banner, Kutuzov.

150 Rifle Division
Units: 469, 674, 756 Rifle, 328 Artillery Regiments.
—Raised at Vyazma, Western Military District, Sep. 1939.
—Odessa Military District w/9 Independent Army, June 1941.
—Coastal Army, Odessa area, July 1941.
—Taganrog, Oct. 1941.
—Southern Front w/9 Independent Army, Oct–Nov 1941.
—Destroyed Izyum, May 1942.
—Second formation raised at Turga, Siberian Military District, Aug. 1942.
—East Pomeranian Op., Jan. 1945.
—Schniedemuhl, Jan. 1945.
—Koenigsberg, Apr. 1945.
—Berlin w/3 Shock Army; took Reichstag, Apr. 1945.
—The 756 Rifle Regiment has the "Banner of Victory," the flag raised over the Reichstag in Berlin, Apr. 1945.
—Rohrburg, Germany w/79 Rifle Corps, 3 Mechanized Army, Oct. 1946 (Feb 1947 OB).
—"Stalin, Idritsk, Pomeranian," Order of Kutuzov.
Key Commanders: Gen-Maj HSU B.M. Shatilov, Apr. 1945.

151 Rifle Division
Units: 581, 626, 683 Rifle, 353 Artillery Regiments.
—Raised at Udshary, Transcaucasus Military District, before June 1941.
—Transcaucasus Military District, June 1941.
—Destroyed at Kiev, Sep. 1941.
—Second formation raised at Udshary, Transcaucasus Military District, Oct. 1941.
—Taman Peninsula w/44 Army, May 1943.
—Turkish border to Terek River w/9 Independent Army, Aug. 1942.
—Terek River, Nov. 1942.
—Zhmerinka, Mar. 1944.
—Stanislav, Aug. 1944.
—Carpathian Mountains w/18 Guards Independent Rifle Corps, 1 Guards Army, Sep. 1944.
—Hungary, Nov. 1944.
—Budapest, Jan. 1945.
—"Carpathian Mtns, Stanislav, Hungarian, Budapest, Zhmerinka."

152 Rifle Division
Units: First and second formations: 480, 544, 644 Rifle, 333 Artillery
    Regiments.
—Raised at Chita, Transbaikal Military District, before 1939.
—One regiment sent to Khalkin Gol, Aug. 1938.
—Transbaikal Military District w/16 Army, May 1941.
—To west w/16 Army, May 1941.
—RVGK w/16 Army, July 1941.
—Smolensk w/6 Army, July 1941.
—Yartsevo area w/16 Army, Sep. 1941.
—Destroyed, Vyazma pocket, Oct. 1941.
—Moscow offensive, Dec. 1941.
—Second formation raised in North Ural Military District, Jan. 1942.
—Karelian front w/26 Army, May 1942.
—Dnepropetrovsk, Sep. 1943.
—Southwest Ukraine w/6 Guards RC, 46 Army, Jan. 1944.
—East Prussian Op. w/28 Army, Jan. 1945.
—Berlin Op. w/128 Rifle Corps, 28 Army, Apr. 1945.
—RVGK (FHO), Apr. 1945.
—"Dnepropetrovsk," Red Banner.

153 Rifle Division
Units: First formation: 435, 505, 666 Rifle, 565 Artillery Regiments;
    Second and third formations: 557, 563, 566 Rifle, 1035 Artillery
    (135 Artillery w/second formation).
—Raised at Sverdlovsk, Ural Military District, before July 1941.
—RVGK w/22 Army, July 1941.
—Reformed as 3 Guards RD, 18 Sep. 1941.
—Second formation raised at Chapayev, Volga Military District, Mar. 1942.
—RVGK w/5 Reserve Army, May 1942.
—Stalingrad w/63 Army, July 1942.
—Stalingrad offensive w/ 1 Guards Army, Nov. 1942.
—Reformed as 57 Guards Rifle Division, Jan. 1943.
—Third formation raised at Rzhev, Moscow Military District from 136 Rifle Brigade, May 1943.
—Smolensk, Sep. 1943.
—Mogilev Op. w/81 Rifle Corps, 49 Army, June 1944.
—"Smolensk."

154 Rifle Division
Units: 437, 473, 510 Rifle, 571 Artillery Regiments.

—Raised at Ulyanovsk, Volga Military District, before June 1941.
—In Volga Military District, June 1941.
—RVGK w/66 Rifle Corps, 22 Army, July 1941.
—Central Front w/5 Cavalry Corps, Sep. 1941.
—Bryansk Pocket w/50 Army, Oct. 1941.
—Kaluga w/50 Army, Nov. 1941.
—Kaluga, Dec. 1941.
—Reformed as 47 Guards Rifle Division, Oct. 1942.
—Second formation raised at Rzhev, Moscow Military District, May 1943.
—"Lunaburg."

155 Rifle Division
Units: 436, 659, 786 Rifle, 306 Artillery Regiments.
—Raised at Opotschka, Moscow Military District, 1939.
—Finnish War w/8 Army, Jan. 1940.
—Baranovichi w/Western Front Reserve, June 1941.
—Central Front w/13 Army, Sep. 1941.
—Destroyed Bryansk, Oct. 1941.
—Second formation raised at Moscow, Moscow Military District from 4 Moscow Home Guard Rifle Division, Jan. 1942.
—Kalinin area w/22 Army, Jan. 1942.
—Yelets area, May 1943.
—Kursk w/26 Guards Rifle Corps, 27 Army, July 1943.
—Akhtyrka w/27 Army, Aug. 1943.
—Southwest Ukraine w/21 Rifle Corps, 38 Army, Jan. 1944.
—Carpathian Uzhgorod Op. w/30 Rifle Corps, 1 Guards Army, Sep. 1944.
—Budapest, Jan. 1945.
—"Stryy, Drohobycz, Borislav, Budapest."

156 Rifle Division
Units: 361, 417, 530 Rifle, 434 Artillery Regiments.
—Raised at Staniza-Petrovska, North Caucasus Military District, before June 1941.
—North Caucasus Military District, June 1941.
—Crimea w/9 Independent Rifle Corps, Aug. 1941.
—RVGK in Crimea w/56 Indepdendent Army, Aug. 1941.
—Perekop, Oct. 1941.
—Kerel, Nov. 1941.
—Crimea w/44 Army, June 1942.
—Dissolved, Aug. 1942.

—Second formation formed from 26, 162 Rifle Brigades, Kalinin, Moscow Military District, Apr. 1943.
—Vitebsk Op. w/60 Rifle Corps, 43 Army, June 1944.

157 Rifle Division
Units: 384, 633, 716 Rifle, 422 Artillery Regiments.
—Raised at Novocherkassk, North Caucasus Military District, 1939.
—North Caucasus Military District, June 1941.
—Odessa, July 1941.
—RVGK, Sep. 1941.
—To Odessa, Sep. 1941.
—Moscow, Nov. 1941.
—Amphibious assault at Feodosiya w/44 Army, Dec. 1941.
—Caucasus w/44 Army, June 1942.
—North Caucasus w/51 Army, Aug. 1942.
—Aksai River, North Caucasus, Aug. 1942.
—Stalingrad w/64 Army, Sep. 1942.
—Reformed as 76 Guards Rifle Division, Mar. 1943.
—Second formation from 148 Rifle Brigade, Kalinin, Moscow Military District, Mar. 1943.
—Chernigov, Sep. 1943.
—Belorussia w/72 Rifle Corps, 33 Army, May 1944.
—Neman, July 1944.
—East Prussian Op., Jan. 1945.
—"Neman, Chernigov, Leszno, Insterburg," Order of Red Banner.

158 Rifle Division
Units: First and second formations: 875, 889, 891 Rifle, 423 Artillery Regiments.
—Raised Yeysk, North Caucasus Military District, 1940.
—RVGK w/19 Army, June 1941.
—Smolensk, July 1941.
—Smolensk pocket w/16 Army, Aug. 1941.
—Second formation at Moscow, Moscow Military District from 5 Moscow Home Guard Rifle Division, Jan. 1942.
—Kalinin w/22 Army, Jan. 1942.
—Kalinin Front w/39 Army, Aug. 1942.
—Vitebsk w/84 Rifle Corps, 39 Army, June 1944.
—"Leszno, Vitebsk," Twice Order of Red Banner.

159 Rifle Division
Units: 491, 558, 631 Rifle, 597 Artillery Regiments.

—Raised at Belaya Tserkov, Kiev Special Military District, June 1940.
—Kiev Special Military District w/6 Rifle Corps, Oct. 1940.
—Przemsyl, w/6 Rifle Corps, 6 Army as a covering division.
—Zhukov: "not fully deployed," June 1941.
—Destroyed Kiev, Sep. 1941.
—Second formation raised in Ural Military District, after Sep. 1941.
—In Stalingrad area, Oct. 1942.
—Stalingrad offensive w/5 Tank Army, Nov. 1942.
—RVGK, Dec. 1942.
—Don Basin w/Southwest Front, Dec. 1942.
—Reformed as 61 Guards Rifle Division, Jan. 1943.
—Third formation raised at Rzhev, Moscow Military District from 20 Rifle and 49 Ski Brigades, June 1943.
—Vitebsk, June 1944.
—East Prussia Op., Jan. 1945.
—"Vitebsk, Insterburg."

160 Rifle Division
Units: First and second formation: 1293, 1295, 1297 Rifle, 973 Artillery Regiments; Third formation: 443, 537, 636 Rifle, 566 Artillery Regiments.
—Raised at Gorki, Moscow Military District from 6 Moscow People's Militia Rifle Division, June 1941.
—One of four double-numbered divisions in Red Army.
—RVGK w/20 Rifle Corps, 16 Army, June 1941.
—Shepetovka w/16 Army, July 1941.
—Central Front w/13 Army, Sep. 1941.
—Second formation raised at Moscow, Moscow Military District, Nov. 1941.
—Mozhaisk w/33 Army, Jan. 1942.
—Vyazma, Jan. 1942.
—Kharkov offensive w/6 Army, June 1942.
—Stalingrad area, Dec. 1942.
—Kharkov w/3 Tank Army, Feb. 1943.
—Reformed as 89 Guards Rifle Division, Apr. 1943.
—Belorussia w/114 Rifle Corps, 70 Army, Jan. 1944.
—Third formation in Gdynia area w/70 Army, Mar. 1945.
—"Torun, Dzherzinskiy."

161 Rifle Division
Units: First formation: 477, 542, 603 Rifle, 628 Artillery Regiments; Second formation: 565, 569, 575 Rifle, 1075 Artillery Regiments.

—Raised at Minsk, Western Special Military District, before June 1941.
—Minsk w/13 Army, June 1941.
—Reformed as 4 Guards Rifle Division, 18 Sep. 1941.
—Second formation raised at Mitschurinsk, Orel Military District, June 1942.
—South of Moscow w/60 Army, July 1942.
—North Caucasus, Jan. 1943.
—Kharkov w/69 Army, Feb. 1943.
—Kursk w/40 Army, July 1943.
—Dnieper River w/40 Army, Sep. 1943.
—Ukraine, Fall 1943.
—Southwest Ukraine w/101 Rifle Corps, 18 Army, Jan. 1944.
—Lvov w/18 Guards Independent Rifle Corps, 1 Guards Army, July 1944.
—Stanislav, Aug. 1944.
—Carpathian Uzgorhod Op. w/18 Guards Independent Rifle Corps, 1 Guards Army, Sep. 1944.
—Poland, Jan. 1945.
—Prague, May 1945.
—"Stanislav."

162 Rifle Division
Units: First and second formation: 501, 627, 720 Rifle, 605 Artillery Regiments; Third formation: 194, 209, 224 Rifle, 369 Artillery Regiments.
—Raised Artemovsk, Kharkov Military District, before June 1941.
—RVGK w/19 Army, July 1941.
—Destroyed Vyazma pocket, Oct. 1941.
—Second formation raised at Verchniy Ufalev, Ural Military District, Jan. 1942.
—Disbanded, July 1942.
—Third formation raised at Tashkent, Central Asia Military District from the Central Asia NKVD Division, Oct. 1942.
—RVGK w/28 Rifle Corps, 70 Army, Feb. 1943.
—Kursk w/28 Rifle Corps, 70 Army, July 1943.
—Novgorod Luga Op., Jan. 1944.
—Baranov bridgehead, July 1944.
—Vistula Oder Op., Jan. 1945.
—Gdynia area w/70 Army, Mar. 1945.
—Berlin Op. w/70 Army, Apr. 1945.
—"Central Asia, Novgorod, Debica, Torun, Ssversk," Order of Red Banner.

163 Rifle Division
Units: 529, 759, 1318 Rifle, 365 Artillery Regiments.
—Raised at Vishny Volochev, Leningrad Military District, July 1930.
—SME says raised Tula, Moscow Military District as 163 Motorized Division, by Sep. 1939.
—Finnish War on Kandalaksha axis, 1939–40 w/9 Independent Army; suffered a bloody defeat at Suomussali, Finland, Nov. 1939.
—Finnish War w/13 Army, Feb. 1940.
—Pskov w/1 Mechanized Corps, 27 Army, June 1941.
—Reformed as a Rifle Division, Sep. 1941.
—Demyansk Pocket w/34 Army, Oct–Dec 1942.
—Demyansk w/11 Army, Feb. 1943.
—Khotin w/40 Army, Mar. 1944.
—RVGK, Apr. 1943.
—Bogodukhov, Ukraine, Aug. 1943.
—Dnieper w/38 Army, Sep. 1943.
—Romny, Sep. 1943.
—Lutezh Bridgehead, Oct. 1943.
—Kiev w/38 and 40 Armies, Nov. 1943.
—Kiev Defensive Op., Dec. 1943.
—Zhitomir Berdichev Op. w/50 Rifle Corps, 40 Army, Jan. 1944.
—Korsun Pocket, Jan. 1944.
—Uman Botosani Op., Mar. 1944.
—Dniester River, Mar. 1944.
—Targul Frumos w/104 Rifle Corps, 40 Army, May 1944.
—Iasi Kishinev Op. w/33 Rifle Corps, 27 Army; took Ploesti, Aug. 1944.
—Cluj, Sep. 1944.
—Carpathian Mountains w/50 Rifle Corps, 40 Army, Sep. 1944.
—Hungary, Dec. 1944.
—Budapest, Jan. 1945.
—Lake Balaton, Mar. 1945.
—Vienna, Apr. 1945.
—Graz, May 1945.
—"Romny, Kiev, Transylvania, Focsani," Orders of Lenin, Red Banner, Suvorov, Kutuzov.

164 Rifle Division
Units: 531, 620, 742 Rifle, 494 Artillery Regiments.
—Raised at Orsha, Western Special Military District, Nov. 1939.
—Chervovtsy w/12 Army, June 1941.
—Southwest Front w/18 Army, June 1941.
—Destroyed in Vyazma pocket, Oct. 1941.

—Second formation at Lenino (near Mogilev) w/33 Army, Oct. 1943.
—Belorussian Op., w/39 Army, June 1944.
—"Vitebsk, Novomoskovsk, u/i honorific."

165 Rifle Division
Units: 562, 641, 751 Rifle, 608 Artillery Regiments.
—Raised at Ordzhonikidze, North Caucasus Military District, before June 1941.
—North Caucasus Military District, June 1941.
—Destroyed, Dec. 1941.
—Second formation raised at Kurgan, Orel Military District, Dec. 1941.
—Gdynia area w/70 Army, Mar. 1945.
—"Torun."

166 Rifle Division
Units: 423, 517, 735 Rifle, 359 Artillery Regiments.
—Raised at Tomsk, Siberian Military District, before June 1941.
—In the east, June 1941.
—RVGK, July 1941.
—Smolensk, July 1941.
—Destroyed at Vyazma, Oct. 1941.
—Second formation raised at Cherbarkul, Ural Military District, Jan. 1942.
—Northwest Front w/53 Army, Apr. 1942.
—Kursk w/26 Guards Rifle Corps, 27 Army, July 1943.
—Akhtyrka (Belgorod Kharkov Op.) w/27 Army, Aug. 1943.
—Order of Red Banner.

167 Rifle Division
Units: 465, 520, 615 Rifle, 576 Artillery Regiments.
—Raised Tula, Moscow Military District, before June 1941.
—RVGK w/63 Rifle Corps, 22 Army, July 1941.
—Destroyed at Rogachev, Aug. 1941.
—Second formation raised at Ssucho Lug, Ural Military District, Feb. 1942.
—RVGK w/3 Reserve (60 Army), July 1942.
—Bryansk Front w/38 Army, Aug. 1942.
—Kursk w/38 Army, July 1943.
—Romny w/38 Army, Sep. 1943.
—Sumy, w/51 Rifle Corps, 13 Army, Sep. 1943.
—Lutezh bridgehead, Kiev w/38 Army, Nov. 1943.
—Korsun Shevchenkovskiy Op. w/47 Rifle Corps, 40 Army, Jan. 1944.
—Iasi Kishinev Op., Aug. 1944.

—Seized Russkiy Pass, Carpathian Uzgorhod Op. w/107 Rifle Corps, 1 Guards Army, Oct. 1944
—Hungary, Dec. 1944.
—"Sumy, Kiev, Carpathian, Hungary, Moscow," Twice Order of Red Banner.

168 Rifle Division
Units: 260, 402, 462 Rifle, 414 Artillery Regiments.
—Raised Sortovala, Archangelsk Military District, before Dec. 1939.
—Finland w/8 Army, Dec. 1939.
—Petrozavodsk axis w/7 Independent Army, June 1941.
—Sortovala, Karelia w/23 Army, July 1941.
—Leningrad w/8 Army, Sep. 1941.
—Stalingrad axis, Aug. 1942.
—Stalingrad w/62 Army; had 4,000 naval riflemen in its composition, Sep. 1942.

169 Rifle Division
Units: 434, 556, 680 Rifle, 307 Artillery Regiments.
—Raised Vinnitsa, Kiev Special Military District, by 1940.
—Kiev Special Military District, June 1941.
—Uman pocket w/6 Army, Aug. 1941.
—Bryansk Front w/4 Reserve (38 Army), July 1942.
—To Stalingrad axis, Aug. 1942.
—Stalingrad axis Sep. 1942.
—Stalingrad w/57 Army; breakthrough division, Nov. 1942.
—Orel w/16 Guards Rifle Corps, 11 Guards Army, July 1943.
—East Prussian Op., Jan. 1945.
—RVGK (FHO), Apr. 1945.
—"Tannenberg,"

170 Rifle Division
Units: 391, 422, 717 Rifle, 294 Artillery Regiments.
—Raised Sterlitamak, Ural Military District, before Feb. 1942.
—Disbanded, Feb. 1942.
—Second formation raised at Molotov, Ural Military District, Feb. 1942.
—Demyansk w/27 Army, Feb. 1943.
—Staraya Russa w/34 Army, Mar. 1943.
—Kursk area w/48 Army, May 1943.
—Kursk, July 1943.
—Rechitsa, Nov. 1943.
—East Prussia w/48 Army, Mar. 1945.
—"Rechitsa, Tannenburg, Insterburg (?)."

171 Rifle Division
Units: 380, 525, 713 Rifle, 357 Artillery Regiments.
—Raised Kamensk, North Caucasus Military District, Sep. 1939.
—RVGK w/19 Army, July 1941.
—Kiev Pocket w/37 Army, Aug. 1941.
—Destroyed at Kiev, Sep. 1941.
—Berlin w/79 Rifle Corps, 3 Shock Army at Reichstag, Apr. 1945.
—Stendal, Germany as 16 Motorized Rifle Division w/79 Rifle Corps, 3 Mechanized Army, Oct. 1946 (Feb. 1947 OB).

172 Rifle Division
Units: 388, 514, 747 Rifle, 134 Artillery Regiments.
—Raised Simferopol, Odessa Military District, before June 1941.
—RVGK w/61 Rifle Corps, 21 Army, June 1941.
—Destroyed at Mogilev, July 1941.
—Second formation raised from 3 Crimean Rifle Division, summer 1941.
—Sevastopol; had two regiments of naval infantry, Nov. 1941.
—Destroyed at Sevastopol with the Independent Coastal Army, July 1942.
—Third formation raised near Moscow, Moscow Military District, Oct. 1942.
—RVGK, Dec. 1942.
—To Stalingrad axis. Dec. 1942.
—Kantemirovka w/6 Army, Dec. 1942.
—Pavlograd, Feb. 1943.
—Southwest front w/12 Army, Apr. 1943.
—Kursk w/1 Guards Army, July 1943.
—Vistula Oder Op., Jan. 1945.
—"Pavlograd, Kielce, Oder."

173 Mountain Rifle Division
Units: First formation: 378, 490, 567 Rifle, 352 Artillery Regiments;
Second and third formation: 1311, 1313, 1315 Rifle, 979 Artillery Regiments.
—Raised Gjassin, Kiev Special Military District, 1940.
—Przemysl area w/8 Rifle Corps, 26 Army as a covering division, June 1941.
—Destroyed at Uman; commander killed, Aug. 1941.
—Second formation raised at Moscow from 21 People's Militia Rifle Division, Sep. 1941.
—Klin Solnechnogorsk as Western Front Reserve, Nov. 1941.
—Tula, Dec. 1941.
—Moscow axis w/26 Army, Dec. 1941.
—Southern Front w/24 Army, Aug. 1942.

—To Stalingrad area, Aug. 1942.
—Stalingrad offensive w/24 Army, Nov. 1942.
—Reformed as 77 Guards Rifle Division, 1 Mar. 1943.
—Third formation raised Staritsa, Moscow Military District from 150 Rifle Brigade, May 1943.
—Chernigov, Sep. 1943.
—Lenino (near Mogilev) w/65 Rifle Corps, 33 Army, Oct. 1943.
—Orsha, Dec. 1943.
—Belorussian Op., June 1944.
—Minsk/Lida, July 1944.
—"Chernigov."

174 Rifle Division
Units: 494, 508, 628 Rifle, 305 (730) Artillery Regiments.
—Raised Kurgan, Ural Military District, Aug. 1940.
—RVGK at Polotsk w/62 Rifle Corps, 22 Army, June 1941.
—Reformed as 20 Guards Rifle Division, 17 Mar. 1942.
—Second formation raised at Starobelsk, Kharkov Military District from 130 Motorized Rifle Brigade, Apr. 1942.
—Storozhevoye Bridgehead, Aug. 1942.
—Reformed as 46 Guards Rifle Division, Oct. 1942.
—Third formation raised from 28 Rifle Brigade at Kaluga, Moscow Military District, Apr. 1943.
—Kursk w/21 Army, July 1943.
—Belorussian Op. w/113 Rifle Corps, 31 Army, June 1944.
—Grodno, July 1944.
—East Prussian Op., Mar. 1945.
—RVGK (FHO), Apr. 1945.
—"Borisov, Masurian," Order of Red Banner.

175 Rifle Division
Units: First and second formations: 560, 632, 728 Rifle, 630 Artillery; Third formation: 277, 278, 282 Rifle, 175 Artillery Regiments.
—Raised Prokladny, North Caucasus Military District, before June 1941.
—North Caucasus Military District, June 1941.
—Kiev pocket w/37 Army, Aug. 1941.
—Destroyed at Kiev, Sep. 1941.
—Second formation raised at Tyumen, Siberian Military District, Mar. 1942.
—Stalingrad axis, June 1942.
—Disbanded, Sep. 1942.
—Third formation raised at Sverdlovsk, Ural Military District from the Ural NKVD Division, after Oct. 1942.
—RVGK w/70 Army, Feb. 1943.

—Demyansk w/70 Army, Feb. 1943.
—Belorussia w/125 Rifle Corps, 47 Army, Mar. 1944.
—Germany, Wernigerode, May 1946 (Aug. 1946 OB).
—"Ural."

176 Rifle Division
Units: First formation: 109, 404, 591 Rifle, 300 Artillery Regiments; Second formation: 52, 55, 63 Rifle, 728 Artillery Regiments.
—Raised Krivoi Rog, Kiev Special Military District, Apr. 1941.
—Odessa Military District w/9 Independent Army, June 1941.
—Ordzhonikidze w/9 Independent Army, Aug. 1942.
—Caucasus, Sep. 1942.
—Novorossiysk, Jan. 1943.
—Nikolayevsk w/18 Army, Feb. 1943.
—Malaya Zemlya, Mar. 1943.
—Novorossiysk, Sep. 1943.
—Reformed as 129 Guards Rifle Division, Oct. 1943.
—Second formation raised at Maselskaya, Leningrad Military District from 65, 80 Naval Rifle Brigades, Mar. 1944.
—Order of Red Banner.

177 Rifle Division
Units: 483, 486, 502 Rifle, 706 Artillery Regiments.
—Raised in Leningrad, Leningrad Military District, before June 1941.
—Luga Line w/23 Army, June 1941.
—Probably on Finnish Front, 1942–44.
—Finland, Aug. 1944.
—Danzig area w/19 Army, Mar. 1945.
—RVGK, Apr. 1945 (FHO).
—Leningrad Military District, Jan. 1946 (EUCOM).
—"Lyubansk."

178 Rifle Division
Units: 386, 693, 709 Rifle, 332 Artillery Regiments.
—Raised Omsk, Siberian Military District, before June 1941.
—RVGK w/19 Army, July 1941.
—Yelnaya area w/24 Army, Sep. 1941.
—Kalinin Front w/39 Army, Aug. 1942.
—RVGK, Apr. 1945 (FHO).
—"Kulagino."

179 Rifle Division
Units: 215, 234, 259 Rifle, 619 Artillery Regiments.
—Raised Vilnius, Western Special Military District, 1940.

—Baltic Special Military District w/16 Rifle Corps, 11 Army, June 1941.
—Toropets area w/22 Army, Sep. 1941.
—Kalinin Front w/41 Army, Aug. 1942.
—Gomel, Nov. 1943.
—Vitebsk Op. w/1 Rifle Corps, 43 Army, June 1944.
—Baltic area, Sep. 1944.
—Memel, Jan. 1945.
—Vilna, Baltic Military District w/11 Guards Army, Nov. 1946 (Feb. 1947 OB).
—"Vitebsk, Memel, Gomel," Order of Red Banner.

180 Rifle Division
Units: 21, 42, 86 Rifle, 627 Artillery Regiments.
—Raised Weissenstein, Ostland before June 1941.
—Baltic Special Military District w/22 Rifle Corps, 27 Army, June 1941.
—Zolsty, July 1941.
—Novgorod Army Group, Leningrad, Nov. 1941.
—Reformed as 28 Guards Rifle Division, May 1942.
—Second formation raised at Tscherepowez, Archangelsk Military District, after May 1942.
—Ostrogosh Rossosh Op., Jan. 1943.
—Kharkov w/69 Army, Feb. 1943.
—Sumy, w/51 Rifle Corps, 38 Army, Sep. 1943.
—Kiev, Nov. 1943.
—Southwest Ukraine w/47 Rifle Corps, 27 Army, Jan. 1944.
—Korsun Shevchenkovskiy Op. w/27 Army Jan. 1944.
—Targul Frumos w/27 Army, May 1944.
—RVGK, Aug. 1944.
—Iasi Kishinev Op., a breakthrough division, Aug. 1944
—Budapest w/46 Army, Dec. 1944.
—Budapest, Feb. 1945.
—Probably an independent division.
—"Kiev, Transylvania," Order of Red Banner.

181 Rifle Division
Units: First and second formation: 186, 195, 243 Rifle, 693 Artillery Regiments; Third formation: 243, 271, 288 Rifle, 375 Artillery Regiments.
—Raised Gulbene, Lettland, 1940.
—Baltic Special Military District w/24 fle Corps, 27 Army, June 1941.
—Destroyed at Staraya Russa, Sep. 1941.
—Second formation raised at Stalingrad, Volga Military District, May 1942.

—RVGK w/7 Reserve Army, June 1942.
—Stalingrad, w/62 Army, July 1942.
—Destroyed at Kalach, Aug. 1942.
—Third formation raised at Chelyabinsk, Ural Military District from 10 NKVD Division, Feb. 1943.
—RVGK w/70 Army, Feb. 1943.
—Demyansk w/70 Army, Feb. 1943.
—Dnieper River w/13 Army, Sep. 1943.
—Korosten, Bekha Railroad Station, Dec. 1943.
—Rovno Lustk w/76 Rifle Corps, 13 Army, Jan. 1944.
—Baltic Military District, Oct. 1945 (Feb. 1947 OB).
—"Stalingrad, Latvian," Orders of Lenin, Red Banner.

182 Rifle Division
Units: 140, 171, 232 Rifle, 625 Artillery Regiments.
—Raised Dorpat, Lettland (Leningrad Military District), before June 1941.
—Novgorod sector w/22 Rifle Corps, 27 Army, June–July 1941.
—Tartu, Leningrad Military District w/15 Guards Rifle Corps, 10 Guards Army, Oct. 1945 (Feb. 1947 OB).

183 Rifle Division
Units: 227, 285, 295 Rifle, 623 Artillery Regiments.
—Raised Wenden, Lettland (Baltic Military District) before June 1941.
—Baltic Special Military District w/24 Rifle Corps, 27 Army, June 1941.
—Sol'tsa w/11 Army, July 1941.
—Kalinin as an independent division, Oct. 1941.
—Rzhev w/39 Army, Dec. 1941.
—Kursk w/69 Army, July 1943.
—Kharkov w/69 Army, Aug. 1943.
—Southwest Ukraine w/74 Rifle Corps, 38 Army, Jan. 1944.
—Lvov, July 1944.
—Carpathian Duklinskiy Op., w/101 Rifle Corps, 38 Army, Sep. 1944.
—Baltic Military District, Nov. 1946 (EUCOM Study).
—Probably an independent division.
—"Kharkov, Lvov," Order of Red Banner.

184 Rifle Division
Units: 262, 294, 297 Rifle, 616 Artillery Regiments.
—Baltic Special Military District w/29 Rifle Corps, 11 Army, June 1941.
—Destroyed at Sevastopol, Nov. 1941.
—Second formation formed at Stalingrad, Volga Military District before June 1942.
—RVGK w/7 Reserve Army, June 1942.

—Stalingrad w/62 Army; encircled at Buzinovka, July 1942.
—Disbanded, Aug. 1942.
—Third formation raised at Penza, Volga Military District, Oct. 1942.
—Ostrogosh Rossosh Op. w/3 Tank Army, Jan. 1943.
—Dukhovschina, Sep. 1943.
—First unit into East Prussia w/5 Army, Aug. 1944.
—East Prussia, Mar. 1945.
—"Dukhovschina, Gumbinnen," Order of Red Banner.

185 Rifle Division
Units: 257, 280, 1319 Rifle, 695 Artillery Regiments.
—Raised at Belgorod, Kharkov Military District, Sep. 1939.
—Moscow Military District, June 1941.
—Baltic Special Military District as a Motorized Division, June 1941.
—Independent division of Kalinin Front, Oct. 1941.
—Moscow axis w/30 Army, Nov. 1941.
—Ryabinki, Dec. 1941.
—Belorussia w/96 Rifle Corps, 70 Army, Mar. 1944.
—Germany, (Aug. 1946 OB).
—"Pankratovo."

186 Rifle Division
Units: 238, 290, 298 Rifle, 327 Artillery Regiments.
—Raised at Ufa, Ural Military District, 1928.
—From Ural Military District to Latvia, June 1941.
—RVGK w/62 Rifle Corps, 22 Army, June 1941.
—One of four double-numbered divisions.
—Formerly 1st Polar Rifle Division, until 28 Sep. 1941.
—Kandalaksha axis w/14 Army, July 1941.
—Leningrad w/32 Army, Mar. 1942.
—Karelian Front w/26 Army, May 1942.
—Gomel w/3 Army, Nov. 1943.
—Rogachev, Feb. 1944.
—Belorussian Op., June 1944.
—Lublin Brest Op., July 1944.
—Vistula Oder Op., Jan. 1945.
—Northern Poland w/65 Army, Mar. 1945.
—Frankenstein, Poland, Mar. 1946 (Aug. 1946 OB).
—"Rogachev, Brest Litovsk, Polar," Order of Red Banner.

187 Rifle Division
Units: 236, 292, 338 Rifle, 325 Artillery Regiments.
—Raised Chernigov, Kiev Special Military Division, by June 1941.

—RVGK w/45 Rifle Corps, 21 Army, June 1941.
—Central Front w/21 Army, Sep. 1941.
—Destroyed at Kiev, Sep. 1941.
—Second formation raised in Far East Military District, after Sep. 1941.
—Stalingrad w/62 Army, had 180 men, Sep. 1942.
—A 187 Rifle Division was identified in 1 Independent Red Banner Army, "Front Command Khabarovsk," Apr. 1943.
—Dnieper River w/37 Army, Sep. 1943.
—A 187 Rifle Regiment was carried in the Far East, Aug. 1944.

188 Rifle Division
Units: 523, 580, 595 Rifle, 234 Artillery Regiments.
—Raised in Kazan, Volga Military District, before June 1941.
—Baltic Special Military District w/16 Rifle Corps, 11 Army as a covering division, June 1941.
—Central Russia w/27 Army, May 1942.
—Southwest Ukraine w/82 Rifle Corps, 37 Army, Jan. 1944.
—Bulgaria w/72 Rifle Corps, 37 Army, Mar. 1946 (Aug. 1946 OB).

189 Rifle Division
Units: 864, 880, 891 Rifle, 431 Artillery Regiments.
—Raised Leningrad, Leningrad Military District, before June 1941.
—Kiev Special Military District Reserve, June 1941.
—Leningrad Front (Pulkovo) w/42 Army, Sep. 1941.
—Leningrad w/42 Army, Sep. 1942.
—Tartu, Sep. 1944.
—RVGK (FHO), Apr. 1945.
—"Kingisepp, Tartu, u/i honorific."

190 Rifle Division
Units: 621, 890 Rifle, 507 Artillery Regiments.
—Raised Cherkassy, Kiev Special Military District, before June 1941.
—Kiev Special Military District Reserve, June 1941.
—Destroyed at Rzhev, Oct. 1941.
—North Korea w/25 Army, Apr. 1946 (Feb. 1947 OB).

191 Rifle Division
Units: 546, 552, 559 Rifle, 504 Artillery Regiments.
—Raised in Leningrad, Leningrad Military District, before June 1941.
—In reserve, Finnish Gulf coast, June 1941.
—Luga Line, Lake Ilmen area, June 1941.
—Kingisepp, July 1941.
—Oranienbaum, Leningrad Front, Sep. 1941.

—Airlifted into Sitomliya, Oct. 1941.
—Leningrad, Nov. 1941.
—Tikhvin, Nov. 1941.
—May have been on the Leningrad Front, 1942–43.
—Novgorod Luga Op. w/14 Rifle Corps, 59 Army, Jan. 1944.
—Narva, Feb. 1944.
—Narva w/2 Shock Army, July 1944.
—Tartu, Sep. 1944.
—Northern Poland, w/65 Army, Mar. 1945.
—"Novgorod, Narva, Tartu, u/i honorific," Order of Red Banner.

192 Mountain Rifle Division
Units: First and second formation: 427, 490, 753 Rifle, 293 Artillery Regiments.
—Raised Rostov, North Caucasus Military District, before Nov. 1940.
—Kiev Special Military District Reserve w/12 Army, June 1941.
—Destroyed at Konotop, Sep. 1941.
—Second formation in the RVGK w/7 Reserve Army, June 1942.
—Encircled at Buzinovka w/62 Army, July 1942.
—Dissolved, Aug. 1942.
—Second formation raised at Ssyteschevka, Moscow Military District, May 1943.
—Belorussia Op. w/71 Rifle Corps, 31 Army, June 1944.

193 Rifle Division
Units: 685, 883, 895 Rifle, 394 Artillery Regiments.
—Raised Korosten, Kiev Special Military District, May 1941.
—Kiev Special Military District Reserve, June 1941.
—Berdichev, July 1941.
—Destroyed at Kiev, Sep. 1941.
—Second formation raised at Sorotschinik, Volga Military District, May 1942.
—To Stalingrad; w/62 Army; had some naval riflemen in its composition, Sep. 1942.
—Stalingrad w/62 Army, Nov. 1942.
—Dnieper, Sep. 1943.
—Belorussia Op., June 1944.
—Vistula Oder Op., Jan. 1945.
—East Pomeranian Op. w/65 Army, Mar. 1945.
—"Dnieper, Baranovichi, Bobruysk," Orders of Lenin, Red Banner, Suvorov, Kutuzov.

194 Mountain Rifle Division
Units: 470, 616, 954 Rifle, 299 Artillery Regiments.

—Raised Tashkent, Central Asian Military District, before Aug. 1941.
—Moscow Military District w/49 Army, Aug. 1941.
—Yelnaya w/49 Army, Sep. 1941.
—RVGK w/24 Army, Sep. 1941.
—From RVGK to Bryansk, Oct. 1941.
—Moscow area w/49 Army, Dec. 1941.
—Stalingrad w/62 Army, Nov 1942–Jan 1943.
—Kursk w/77 Rifle Corps, 65 Army, July 1943.
—Belorussia Op., June 1944.
—East Prussian Op., Jan. 1945.
—"Rechitsa, Slonim, Luminets, Tannenburg," Order of Red Banner.

195 Rifle Division
Units: 564, 573, 604 Rifle, 475 Artillery Regiments.
—Raised Ovruch, Kiev Special Military District, before June 1941.
—In the Kiev Special Military District Reserve, June 1941.
—Berdichev area, July 1941.
—Destroyed at Kiev, Sep. 1941.
—Second formation raised in Ural Military District, Mar. 1942.
—RVGK w/3 Reserve (later 60 Army), July 1942.
—To Stalingrad, Nov. 1942.
—Stalingrad offensive, Nov. 1942.
—Novomoskovsk, Feb. 1943.
—Southwest Ukraine w/34 Rifle Corps, 46 Army, Jan. 1944.
—"Novomoskovsk," Order of Red Banner.

196 Rifle Division
Units: 863, 884, 893 Rifle, 725 Artillery Regiments.
—Raised at Dnepropetrovsk, Odessa Military District (FHO), July 1941.
—SME says in North Caucasus Military District, June 1941.
—RVGK to Zhitomir, July 1941.
—Destroyed in Kiev Pocket, Sep. 1941.
—Second formation raised at Kisner, Ural Military District, Jan. 1942.
—RVGK w/7 Reserve Army, June 1942.
—Stalingrad w/62 Army, July 1942.
—Stalingrad w/62 Army, had 800 men, Sep. 1942.
—Oranienbaum w/2 Shock Army, Jan. 1944.
—Krasnogvardeysk, Jan. 1944.
—East Prussia, Jan. 1945.
—RVGK (FHO), Apr. 1945.
—"Gatchina, Krasnogvardeysk," Order of Red Banner.

197 Rifle Division
Units: 828, 862, 889 Rifle, 261 Artillery Regiments.

—Raised Kiev, Kiev Special Military District, Apr. 1941
—In the Kiev Special Military District Reserve, June 1941.
—Destroyed at Uman, Aug. 1941.
—Second formation from Krasnodar, North Caucasus Military District w/7 Reserve Army, Mar. 1942.
—RVGK w/5 Reserve Army, July 1942.
—Stalingrad w/63 Army, July 1942.
—Stalingrad Offensive w/1 Guards Army, Nov. 1942.
—Reformed as 59 Guards Rifle Division, Jan. 1943.
—Third formation raised at Kubyshev, Volga Military District, Feb. 1943.
—Bryansk, Aug. 1943.
—In Weichsel Bridgehead w/3 Guards Army, Aug. 1944.
—Vistula Oder Op., Jan. 1945.
—"Bryansk, Oder," Order of Red Banner.

198 Rifle Division
Units: 506, 1027, 1029 Rifle, 704 Artillery Regiments.
—Raised in Leningrad, Leningrad Military District as a Motorized Division, June 1941.
—Khitola, June 1941.
—To 23 Army in Karelia, July 1941.
—Trapped against Lake Ladoga, Aug. 1941.
—Dissolved, Dec. 1941.
—Second formation raised at Rybinsk, Moscow Military District as a rifle division, after Dec. 1941.

199 Rifle Division
Units: 492, 584, 617 Rifle, 500 Artillery Regiments.
—Raised at Novossibirsk, Siberian Military District, May 1941.
—In the Kiev Special Military District Reserve, June 1941.
—Lake Ilmen w/38 Army, Aug. 1941.
—Kharkov sector w/38 Army, Oct. 1941.
—Severskiy Donets, Jan. 1942.
—Dissolved, Sep. 1942.
—Second formation formed at Kalinin, Moscow Military District from 126, 128 Rifle Brigades, Feb. 1943.
—Reported by Germans at Platono-Alexandrovskaya w/1 Independent Red Banner Army, "Front Command Khabarovsk," Apr. 1943.
—Smolensk, Sep. 1943.
—Novgorod Luga Op. w/54 Army, Jan. 1944.
—East Pomeranian Op., Mar. 1945.
—"Smolensk."

200 Rifle Division
Units: 642, 648, 661 Rifle, 650 Artillery Regiments.
—Raised Belokorovichi, Kiev Special Military District, before June 1941.
—Kovel, in the Kiev Special Military District reserve, June 1941.
—Destroyed at Kiev, Sep. 1941.
—Second formation raised at Busuluk, Volga Military District, Feb. 1942.
—Belorussian Op., June 1944.
—Gdynia area w/70 Army, Mar. 1945.
—Berlin Op. w/49 Army, Apr. 1945.
—"Borisov."

201 Rifle Division
Units: 92, 122, 191 Rifle, 220 Artillery Regiments.
—Raised Gorki, Moscow Military District, Aug. 1941.
—Western Front, Dec. 1941.
—Borovsk, Jan. 1942.
—Mozhaisk w/33 Army, Jan. 1942.
—Reformed as 43 Guards Rifle Division, Oct. 1942.
—Second formation from 27 Rifle Brigade, Schlusselburg, Leningrad Military District, Nov. 1943.
—Received 191 Rifle Regiment from 22 Rifle Division.
—"Gatschina, Latvian," Order of Red Banner.

202 Rifle Division
Units: 645, 682, 1317 Rifle, 652 Artillery Regiments.
—Raised Leningrad, Leningrad Military District as a Motorized Rifle Division in 1940 or 1941.
—Sol'tsa w/12 Mechanized Corps, 8 Army, June 1941.
—RVGK w/70 Army as a rifle division, Oct. 1943.
—Kiev Op. w/60 Army, Nov. 1943.
—Korsun Shevchenkovskiy Op., Jan. 1944.
—Targul Frumos w/33 Rifle Corps, 27 Army, May 1944.
—Probably in the Iasi Kishinev Op., Aug. 1944.
—"Korsun."

203 Rifle Division
Units: 592, 610, 619 Rifle, 1037 Artillery Regiments.
—Raised Voroshilovsk, North Caucasus Military District, Feb. 1941.
—North Caucasus Military District, June 1941.
—Second formation formed in North Caucasus Military District, Apr. 1942.
—RVGK w/5 Reserve Army, May 1942.
—Stalingrad axis, July 1942.

—Stalingrad offensive w/1 Guards Army, Nov. 1942.
—Southwest front w/12 Army, Aug. 1943.
—Zaporozhye, Sep. 1943.
—Dnieper River w/12 Army, Sep. 1943.
—Southwest Ukraine w/66 Rifle Corps, 6 Army, Jan. 1944.
—Iasi Kishinev Op., Aug. 1944.
—"Zaporozhye, Bucharest," Order of Red Banner.

204 Rifle Division
Units: 700, 706, 730 Rifle, 657 Artillery Regiments.
—Raised as 204 Motorized Division at Volkhovsk, Western Special Military District, Apr. 1941.
—Western Special Military Disrict w/11 Mechanized Corps, 3 Army, June 1941.
—Volkhovsk, July 1941.
—Destroyed at Yelnya, Aug. 1941.
—Second formation raised at Blagoveshensk/Kuibyshevka, Far East Military District, Nov. 1941.
—RVGK in Siberia Military District as an independent division, June 1942.
—To Stalingrad, July 1942.
—Stalingrad front w/64 Army, Aug. 1942.
—Reformed as 78 Guards Rifle Division, Mar. 1943.
—Third formation raised at Nelidovo, Moscow Military District from 37 Rifle Brigade, July 1943.
—Kursk w/38 Army, July 1943.
—Belorussian Op. w/92 Rifle Corps, 43 Army, June 1944.
—Dobele area, Sep. 1944.
—Probably an independent division.
—"Vitebsk."

205 Rifle Division
Units: 577, 721, 731 Rifle, 672 Artillery Regiments.
—Raised Khabarovsk, Far East Military District, before June 1941.
—Bereza Western Special Military District w/14 Mechanized Corps, 4 Army as a motorized division, June 1941.
—Second unit w/same number raised at Murmansk, Archangelsk Military District, Oct. 1941.
—RVGK in Siberia Military District as an independent division, June 1942.
—To Stalingrad area, July 1942.
—Kletskaya w/4 Tank Army, July 1942.
—Destroyed at Stalingrad, Oct. 1942.

—Second formation raised from 1 Polar Rifle Division and 186 Rifle Division, after Oct. 1942.
—Danzig area w/19 Army, Mar. 1945.
—RVGK (FHO), Apr. 1945.

206 Rifle Division
Units: 722, 737, 748 Rifle, 661 Artillery Regiments.
—Raised Pavlograd, Odessa Military District, before June 1941.
—Odessa Military District w/9 Independent Army, June 1941.
—Kiev, July 1941.
—Destroyed at Kiev w/37 Army, Sep. 1941.
—Second formation raised at Buguruslan, Volga Military District, Jan. 1942.
—Stalingrad axis, June 1942.
—Korsun Shevchenkovskiy Op., Jan. 1944.
—Uman Botosani Op.; crossed Pruth, Mar. 1944.
—Targul Frumos w/33 Rifle Corps, 27 Army, May 1944.
—Breakthrough division for Iasi Kishinev Op., Aug. 1944.
—"Korsun," Order of Red Banner.

207 Rifle Division
Units: 594, 597, 598 Rifle, 780 Artillery Regiments.
—Raised Ivanovo, Moscow Military District, Aug. 1942.
—To Stalingrad axis w/24 Army, Aug. 1942.
—Destroyed at Stalingrad, Oct. 1942.
—Second formation raised at Yelnaya, Western Special Military District, June 1943.
—Baltic Coast, Aug. 1944.
—Berlin, at Reichstag w/3 Shock Army, Apr. 1945.
—Stendahl, Germany w/79 Rifle Corps, 3 Mechanized Army, 1947 (Feb. 1947 OB).
—Order of Red Banner.

208 Rifle Division
Units: 435, 578, 760 Rifle, 662 Artillery Regiments.
—Raised as 208 Mechanized Division at Gaynovka, Western Special Military Division, Apr. 1941.
—At the front, June–Sep. 1941.
—Disbanded, Sep. 1941.
—Fought behind German lines as "Partisan Detachment 208," Oct. 1941.
—Second formation raised at Vladivostok/Slavyansk, Far East Military District, Oct. 1941.

—RVGK in Siberia Military District as an independent division, June 1942.
—To Stalingrad, heavily bombed by Luftwaffe; division dissolved, July 1942.
—Third formation raised at Dorogobush, Western Military District from 35 and 49 Rifle Brigades, June 1943.
—Riga area, Sep. 1944.
—The 435 Rifle Regiment is associated w/153 Rifle Division.

209 Rifle Division
Units: 67 Rifle Regiment.
—Raised Ivye, Western Military District as 209 Motorized Division, Apr. 1941.
—In Moscow Military District, June 1941.
—Destroyed at Minsk, July 1941.
—Officially disbanded, Sep. 1941.
—Second formation rifle division formed in Far East Military District; w/17 Army, Aug 1944–Aug 1945.

210 Motorized Division
—Western Special Military District, in reserve w/20 Mechanized Corps, June 1941.
—Rzhev w/30 Army, Aug. 1941.
—Bayan Tumen w/17 Army, "Front Command Chita," Apr. 1943.
—Far East as 210 Motorized Division, Aug. 1944.

211 Rifle Division
Units: 887, 894, 896 Rifle, 829 Artillery Regiments.
—Raised at Zagorsk, Moscow Military District, before June 1941.
—In Moscow Military District, June 1941.
—RVGK in Reserve Front w/43 Army, July 1941.
—Yelnaya w/43 Army, Sep. 1941.
—Destroyed at Vyazma, Oct. 1941.
—Second formation raised at Novossil, Orel Military District, Jan. 1942.
—Bryansk Front w/48 Army, Apr. 1942.
—Voronezh, Jan. 1943.
—Reported by Germans at Sretensk w/36 Army, "Front Command Chita," Apr. 1943.
—Bolkhov (Kursk), w/11 Guards Army, July 1943.
—Chernigov, Sep. 1943.
—Dnieper River w/13 Army, Sep. 1943.
—Southwest Ukraine w/17 Guards Rifle Corps, 38 Army, Jan. 1944.
—Carpathian Duklinskiy Op. w/101 Rifle Corps, 38 Army, Sep. 1944.
—"Chernigov."

212 Rifle Division
Units: 587, 669, 692 Rifle, 665 Artillery Regiments.
—Raised at Cherkassy, Kiev Special Military District, June 1941.
—Brody, in Kiev Special Military District Reserve w/15 Mechanized Corps as a Motorized Division, June 1941.
—Moscow axis w/10 Army, Dec. 1941.
—Kharkov offensive w/6 Army, June 1942.
—To Stalingrad, Oct. 1942.
—Disbanded, Nov. 1942.
—Second formation raised at Ssuschinitschi, Western Military District from 4, 125 Rifle Brigades. June 1943.
—Kursk w/50 Army, July 1943.
—"Krichev," Orders of Red Banner, Suvorov.

213 Rifle Division
Units: 585, 702, 793 Rifle, 671 Artillery Regiments.
—Raised at Vinnitsa, Kiev Special Military District as a Motorized Division, Mar. 1941.
—In the Kiev Special Military District Reserve, June 1941.
—Shepetovka, July 1941.
—Destroyed at Uman, Aug. 1941.
—Second formation raised at Katta Kurgan, Central Asia Military District, Jan. 1942.
—Kursk w/7 Guards Army, July 1943.
—Dnieper River w/49 Rifle Corps, 7 Guards Army, Sep. 1943.
—Kirovograd w/75 Rifle Corps, 53 Army, Jan. 1944.
—Zvenigorod w/53 Army, Feb. 1944.
—Targul Frumos, May 1944.
—Vistula Oder Op., Jan. 1945.
—Constanta, Rumania, Sep. 1946 (Feb. 1947 OB).
—"Oder."

214 Rifle Division
Units: 776, 780, 788 Rifle, 683 Artillery Regiments.
—Raised at Voroshilovgrad, Kharkov Military District, Apr. 1941.
—RVGK w/20 Army, June 1941.
—Toropets area w/22 Army, Sep. 1941.
—Destroyed at Vyazma, Oct. 1941.
—Second formation raised at Ufa, Ural Military District, Jan. 1942.
—RVGK w/7 Reserve Army, June 1942.
—Stalingrad Front w/64 Army, July 1942.
—Stalingrad Offensive w/24 Army, Nov. 1942.
—Voronezh w/24 Army, Mar. 1943.
—Kremenchug, Sep. 1943.

—Vorskla River w/53 Army, Sep. 1943.
—Znamenka, Dec. 1943.
—Alexandrija, Dec. 1943.
—Kirovograd w/32 Guards Rifle Corps, 5 Guards Army, Jan. 1944.
—Zvenigorod w/53 Army, Feb. 1944.
—Pulawy bridgehead w/25 Rifle Corps, 69 Army, Jan. 1945.
—Probably an independent division.
—"Kremenchug, Alexandrija, Znamenka, u/i honorific," Order of Red Banner.

215 Rifle Division
Units: 618, 711, 771 Rifle, 781 Artillery Regiments.
—Raised at Rovno, Kiev Special Military District, Apr. 1941.
—Brody w/22 Mechanized Corps as a Motorized Division, June 1941.
—Destroyed Kiev, Sep. 1941.
—Second formation raised at Nelidovo, Moscow Military District, Apr. 1942.
—Terek River, North Caucasus, Aug. 1942.
—Baltic area w/36 Rifle Corps, 31 Army, June 1943.
—Smolensk, Sep. 1943.
—Vitebsk Op. w/39 Army, June 1944.
—Vilnius w/42 Rifle Corps, 5 Army, Aug. 1944.
—"Smolensk," Order of Red Banner.

216 Rifle Division
Units: 589, 647, 665 Rifle, 656 Artillery Regiments.
—Raised at Staro Konstantinov, Kiev Special Military District, May 1941.
—In the Kiev Special Military District Reserve as a Motorized Division, June 1941.
—Kharkov w/38 Army, Oct. 1941.
—Southern Front w/37 Army, Nov. 1941.
—Karelian Front w/26 Army, May 1942.
—Koisog Bataiysk area w/18 Army, Aug. 1942.
—Novorossiysk w/56 Army, Aug. 1942.
—Novorossiysk w/47 Army, Sep. 1942.
—Nikolayevsk, Feb. 1943.
—Krimskaya, Mar. 1943.
—Reported by Germans at Razdolnoye w/25 Army, "Front Command Khabarovsk," Apr. 1943.
—Southern Ukraine w/10 Rifle Corps, 51 Army, Jan. 1944.
—Crimea w/10 Rifle Corps, 51 Army, May 1944.
—Order of Red Banner.

217 Rifle Division
Units: 740, 755, 766 Rifle, 688 Artillery Regiments.
—Raised Voronezh, Orel Military District, June 1941.
—RVGK in Reserve Front w/43 Army, July 1941.
—Bryansk front w/50 Army, Aug. 1941.
—Yelnaya area w/43 Army, Sep. 1941.
—Destroyed Bryansk Pocket, Oct. 1941.
—Second formation raised at Pavlograd, Odessa Military District, Oct. 1941.
—Malyshevo Glebevo, w/50 Army, Nov. 1941.
—Kaluga w/50 Army, Dec. 1941.
—Bolkhov (Kursk) w/11 Guards Army, July 1943.
—Belorussian Op., June 1944.
—East Prussia, Mar. 1945.
—Germany 1946, (Feb. 1947 OB); believed inactivated by publication of the Feb. 1948 OB.
—"Unechka, Zhlobin, Bobruysk, Tannenberg," Order of Red Banner.

218 Rifle Division
Units: First formation: 182, 658, 667 Rifle, 663 Artillery Regiments;
    Second formation: 372, 658, 667 Rifle, 663 Artillery Regiments.
—Raised at Gusyatin, Kiev Special Military District, before June 1941.
—Odessa Military District w/18 Mechanized Corps, 9 Independent Army, as a motorized division, June 1941.
—Dissolved, July 1942.
—Second formation at Kiev as an independent division of the 1 Ukrainian Front, Nov. 1943.
—Zhitomir, Dec. 1943.
—Probably an independent division.
—"Romodan, Kiev, Zhitomir," Order of Red Banner.

219 Rifle Division
Units: 375, 710, 727 Rifle, 673 Artillery Regiments.
—Formed as 219 Motorized Division at Kharkov, Apr. 1941.
—RVGK w/25 Mechanized Corps, 21 Army, June 1941.
—Destroyed at Kiev; commander captured, Sep. 1941.
—Second formation raised at Kirssanov, Orel Military District, May 1942.
—Kharkov offensive w/6 Army, May 1942.
—Stalingrad axis, July 1942.

220 Rifle Division
Units: 376, 653, 673 Rifle, 660 Artillery Regiments.
—Raised at Vyazma, Western Special Military District, 1941.

—RVGK w/23 Mechanized Corps, 19 Army, June 1941.
—Vitebsk, July 1941.
—Had been motorized division, until July 1941.
—Moscow w/49 Army, Aug. 1941.
—Yelnaya area w/49 Army, Sep. 1941.
—Vyazma, Oct. 1941.
—Rzhev w/39 Army, Dec. 1941.
—Torzhok w/39 Army, Jan. 1942.
—Baltic area, June 1943.
—Belorussia Op. w/36 Rifle Corps, 31 Army, June 1944.
—Grodno, July 1944.
—Minsk Lida, July 1944.
—RVGK (FHO), Apr. 1945.
—"Orsha, Minsk, Grodno," Order of Red Banner.

221 Rifle Division
Units: First and second formations: 625, 671, 695 Rifle, 659 Artillery Regiments.
—Raised at Krasnoufinsk, Ural Military District, Mar. 1942.
—Stalingrad w/24 Army, Aug–Nov. 1942.
—Dissolved, Nov. 1942.
—Second formation raised from 79 Rifle Brigade, June 1943.
—Ukraine w/28 Army, Nov. 1943.
—Gvardeysk (East Prussia), Jan. 1945.
—Transcaucasus Military District w/45 Army, Mar. 1946 (Feb. 1947 OB).
—"Mariupol."

222 Rifle Division
Units: 757, 774, 787 Rifle, 666 Artillery Regiments.
—Raised at Starodub, Orel Military District, Apr. 1941.
—In Orel Military District, June 1941.
—RVGK in Reserve Front w/43 Army, Aug. 1941.
—Yelnaya area w/43 Army, Sep. 1941.
—Moscow axis w/33 Army, Dec. 1941.
—Mozhaisk w/33 Army, Jan. 1942.
—Smolensk, Sep. 1943.
—Lenino (near Mogilev) w/33 Army, Oct. 1943.
—Kalinin area, Nov. 1943.
—Belorussia w/33 Army, May 1944.
—Mogilev Op. w/69 Rifle Corps, 49 Army, June 1944.
—"Smolensk," Order of Red Banner.

223 Rifle Division
Units: 1037, 1039, 1041 Rifle, 818 Artillery Regiments.
—Raised at Kuba, North Caucasus Military District; Azerbaijani division, Sep. 1941.
—Terek River w/44 Army, Nov. 1942.
—North Caucasus w/44 Army, Jan. 1943.
—Southwest Ukraine w/49 Rifle Corps, 57 Army, Jan. 1944.

224 Rifle Division
Units: First and second formations: 143, 160, 185 Rifle, 111 Artillery Regiments.
—Raised at Suchum, Transcaucasus Military District, by Dec. 1941.
—Kerch Feodosiya Op., Dec. 1941.
—Destroyed near Kerch, May 1942.
—Second formation raised at Onenga, Archangelsk Military District, June 1942.
—"Gatchina," Order of Red Banner.

225 Rifle Division
Units: 299, 1347, 1349 Rifle, 1009 Artillery Regiments.
—Raised at Yerevan, Transcaucasus Military District, by Oct. 1941.
—Possibly on Leningrad Front, 1942–44.
—Novgorod Luga Op., Jan. 1944.
—Vistula Oder Op., Jan. 1945.
—Opole w/21 Army, Feb. 1945.
—"Novgorod, Kattowice, Oder, Dombrowa."

226 Rifle Division
Units: All formations: 985, 987, 989 Rifle, 875 Artillery Regiments.
—Raised at Orochevo, Moscow Military District (SME), June 1941.
—Raised Zaporozhye, Odessa Special Military District (FHO), July–Aug 1941.
—Uman pocket w/6 Army, Aug. 1941.
—Kharkov sector w/38 Army, Oct. 1941.
—To Southwest Front, Oct. 1941.
—Probably in Kharkov Offensive Op. w/38 Army, June 1942.
—To Stalingrad axis from 38 Army, July 1942.
—Dissolved, July 1942.
—Second formation raised at Bugurusslan, Volga Military District, Sep. 1942.
—Stalingrad offensive w/1 Guards Army, Sep. 1942.
—Reformed as 95 Guards Rifle Division, 4 May 1943.
—Third formation raised at Lgov, Orel Military District, July 1943.

—Glukhov, Aug. 1943.
—Kiev Op. w/60 Army, Nov. 1943.
—Probably Kiev Defensive Op., Dec. 1943.
—Southwest Ukraine w/23 Rifle Corps, 60 Army, Jan. 1944.
—Rovno Lutsk Op. w/23 Rifle Corps, 13 Army, Feb. 1944.
—Poland, Feb. 1945.
—Tunskirck, Germany, Apr. 1945.
—"Glukhov, Kiev, Debica," Orders of Lenin, Red Banner, Suvorov.

227 Rifle Division
Units: First and second formations: 777, 789, 794 Rifle, 711 Artillery Regiments.
—Raised at Sslavyansk, North Caucasus Military District, Apr. 1941.
—In North Caucasus Military District, June 1941.
—From RVGK to Zhitomir, July 1941.
—Zhitomir area w/26 Army, July 1941.
—Destroyed near Kharkov, May 1942.
—Second formation raised from 19 Rifle and 84 Naval Rifle Brigades (SME), July–Aug. 1942.
—Kursk w/47 Army, July 1943.
—Kurchnskaya, Sep. 1943.
—Taman area w/56 Army, Nov. 1943.
—Kerch w/16 Rifle Corps, Independent Coastal Army, Jan. 1944.
—Crimea w/Independent Coastal Army as mobile group, Apr. 1944.
—Sevastopol, May 1944.
—Probably an independent division.
—"Feodosiya, Temruk, Yalta."

228 Rifle Division
Units: First and second formations: 767, 795, 799 Rifle, 669 Artillery Regiments.
—Raised at Zhitomir, Kiev Special Military District, by June 1941.
—In the Kiev Special Military District Reserve, June 1941.
—Mlyrov region w/36 Rifle Corps, June 1941.
—Rovno, Aug. 1941.
—Destroyed near Kiev, Sep. 1941.
—Second formation raised at Kansk, Siberia Military District, Nov. 1941.
—Southern Front w/24 Army, May 1942.
—Stalingrad axis, July 1942.
—Southwest Ukraine w/57 Rifle Corps, 37 Army, Jan. 1944.
—RVGK (FHO), Apr. 1945.

229 Rifle Division
Units: First and second formations: 783, 804, 811 Rifle, 237 Artillery Regiments.
—Raised at Noginsk, Moscow Military District, May 1941.
—In Moscow Military District, July 1941.
—Solovev, Dnieper River w/16 Army, Aug. 1941.
—RVGK w/1 Reserve Army, June 1942.
—Stalingrad w/64 Army, July 1942.
—Destroyed near Kalatsch, Aug. 1942.
—Second formation raised at Volokolamsk, Moscow Military District, Dec. 1942.
—Opole w/21 Army, Feb. 1945.

230 Rifle Division
Units: First and second formation: 986, 988, 990 Rifle, 805 Artillery Regiments.
—Raised at Dnepropetrovsk, Odessa Military District, July 1941.
—Uman Pocket w/6 Army, Aug. 1941.
—North Caucasus, July 1942.
—Dissolved, Aug. 1942.
—Second formation raised from 229 Rifle Brigade, June 1943.
—Stalino, Sep. 1943.
—Southwest Ukraine w/9 Rifle Corps, 28 Army, Jan. 1944.
—Berlin w/5 Shock Army, Apr. 1945.
—"Stalino."

231 Rifle Division
Units: First and second formation: 607, 623, 639 Rifle Regiments.
—Raised at Kungur, Ural Military District, in 1941.
—RVGK w/66 Army, Aug. 1942.
—Stalingrad area w/66 Army, Aug. 1942.
—Dissolved, Nov. 1942.
—Second formation division in Far East w/1 Independent Red Banner Army, Aug. 1945.

232 Rifle Division
Units: First and second formation: 764, 794, 797 Rifle, 684 Artillery Regiments.
—Raised at Chernigov, Kiev Special Military District before June 1941.
—RVGK in Moscow Military District w/22 Army, June 1941.
—RVGK w/66 Rifle Corps, 21 Army, July 1941.
—Berezina River, July 1941.

—Destroyed at Kiev, Sep. 1941.
—Second formation raised at Biysk, Siberian Military District, Jan. 1942.
—RVGK w/3 Reserve later 60 Army, July 1942.
—Voronezh w/60 Army, Jan. 1943.
—Sumy w/51 Rifle Corps, 38 Army, Sep. 1943.
—Kiev, Nov. 1943.
—Southwest Ukraine w/51 Rifle Corps, 40 Army, Jan. 1944.
—Targul Frumos w/7 Guards Army, May 1944.
—Iasi Kishinev Op., Aug. 1944.
—Western Carpathian Mountains., Mar. 1945.
—"Sumy, Kiev, Transylvania," Orders of Red Banner, Suvorov, Bogdan Khmelnitskiy.

233 Rifle Division
Units: First and second formation: 703, 724, 734 Rifle, 684 Artillery Regiments.
—Raised at Zvenigorod, Moscow Military District, May 1941.
—In Moscow Military District, June 1941.
—Destroyed near Smolensk, Aug. 1941.
—Moscow axis w/26 Army, Dec. 1941.
—Second formation raised at Naro Fominsk, Moscow Military District, Aug. 1942.
—To Stalingrad area, Sep. 1942.
—Stalingrad offensive w/24 Army, Nov. 1942.
—Voronezh w/24 Army, Apr. 1943.
—Kremenchug, Sep. 1943.
—Vorskla River w/53 Army, Sep. 1943.
—Znamenka, Dec. 1943.
—Kirovograd w/75 Rifle Corps, 53 Army, Jan. 1944.
—Iasi Kishinev Op., Aug. 1944.
—RVGK, Aug. 1944 (FHO).
—Tekiya (?), Sep. 1944.
—Lake Balaton, Mar. 1945.
—Bulgaria as 19 Mechanized Division, 1946–47 (Feb. 1947 OB).
—"Kremenchug, Znamenka, Iasi, Kishinev."

234 Rifle Division
Units: 1340, 1342, 1350 Rifle, 592 Artillery Regiments.
—Raised at Kostroma, Moscow Military District, from Yaroslavl Home Guard Division, June 1941.
—Crimea w/9 Independent Rifle Corps, June 1941.
—RVGK w/3 Reserve (60 Army), May 1942.
—Central Front w/11 Guards Army, Dec. 1943.

—Warsaw, Jan. 1945.
—"Communist, Lomonosovo, Praga."

235 Rifle Division
Units: First and second formation: 732, 801, 806 Rifle, 541 Artillery
    Regiments.
—Raised at Nikopol, Odessa Military District, May 1941.
—RVGK w/41 Rifle Corps, June 1941.
—Baltic Special Military District w/41 Rifle Corps, June 1941.
—Destroyed near Luga, Sep. 1941.
—Second formation raised at Novosibirsk, Siberia Military District, Mar. 1942.
—Northwest Front w/53 Army, Apr. 1942.
—RVGK w/2 Reserve (63 Army), Mar. 1943.
—Central Front w/11 Guards Army, Dec. 1943.
—Vitebsk Op. w/60 Rifle Corps, 43 Army, June 1944.
—Assault division at Koenigsberg (Kaliningrad); 801 Rifle Regiment the assault regiment, Apr. 1945.

236 Rifle Division
Units: 177, 509, 814 Rifle, 687 Artillery Regiments.
—Raised at Kazakh, Transcaucasus Military District, Feb. 1941.
—Transcaucasus Military District w/47 Army as a Motorized Division, July 1941.
—Amphibious landing at Feodosiya w/44 Army, Dec. 1941.
—Caucasus w/44 Army, June 1942.
—Serafimovich, July 1942.
—Maikop Tuapse Road, Aug. 1942.
—Tuapse Defensive Op., Sep–Dec 1942.
—Kuban w/18 Army, Jan. 1943.
—Kuban w/56 Army, Feb. 1943.
—Dnieper River w/46 Army, Sep. 1943.
—Dnepropetrovsk, Sep. 1943.
—Southwest Ukraine w/34 Rifle Corps, 46 Army, Jan. 1944.
—Belgrade w/57 Army, Oct. 1944.
—"Dnepropetrovsk."

237 Rifle Division
Units: First and second formation: 835, 838, 841 Rifle, 691 Artillery
    Regiments.
—Raised at Petrozavodsk, Archangelsk Military District, Apr. 1941.
—Leningrad Military District w/55 Army, Apr. 1941.
—Leningrad area w/7 Independent Army, June 1941.

—Novgorod sector, July 1941.
—Sol'tsa, w/11 Army, July 1941.
—Leningrad Front w/14 Army, Aug. 1941.
—Destroyed near Leningrad, Sep. 1941.
—Second raised at Stalinsk, Siberia Military District, Feb. 1942.
—RVGK w/3 Reserve (60 Army), July 1942.
—Southwest Front w/38 Army, July 1942.
—Yerevan, Jan. 1943.
—Dnieper River w/40 Army, Sep. 1943.
—Carpathian Uzhgorod Op. w/30 then 18 Guards Independent Rifle Corps, 1 Guards Army, Sep. 1944.
—Possibly an independent division.
—"Piryatin," Order of Red Banner.

238 Rifle Division
Units: First and second formation: 830, 837, 843 Rifle, 693 Artillery Regiments.
—Raised at Kazakstan, Central Asia Military District, 1941.
—To western front, Oct. 1941.
—Moscow axis w/49 Army, Nov. 1941.
—Reformed as 30 Guards Rifle Division, May 1942.
—Second formation raised at Arzamas, Moscow Military District, June 1942.
—Stalingrad axis, July 1942.
—Karachev, Aug. 1943.
—Belorussian Op., June 1944.
—Vistula Oder Op., Jan. 1945.
—East Prussia w/49 Army, Mar. 1945.
—North Korea w/25 Army, Feb. 1947 OB.
—"Karachev, Mogilev, Lomza, Osowiec," Orders of Red Banner, Suvorov.

239 Rifle Division
Units: 511, 813, 817 Rifle, 688 Artillery Regiments.
—Raised at Tambov, Orel Military District, before Aug. 1941.
—In Eastern Russia, Aug. 1941.
—Jenev area, Nov. 1941.
—Moscow area w/50 Army, Dec. 1941.
—Novgorod Luga Op. w/6 "Stalin," Rifle Corps, 59 Army, Jan. 1944.
—Carpathian Mountains, Sep. 1944.
—Chop, Oct. 1944.

240 Rifle Division
Units: First and second formation: 836, 842, 931 Rifle, 692 Artillery Regiments.
—Raised at Kupyansk, Kharkov Military District, before June 1941.
—In Kiev Special Military District Reserve, June 1941.
—Destroyed near Kiev, Sep. 1941.
—Second formation raised at Kupyansk, Kharkov Military District, Oct. 1941.
—Southwest Front w/38 Army, Aug. 1942.
—Kursk w/50 Rifle Corps, 38 Army, July 1943.
—Assault crossing of Dnieper at Lutezh, Sep. 1943.
—Sumy w/51 Rifle Corps, 38 Army, Sep. 1943.
—Kiev w/38 Army, Nov. 1943.
—Probably in the Kiev Defensive Op., Dec. 1943.
—Southwest Ukraine w/18 Guards Independent Rifle Corps, 60 Army, Jan. 1944.
—Khotin w/40 Army, Mar. 1944.
—Targul Frumos w/7 Guards Army, May 1944.
—Iasi Kishinev Op., Aug. 1944.
—Carpathian Mts. Sep. 1944.
—Vistula Oder Op., Jan. 1945.
—Probably an independent division.
—"Kiev, Dnieper, Carpathian, Transylvania."

241 Rifle Division
Units: 264, 318, 332 Rifle, 1010 Artillery Regiments.
—Raised at Vishni Volochek, Moscow Military District, Oct. 1941.
—Formed from 28 Tank Division; 264 Rifle Regiment associated w/3 Rifle Division, Oct. 1941.
—Northwest Front w/53 Army, Apr. 1942.
—Kursk w/26 Guards Rifle Corps, 27 Army, July 1943.
—Akhtyrka w/27 Army, Aug. 1943.
—Southwest Ukraine w/17 Guards Rifle Corps, 38 Army, Jan. 1944.
—Vinnitsa, Mar. 1944.
—Carpathian Duklinskiy Op. w/67 Rifle Corps, 38 Army, Sep. 1944.
—Czechoslovakia, Jan. 1945.
—"Vinnitsa."

242 Mountain Rifle Division
Units: First formation: 897, 900, 903 Rifle, 679 Artillery Regiments; Second formation: 819, 897, 900, 903 Rifle, 679 Artillery Regiments.

—Raised in Moscow Military District, July 1941.
—RVGK w/30 Army, July 1941.
—Smolensk w/30 Army, July 1941.
—Olenino area, Sep. 1941.
—Dissolved, Oct. 1941.
—Second formation raised at Grozny, North Caucasus Military District as a Mountain Rifle Division, Mar. 1942.
—Stalingrad, June 1942.
—Mt. Elbrus, Aug. 1942.
—Yerevan, Jan. 1943.
—Kuban area, Jan. 1943.
—Novorossiysk, Feb. 1943.
—Krimskaya, Mar. 1943.
—Taman, Nov. 1943.
—Kerch w/Independent Coastal Army, Jan. 1944.
—Crimea w/3 Mountain Rifle Corps, 4 Ukrainian Front, Apr. 1944.
—Sevastopol, May 1944.
—"Taman, Rotthamer."

243 Rifle Division
Units: 906, 910, 912 Rifle, 975 Artillery Regiments.
—Raised at Yaroslavl, Moscow Military District, July 1941.
—RVGK w/30 Army, July 1941.
—Smolensk w/30 Army, July 1941.
—Western Dvina River w/29 Army, Aug. 1941.
—Toropets area w/29 Army, Sep. 1941.
—Zaporozhye bridgehead w/3 Guards Army, Oct. 1943.
—South Ukraine w/34 Guards Rifle Corps, 3 Guards Army, Jan. 1944.

244 Rifle Division
Units: First and second formations: 907, 911, 913 Rifle, 776 Artillery Regiments.
—Raised at Dimitrov, Moscow Military District, July 1941.
—RVGK in Moscow Military District w/31 Army, July 1941.
—In Reserve Front w/31 Army, Sep. 1941.
—Roslavl w/19 Army, Oct. 1941.
—Destroyed at Vyazma, Oct. 1941.
—Second formation merged w/469 Rifle Division at Stalingrad as an independent division of the RVGK, Jan. 1942.
—In the RVGK as an independent division, June 1942.
—To Stalingrad, June 1942.
—Southwest front w/12 Army, Apr. 1943.
—Dnieper River w/12 Army, Oct. 1943.

—Zaporozhye bridgehead w/12 army, Oct. 1943.
—Southwest Ukraine w/66 Rifle Corps, 6 Army, Jan. 1944.
—Probably an independent division.
—"Zaporozhye," Orders of Red Banner, Suvorov.

245 Rifle Division
Units: 898, 901, 904 Rifle, 770 Artillery Regiments.
—Raised at Vishniy Volochek, Moscow Military District, July 1941.
—RVGK w/29 Army, July 1941.
—Toropets w/29 Army, Sep. 1941.
—Poland, Jan. 1945.
—"Lombrova, Kattowice."

246 Rifle Division
Units: 908, 914, 915 Rifle, 777 Artillery Regiments.
—Raised at Rybinsk, Moscow Military District, July 1941.
—RVGK in Moscow area w/31 Army, July 1941.
—Reserve Front w/31 Army, Sep. 1941.
—Kursk w/77 Rifle Corps, 65 Army, July 1943.
—Southwest Ukraine w/28 Rifle Corps, 13 Army, Jan. 1944.
—Crimea w/1 Guards Rifle Corps, 51 Army, Apr. 1944.
—Krakow, Jan. 1945.
—Lower Silesian Op., Feb. 1945.
—North Caucasus Military District, Oct. 1947 (EUCOM Study).
—"Osowiec, Krakow, Kattowice, u/i honorific."

247 Rifle Division
Units: 909, 916, 920 Rifle, 778 Artillery Regiments.
—Raised at Murom, Moscow Military District, July 1941.
—RVGK in Moscow area w/31 Army, July 1941.
—Reserve Front w/24 Army, Sep. 1941.
—Kursk w/10 Army, July 1943.
—Pulawy bridgehead w/61 Rifle Corps, 69 Army; had six rifle battalions, Jan. 1945.
—Berlin Op. w/61 Rifle Corps, 69 Army, Apr. 1945.
—Brandenberg, Apr. 1945.
—"Roslavl, Radom, Brandenberg."

248 Rifle Division
Units: All formations: 899, 902, 905 Rifle, 771 Artillery Regiments.
—Raised at Vyazma, Moscow Military District, July 1941.
—Moscow Military District w/49 Army, Aug. 1941.
—Reserve Front w/24 Army, Sep. 1941.

—Destroyed Vyazma, Oct. 1941.
—Second formation raised at Astrakhan, North Caucasus Military District, May 1942.
—Kharkov offensive w/6 Army, May 1942.
—Destroyed at Izyum, May 1942.
—Third formation raised at Astrakhan, North Caucasus Military District, July 1942.
—To Stalingrad area, Aug. 1942.
—Stalingrad area, Sep. 1942.
—Stalingrad offensive w/28 Army, Nov. 1942.
—Ukraine w/28 Army, Nov. 1943.
—South Ukraine w/37 Rifle Corps, 3 Guards Army, Jan. 1944.
—Pomeranian Op., Feb. 1945.
—Berlin w/5 Shock Army, Apr. 1945.
—Barth, Germany w/5 Mechanized Army, July 1946 (Aug. 1946 OB).
—"Pomeranian," Order of Suvorov.

249 Rifle Division
Units: All formations: 917, 921, 925 Rifle, 786 Artillery Regiments.
—Raised in Ural Military District from "picked frontier guards," before July 1941.
—RVGK w/31 Army, July 1941.
—Reserve Front w/31 Army, Sep. 1941.
—Demyansk w/4 Shock Army; covered concentration of Army, Dec. 1941.
—Kalinin area w/4 Shock Army, Jan. 1942.
—Toropets, Jan. 1942.
—Andreopol, Jan. 1942.
—Reformed as 16 Guards Rifle Division, Feb. 1942.
—Second formation raised at Cherbarkul, Ural Military District, Mar. 1942.
—Reformed as 122 Guards Rifle Division, 28 June 1945 (Pravda).
—Southern Leningrad w/8 Guards Rifle Corps, 10 Guards Army, Apr. 1946, (Feb. 1947 OB).
—"Estonian."

250 Rifle Division
Units: 918, 922, 926 Rifle, 790 Artillery Regiments.
—Raised at Vladimir, Moscow Military District, July 1941.
—Smolensk, July 1941.
—Northwest Front w/53 Army, Apr. 1942.
—RVGK w/2 reserve (63 Army), Mar. 1943.
—Kursk, w/28 Rifle Corps, 70 Army, July 1943.
—Gomel Op., Nov. 1943.

—Belorussian Op., June 1944.
—RVGK, Apr. 1945 (FHO).
—"Bobruysk, Bialystok, Gomel," Order of Red Banner.

251 Rifle Division
Units: 919, 923, 927 Rifle, 790 Artillery Regiments.
—Raised at Kolomna, Moscow Military District, July 1941.
—RVGK w/30 Army, July 1941.
—Smolensk w/30 Army, July 1941.
—Olenino area w/30 Army, Sep. 1941.
—Moscow axis w/30 Army, Nov. 1941.
—Klin, Dec. 1941.
—Pogorole Gorodische Op. w/20 Army; breakthrough RD, Aug. 1942.
—Iasi w/52 Army, Apr. 1944.
—Targul Frumos w/52 Army, May 1944.
—Belorussian Op. w/39 Army, June 1944.
—"Vitebsk."

252 Rifle Division
Units: First and second formation: 924, 928, 952 Rifle, 787 Artillery Regiments.
—Raised at Serpukhov, Moscow Military District, July 1941.
—Smolensk, w/29 Army, July 1941.
—Western Dvina River w/29 Army, Aug. 1941.
—Kalinin, Jan. 1942.
—Destroyed near Belyi, May 1942.
—Second formation raised at Molotov, Ural Military District, Aug. 1942.
—To Stalingrad area, Oct. 1942.
—Stalingrad offensive w/65 Army, Nov. 1942.
—Voronezh w/24 Army, Mar. 1943.
—Kursk w/53 Army, July 1943.
—Kharkov w/69 Army, Aug. 1943.
—Kirovograd w/48 Rifle Corps, 53 Army, Jan. 1944.
—Iasi, Apr. 1944.
—Targul Frumos, May 1944.
—Hungary w/4 Guards Army, Nov. 1944.
—Probably an independent division.
—"Kharkov, Pressburg," Orders of Red Banner, Suvorov, Bogdan Khmelnitskiy.

253 Rifle Division
Units: First and second formations: 979, 981, 983 Rifle, 808 Artillery Regiments.
—Raised at Volochansk, Kharkov Military District, July 1941.

—Toropets area w/29 Army, Sep. 1941.
—Rostov w/37 Army, Nov. 1941.
—Kharkov offensive w/6 Army, May 1942.
—Destroyed at Izyum, May 1942.
—Second formation raised at Chapayevsk, Volga Military District, Sep. 1942.
—Dnieper River w/40 Army, Sep. 1943.
—Kalinkovichi, Jan. 1944.
—Had some naval infantry in its composition.
—"Kalinkovichi."

254 Rifle Division
Units: 929, 933, 936 Rifle, 791 Artillery Regiments.
—Raised at Tula, Moscow Military District, July 1941.
—RVGK in the Reserve Front w/29 Army, July 1941.
—To 11 Army, Northwest Front, July 1941.
—Staraya Russa, Aug. 1941.
—Toropets area w/29 Army, Sep. 1941.
—Northwest Front w/11, 1 Shock, 34 and 27 Armies, 1942–43.
—Demyansk, w/27 Army, May 1942–Feb. 1943.
—Reequipped, probably in the RVGK, Mar–May 1943.
—RVGK w/53 Army, May 1943.
—Kursk w/13 Army, July 1943.
—Voronezh Front w/52 Army, Aug. 1943.
—Cherkassy, Dec. 1943.
—Kirovograd w/4 Guards Army, Jan. 1944.
—Korsun Shevchenkovskiy Op., Jan. 1944.
—To 52 Army (rest of war), Feb. 1944.
—Uman Botosani Op., Mar. 1944.
—Prut and Dniester Rivers, Mar–Apr 1944.
—In action versus German 24 Panzer Division at Vulturul, Rumania, 7 May 1944.
—Targul Frumos, May 1944.
—Iasi Kishinev Op., Aug. 1944.
—RVGK, Sep. 1944.
—Poland, Oct. 1944.
—Sandomir Silesian Op., Jan. 1945.
—Lower Silesian Op., Feb. 1945.
—Berlin Op., Apr. 1945.
—Prague, May 1945.
—"Cherkassy, Roman, Iasi, Czestochowa, Cherkassk," Orders of Lenin, Red Banner, Suvorov, Kutuzov, Bogdan Khmelnitskiy.

255 Rifle Division
Units: 968, 970, 972 Rifle, 811 Artillery Regiments.
—Raised at Pavlograd, Odessa Military District, Aug. 1941.
—Uman Pocket w/6 Army, Aug. 1941.
—Southwest Front w/24 Army, May 1942.
—Dissolved, July 1942.

256 Rifle Division
Units: 930, 934, 937 Rifle, 792 Artillery Regiments.
—Smolensk w/29 Army, July 1941.
—Toropets area w/29 Army, Sep. 1941.
—Moscow axis w/30 Army, Nov. 1941.
—Leningrad offensive w/2 Shock Army, Jan. 1943.
—Kursk w/53 Army, July 1943.
—Red Banner.

257 Rifle Division
Units: All formations: 943, 948, 953 Rifle, 793 Artillery Regiments.
—Raised at Tula, Moscow Military District, July 1941.
—SME states raised as 257 RD (2nd form), Kalinin, Moscow Military District, 1941.
—Moscow area w/34 Army, July 1941.
—Kerch, Nov. 1941.
—RVGK w/3 Shock Army, Dec. 1941.
—Velikiye Luki w/3 Shock Army, Jan. 1943.
—Reformed as 91 Guards Rifle Division, 18 Apr. 1943.
—Second formation raised at Krimskaya, North Caucasus Military District from 9, 60 Rifle, 62 Red Banner Naval Rifle Brigades, June 1943.
—Southern Ukraine w/10 Rifle Corps, 51 Army, Jan. 1944.
—Crimea w/10 Rifle Corps, 51 Army, May 1944.
—Memel w/1 Guards Rifle Corps, Oct. 1944.
—U/i honorific, Orders of Red Banner, Suvorov.

258 Rifle Division
Units: First formation: 954, 991, 999 Rifle, 841 Artillery Regiments;
Second formation: 405, 991, 999 Rifle, 782 Artillery Regiments;
Third formation unknown.
—Raised at Orel, Orel Military District, July 1941.
—Bryansk Front w/50 Army, Aug. 1941.
—Roslavl w/50 Army, Sep. 1941.
—Bryansk Pocket w/5 Army, Oct. 1941.
—Tula w/49 Army, Dec. 1941.
—Reformed as 12 Guards Rifle Division, Jan. 1942.

—Second formation raised as 43 Independent Rifle Brigade at Novosibirsk, Siberia Military District; reformed as 258 Rifle Division at Mozhaisk, Moscow Military District, May 1942.
—To Stalingrad area, Sep. 1942.
—Stalingrad w/24 Army, Oct. 1942.
—Stalingrad offensive w/65 Army, Nov. 1942.
—Reformed as 96 Guards Rifle Division, 4 May 1943.
—Third formation in North Korea w/25 Army, Sep. 1946 (Feb. 1947 OB).

259 Rifle Division
Units: 939, 944, 949 Rifle, 801 Artillery Regiments.
—Raised at Serpukhov, Moscow Military District, July 1941.
—Moscow area w/34 Army, July 1941.
—Leningrad w/52 Army of the RVGK, Nov. 1941.
—South Ukraine w/32 Rifle Corps, 3 Guards Army, Jan. 1944.
—"Artemovsk."

260 Rifle Division
Units: First and second formation: 1026, 1028, 1030 Rifle, 689 Artillery Regiments.
—Raised at Kalinin, Moscow Military District, July 1941.
—Bryansk Front w/50 Army, Aug. 1941.
—Roslavl w/50 Army, Sep. 1941.
—Destroyed in the Bryansk Pocket, Oct. 1941.
—Second formation raised at Volokolamsk, Moscow Military District, after Oct. 1941.
—Moscow axis w/50 Army, Nov. 1941.
—To Stalingrad area, Sep. 1942.
—Stalingrad offensive w/24 Army, Nov. 1942.
—Belorussia w/11 Army, Feb. 1943.
—RVGK w/11 Army, May 1943.
—Kovel Lutsk Op., Feb. 1944.
—Belorussia w/77 Rifle Corps, 47 Army, Mar. 1944.
—Opposed II SS Panzer Korps relief of 1 Panzer Army w/18 Guards Independent Rifle Corps, Apr. 1944.
—Warsaw Poznan Op. w/129 Rifle Corps, 47 Army, Jan. 1945.
—Quedlinburg, Germany w/3 Mechanized Army, Aug. 1946 (Feb. 1947 OB).
—"Kovel."

261 Rifle Division
Units: First and second: 974, 976, 978 Rifle, 809 Artillery Regiments.

—Raised at Berdyansk, Odessa Military District, July 1941.
—Dissolved; remnants to 30 Rifle Division (FHO), Oct. 1942.
—Second formation raised at Yerevan, Transcaucasus Military District, after Oct. 1942.
—Probably in the Caucasus, 1943.
—Transcaucasus Military District, Oct. 1945 (EUCOM Study).
—"Armenian, Yerevan."

262 Rifle Division
Units: 940, 945, 950 Rifle, 788 Artillery Regiments.
—Raised at Vladimir, Moscow Military District, July 1941.
—Moscow Military District w/34 Army, July 1941.
—Demidov, Sep. 1943.
—Belorussian Op., June 1944.
—Tilsit, Oct. 1944.
—Khingan Mukden Op., Aug. 1945.
—"Demidov, Vitebsk, Tilsit," Orders of Red Banner, Suvorov (FHO).
—"Demidov, Khingan," Orders of Red Banner, Suvorov (Military Intelligence Magazine Jan–Feb 1983).

263 Rifle Division
Units: 993, 995, 997 Rifle, 853 Artillery Regiments.
—Raised at Vologda, Archangelsk Military District, Nov. 1941.
—Lake Khizh, Leningrad Front w/32 Army, Jan. 1942.
—Leningrad area w/32 Army, Mar. 1942.
—South Ukraine w/10 Rifle Corps, 51 Army, Jan. 1944.
—Crimea w/63 Rifle Corps, 51 Army, Apr. 1944.
—Sivash River, Apr. 1944.
—"Sivash."

264 Rifle Division
Units: First and second formation: 1056, 1058, 1060 Rifle Regiments; Third formation: unknown.
—Raised at Poltava, Kharkov Military District, July 1941.
—Destroyed at Kiev, Sep. 1941.
—Second formation raised at Svyatogorsk, Kharkov Military District, May 1942.
—Reformed as 48 Guards Rifle Division, Oct. 1942.
—Third formation raised; in Far East, Aug. 1945.

265 Rifle Division
Units: 450, 941, 951 Rifle, 798 Artillery Regiments.
—Raised in Leningrad, Leningrad Military District, probably in 1941.

—Vyborg axis, June 1941.
—RVGK to 23 Army, Kerkholm area, July 1941.
—Tortolovo, Leninrgad Front w/8 Army, Sep. 1942.
—Probably on the Leningrad Front, 1943–44.
—Vyborg, June 1944.
—"Vyborg, u/i honorific."

266 Rifle Division
Units: First and third formation: 1006, 1008, 1010 Rifle, 832 Artillery Regiments; Second formation: 1000, 1006, 1008 Rifle, 832 Artillery Regiments.
—Raised at Kaluga, Moscow Military District as a motorized division, July 1941.
—Destroyed at Kiev, Sep. 1941.
—Second formation raised at Stalingrad, North Caucasus Military District, Jan. 1942.
—Kharkov offensive w/6 Army, May 1942.
—Merged w/417 Rifle Division; 1000 Rifle Regiment to 305 Rifle Division (FHO), May 1942.
—Third formation raised at Kuibyshev, Volga Military District, Aug. 1942.
—To Stalingrad area, Nov. 1942.
—Zaporozhye bridgehead w/3 Guards Army, Oct. 1943.
—South Ukraine w/32 Rifle Corps, 3 Guards Army, Jan. 1944.
—Lvov Sandomir Op. w/11 Guards Rifle Corps, 1 Guards Army, July 1944.
—Iasi Kishinev Op., Aug. 1944.
—Berlin w/5 Shock Army, Apr. 1945.
—Probably an independent division.
—"Artemovsk, Kishinev, Pomeranian," Orders of Red Banner, Suvorov.

267 Rifle Division
Units: First and second formation: 844, 846, 848 Rifle, 845 Artillery Regiments.
—Raised at Stary Oskol, Orel Military District, Aug. 1941.
—RVGK w/52 Army, Aug. 1941.
—Southwest Front w/52 Army, Aug. 1941.
—Maselga, Karelian Front, Dec. 1941.
—Destroyed at Volchov, June 1942.
—Second formation raised at Serpukhov, Moscow Military District, Sep. 1942.
—RVGK, Dec. 1942.
—To Stalingrad, Dec. 1942.

—Kantemirovka w/6 Army, Dec. 1942.
—In Pavlograd Pocket, Feb. 1943.
—South Ukraine w/63 Rifle Corps, 5 Shock Army, Jan. 1944.
—Crimea w/63 Rifle Corps, 51 Army, Apr. 1944.
—Sivash River, Apr. 1944.
—Panevyzys, July 1944.
—Riga, Oct. 1944.
—Memel w/1 Guards Rifle Corps, Oct. 1944.
—"Sivash."

268 Rifle Division
Units: 942, 947, 952 Rifle, 799 Artillery Regiments.
—Raised at Mozyr, Western Special Military District, July 1941.
—RVGK to 8 Army, July 1941.
—Krasnoye Selo, Sep. 1941.
—Leningrad Front w/52 Army, Nov. 1941.
—Tosno River, Leningrad Front w/55 Army, Aug. 1942.
—Probably on the Leningrad Front, 1942–43.
—Leningrad offensive, Neva River w/67 Army, Jan. 1943.
—Mga, July 1943.
—Riga area, Sep. 1944.
—"Mga."

269 Rifle Division
Units: 1018, 1020, 1022 Rifle, 836 Artillery Regiments.
—Raised at Kolomna, Moscow Military District, July 1941.
—Bryansk Front w/50 Army, Aug. 1941.
—Central Front w/13 Army, Sep. 1941.
—Moscow axis w/10 Army, Dec. 1941.
—Orel w/3 Army, Aug. 1943.
—Gomel w/3 Army, Nov. 1943.
—Rogachev, Feb. 1944.
—Belorussian Op., June 1944.
—Bialystok, July 1944.
—RVGK, Apr. 1945 (FHO).
—"Bialystok, Rogachev, Ostrolenka," Order of Red Banner.

270 Rifle Division
Units: First and second formation: 973, 975, 977 Rifle, 810 Artillery Regiments.
—Raised at Melitopol, Odessa Military District, July 1941.
—Southwest Front w/12 Army, Aug. 1941.
—Destroyed at Izyum, May 1942.

—Second formation raised at Voronezh, Ural Military District, Oct. 1942.
—Stalingrad area, Nov. 1942.
—Kharkov w/69 Army, Feb. 1943.
—Kursk w/69 Army, July 1943.
—Demidov, Sep. 1943.
—Belorussian Op., June 1944.
—"Demidov, Polotsk," Order of Red Banner.

271 Rifle Division
Units: 865, 867, 869 Rifle, 850 Artillery Regiments.
—Raised at Orel, Orel Military District, July 1941.
—Crimea w/9 Independent Rifle Corps, Aug. 1941.
—RVGK in Crimea w/51 Independent Army, Aug. 1941.
—Moscow Front w/30 Army, Nov. 1941.
—Makhachkala direction, Nov. 1942.
—Mozdok w/44 Army, Jan., 1943.
—Kursk w/40 Rifle Corps, 63 Army, July 1943.
—Southwest Ukraine w/11 Rifle Corps, 1 Guards Army, Jan. 1944.
—Destroyed at Dolina (Ultra, FHO); reformed, Aug. 1944.
—Carpathian Mountains, Sep. 1944.
—Budapest, Jan. 1945.
—East Prussia w/42 Army, Feb. 1945.
—Possibly an independent division.
—"Gorlovka, High Carpathian, Budapest, Rotthamer," Orders of Red Banner, Suvurov, Bogdan Khmelnitskiy.

272 Rifle Division
Units: 1061, 1063, 1065 Rifle, 815 Artillery Regiments.
—Raised at Tikhvin, Leningrad Military District in the RVGK, July 1941.
—Petrozavodsk axis w/7th Independent Army, July–Sep 1941.
—Svir River, June 1944.
—Danzig area w/19 Army, Mar. 1945.
—RVGK (FHO), Apr. 1945.
—"Svir, Petrozavodsk."

273 Rifle Division
Units: First and second formation: 967, 969, 971 Rifle, 812 Artillery Regiments.
—Raised at Dnepropetrovsk, Odessa Military District, Aug. 1941.
—Uman pocket w/6 Army, Aug. 1941.
—Destroyed near Dnepropetrovsk, Sep. 1941.
—Second formation raised near Podolsk, Moscow Military District, July 1942.

—To Stalingrad area, Sep. 1942.
—Stalingrad offensive w/24 Army, Nov. 1942.
—Belorussia w/11 Army, Feb. 1943.
—RVGK w/11 Army, May 1943.
—"Beshiza."

274 Rifle Division
Units: 961, 963, 965 Rifle, 814 Artillery Regiments.
—Raised at Zaporozhye, Kiev Special Military District, Aug. 1941.
—Southern Front w/12 Army, Aug. 1941.
—Baltic area w/36 Rifle Corps, 31 Army, Western Front, June 1943.
—Pulawy bridgehead w/61 Rifle Corps, 69 Army; breakthrough division, had six rifle battalions, Jan. 1945.
—Berlin Op. w/61 Rifle Corps, 69 Army, Apr. 1945.
—"Jarzevo, Radom."

275 Rifle Division
Units: First and second formation: 980, 982, 984 Rifle, 802 Artillery Regiments.
—Raised at Novo-Moskovsk, Odessa Military District, Aug. 1941.
—Digora, North Caucasus, Nov. 1942.
—Destroyed or dissolved, remnants to 10 Rifle Brigade, Dec. 1942.
—Second formation raised in Far East, Aug. 1944.

276 Rifle Division
Units: First and second formation: 871, 873, 876 Rifle, 852 Artillery Regiments.
—Raised Simferopol, Odessa Military District, Mar. 1941.
—Crimea w/9 Independent Rifle Corps, Aug. 1941.
—RVGK in Crimea w/51 Independent Army, Aug. 1941.
—Destroyed at Kerch, May 1942.
—Second formation raised at Kutaisi, Transcaucasus as a Georgian Rifle Division, Oct. 1942.
—Ordzhonikidze w/9 Army, Nov. 1942.
—Terek River, North Caucasus, Jan. 1943.
—Kurchanskaya, Sep. 1943.
—Southwest Ukraine w/11 Rifle Corps, 1 Guards Army, Jan. 1944.
—Carpathian Uzhgorod Op. w/1 Guards Army, Sep. 1944.
—"Temruk, Stryy, Drogobycz."

277 Rifle Division
Units: First and second formation: 850, 852, 854 Rifle, 846 Artillery Regiments.

—Raised at Dmitriyev, Orel Military District, Aug. 1941.
—Uman Pocket w/6 Army, Aug. 1941.
—Destroyed near Korep, Sep. 1941.
—Second formation raised at Frolov, North Caucasus Military District, Jan. 1942.
—Probably in the Kharkov Offensive Op. w/38 Army, June 1942.
—To Stalingrad axis from 38 Army, July 1942.
—To Stalingrad, Oct. 1942.
—Stalingrad offensive w/21 Army, Nov. 1942.
—Borodino area, June 1944.
—Belorussian Op., June 1944.
—Vilnius w/72 Rifle Corps, 5 Army, Aug. 1944.
—"Rosslavl, Vitebsk, Borisov, Vilnius, Kaunas."

278 Rifle Division
Units: First and second formation: 851, 853, 855 Rifle, 847 Artillery Regiments; Third formation: unknown.
—Raised at Livny, Orel Military District, Aug. 1941.
—Bryansk Front w/50 Army, Aug. 1941.
—Roslavl area w/50 Army, Sep. 1941.
—Destroyed in Bryansk Pocket w/50 Army, Oct. 1941.
—Second formation raised near Stalingrad, Volga Military District, Jan. 1942.
—Probably in Kharkov Offensive Op. w/38 Army, June 1942.
—To Stalingrad axis from 38 Army, July 1942.
—Stalingrad offensive w/1 Guards Army, Nov. 1942.
—Reformed as 60 Guards Rifle Division, Jan. 1943.
—Third formation raised; in Far East w/17 Army, Aug. 1945.

279 Rifle Division
Units: First and second formation: 1001, 1003, 1005 Rifle, 831 Artillery Regiments.
—Raised at Dzerzhinsk, Moscow Military District, July 1941.
—RVGK in Reserve Front w/43 Army, July 1941.
—Bryansk Front w/50 Army, Aug. 1941.
—Yelnaya area w/43 Army, Sep. 1941.
—Destroyed Bryansk Pocket w/50 Army, Oct. 1941.
—Second formation raised at Balachina, Moscow Military District, Aug. 1942.
—Zaporozhye Bridgehead w/3 Guards Army, Oct. 1943.
—South Ukraine w/32 Rifle Corps, 3 Guards Army, Jan. 1944.
—Crimea w/10 Rifle Corps, 51 Army, May 1944.
—Riga area w/51 Army, Aug. 1944.

—Memel w/10 Rifle Corps, Oct. 1944.
—"Lisichansk, Mitau."

280 Rifle Division
Units: First and second formation: 1031, 1033, 1035 Rifle, 840 Artillery Regiments.
—Raised at Tula, Moscow Military District, probably in July 1941.
—Bryansk Front w/50 Army, Aug. 1941.
—Roslavl area w/50 Army, Sep. 1941.
—Destroyed in Bryansk pocket, Oct. 1941.
—Stalingrad axis, June 1942.
—Second formation raised at Voronezh, Jan. 1943.
—Kursk w/28 Rifle Corps, 70 Army, July 1943.
—Korosten, Dec. 1943.
—Shepetovka, Mar. 1944.
—"Konotop, Korosten, Shepetovka," Orders of Red Banner, Suvorov.

281 Rifle Division
Units: 1062, 1064, 1066 Rifle, 816 Artillery Regiments.
—Probably raised in Leningrad, Leningrad Military District, July 1941.
—RVGK, July 1941.
—Kingisepp, July 1941.
—Krasnoye Selo, Sep. 1941.
—Volkhov w/4 Army, Nov. 1941.
—Probably on Leningrad Front, 1941–44.
—Novgorod Luga Op., Jan. 1944.
—Danzig area w/2 Shock Army, Mar. 1945.
—"Lyuban, Luga."

282 Rifle Division
Units: First and second formation: 872, 874, 877 Rifle, 826 Artillery Regiments.
—Raised in Moscow Military District, July 1941.
—Central Front w/13 Army, Sep. 1941.
—Destroyed in Bryansk pocket, Oct. 1941.
—Second formation raised at Omsk, Siberia Military District, Feb. 1942.
—Poland, Feb. 1945.
—"Walcz, Dorpat."

283 Rifle Division
Units: 856, 858, 860 Rifle, 9 Guards Artillery Regiments.
—Raised at Schtschigry, Orel Military District, Sep. 1941.
—Central Front w/13 Army, Sep. 1941.

—Gomel w/3 Army, Nov. 1943.
—Belorussian Op., June 1944.
—Bialystok, July 1944.
—East Prussian Op., Mar. 1945.
—RVGK (FHO), Apr. 1945.
—"Gomel, Bialystok, Tannenberg," Orders of Red Banner, Suvorov.

284 Rifle Division
Units: First and second formation: 1043, 1045, 1047 Rifle, 820 Artillery Regiments; third formation: unknown.
—Raised at Romny, Kharkov Military District, July 1941.
—Kiev Pocket w/37 Army, Aug. 1941.
—Destroyed near Kiev, Sep. 1941.
—Second formation raised at Tomsk, Siberian Military District, Mar. 1942.
—Bryansk Front w/48 Army, Apr. 1942.
—To Stalingrad, Sep. 1942.
—Mamaev Hill, Stalingrad w/62 Army, Sep. 1942.
—Reformed as 79 Guards Rifle Division, Mar. 1943.
—Third formation raised; in Far East w/17 Army, Aug. 1945.

285 Rifle Division
Units: 1013, 1015, 1017 Rifle, 835 Artillery Regiments.
—Raised at Kostroma, Moscow Military District, July 1941.
—RVGK w/52 Army, Aug. 1941.
—Southwest Front w/52 Army, Aug. 1941.
—RVGK, Moscow Military District w/54 Army, Aug. 1941.
—RVGK w/54 Army, Sep. 1941.
—Volkhov w/4 Army, Nov. 1941.
—Probably on Leningrad Front 1942–44.
—Opole w/21 Army, Feb. 1945.
—"Kattowice, Oder."

286 Rifle Division
Units: 994, 996, 998 Rifle, 854 Artillery Regiments.
—Raised at Cherepovets, Archangelsk Military District, July 1941.
—RVGK, Moscow Military District w/54 Army, Aug–Sep 1941.
—Tikhvin w/54 Army, Oct. 1941.
—Probably on Leningrad Front, 1941–44.
—Poland, Feb. 1945.
—"Leningrad, Kattowice, u/i honorific."

287 Rifle Division

Units: First and second formation: 866, 868, 870 Rifle, 851 Artillery Regiments.
—Raised at Yelez, Orel Military District, July 1941.
—On Central Front, Sep. 1941.
—Destroyed in Bryansk pocket, Oct. 1941.
—Second formation raised at Lipetsk, Orel Military District; w/61 Army, Dec. 1941.
—Central front w/3 Army, Jan. 1942.
—Mtsensk region, Feb. 1942–July 1943.
—Orel area w/63 Army, Aug. 1943.
—Novosybkov, Sep. 1943.
—Gomel area, Oct. 1943.
—Gomel Rechitsa Op., Nov. 1943.
—To 13 Army, Dec. 1943.
—Zhitomir Berdichev Op. w/24 Rifle Corps, 13 Army, Jan. 1944.
—Novograd Volynskiy, Jan. 1944.
—Rovno Lutsk Op. w/24 Rifle Corps, 13 Army, Feb. 1944.
—Proskurov Chernovtsy Op., Mar. 1944.
—Lvov Sandomir Op., July 1944.
—Przemysyl, July 1944.
—To 3 Guards Army (rest of war), Nov. 1944.
—Sandomir Silesian Op., Jan. 1945.
—Lower Silesian Op., Feb. 1945.
—Berlin Op., Apr. 1945.
—Prague Op., May 1945.
—Oster, Kiev Military District as a training motorized rifle division, 1960's (Suvorov, *The Liberators*).
—"Novograd Volyinskiy, Kielce," Twice Order of the Red Banner, Orders of Suvorov, Kutuzov, Bogdan Khmelnitskiy.

288 Rifle Division

Units: 1012, 1014, 1016 Rifle, 834 Artillery Regiments.
—Raised at Yaroslavl, Moscow Military District, July 1941.
—RVGK w/52 Army, Aug. 1941.
—Southwest Front w/52 Army, Aug. 1941.
—Tikhvin, Leningrad Front, Oct. 1941.
—Probably on Leningrad Front, 1941–44.
—Ostrov, July 1944.
—Tartu, Sep. 1944.
—"Ostrov, Tartu, Dorpat."

289 Rifle Division
Units: First and second formation: 1044, 1046, 1048 Rifle, 281 Artillery Regiments.
—Probably raised at Lubny, Kharkov Military District, July 1941.
—Destroyed in Kiev Pocket, Sep. 1941.
—Second formation raised at an unknown location, Oct. 1941.
—Karelian Front, Dec. 1941.
—Leningrad Front w/32 Army, Mar. 1942.

290 Rifle Division
Units: 878, 882, 885 Rifle, 1420 Artillery Regiments.
—Raised at Kaljasin, Moscow Military District, Aug. 1941.
—Bryansk Front w/50 Army, Aug. 1941.
—Roslavl area w/50 Army, Sep. 1941.
—Bryansk Pocket w/50 Army, Oct. 1941.
—Moscow axis w/49 Army, Nov. 1941.
—Lenino (near Mogilev) w/33 Army, Oct. 1943.
—Mogilev Op. w/70 Rifle Corps, 49 Army, June 1944.
—RVGK (FHO), Apr. 1945.
—"Mogilev, Osowiec," Orders of Red Banner, Kutuzov.

291 Rifle Division
Units: 181, 309, 1025 Rifle, 838 Artillery Regiments.
—Raised at Rybinsk, Moscow Military District, Aug. 1941.
—Leningrad Front w/55 Army, Aug. 1941.
—Krasnogvardeysk, Sep. 1941.
—Probably on Leningrad Front, 1941–44.
—Vistula Oder Op., Jan. 1945.
—"Plaskow, Kattowice, Gatchina."

292 Rifle Division
Units: First formation: 1007, 1009, 1011 Rifle, 13 Guards Artillery; Second formation: 1000, 1007, 1011 Rifle, 833 Artillery Regiments.
—Raised at Krasnogvardeysk, Leningrad Military District, July 1941.
—RVGK w/52 Army, Aug. 1941.
—Southwest front w/52 Army, Aug. 1941.
—RVGK w/4 Army, Sep. 1941.
—Volkhov w/4 Army, Nov. 1941.
—Stalingrad area w/24 Army, July 1942.
—Stalingrad area, Sep. 1942.
—Dissolved; absorbed into 173 Rifle Division (FHO), Nov. 1942.
—Second formation raised; in Manchuria, Aug. 1945.

293 Rifle Division
Units: First and second formation: 1032, 1034, 1036 Rifle, 817 Artillery Regiments.
—Raised at Sumy, Kharkov Military District, July 1941.
—Kharkov w/40 Army, Aug. 1941.
—Southwest Front w/40 Army, Sep. 1941.
—Southwest Front w/3 Army, Oct–Nov 1941.
—Tula, W/50 Army, Nov. 1941.
—Probably in the Kharkov Offensive Op. w/38 Army, June 1942.
—To Stalingrad axis from 38 Army, July 1942.
—In reserve in Stalingrad area, July–Sep 1942.
—To Stalingrad, Oct. 1942.
—Stalingrad offensive w/21 Army, Nov. 1942.
—Reformed as 66 Guards Rifle Division, Jan. 1943.
—Second formation raised; w/36 Army, Far East, Aug. 1945.

294 Rifle Division
Units: 857, 859, 861 Rifle, 849 Artillery Regiments.
—Raised at Lipetsk, Orel Military District, Sep. 1941.
—Tikhvin, Leningrad Front w/54 Army, Oct. 1941.
—Korsun Shevchenkovskiy Op., Jan. 1944.
—Targul Frumos w/52 Army May 1944.
—"Cherkassy."

295 Rifle Division
Units: 1038, 1040, 1042 Rifle, 819 Artillery Regiments.
—Raised at Chuguyev, Kharkov Military District, Sep. 1941.
—Kiev Pocket w/37 Army, Aug. 1941.
—Terek River, North Caucasus, Nov. 1942.
—Nalchik, North Caucasus, Jan. 1943.
—South Ukraine w/13 Guards Rifle Corps, 2 Guards Army, Jan. 1944.
—Kherson, Mar. 1944.
—Nikolayev, Apr. 1944.
—Berlin w/5 Shock Army, Apr. 1945.
—"Nikolayev, Kherson," Orders of Red Banner, Suvorov.

296 Rifle Division
Units: 962, 964, 966 Rifle, 813 Artillery Regiments.
—In Eastern Russia, Aug. 1941.
—Stalingrad axis, June 1942.
—Dissolved; remnants to 242 Rifle Division (FHO), Aug. 1942.

297 Rifle Division
Units: 1055, 1057, 1059 Rifle, 824 Artillery Regiments.
—Raised at Lubny, Kharkov Military District, July 1941.
—Khorol, Southwest Front w/38 Army, Sep. 1941.
—Southwest Ukraine w/33 Rifle Corps, 2 Ukrainian Front, Jan. 1944.
—Kirovograd, Jan. 1944.
—Iasi, Apr. 1944.
—Targul Frumos, May 1944.
—Budapest, Jan. 1945.
—"Slavyansk, Kirovograd, Budapest."

298 Rifle Division
Units: First and second formation: 886, 888, 892 Rifle, 828 Artillery Regiments; Third formation: unknown.
—Moscow Military District w/49 Army, Aug. 1941.
—Destroyed at Bryansk, Oct. 1941.
—Second formation raised at Barnaul, Siberia Military District, Jan. 1942.
—To Stalingrad area, Aug. 1942.
—Stalingrad offensive w/24 Army, Nov. 1942.
—Reformed as 80 Guards Rifle Division, Mar. 1943.
—Third formation raised; in Far East w/36 Army, Aug. 1945.

299 Rifle Division
Units: First and second formation: 956, 958, 960 Rifle, 843 Artillery Regiments.
—Raised at Belgorod, Orel Military District, July 1941.
—On Central Front, Sep. 1941.
—Destroyed in Bryansk pocket, Oct. 1941.
—Tula w/50 Army, Nov. 1941.
—Moscow area, Dec. 1941.
—Second formation raised at Kovrov, Moscow Military District, possibly in Aug. 1942.
—RVGK w/66 Army, Aug. 1942.
—To Stalingrad, Aug. 1942.
—Stalingrad offensive w/66 Army, Nov. 1942.
—Kharkov w/53 Army, Aug. 1943.
—Vorskla River w/53 Army, Sep. 1943.
—Kirovograd w/48 Rifle Corps, 53 Army, Jan. 1944.
—Iasi, Apr. 1944
—Targul Frumos, May 1944.
—RVGK (FHO), Apr. 1945.
—"Kharkov."

300 Rifle Division
Units: 1049, 1051, 1053 Rifle Regiments.
—Probably raised Kharkov Military District, July 1941.
—Lake Ilmen w/38 Army, Aug. 1941.
—Kharkov sector w/38 Army, Oct. 1941.
—Kharkov Offensive Op. w/38 Army, May–June 1942.
—To Stalingrad area, Aug. 1942.
—Stalingrad, on Volga Islands, Oct. 1942.
—Stalingrad as front reserve, 20 Nov. 1942.
—RVGK w/5 Shock Army, Dec. 1942.
—Reformed as 86 Guards Rifle Division, Apr. 1943.
—Second formation in Far East w/1 Independent Red Banner Army, Aug. 1945.

301 Rifle Division
Units: First and second formations: 1050, 1052, 1054 Rifle, 823 Artillery Regiments.
—Raised at Poltava, Kharkov Military District, Aug. 1941.
—Destroyed at Kiev, Sep. 1941.
—Second formation raised at Krasnoyarsk, Siberia Military District, Mar. 1942.
—Stalino, Sep. 1943.
—South Ukraine w/9 Rifle Corps, 28 Army, Jan. 1944.
—Seelow Heights w/5 Shock Army, Apr. 1945.
—Berlin w/5 Shock Army; took Reich Chancellery, Apr. 1945.
—Ludwigslust, Germany, w/9 Rifle Corps, 5 Mechanized Army, 1946 (Feb. 1947 OB).
—"Stalino."

302 Mountain Rifle Division
Units: 823, 825, 827, 831 Rifle, 865 Artillery Regiments.
—Raised at Krasnodar, North Caucasus Military District, July 1941.
—RVGK in North Caucasus w/51 Independent Army, Oct. 1941.
—Amphibious landing, Feodosiya area, Dec. 1941.
—Reformed as a rifle division, May 1942.
—Crimea w/44 Army, June 1942.
—Stalingrad area w/51 Army, July 1942.
—Nikolayevskaya, North Caucasus, Aug. 1942.
—Stalingrad area w/51 Army, Oct. 1942.
—Stalingrad area; opposed German counterattack w/51 Army, Dec. 1942.
—Ternopol w/60 Army, Mar. 1944.
—Debica, Poland, Jan. 1945.

—Lower Silesian Op., Krakow, Feb. 1945.
—Mobile group of 4 Ukrainian Front as a Motorized Rifle Division in Czechoslovakia, May 1945.
—"Lvov, Tarnopol, Debica, Krakow."

303 Rifle Division
Units: 845, 847, 849 Rifle, 844 Artillery Regiments.
—Raised Voronezh, Orel Military District, July 1941.
—RVGK w/43 Army, July 1941.
—Reserve Front w/24 Army, Sep. 1941.
—Destroyed at Kiev, Sep. 1941.
—Second formation raised at Typki, Siberia Military District, Mar. 1942.
—RVGK w/3 Reserve (later 60 Army), July 1942.
—Voronezh w/60 Army, Jan. 1943.
—Kursk w/57 Army, July 1943.
—Kirovograd w/7 Guards Army, Jan. 1944.
—Iasi, Apr. 1944.
—Targul Frumos, May 1944.
—Iasi Kishinev Op., Aug. 1944.
—"Verchnedneprovsk (Dneprovsk), Iasi Kishinev," Order of Red Banner.

304 Rifle Division
Units: First and second formations: 807, 809, 812 Rifle, 560 Artillery Regiments.
—Raised at Solotnoscha, Kharkov Military District, Aug. 1941.
—Lake Ilmen w/38 Army, Aug. 1941.
—Kharkov sector, probably w/38 Army, Oct. 1941.
—Probably in Kharkov Offensive Op. w/38 Army, June 1942.
—To Stalingrad axis from 38 Army, June 1942.
—Don Front w/65 Army, Oct. 1942.
—Stalingrad offensive w/65 Army, Nov. 1942.
—Reformed as 67 Guards Rifle Division, Jan. 1943.
—Second formation raised from 43, 256 Rifle Brigades, about June 1943.
—Temruk and Kerchnskaya w/9 Army, Sep. 1943.
—Zaporozhye bridgehead w/12 Army, Oct. 1943.
—Taman area w/11 Rifle Corps, Nov. 1943.
—Kiev Zhitomir Defensive Op., Dec. 1943.
—Zhitomir Berdichev Op. w/107 Rifle Corps, 13 Army, Jan. 1944.
—Carpathian Duklinskiy Op. w/52 Rifle Corps, 38 Army, Sep. 1944.
—"Zhitomir."
Key Commanders: Gen-Major M.P. Pukhov, Oct. 1941.

305 Rifle Division
Units: First and second formations: 1000, 1002, 1004 Rifle, 830 Artillery Regiments.
—Raised Dmitrov, Moscow Military District, July 1941.
—Novgorod Army Group, Leningrad, Nov. 1941.
—Destroyed at Volkhov, June 1942.
—Second formation raised at Voronezh, Orel Military District, Oct. 1942.
—Stalingrad area, Nov. 1942.
—Ostrogosh Rossosh Op. w/40 Army, Jan. 1943.
—Kursk w/69 Army, July 1943.
—Belgorod, 5 Aug. 1943.
—Southwest Ukraine w/74 Rifle Corps, 38 Army, Jan. 1944.
—Baranow Bridgehead w/13 Army, Aug. 1944.
—Carpathian Duklinskiy Op. w/52 Rifle Corps, 38 Army, Sep. 1944.
—The 1000 Rifle Regiment is associated w/266 Rifle Division.
—"Belgorod," Order of Red Banner.

306 Rifle Division
Units: 935, 938, 992 Rifle, 1043 Artillery Regiments.
—Raised Yuriev, Moscow Military Division, Sep. 1941.
—Vitebsk Op. w/1 Rifle Corps, 43 Army, June 1944.
—Baltic area, Sep. 1944.
—"Ribschevo, Vitebsk."

307 Rifle Division
Units: 1019, 1021, 1023 Rifle, 837 Artillery Regiments.
—Raised Ivanovo, Moscow Military District, July 1941.
—Central Front w/13 Army, Sep. 1941.
—Yelets, Dec. 1941.
—Voronezh, Jan. 1943.
—Kursk (Ponyri), w/29 Rifle Corps, 13 Army, July 1943.
—Poland, July 1944.
—Brandenberg, Apr. 1945.
—"Novosybkov, Brandenberg."

308 Rifle Division
Units: First formation: 339, 347, 351 Rifle, 1011 Artillery Regiments; Second formation: 319, 323, 355 Rifle Regiments.
—Raised Omsk, Siberia Military District, Mar–May 1942.
—Stalingrad area w/62 Army, July 1942.
—Stalingrad area w/24 Army, Aug. 1942.
—Stalingrad, Sep. 1942.

—Barrikady Factory w/62 Army, Nov. 1942.
—Dnieper River w/40 Army, Sep. 1943.
—Reformed as 120 Guards Rifle Division, Sep. 1943.
—Second formation received 355 Rifle Regiment from 100 Rifle Division.
—Latvia, Oct. 1944.
—"Latvian," Order of Red Banner, Suvorov.

309 Rifle Division
Units: First and second formations: 955, 957, 959 Rifle, 842 Artillery Regiments.
—Raised Kursk, Orel Military District, July 1941.
—Reserve Front w/24 Army, Sep. 1941.
—Destroyed in Vyazma pocket, Oct. 1941.
—Moscow axis w/26 Army, Dec. 1941.
—Second formation raised at Abakan, Siberia Military District, Jan. 1942.
—Kharkov offensive w/6 Army, June 1942.
—Kursk w/40 Army, July 1943.
—Dnieper, Kanev bridgehead w/40 Army; repulsed 84 German attacks, Sep. 1943.
—Stanislav, Aug. 1944.
—Vistula Oder Op., Jan. 1945.
—Komarno, Hungary as Motorized Rifle Division, 1946 (Feb. 1947 OB).
—"Piryatin, Stanislav, Oder."

310 Rifle Division
Units: 1080, 1082, 1084 Rifle, 860 Artillery Regiments.
—Raised Akmolinsk, Kazakhstan, Central Asia Military District, July 1941.
—RVGK w/54 Army, Aug–Sep 1941.
—Tikhvin, Leningrad Front w/54 Army, Oct. 1941.
—Volkhov w/4 Army, Nov. 1941.
—Probably on Leningrad Front 1941–44.
—Novgorod Luga Op. w/6 "Stalin" Rifle Corps, 59 Army, Jan. 1944.
—Danzig area w/19 Army, Mar. 1945.
—RVGK (FHO), Apr. 1945.
—"Novgorod," Order of Red Banner.

311 Rifle Division
Units: 1067, 1069, 1071 Rifle, 855 Artillery Regiments.
—Raised Kirov, Ural Military District, July 1941.
—Smolensk w/4 Army, July 1941.
—Mga w/48 Army, Aug–Sep 1941.

—Volkhov w/4 Army, Nov. 1941.
—Probably on Leningrad Front, 1941–44.
—Arnswalde, Feb. 1945.

312 Rifle Division
Units: First and second formations: 1079, 1081, 1083 Rifle, 859 Artillery Regiments.
—Raised Aktubinsk, Central Asia Military District, July 1941.
—RVGK w/52 Army, Aug. 1941.
—To west, Oct. 1941.
—Malojaroslavl, Oct. 1941.
—Destroyed at Maloyaroslavl w/30 Army, Nov. 1941.
—Second formation raised at Slavgorod, Siberia Military District, Jan. 1942.
—Pogorole Gorodische Op. w/20 Army, Aug. 1942.
—Smolensk, Sep. 1943.
—Pulawy bridgehead, w/91 Rifle Corps, 69 Army; had only six rifle battalions, Jan. 1945.
—Posen, Feb. 1945.
—Berlin w/91 Rifle Corps, 69 Army, Apr. 1945.
—"Smolensk, Cholm, Posnan," Orders of Lenin, Red Banner.

313 Rifle Division
Units: 1068, 1070, 1072 Rifle, 856 Artillery Regiments.
—Raised Turkestan, Central Asia Military District; June 1941.
—In combat with basic training only on Leningrad Front, Aug. 1941.
—Petrozavodsk, Sep. 1941.
—Leningrad area w/32 Army, Mar. 1942.
—Probably on Leningrad Front, 1941–44.
—Danzig area w/19 Army, Mar. 1945.
—RVGK (FHO), Apr. 1945.
—"Petrozavodsk."

314 Rifle Division
Units: 1074, 1076, 1078 Rifle, 858 Artillery Regiments.
—Raised Petropavlovsk, Far East Military District, July 1941.
—RVGK w/52 Army, Aug. 1941.
—RVGK w/54 Army in Moscow Military District, Aug–Sep 1941.
—Finnish Front (FHO), Sep. 1942–June 1944.
—"Kingisepp."

315 Rifle Division
Units: 362, 724, 1324 Rifle, 1012 Artillery Regiments.

—Raised Barnaul, Siberia Military District, July 1942.
—RVGK to Stalingrad, Aug. 1942.
—Volga Corridor w/1 Guards Army, Sep. 1942.
—RVGK in Stalingrad area w/5 Shock Army, Nov. 1942.
—Melitopol Op., Oct. 1943.
—South Ukraine w/54 Rifle Corps, 51 Army, Jan. 1944.
—Crimea w/54 Rifle Corps, 2 Guards Army, Apr. 1944.
—RVGK (FHO), Aug. 1944.
—"Melitopol."

316 Rifle Division
Units: All formations: 1073, 1075, 1077 Rifle, 857 Artillery Regiments.
—Raised at Alma Ata, Central Asia Military District, July 1941.
—Deployed to Western Front, July 1941.
—RVGK w/52 Army, Aug. 1941.
—To western front, Oct. 1941.
—Volokolamsk Highway, Nov. 1941.
—Reformed as 8 Guards Rifle Division, 18 Nov. 1941.
—Second formation raised at Vjasniki, Moscow Military District, July 1942.
—RVGK w/66 Army, Aug. 1942.
—Stalingrad area w/66 Army, Aug. 1942.
—Stalingrad area w/24 Army, Oct. 1942.
—Dissolved; troops to 260 Rifle Division, Nov. 1942.
—Third formation raised from 57, 131 Rifle Brigades at Krasnodar, North Caucasus Military District, Sep. 1943.
—Kurchanskaya, Sep. 1943.
—Temruk, w/9 Army, Sep. 1943.
—Taman area w/16 Rifle Corps, Nov. 1943.
—Southwest Ukraine w/11 Rifle Corps, 1 Guards Army, Jan. 1944.
—"Temruk, Rechitsa," Orders of Lenin, Red Banner, Suvorov.
Key Commanders: MG I.V. Panfilov, Nov. 1941.

317 Rifle Division
Units: First and second formations: 571, 606, 761 Rifle, 773 Artillery Regiments.
—Raised at Baku, Transcaucasus Military District, Aug. 1941.
—RVGK w/56 Independent Army, North Caucasus, Oct. 1941.
—Rostov w/56 Independent Army, Nov. 1941.
—Destroyed at Izyum, May 1942.
—Second formation raised at Makhachkala, North Caucasus Military District, Aug. 1942.
—Stalingrad area, Oct. 1942.

—Ordzhonikidze w/9 Army, Nov. 1942.
—North Caucasus w/58 Army, Jan. 1943.
—Krasny Oktyabr; suffered heavy losses, Feb. 1943.
—Kerch, w/22 Rifle Corps, 18 Army, Nov. 1943.
—Southwest Ukraine w/22 Rifle Corps, 18 Army, Jan. 1944.
—Uzhgorod Mukachevo Op. w/1 Guards Army, Sep. 1944.

318 Mountain Rifle Division
Units: 1331, 1337, 1339 Rifle, 796 Artillery Regiments.
—Raised Rostov, North Caucasus Military District from 78 Rifle Brigade, June 1942.
—Novo Mikhailovskiy w/12 Army, Aug. 1942.
—Novorossiysk, Sep. 1942.
—Tuapse w/47 Army, Sep. 1942.
—North Caucasus w/18 Army, Feb. 1943.
—Krasnodar area w/47 Army, Feb. 1943.
—Novorossiysk w/18 Army, Sep. 1943.
—Assault landing at Kerch w/22 Rifle Corps, 18 Army, Nov. 1943.
—Crimea w/3 Mountain Rifle Corps, 4 Ukrainian Front, Apr. 1944.
—RVGK (FHO), Aug. 1944.
—Carpathian Mountains, Sep. 1944.
—Carpathian Military District w/3 Mountain Rifle Corps, 1947 (Feb. 1948 OB).
—Had some naval infantry/riflemen in its composition.
—"Novorossiysk, Carpathian Mountains."

319 Rifle Division
Units: First and second formations: 1336, 1341, 1344 Rifle, 1014 Artillery Regiments.
—Raised Makhachkala, North Caucasus Military District, Aug. 1942.
—Ardon River, North Caucasus w/58 Army, Oct. 1942.
—Makhachkala direction, Nov. 1942.
—Dissolved; remnants to 131 Rifle Brigade, Feb. 1943.
—Second formation from 32, 33 Rifle Brigades at Cholm, Leningrad Military District, Oct. 1943.

320 Rifle Division
Units: First and second formations: 476, 478, 481 Rifle, 585 Artillery Regiments.
—Raised Crimea, Odessa Military District, Sep. 1941.
—Simferopol, Aug. 1941.
—In combat versus Heeresgruppe South, Oct. 1941.
—Kerch, Nov. 1941.

—Destroyed at Kerch, May 1942.
—Second formation raised at Leninakan, Transcaucasus Military District, Sep. 1942.
—Stalingrad area, Dec. 1942.
—North Caucasus w/44 Army, Jan. 1943.
—Jenakijevo, Sep. 1943.
—Germans claim to have destroyed it at Vascati, Rumania, 13 May 1944, (Ultra).
—Hungary w/37 Rifle Corps, 46 Army, Nov. 1944.
—"Jenakijevo," Orders of Red Banner, Suvorov.

321 Rifle Division
Units: All formations: 484, 488, 493 Rifle, 986 Artillery Regiments.
—Raised Voronezh, Orel Military District, Sep. 1941.
—Destroyed near Kerch, Nov. 1941.
—Second formation raised at Borzya, Far East Military District, Apr. 1942.
—RVGK in Siberia as an independent rifle division, June 1942.
—To Stalingrad area, July 1942.
—Southern Front w/64 Army, Aug. 1942.
—Don front w/5 Mechanized Corps of 65 Army, Oct. 1942.
—Stalingrad offensive w/65 Army, Nov. 1942.
—Reformed as 82 Guards Rifle Division, Mar. 1943.
—Third formation raised from 137 Rifle Brigade, Apr. 1944.
—Danzig area w/2 Shock Army, Mar. 1945.
—Probably an independent division.
—"Tschudowo, Elblag, u/i honorific," Order of Red Banner.

322 Rifle Division
Units: 1085, 1087, 1089 Rifle, 886 Artillery Regiments.
—Raised at Gorki, Moscow Military District, July 1941.
—Moscow, w/10 Army, Dec. 1941.
—Lyudinovo w/10 Army, Jan. 1942.
—Sukinichi w/16 Army, Feb. 1942.
—Trapped at Sukelnichi; rescued, Aug. 1942.
—Voronezh w/60 Army, Jan. 1943.
—Kursk, July 1943.
—Pripet River, Oct. 1943.
—Kiev, Nov. 1943.
—Kiev Zhitomir Defensive Op., Dec. 1943.
—Zhitomir Berdichev Op. w/15 Rifle Corps, 60 Army, Jan. 1944.
—Ternopol w/15 Rifle Corps, 60 Army, Mar. 1944.
—Lvov Sandomir Op., July 1944.

—Vistula Oder Op., Jan. 1945.
—"Zhitomir, Krakow, Kattowice," Order of Red Banner.

323 Rifle Division
Units: 1086, 1088, 1090 Rifle, 886 Artillery Regiments.
—Raised at Tambov, Orel Military District, Aug. 1941.
—Mikhalov w/10 Army, Dec. 1941.
—Sukinichi w/16 Army, Feb. 1942.
—RVGK w/11 Army, May 1943.
—Bryansk, Aug. 1943.
—"Bryansk."

324 Rifle Division
Units: 1091, 1093, 1095 Rifle, 887 Artillery Regiments.
—Raised Tscherbokkasary, Moscow Military District, Oct. 1941.
—Mikhalov w/10 Army, Dec. 1941.
—Sukinichi w/16 Army, Feb. 1942.
—Kursk w/50 Army, July 1943.

325 Rifle Division
Units: First and second formations: 1092, 1094, 1096 Rifle, 893 Artillery Regiments.
—Raised Morschansk, Orel Military District, Oct. 1941.
—Moscow axis w/10 Army, Dec. 1941.
—Reformed as 90 Guards Rifle Division, Apr. 1943.
—Second formation raised at Luknja, Moscow Military District from 23 and 54 Rifle Brigades, Apr–May 1943.
—Kursk, w/50 Army, July 1943.
—Pobeten (?), Apr. 1945.
—Poland w/105 Rifle Corps, 65 Army, June 1946 (Aug. 1946 OB).

326 Rifle Division
Units: 1097, 1099, 1101 Rifle, 888 Artillery Regiments.
—Raised Saransk, Moscow Military District, Aug. 1941.
—Only 4,000 of its 7-8000 men had weapons when committed to combat in 1941.
—Moscow offensive w/10 Army, Dec. 1941.
—Danzig area w/2 Shock Army, Mar. 1945.
—"Rosslau, Roslavl."

327 Rifle Division
Units: First and second formations: 1098, 1100, 1102 Rifle, 894 Artillery Regiments.

—Raised at Voronezh, Orel Military District, Nov. 1941.
—RVGK in Volga Military District w/26 Army, Nov. 1941.
—Moscow axis w/10 Army, Dec. 1941.
—Leningrad offensive w/2 Shock Army, Jan. 1943.
—Named 64 Guards Rifle Division, Jan. 1943.
—Second formation on Finnish front, 1943–44.
—RVGK (FHO), Apr. 1945.

328 Rifle Division
Units: First and second formations: 1103, 1105, 1107 Rifle, 889 Artillery
    Regiments.
—Raised Yaroslavl, Moscow Military District, Sep. 1941.
—Moscow offensive (Mikhalov) w/10 Army, Dec. 1941.
—Sukinichi w/16 Army, Feb. 1942.
—Reformed as 31 Guards Rifle Division, Mar. 1942.
—Second formation raised at Besslan, North Caucasus Military District, July 1942.
—Tuapse w/45 Army, Aug. 1942.
—Tuapse w/18 Army, Sep. 1942.
—South of Krimskaya, May 1943.
—Southwest Ukraine w/107 Rifle Corps, 1 Guards Army, Jan. 1944.
—Belorussia w/125 Rifle Corps, 47 Army, Mar. 1944.
—Warsaw Poznan Op. w/77 Rifle Corps, 47 Army, Jan. 1945.
—Berlin w/77 Rifle Corps, 47 Army, Apr. 1945.
—Potsdam w/47 Army, Apr. 1945.
—"Warsaw."

329 Rifle Division
Units: 1110, 1112, 1114 Rifle, 895 Artillery Regiments.
—Raised at Voronezh, Orel Military District, Sep. 1941.
—RVGK, Volga Military District w/26 Army, Nov. 1941.
—Western Front, Dec. 1941.
—Mozhaisk w/5 Army, Jan. 1942.
—Second formation raised at Lutsk, Kiev Military District, Apr. 1944.

330 Rifle Division
Units: 1109, 1111, 1113 Rifle, 890 Artillery Regiments.
—Raised at Tula, Moscow Military District, Aug. 1941.
—Moscow axis w/49 Army, Nov. 1941.
—Moscow offensive (Mikhalov), w/10 Army, Dec. 1941.
—Kursk, July 1943.
—Mogilev Op. w/62 Rifle Corps, 49 Army, June 1944.
—Danzig area w/2 Shock Army, Mar. 1945.

331 Rifle Division
Units: 1104, 1106, 1108 Rifle, 896 Artillery Regiments.
—Activated Tambov, Moscow Military District on basis of workers of Bryansk province as 331 "Bryansk, Proletarian" Rifle Division, Oct–Nov 1941.
—RVGK with reconstituted 20 Army, Nov. 1941.
—Assault division for 20 Army, Moscow offensive, Dec. 1941.
—Pogorelo Gorodische Op. w/20 Army, Jan. 1942.
—Gzhatsk axis w/5 and 20 Armies, Mar–June 1942.
—Pogorelo Gorodische Op. w/20 Army, Aug. 1942.
—Rhzev Vyazma Op., Mar. 1943.
—To 31 Army (rest of war) Belorussia, Mar. 1943.
—Bryansk, Aug. 1943.
—Smolensk, Sep. 1943.
—Belorussian Op., w/71 Rifle Corps, June 1944.
—Borisov, July 1944.
—Neman River, July 1944.
—Front Reserve, Aug. 1944.
—East Prussia, Oct. 1944.
—East Prussian Op., Jan. 1945.
—Masurian Lakes, Jan–Feb 1945.
—RVGK (FHO), Apr. 1945.
—Prague Op., May 1945.
—"Proletarian, Bryansk, Smolensk, Minsk, Orsha, Borisov, Neman, Masurian," Twice Order of Red Banner, Order of Suvorov.

332 Rifle Division
Units: 1115, 1117, 1119 Rifle, 891 Artillery Regiments.
—Raised Nanovo, Moscow Military District, Aug. 1941.
—Mikhalov w/10 Army, Dec. 1941.
—Demidev w/4 Shock Army, Jan. 1942.
—Lvov Sandomir Op., July 1944.
—"Ivanovo, Polotsk (?)."

333 Rifle Division
Units: 1116, 1118, 1120 Rifle, 897 Artillery Regiments.
—Raised Kamychin, North Caucasus Military District, Aug. 1941.
—RVGK, in North Caucasus w/57 Independent Army, Oct. 1941.
—Moscow axis w/10 Army, Dec. 1941.
—Stalingrad axis, June 1942.
—To Stalingrad, Oct. 1942.
—Stalingrad offensive w/4 Tank Corps, 21 Army, Nov. 1942.
—Sinelnikovo, Sep. 1943.

—Dnieper River w/12 Army, Oct. 1943.
—Zaporozhye bridgehead w/12 Army, Oct. 1943.
—Southwest Ukraine w/66 Rifle Corps, 6 Army, Jan. 1944.
—Lower Dniester River, Apr. 1944.
—"Sinelnikovo, Lower Dniester, " Orders of Red Banner, Suvorov.

334 Rifle Division
Units: 1122, 1124, 1126 Rifle, 908 Artillery Regiments.
—Raised Kazan, Volga Military District, Oct. 1941.
—RVGK w/60 Army, Moscow Military District, Nov. 1941.
—Orel Kursk area w/4 Shock Army, Jan. 1942.
—Vitebsk, Belorussia w/60 Rifle Corps, 43 Army, June 1943.

335 Rifle Division
Units: 1121, 1123, 1125 Rifle, 898 Artillery Regiments.
—Raised Stalingrad, Volga Military District, Sep. 1941.
—RVGK, North Caucasus Military District w/57 Independent Army, Oct. 1941.
—Southern Front w/24 Army, May 1942.
—Stalingrad axis, July 1942.
—Disbanded, Aug. 1942.

336 Rifle Division
Units: 1128, 1130, 1132 Rifle, 909 Artillery Regiments.
—Raised Gorki, Moscow Military District, Nov. 1941.
—RVGK w/60 Army, Nov. 1941.
—Moscow, Dec. 1941.
—Mozhaisk w/5 Army, Jan. 1942.
—Mtsenk w/61 Army, June 1943.
—Orel, Aug. 1943.
—Zhitomir, Dec. 1943.
—Zhitomir Berdichev Op., Jan. 1944.
—Southwest Ukraine w/15 Rifle Corps, 60 Army, Jan. 1944.
—Ternopol w/15 Rifle Corps, 60 Army, Mar. 1944.
—Lvov Sandomir Op., July 1944.
—Poland, Feb. 1945.
—The 1125 and 1130 Rifle Regiments have honorific "Ternopol."
—"Zhitomir, Kattowice."

337 Rifle Division
Units: 1127, 1129, 1131 Rifle, 899 Artillery Regiments.
—Raised Astrakhan, North Caucasus Military District, Sep. 1941.
—RVGK in North Caucasus w/57 Independent Army, Oct. 1941.

—Kharkov w/6 Army, May 1942.
—Stalingrad axis, June 1942.
—Caucasus Mountains, Oct. 1942.
—Kuban w/58 Army, Jan. 1943.
—Nikolayevsk, Feb. 1943.
—Dnieper River w/40 Army, Sep. 1943.
—Korsun Shevchenkovskiy Op. w/27 Army, Jan. 1944.
—Targul Frumos; exceptionally high losses in April; unit equipped with captured German machine guns, May 1944.
—Lvov Sandomir Op. w/73 Rifle Corps, 37 Army, July 1944.
—Iasi Kishinev Op. w/33 Rifle Corps, 6 Tank Army, Aug. 1944.
—Debrecen, Hungary w/33 Rifle Corps, 6 Guards Tank Army, Oct. 1944.
—Budapest, Dec. 1944.
—Probably an independent division.
—"Lubny, Grosswardein, Budapest, Debrecen."

338 Rifle Division
Units: 1134, 1136, 1138 Rifle, 910 Artillery Regiments.
—RVGK when Raised Penza, Volga Military District, Nov. 1941.
—Naro Fominsk, Dec. 1941.
—Vyazma, Jan. 1942.
—Mozhaisk w/33 Army, Jan. 1942.
—Lenino (near Mogilev) w/70 Rifle Corps, 33 Army, Oct. 1943.
—Belorussian Op., June 1944.
—Neman River, July 1944.
—"Neman," Order of Red Banner.

339 Rifle Division
Units: 1133, 1135, 1137 Rifle, 900 Artillery Regiments.
—Raised Rostov, North Caucasus Military District, Aug. 1941.
—Taganrog, Oct. 1941.
—In first echelon of 9 Independent Army, Southern Front, Oct–Nov 1941.
—Rostov, Nov. 1941.
—Rostov w/Independent 56 Army, Jan. 1942.
—Taganrog Offensive Op. w/56 Independent Army; had some naval infantry in its composition, Mar. 1942.
—Southern Front w/56 Independent Army, June 1942.
—Tuapse, North Caucasus Military District, Sep. 1942.
—Abinskaya, North Caucasus, Mar. 1943.
—Taman area w/56 Army, Nov. 1943.
—Kerch, w/16 Rifle Corps, Independent Coastal Army, Jan. 1944.
—Crimea w/16 Rifle Corps, 4 Ukrainian Front, Apr. 1944.

—Sevastopol, May 1944.
—RVGK (FHO), Aug. 1944.
—Probably an independent division.
—"Taman."

340 Rifle Division
Units: 1140, 1142, 1144 Rifle, 911 Artillery Regiments.
—Raised Balaschov, Volga Military District, Sep. 1941.
—Kashira w/50 Army, Nov. 1941.
—Moscow axis w/26 Army, Dec. 1941.
—Southwest axis w/38 Army, Aug. 1942.
—Ostrogosh Rossosh Op. w/40 Army, Jan. 1943.
—Kharkov, had 275 man effective strength, Feb. 1943.
—Belgorod Kharkov Op., Aug. 1943.
—Sumy w/51 Rifle Corps, 38 Army, Sep. 1943.
—Nevel Op., Oct. 1943.
—Kiev Op., Nov. 1943.
—Korsun Shevchenkovskiy Op. w/51 Rifle Corps, 40 Army, Jan. 1944.
—Carpathian Duklinskiy Op. w/52 Rifle Corps, 38 Army, Sep. 1944.
—"Sumy, Kiev," Order of Red Banner.

341 Rifle Division
Units: 1139, 1141, 1143 Rifle, 901 Artillery Regiments.
—Raised Stalingrad, North Caucasus Military District, Dec. 1941.
—RVGK w/57 Ind. Army in North Caucasus, Oct. 1941.
—Southern front w/24 Army, May 1942.
—Destroyed in Izyum pocket, May 1942.

342 Rifle Division
Units: 1146, 1148, 1150 Rifle, 912 Artillery Regiments.
—Raised Saratov, Volga Military District, Nov. 1941.
—RVGK w/61 Army in Volga Military District, Nov. 1941.
—Orel area w/61 Army, Dec. 1941.
—Bolkhov, Nov. 1942.
—Reformed as 121 Guards Rifle Division, Sep. 1943.

343 Rifle Division
Units: First and second formation: 1151, 1153, 1155 Rifle, 903 Artillery Regiments.
—Raised Voroshilovsk, North Caucasus Military District, Sep. 1941.
—In combat by 14 Oct. 1941.
—RVGK w/56 Independent Army, North Caucasus, Oct. 1941.
—Rostov w/56 Independent Army, Nov. 1941.

—Probably in Kharkov Offensive w/38 Army, May–June 1942.
—To Stalingrad axis from 38 Army, June 1942.
—Stalingrad offensive w/66 Army, Nov. 1942.
—Reformed as 97 Guards Rifle Division, May 1943.
—Second formation raised at Mogilev, Western Military District; may have had different regiments than first formation, Feb. 1944.

344 Rifle Divisions
Units: First and second formation: 1152, 1154, 1156 Rifle, 913 Artillery Regiments.
—Raised Moscow, Moscow Military District, Oct. 1941.
—RVGK w/26 Army, Volga Military District, Nov. 1941.
—RVGK to Gzhatsk, Jan. 1942.
—Reformed as 58 Guards Rifle Division, 31 Dec. 1942.
—Had second formation created after 1942.
—Belorussia w/72 Rifle Corps, 33 Army, May 1944.
—Memel, Mar. 1945.
—"Roslavl, Memel."

345 Rifle Division
Units: 1163, 1165, 1167 Rifle, 905 Artillery Regiments.
—Raised at Makhachkala, North Caucasus Military District, Sep. 1941.
—RVGK to Odessa, Sep. 1941.
—In the RVGK at Tuapse, Dec. 1941.
—From Tuapse to Sevastopol, Dec. 1941.
—Destroyed at Sevastopol w/Independent Coastal Army, July 1942.

346 Rifle Division
Units: 1164, 1166, 1168 Rifle, 915 Artillery Regiments.
—Raised at Volsk, Volga Military District, Aug. 1941.
—RVGK w/61 Army, Nov. 1941.
—Orel, Dec. 1941.
—To Stalingrad area, Oct. 1942.
—Stalingrad offensive as 5 Tank Army reserve, Nov. 1942.
—Donets Basin w/51 Army, Mar.–Apr. 1943.
—South Ukraine w/10 Rifle Corps, 51 Army, Jan. 1944.
—Crimea w/1 Guards Rifle Corps, 51 Army, Apr. 1944.
—Riga area w/51 Army, Aug. 1944.
—Memel w/1 Guards Rifle Corps, Oct. 1944.
—"Debalzev," Order of Red Banner.

347 Rifle Division
Units: 1175, 1177, 1179 Rifle, 907 Artillery Regiments.

—Raised Krasnodar, North Caucasus Military District, Sep. 1941.
—RVGK in North Caucasus w/56 Independent Army, Oct. 1941.
—Rostov w/56 Independent Army, Nov. 1941.
—Caucasus, Sep. 1942.
—Mozdok w/44 Army, Jan. 1943.
—Melitopol Op., Oct. 1943.
—South Ukraine w/55 Rifle Corps, 51 Army, Jan. 1944.
—Crimea w/1 Guards RC, 51 Army, Apr. 1944.
—Memel w/10 Rifle Corps, Oct. 1944.
—"Melitopol," Orders of Red Banner, Suvorov.

348 Rifle Division
Units: 1170, 1172, 1174 Rifle, 916 Artillery Regiments.
—Raised Kubyshev, Volga Military District, Oct. 1941.
—RVGK w/60 Army, Moscow area, Nov. 1941.
—Klin, Dec. 1941.
—Kalinin Front w/39 Army, Aug. 1942.
—RVGK w/2 Reserve (63 Army), Mar. 1943.
—Kursk w/40 Rifle Corps, 63 Army, July 1943.
—Vistula Oder Op., Jan. 1945.
—RVGK (FHO), Apr. 1945.
—"Bialystok, u/i honorific," Order of Red Banner.

349 Rifle Division
Units: 1169, 1171, 1173 Rifle, 906 Artillery Regiments.
—Raised Astrakhan, North Caucasus Military District, Sep. 1941.
—RVGK in the North Caucasus w/57 Independent Army, Oct. 1941.
—Stalingrad axis, June 1942.
—Tuapse, Sep. 1942.
—Disbanded; remnants to 353 Rifle Division, Oct. 1942.
—May have had a second formation in the Transcaucasus Military District, Oct. 1945 (EUCOM Study).

350 Rifle Division
Units: 1176, 1178, 1180 Rifle, 917 Artillery Regiments.
—Raised Atkarsk, Volga Military District, Aug. 1941.
—RVGK w/61 Army, Nov. 1941.
—Orel area w/61 Army, Dec. 1941.
—RVGK, Dec. 1942.
—To Stalingrad area, Dec. 1942.
—Kantemirovka w/6 Army, Dec. 1942.
—Kharkov w/3 Tank Army, Feb. 1943.
—Southwest Front w/12 Army, Apr. 1943.

—Zhitomir, Dec. 1943.
—Southwest Ukraine w/94 Rifle Corps, 1 Guards Army, Jan. 1944.
—Baranov bridgehead w/13 Army, July 1944.
—Vistula Oder Op., Jan. 1945.
—Potsdam w/13 Army, Apr. 1945.
—Berlin Op. w/28 army, Apr. 1945.
—Carpathian Military District, Mar. 1946 (EUCOM Study).
—Probably an independent division.
—"Zhitomir, Oder."

351 Rifle Division
Units: First and second formation: 1157, 1159, 1161 Rifle, 904 Artillery Regiments.
—Raised Stalingrad, North Caucasus Military District, Sep. 1941.
—RVGK, North Caucasus w/57 Independent Army, Oct. 1941.
—Destroyed in Izyum pocket, May 1942.
—Second formation raised at Ordzhonikidze, North Caucasus Military District, Aug. 1942.
—Ordzhonikidze w/9 Army, Nov. 1942.
—Alagir, Dec. 1942.
—Nalchik, Jan. 1943.
—Krasny Oktybar; heavy losses, Feb. 1943.
—Southwest Ukraine w/18 Guards RC, 60 Army, Jan. 1944.
—Proskurov Chernovtsy Op., Mar. 1944.
—Lvov Sandomir Op. w/1 Guards Army, July 1944.
—Had some naval infantry/rifle troops in its composition.
—Probably an independent division.
—"Shepetovka," Order of Red Banner.

352 Rifle Division
Units: 1158, 1160, 1162 Rifle, 914 Artillery Regiments.
—Raised Bugulma, Volga Military District, Aug. 1941.
—RVGK w/60 Army in Moscow Military District, Nov. 1941.
—Moscow, Dec. 1941.
—Breakthrough division for 20 Army in Rzhev-Vyazma Op., Jan. 1942.
—Belorussia Op. w/36 and 113 Rifle Corps, 31 Army, June 1944.
—Grodno, July 1944.
—Order of Red Banner.

353 Rifle Division
Units: 1145, 1147, 1149 Rifle, 902 Artillery Regiments.
—Raised, Krasnodar, North Caucasus Military District, Sep. 1941.
—RVGK in North Caucasus w/56 Independent Army, Oct. 1941.

—Rostov w/56 Independent Army, Nov. 1941.
—Tuapse Op.; absorbed troops of 349 Rifle Division, Sep–Dec 1942.
—Kuban w/18 Army, Jan. 1943.
—Krasnodar w/56 Independent Army, Feb. 1943.
—Southwest Ukraine w/6 Guards Rifle Corps, 46 Army, Jan. 1944.
—Dniester River, Apr. 1944.
—Budapest, Dec. 1944.
—"Lower Dniester, Izmail, Budapest."

354 Rifle Division
Units: 1199, 1201, 1203 Rifle, 921 Artillery Regiments.
—Raised at Kuibyshev, Volga Military District, Oct. 1941.
—Probably part of RVGK army when raised (based on pattern of similar divisions in the RVGK), Oct. 1941.
—On Moscow-Volga Canal, Nov. 1941.
—Moscow axis w/26 Army, Dec. 1941.
—Istra, Moscow area, Jan. 1942.
—Pogorole Gorodische Op. w/20 Army, Aug. 1942.
—Kursk w/77 Rifle Corps, 65 Army, July 1943.
—Kalinkovichi, Jan. 1944.
—Belorussian Op., June 1944.
—Narev River, Aug. 1944.
—Vistula Oder Op. w/65 Army, Jan. 1945.
—Northern Poland w/65 Army, Mar. 1945.
—Transcaucasus Military District, Jan. 1946 (EUCOM Study).
—"Kalinkovichi, Bobruysk, Baranovichi, Slonim, Luminets."

355 Rifle Division
Units: First and second formation: 1182, 1184, 1186 Rifle, 922 Artillery Regiments.
—Raised Kirov, Ural Military District, Sep. 1941.
—RVGK w/39 Army, Dec. 1941.
—Rzhev w/39 Army, Dec. 1941.
—Torzhok w/39 Army, Jan. 1942.
—Destroyed at Rzhev, July 1942.
—Second formation division in Finland, Aug. 1944.

356 Rifle Division
Units: 1181, 1183, 1185 Rifle, 918 Artillery Regiments.
—Raised Kuibyshev, Volga Military District, Nov. 1941.
—RVGK w/61 Army, Volga Military District, Nov. 1941.
—Orel, Dec. 1941.
—Mtsenk w/61 Army, June 1943.

—Kursk w/41 Rifle Corps, 3 Army, July 1943.
—Kalinkovichi, Jan. 1944.
—Belorussia w/89 Rifle Corps, 61 Army, Mar. 1944.
—Riga, Oct. 1944.
—Berlin w/61 Army, Apr. 1945.
—"Kalinkovichi, Riga," Orders of Red Banner, Suvorov.

357 Rifle Division
Units: 1188, 1190, 1192 Rifle, 923 Artillery Regiments.
—Raised Sarapul, Ural Military District, Oct. 1941.
—RVGK w/39 Army, Nov. 1941.
—Rzhev w/39 Army, Dec. 1941.
—Velikiye Luki w/3 Shock Army, Dec. 1942.
—Nevel w/3 Shock Army, Oct. 1943.
—Vitebsk Op. w/1 Rifle Corps, 43 Army, June 1944.
—Possibly an independent division.

358 Rifle Division
Units: 1187, 1189, 1191 Rifle, 919 Artillery Regiments.
—Raised Bugurusslan, Volga Military District, Aug. 1941.
—RVGK w/60 Army in Moscow area, Nov. 1941.
—Orel Kursk area w/4 Shock Army, Jan. 1942.
—Finland, Aug. 1944.
—Kwantung Peninsula w/5 Guards Rifle Corps, 39 Army, July 1947 (Feb. 1948 OB).

359 Rifle Division
Units: 1194, 1196, 1198 Rifle, 924 Artillery Regiments.
—Raised Krasnodar, North Caucasus Military District, Oct. 1941.
—Moscow area w/28 Army, Nov. 1941.
—RVGK w/39 Army, Dec. 1941.
—Rzhev w/39 Army, Dec. 1941.
—Kalinin Front w/39 Army, Aug. 1942.
—Korsun Shevchenkovskiy Op. w/47 Rifle Corps, 40 Army, Jan. 1944.
—Carpathian Duklinskiy Op. w/38 Army, Sep. 1944.
—Vistula Oder Op., Jan. 1945.
—"Jarzewo, Oder," Order of Lenin.

360 Rifle Division
Units: 1193, 1195, 1197 Rifle, 920 Artillery Regiments.
—Raised Chkalov, Volga Military District, Sep. 1941.
—RVGK w/60 Army Moscow Military District, Nov. 1941.
—Orel Kursk w/4 Shock Army, Jan. 1942.

—Velizh w/4 Shock Army, Jan. 1942.
—Nevel Op. w/3 Shock Army, Oct. 1943.
—Central Front w/83 Rifle Corps, 11 Guards Army, Dec. 1943.
—Belorussian Op., June 1944.
—Termez, Turkestan Military Disrict, June 1946 (Apr. 1948 OB).
—Probably an independent division.
—"Nevel, Polotsk," Order of Red Banner.

361 Rifle Division
Units: 1200, 1202, 1204 Rifle, 925 Artillery Regiments.
—Raised Ufa, Ural Military District, Oct. 1941.
—RVGK w/39 Army, Nov. 1941.
—Rzhev, w/39 Army, Dec. 1941.
—Torzhok w/39 Army, Jan. 1942.
—Reformed as 21 Guards Rifle Division, Mar. 1942.
—Second formation in Manchurian Campaign w/15 Army, Aug. 1945.

362 Rifle Division
Units: 1206, 1208, 1210 Rifle, 936 Artillery Regiments.
—Raised Archangelsk, Archangelsk Military District (FHO), Sep. 1941.
—Pattern of similar divisions indicates it was probably raised in Siberia Military District, Sep. 1941.
—RVGK in Siberia Military District w/58 Army, Nov. 1941.
—To Archangelsk Military District w/58 Army, Nov. 1941.
—Belorussian Op., June 1944.
—East Prussian Op., Jan. 1945.
—"Osowiec, Masurian."

363 Rifle Division
Units: First and second formation: 1205, 1207, 1209 Rifle, 926 Artillery Regiments.
—Raised Sverdlovsk, Ural Military District, Sep. 1941.
—Moscow area w/28 Army, Nov. 1941.
—RVGK w/39 Army, Dec. 1941.
—Rzhev w/39 Army, Dec. 1941.
—Possibly at Torzhok w/39 Army, Jan. 1942.
—Reformed as 22 Guards Rifle Division, Mar. 1942.
—Second formation raised; Far East w/35 Army, Aug. 1945.

364 Rifle Division
Units: 1212, 1214, 1216 Rifle, 937 Artillery.
—Raised Omsk, Siberia Military District, Sep. 1941.
—RVGK, in Siberia Military District w/58 Army, Nov. 1941.

—To Archangelsk Military District w/58 Army, Nov. 1941.
—Probably on Leningrad Front, 1941–44.
—Pulawy bridgehead as an independent division w/69 Army; had six rifle battalions, Jan. 1945.
—"Tossno."

365 Rifle Division
Units: 1211, 1213, 1215 Rifle, 927 Artillery Regiments.
—Raised Sverdlovsk, Ural Military District, Oct. 1941.
—Moscow offensive (Klin) w/26 Army; breakthrough division, Dec. 1941.
—Destroyed near Rzhev, Feb. 1942.
—Second formation probably raised; w/1 Independent Red Banner Army, Far East, Aug. 1945.

366 Rifle Division
Units: 1218, 1220, 1222 Rifle, 938 Artillery Regiments.
—Raised Tomsk, Siberia Military District, Aug–Sep. 1941.
—RVGK in Siberia w/59 Army, Nov. 1941.
—To Archangelsk Military District w/59 Army, Nov. 1941.
—Leningrad area w/2 Shock Army, Jan–Apr 1942.
—Reformed as 19 Guards Rifle Division, 17 Mar. 1942.

367 Rifle Division
Units: 1217, 1219, 1221 Rifle, 928 Artillery Regiments.
—Raised Shandansk, Volga Military District, Aug. 1941.
—Moscow area w/28 Army, Nov. 1941.
—Finland, Aug. 1944.
—Petsamo Kirkenes Op. w/31 Rifle Corps, 14 Army; had 5,971 personnel, Oct. 1944.
—RVGK (FHO), Apr. 1945.

368 Rifle Division
Units: 1224, 1226, 1228 Rifle, 939 Artillery Regiments.
—Probably raised in Siberia Military District, Sep. 1941.
—RVGK in Siberia Military District w/58 Army (SME), Nov. 1941.
—Raised Archangelsk, Archangelsk Military District (FHO), Dec. 1941.
—To Archangelsk Military District w/58 Army, Nov. 1941.
—Probably on Finnish Front, 1941–44.
—Petsamo Kirkenes Op. w/99 Rifle Corps, 14 Army; had 6,098 personnel, Oct. 1944.
—RVGK (FHO), Apr. 1945.
—White Sea Military District, Oct. 1946 (Feb. 1947 OB).
—"Petrozavodsk, Kirkenes."

369 Rifle Division
Units: 1223, 1225, 1227 Rifle, 929 Artillery Regiments.
—Raised Kurgan, Ural Military District, Sep. 1941.
—RVGK w/39 Army, Nov. 1941.
—Rzhev w/39 Army, Dec. 1941.
—RVGK w/11 Army, May 1943.
—Kursk w/53 Rifle Corps, 11 Army, July 1943.
—Karachev, Aug. 1943.
—Belorussian Op., w/62 Rifle Corps, 49 Army, June 1944.
—Danzig area w/70 Army, Mar. 1945.
—"Karachev."

370 Rifle Division
Units: 1230, 1232, 2134 Rifle, 940 Artillery Regiments.
—Raised Tomsk, Siberia Military District, Sep. 1941.
—RVGK in Siberia Military District w/58 Army, Nov. 1941.
—To Archangelsk Military District w/58 Army, Nov. 1941.
—Demyansk w/27 Army, Feb. 1943.
—Staraya Russa area w/34 Army, Mar. 1943.
—Pulawy bridgehead w/91 Rifle Corps, 69 Army, Jan. 1945.
—Berlin Op. w/91 Rifle Corps, 69 Army; had six rifle battalions, Apr. 1945.

371 Rifle Division
Units: 1229, 1231, 1233 Rifle, 930 Artillery Regiments.
—Raised Sverdlovsk, Ural Military District, Oct. 1941.
—RVGK w/39 Army, Nov. 1941.
—Klin as breakthrough division w/26 Army, Dec. 1941.
—Kursk w/10 Army, July 1943.
—Lenino (near Mogilev), w/70 Rifle Corps, 33 Army, Oct. 1943.
—Belorussian Op., June 1944.
—Vilnius w/65 Rifle Corps, 5 Army, July 1944.
—"Vitebsk, Borisov, Vilnius, Kaunas."

372 Rifle Division
Units: 1236, 1238, 1240 Rifle, 941 Artillery Regiments.
—Raised Barnaul, Siberia Military District, Sep. 1941.
—RVGK in Siberia Military District w/59 Army, Nov. 1941.
—To Archangelsk Military District w/59 Army, Nov. 1941.
—Leningrad offensive (Schlusselburg), w/2 Shock Army; broke the Leningrad blockade, 18 Jan. 1943.
—Novgorod Luga Op., Jan. 1944.
—Vyborg, Aug. 1944.

—East Pomeranian Op., Mar. 1945.
—Danzig area w/2 Shock Army, Mar. 1945.
—"Novgorod, Vyborg, u/i honorific."

373 Rifle Division
Units: 1235, 1237, 1239 Rifle, 931 Artillery Regiments.
—Raised Cherbarkul, Ural Military District, Aug. 1941.
—RVGK w/39 Army, Nov. 1941.
—Rzhev w/39 Army, Dec. 1941.
—Torzhok w/39 Army, Jan. 1942.
—Korsun Shevchenkovskiy Op. w/78 Rifle Corps, 52 Army, Jan. 1944.
—Targul Frumos at 30% strength, May 1944.
—"Mirgorod, Cherkassy," Orders of Red Banner, Suvorov.

374 Rifle Division
Units: 1242, 1244, 1246 Rifle, 942 Artillery Regiments.
—Raised Bogolovo, Siberia Military District, probably Aug. 1941.
—RVGK in Siberia w/59 Army, Nov. 1941.
—To Archangelsk Military District w/59 Army, Nov. 1941.
—Possibly on Finnish Front, 1941–44.
—"Ljuban."

375 Rifle Division
Units: 1241, 1243, 1245 Rifle, 932 Artillery Regiments.
—Raised Kamyshlov, Ural Military District, Aug. 1941.
—Moscow area w/28 Army, Nov. 1941.
—RVGK w/39 Army, Dec. 1941.
—Rzhev w/39 Army, Dec. 1941.
—Northwest Front w/53 Army, Apr. 1942.
—Belgorod, Mar. 1943.
—Kursk w/23 Guards Rifle Corps, 6 Guards Army, July 1943.
—Belgorod, Aug. 1943.
—Vorskla River w/53 Army, Sep. 1943.
—Korsun Shevchenkovskiy Op. w/20 Guards Rifle Corps, 4 Guards Army, Jan. 1944.
—Zvenigorod w/49 Rifle Corps, 5 Guards Tank Army, Feb. 1944.
—Iasi, Apr. 1944
—Targul Frumos, May 1944.
—Iasi Kishinev Op., Aug. 1944.
—North Caucasus Military District, Apr. 1946 (EUCOM Study).
—Probably an independent division.
—"Belgorod, Kharkov, Bucharest, Pressburg."

376 Rifle Division
Units: 1248, 1250, 1252 Rifle, 943 Artillery Regiments.
—Raised Novosibirsk, Siberia Military District, from Kuznetsk Basin, Aug. 1941.
—RVGK in Siberia Military Districtw/59 Army, Nov. 1941.
—To Archangelsk Military District w/59 Army, Nov. 1941.
—Leningrad w/2 Shock Army, Dec. 1942.
—Kursk, called crack formation, July 1943.
—Riga, Oct. 1944.
—Vistula Oder Op. w/67 Army, Jan. 1945.
—Postwar museum in Kuzbas, Siberia Military District (MHJ), 1982.
—"Plaskow, Walcz, Riga, Kuzbas, Pskov," Order of Red Banner.

377 Rifle Division
Units: 1247, 1249, 1251 Rifle, 933 Artillery Regiments.
—Raised Cherbarkul Ural Military District, Sep. 1941.
—RVGK w/39 Army, Nov. 1941.
—RVGK to 4 Army, Dec. 1941.
—Novgorod Luga Op. w/112 Rifle Corps, 59 Army, Jan. 1944.
—"Ural."

378 Rifle Division
Units: 1254, 1256, 1258 Rifle, 944 Artillery Regiments.
—Raised Achinsk, Siberia Military District, Sep. 1941.
—RVGK in Siberia Military District w/59 Army, Nov. 1941.
—To Archangelsk Military District w/59 Army, Nov. 1941.
—Probably on Finnish Front, 1941–44.
—Nogorod Luga Op. w/14 Rifle Corps, 59 Army; breakthrough division, Jan. 1944.
—"Novgorod," Order of Red Banner.

379 Rifle Division
Units: 1253, 1255, 1257 Rifle, 934 Artillery Regiments.
—Raised at Molotov or Perm, Ural Military District; in combat within 30 days, Aug. 1941.
—RVGK w/39 Army, Dec. 1941.
—Rzhev w/39 Army, Dec. 1941.
—Klin, Dec. 1941.
—Baltic area, Sep. 1944.
—Riga, Oct. 1944.
—"Riga."

380 Rifle Division
Units: 1260, 1262, 1264 Rifle, 945 Artillery Regiments.
—Raised Slavgorod, Siberia Military District, Sep. 1941.
—To western front, Jan. 1942.
—RVGK w/2 Reserve (63 Army), Mar. 1943.
—Orel; distinguished itself (Zhukov), Aug. 1943.
—Vistula Oder Op., Jan. 1945.
—Gdynia area w/49 Army, Mar. 1945.
—"Orel, Lomza."

381 Rifle Division
Units: 1259, 1261, 1263 Rifle, 935 Artillery Regiments.
—Raised Zlatoust, Siberia Military District, Aug. 1941.
—RVGK w/39 Army, Nov. 1941.
—Rzhev w/39 Army, Dec. 1941.
—Velikiye Luki w/3 Shock Army, Nov. 1942.
—Finland, Aug. 1944.
—Danzig area w/2 Shock Army, Mar. 1945.
—Rugen Island, Germany w/5 Mechanized Army, July 1946 (Aug. 1946 OB).
—"Elblag, u/i honorific."

382 Rifle Division
Units: 1265, 1267, 1269 Rifle, 946 Artillery Regiments.
—Raised Kansk, Siberia Military District, Oct. 1941.
—RVGK w/58 Army in Siberia Military District, Nov. 1941.
—Archangelsk Military District w/58 Army, Dec. 1941.
—Orel/Kursk area w/4 Shock Army, Jan. 1942.
—Novgorod Luga Op., Jan. 1944.
—Finland, Aug. 1944.
—"Novgorod."

383 Rifle Division
Units: 691, 694, 696 Rifle, 966 Artillery Regiments.
—Raised Stalino, Kharkov Military District from home guards and assault battalions, Sep. 1941.
—Laba River, North Caucasus w/18 Army, Aug. 1942.
—Tuapse w/18 Army Sep–Dec 1942.
—Novorossiysk, Jan. 1943.
—Nikolayev, Feb. 1943.
—Krimskaya w/56 Independent Army, Mar. 1943.
—Taman area w/56 Independent Army, Nov. 1943.

—Kerch Peninsula w/16 Rifle Corps, Independent Coastal Army, Jan. 1944.
—Crimea w/16 Rifle Corps, Independent Coastal Army, Apr. 1944.
—East Prussia, Jan. 1945.
—"Brandenburg," Order of Red Banner.

384 Rifle Division
Units: First and second: 1272, 1274, 1276 Rifle, 947 Artillery Regiments.
—Raised at Omsk, Siberia Military District, Aug. 1941.
—RVGK w/58 Army in Siberia Military District, Nov. 1941.
—Archangelsk Military District w/58 Army, Dec. 1941.
—Northwest front w/27 Army, May 1942.
—Ordzhonikidze, North Caucasus w/9 Independent Army, Aug. 1942.
—Disbanded; troops to 202 Rifle Division, Dec. 1942.
—Had second formation division after 1942.
—RVGK (FHO), Apr. 1945.
—In Far East w/25 Army, Aug. 1945.

385 Rifle Division
Units: 1266, 1268, 1270 Rifle, 948 Artillery Regiments.
—Raised Frunze, Central Asia Military District, Sep. 1941.
—RVGK w/61 Army, Nov. 1941.
—Moscow area w/24 Army, Dec. 1941.
—RVGK to Gzhatsk area, Jan. 1942.
—Kursk w/10 Army, July 1943.
—Vistula Oder Op., Jan. 1945.
—Gdynia area w/49 Army, Mar. 1945.
—"Krichev, Lomza, Osowiec."

386 Rifle Division
Units: 769, 772, 775 Rifle, 952 Artillery Regiments.
—Raised Tiflis (Tblisi), Transcaucasus Military District, Sep. 1941.
—To western front, Dec. 1941.
—Mount Sapun, Sevastopol, June 1942.
—Destroyed at Sevastopol w/Independent Coastal Army, July 1942.

387 Rifle Division
Units: 1271, 1273, 1275 Rifle, 949 Artillery Regiments.
—Raised in Akmolinsk, Central Asia Military District, Nov. 1941.
—RVGK w/61 Army, Nov. 1941.
—Orel area w/61 Army, Dec. 1941.
—Stalingrad area, Dec. 1942.

—South Ukraine w/55 Rifle Corps, 51 Army, Jan. 1944.
—Crimea w/55 Rifle Corps, 2 Guards Army, Apr. 1944.
—RVGK (FHO), Aug. 1944.

388 Rifle Division
Units: 773, 778, 782 Rifle, 953 Artillery Regiments.
—Raised at Kutaisi, Transcaucasus Military District, Nov. 1941.
—To Sevastopol, Dec. 1941.
—Destroyed at Sevastopol w/Independent Coastal Army, July 1942.
—Second formation in the Manchurian Campaign w/15 Army, Aug. 1945.

389 Rifle Division
Units: 545, 1277, 1279 Rifle, 950 Artillery Regiments.
—Raised at Tashkent, Central Asia Military District, Aug. 1941.
—RVGK to Transcaucasus Front, Apr. 1942.
—From Turkish frontier to Terek River, Aug. 1942.
—Terek River w/44 Army, Nov. 1942.
—Terek River, Jan. 1943.
—Armarvir w/9 Independent Army; w/37 Army after 11 January 1943.
—Kuban, Mar. 1943.
—Keslerovo, Sep. 1942.
—Berdichev, Jan. 1944.
—Lvov Sandomir Op. w/22 Rifle Corps, 3 Guards Army, July 1944.
—Vistula River (Winjarka bridgehead), 22 July 1944.
—Received Order of Red Banner, 9 Aug. 1944.
—Vistula Oder Op., Jan. 1945.
—Usti Nad Labem, Czechoslovakia, May 1945.
—"Berdichev, Kielce, Oder," Order of Red Banner.
Key Commanders: Gen-Maj HSU L.A. Kolobov, Sep. 1942–May 1945.

390 Rifle Division
Units: First and second formation: 784, 790, 792 Rifle, 954 Artillery Regiments.
—From eastern Russia to the West, Dec. 1941.
—In combat versus HeeresGruppe South, Jan. 1942.
—Destroyed at Kerch, May 1942.
—Second formation at Stalingrad; had 300 men, Sep. 1942.
—The 790 Rifle Regiment to 392 Rifle Division.

391 Rifle Division
Units: 1024, 1278, 1280 Rifle, 951 Artillery Regiments.
—Raised at Alma Ata, Central Asia Military District, Sep. 1941.
—RVGK w/61 Army, Nov. 1941.

—In combat in west, Jan. 1942.
—Riga, Oct. 1944.
—"Riga."

392 Rifle Division
Units: 790, 802, 805 Rifle, 955 Artillery Regiments.
—Raised at Gori, Transcaucasus Military District; a Georgian division, Aug. 1941.
—The 790 Rifle Regiment was from 390 Rifle Division.
—Terek River, Nov. 1941.
—Distinguished itself on Terek River, Aug. 1942.

393 Rifle Division
Units: First and second formation: 697, 699, 704 Rifle, 967 Artillery Regiments.
—Raised at Svyatogorsk, Kharkov Military District, Sep. 1941.
—Kharkov, w/6 Army, May 1942.
—Destroyed in Izyum Pocket, May 1942.
—Second formation in the Far East w/25 Army, Aug. 1945.

394 Rifle Division
Units: 808, 810, 815 Rifle, 956 Artillery Regiments.
—Raised at Tiflis, Transcaucasus Military District, Aug. 1941.
—Caucasus Mountains., June 1942.
—North Caucasus Mountain passes, Aug. 1942.
—Yerevan, Jan. 1943.
—Novorossiysk, Feb. 1943.
—Abinskaya, Mar. 1943.
—Southwest Ukraine w/34 Rifle Corps, 46 Army, Jan. 1944.
—Rumania, Aug. 1944.
—"Constanza," Order of Red Banner.

395 Rifle Division
Units: 714, 723, 726 Rifle, 968 Artillery Regiments.
—Raised at Voroshilovgrad, Kharkov Military District from home guard units, Sep. 1941.
—Caucasus Front w/51 Army, July 1942.
—Bataisk area w/18 Army, Aug. 1942.
—Tuapse Defensive Op. w/18 Army, Sep–Dec 1942.
—Kuban w/18 Army, Jan. 1943.
—North Caucasus w/56 Independent Army, Feb. 1943.
—Taman area, Nov. 1943.
—Southwest Ukraine w/52 Rifle Corps, 18 Army, Jan. 1944.

—Stanislav, Aug. 1944.
—Berlin Op., Apr. 1945.
—Transcaucasus Military District, Apr. 1946 (EUCOM Study).
—"Mountain Workers, Stanislav, Taman," Orders of Red Banner, Suvorov.

396 Rifle Division
Units: First and second: 803, 816, 819 Rifle, 957 Artillery Regiments.
—Raised at Kussary, Transcaucasus Military District, Sep. 1941.
—The 819 Rifle Regiment to the 242 Mountain Rifle Division.
—To western front, Dec. 1941.
—Destroyed at Kerch, May 1942.
—Second formation in Far East w/2 Independent Red Banner Army, Apr. 1945.

397 Rifle Division
Units: 446, 447, 448 Rifle, 1015 Artillery Regiments.
—Raised at Atkarsk, Volga Military District, Jan. 1942.
—To western front, Jan. 1942.
—RVGK w/2 Reserve Army (later 40 Rifle Corps, 63 Army), Mar. 1943.
—Kursk, July 1943.
—Rovno Lutsk Op. w/77 Rifle Corps, 13 Army, Jan. 1944.
—Pinsk, July 1944.
—Pomerania, Feb. 1945.
—"Pinsk, Pomeranian."

398 Rifle Division
Units: 821, 824, 826 Rifle, 958 Artillery Regiments.
—Raised at Kirovobad, Transcaucasus Military District, Sep. 1941.
—To the front, Jan. 1942.
—Destroyed at Kerch, May 1942.

399 Rifle Division
Units: 1343, 1345, 1348 Rifle, 1046 Artillery Regiments.
—Raised at Chita, Transbaikal Military District, Mar. 1942.
—RVGK in Siberia Military District as an independent division, June 1942.
—Stalingrad w/62 Army, Aug. 1942.
—Kursk area w/48 Army, May 1943.
—Kursk, July 1943.
—East Prussian Op., Jan. 1945.
—Berlin, w/48 Army, Apr. 1945.
—"Novosybkov, Tannenberg, u/i honorific."

400 Rifle Division
Units: 829, 832, 834 Rifle, 959 Artillery Regiments.
—Raised at Yevlak, Transcaucasus Military District, Oct. 1941.
—To the front, Jan. 1942.
—Stalingrad axis, June 1942.
—Caucasus, Aug. 1944.
—Baku, Transcaucasus Military District w/13 Rifle Corps, 45 Army, Mar. 1946 (Apr. 1947 OB).

402 Rifle Division
Units: 833, 839, 840 Rifle, 960 Artillery Regiments.
—Raised at Agdam, Transcaucasus Military District; an Azerbaijani division, Sep. 1941.
—Terek River w/44 Army, Aug. 1942.
—Caucasus, Nov. 1942.
—Titarov, Dec. 1942.
—Caucasus, Aug. 1944.
—Nakichevan, Transcaucasus Military District w/45 Army, Mar. 1946 (Feb. 1947 OB).

404 Rifle Division
Units: 643, 652, 655 Rifle, 961 Artillery Regiments.
—Raised at Sumgait, Transcaucasus Military District, Oct. 1941.
—To the front, Dec. 1941.
—Destroyed at Kerch, May 1942.
—Second formation in the Transcaucasus Military District; units unknown, Dec. 1945 (EUCOM Study).

406 Rifle Division
Units: 660, 662, 668 Rifle, 962 Artillery Regiments.
—Raised at Kirovakan, Transcaucasus Military District, Sep. 1941.
—Caucasus, Oct. 1942.
—Caucasus, Aug. 1943.

407 Rifle Division
—Raised at Alkakalaki, Transcaucasus Military District, 1941.
—Caucasus, Aug. 1944.

408 Rifle Division
Units: 663, 670, 672 Rifle, 973 Artillery Regiments.
—Raised at Yerevan, Transcaucasus Military District; an Armenian division, Mar. 1942.
—Turkish frontier, Aug. 1942.

—Tuapse Defensive Op. w/18 Army, Sep–Dec. 1942.
—Probably converted into 408 Rifle Brigade (FHO), Dec. 1942.

409 Rifle Division
Units: 675, 677, 684 Rifle, 964 Artillery Regiments.
—Raised at Stepanavan, Transcaucasus Military District; an Armenian division, 1941.
—Kirovograd w/25 Guards Rifle Corps, 7 Guards Army, Jan. 1944.
—Iasi, Apr. 1944.
—Targul Frumos, May 1944.
—RVGK (FHO), Aug. 1944.
—Bratislava, Apr. 1945.
—"Kirovograd, Prepwitz (?)."

411 Rifle Division
Units: 678, 686, 689 Rifle, 965 Artillery Regiments.
—Raised at Chuguyev, Kharkov Military District, Sep. 1941.
—Kharkov w/6 Army, May 1942.
—Destroyed in Izyum pocket, May 1942.

413 Rifle Division
Units: 1320, 1322, 1324 Rifle, 982 Artillery Regiments.
—Raised at Svobodny/Spassk, Far East Military District, July 1941.
—To western front (central sector), Nov. 1941.
—Distinguished itself in the Venev sector; had full strength of 12,000 men, Nov. 1941.
—Tula w/50 Army, Nov. 1941.
—Kaluga w/50 Army, Dec. 1941.
—Moscow, Jan. 1942.
—Lublin Brest Op., July 1944.
—RVGK (FHO), Aug. 1944.
—Northern Poland w/65 Army, Mar. 1945.
—"Brest, u/i honorific."

414 Rifle Division
Units: 1367, 1371, 1375 Rifle, 1053 Artillery Regiments.
—Raised at Makhachkala, North Caucasus Military District; a Georgian division, Mar. 1942.
—Kerch, May 1942.
—Caucasus, Aug. 1942.
—Terek River w/44 Army, Nov. 1942.
—North Caucasus w/44 Army, Jan. 1943.
—Novorossiysk, Sep. 1943.

—Kerch, as a reserve of the Independent Coastal Army, Jan. 1944.
—Crimea w/11 Guards Rifle Corps, 4 Ukrainian Front, Apr. 1944.
—RVGK (FHO), Aug. 1944.
—Transcaucasus Military District, Jan. 1947 (Feb. 1948 OB).
—Possibly an independent division.
—"Grunische, Anapa."

415 Rifle Division
Units: 1321, 1323, 1326 Rifle, 686 Artillery Regiments.
—Raised at Vladivostok, Far East Military District, July 1941.
—The 1326 Rifle Regiment is also associated w/422 Rifle Division.
—To western front (central sector), Nov. 1941.
—Serpukhov w/49 Army, Nov. 1941.
—Moscow w/49 Army, Dec. 1941.
—Pogorole Gorodische Op. w/20 Army, Aug. 1942.
—Kursk, July 1943.
—Southwest Ukraine w/28 Rifle Corps, 13 Army, Jan. 1944.
—Belorussia w/89 Rifle Corps, 61 Army, Mar. 1944.
—"Mozyr."

416 Rifle Division
Units: 1368, 1373, 1374 Rifle, 1054 Artillery Regiments.
—Raised at Sumgait, Transcaucasus Military District; as an Azerbaijani division w/23 Rifle Corps, Mar. 1942.
—Makhachkala direction, Nov. 1942.
—North Caucasus w/44 Army, Jan. 1943.
—Taman area w/44 Army, May 1943.
—Taganrog, Aug. 1943.
—Southwest Ukraine w/37 Rifle Corps, 3 Guards Army, Jan. 1944.
—Iasi Kishinev Op., Aug. 1944.
—Berlin w/5 Shock Army, Apr. 1945.
—The 1374 Rifle Regiment is Order of the Red Banner.
—"Azerbaijan, Taganrog, Kishinev," Order of Red Banner.

417 Rifle Division
Units: 1369, 1372, 1376 Rifle, 1055 Artillery Regiments.
—Raised at Tiflis, Transcaucasus Military District, Mar. 1942.
—Krimskaya, Apr. 1942.
—Turkish frontier to Terek River, Aug. 1942.
—North Caucasus w/58 Army, Jan. 1943.
—Southwest Ukraine w/37 Rifle Corps, 3 Guards Army, Jan. 1944.
—Crimea w/63 Rifle Corps, 51 Army, Apr. 1944.
—Panevyzys, July 1944.

—Shauliai, Sep. 1944.
—Riga, Oct. 1944.
—Memel w/63 Rifle Corps, Oct. 1944.
—"Sivash, Ponowiek, Shauliai, Svesk," Orders of Red Banner, Suvorov.

418 Rifle Division
Units: 311 Artillery Regiment.
—Raised at Gorki, Moscow Military District.
—In combat versus Heeresgruppe North, Aug. 1944.
—RVGK (FHO), Apr. 1945.

421 Rifle Division
Units: 1327, 1330 Rifle Regiments.
—Raised at Simferopol, Odessa Military District from home guard units, Oct. 1941.
—Perekop, Oct. 1941.
—The 1 Naval Infantry Regiment merged with the division; unit became 1330 Rifle Regiment, Oct. 1941.
—Sevastopol, Dec. 1941.
—Disbanded, Feb. 1942.

422 Rifle Division
Units: 1326, 1334, 1392 Rifle, 1061 Artillery Regiments.
—Raised at Bikin/Khabarovsk, Far East Military District, Apr. 1942.
—RVGK in Siberia Military District as an independent rifle division, June 1942.
—To western front, July 1942.
—Stalingrad area, July 1942.
—Stalingrad w/64 Army, Sep. 1942.
—Stalingrad Offensive w/57 Army, Nov. 1942.
—Reformed as 81 Guards Rifle Division, Mar. 1943.
—The 1326 Rifle Regiment sent to 415 Rifle Division.

443 Rifle Division
—Raised at Tomsk, Siberia Military District, Dec. 1941.
—Redesignated 284 Rifle Division (later 79 Guards Rifle Division), Mar. 1942.

446 Rifle Division
—Raised Leninakan, Transcaucasus Military District; an Armenian division (FHO), Jan. 1944.
—Caucasus, Aug. 1942.

—Transcaucasus Military District, Jan. 1946 (EUCOM Study).
—"Armenian."

469 Rifle Division
—Raised at Leninakan, Transcaucasus Military District, before Jan. 1942.
—Merged w/244 Rifle Division at Stalingrad, Jan. 1942.
—Second formation in the Caucasus, Aug. 1944.